W0115377

THE
WORLD'S
GAME

THE WORLD'S GAME

Reflections on Western Culture

FREDERIC RAPHAEL

An Apollo Book

First published in the UK in 2025 by Head of Zeus Ltd,
part of Bloomsbury Publishing Plc

Copyright © Frederic Raphael, 2025

The moral right of Frederic Raphael to be identified
as the author of this work has been asserted in accordance with
the Copyright, Designs and Patents Act of 1988.

All rights reserved. No part of this publication may be: i) reproduced or
transmitted in any form, electronic or mechanical, including photocopying,
recording or by means of any information storage or retrieval system without
prior permission in writing from the publishers; or ii) used or reproduced in
any way for the training, development or operation of artificial intelligence
(AI) technologies, including generative AI technologies. The rights holders
expressly reserve this publication from the text and data mining exception
as per Article 4(3) of the Digital Single Market Directive (EU) 2019/790.

9 7 5 3 1 2 4 6 8

A catalogue record for this book is available from the British Library.

ISBN (HB): 9781837933389
ISBN (E): 9781837933365

Typeset by DivAddict Solutions Ltd

Printed and bound in Great Britain by
CPI Group (UK) Ltd, Croydon CR0 4YY

Bloomsbury Publishing Plc
50 Bedford Square, London, WC1B 3DP, UK
Bloomsbury Publishing Ireland Limited,
29 Earlsfort Terrace, Dublin 2, D02 AY28, Ireland

HEAD OF ZEUS LTD
5–8 Hardwick Street
London EC1R 4RG

To find out more about our authors and books
visit www.headofzeus.com

For product safety related questions contact productsafety@bloomsbury.com

For Beetle, always.

'While I cannot be regarded as a pillar, I must be regarded as a buttress of the church, because I support it from the outside.' – *William Lamb, Viscount Melbourne*

'Mutatis mutandis.' – *F.R.*

'The Pope is resolved to be lord and master of the world's game.' – *Pope Clement III*

'Everything is what it is and not another thing.' – *Bishop Butler*

'Wanna bet?' – *Failed US TV game show*

1

Aristophanes' comedy *The Clouds* opens with Socrates a literal basket case, suspended in airy eminence above the ancient Athenian audience. Was the original question-master prone to the haughty contemplation implied by *meteora phrontistes*, celestial pundit? Not a bit. One of the earliest habits of show biz is anything for a laugh. 'Sent 'er up', literally in this case, is camp for taking the piss. The Athenians of 423 BCE, their city's eminence still intact, were not greatly amused to have their prime celebrity derided. The original version of *The Clouds* came third and last in the competition. Ah, rewrites! How many dramatists, of all sizes, have followed the great Aristophanes into the business of try-again-and-again?

More street than starry-eyed, the mundane Socrates kept his feet on the ground. When smug Athenians affected to define terms such as courage or justice, he punctured their conceits, supplied no answers. His sole boast was that, to his amazement, the Delphic oracle had named him wisest of mortals: he alone of men, it declared, had the intelligence not to affect certainty. Inscribed on the temple of Apollo, where the priestess, high on earthy exhalations, chewed out her *ainaigmata* (crafty ambiguities), was *gnōthi seauton*, 'Know Thyself'. Two and a half thousand years and billions of words later from generations of know-it-alls, Wittgenstein declared, 'Whereof one cannot speak, thereof one should be silent.' That'll be the day, possibly.

Greek gods could also be jokers. Zeus' express messenger Hermes doubled as cracksman. Crafty Hephaestus snared his exquisite wife Aphrodite in a golden filigree while she was bumping her daisy with Ares. The other Olympians mocked the lame cuckold no less than the god of war and his divine piece. Male gods were forever up for carnal favours from mortal females, seldom *philia*, the chaste devotion advocated by Christians. Goddesses too had choice human protégés. Thwarting Hera's malice, virgin Athene saw Odysseus home safely, slowly, to Ithaca after his wooden equine troop-carrier, bellyful of commandos aboard, had conned its way through the Trojan walls. Priam's city on fire, Aphrodite saved Aeneas, her son by mortal Anchises, and translated him, via Dido's Carthage, into Latin myth as founder of Rome. In pettish mood, she did for Hippolytus, having taken his aversion from sex as a personal slight. Fate implicit in his name, the Horse-Looser was fatally thrown when his chariot-team bolted at the shock surge of a sea-monster commissioned by the jilted goddess.

Ever since the golden age of Athenian democracy, in the late fifth century BCE, when laurel crowns topped official prizes, lampoonery has shone a light to enrage prudes, pique pretensions. Laughter remains the common man's tribute, farcical playwrights its shameless prompters. In 404 BCE, once-imperious Athens slumped in shock after conclusive defeat at Aegospotami ended the long-off-and-on Peloponnesian Wars. From 404 to 403, Plato's relative Critias (no mean tragedian), leader of the Thirty Tyrants, lorded it over the sorry city and its flattened walls. The proto-quislings were then overthrown, their Spartan back-up sent packing, Critias killed. Restored democracy, like the old, had no public prosecutor. Its citizens passed a law *mê mnêsikakein*, against hawking bitter memories, reopening wounds. Over two thousand years later, Nelson Mandela did likewise in post-Apartheid South Africa. Magnanimity did not preclude issuing his own fatwa against Israel. What fun some neo-Aristophanes might have with a sky-pilot called Archbishop Tutu, as in too-too divine!

In 399 BCE, Meletus and Anytus and their friends, who had had family members murdered by Critias and his crew, persisted in bringing charges against the allegedly collusive Socrates. Arraigned before a jury of male citizens, he was voted guilty of having sided with the deposed tyranny, of flaunting his personal daimon (non-curricular mini-god) and corrupting the young with scepticism. Invited to exercise a convicted man's right to propose a suitable penalty, he dared to suggest that, like an Olympic champion, he should receive a state pension and free meals for life. Things had changed. His reward for skittishness was to be sentenced to death by a larger majority than had deemed him guilty of impiety. He had provoked, if not rigged, martyrdom at the hands of his own people; so too Jesus of Nazareth, Hugh J. Schonfield suggested, in *The Passover Plot* (1965). Democracy was to be damned in the first case, 'the Jews' in the second. Both charges have had a long run.

2

From its beginnings in sixth-century-BCE Asia Minor, philosophy – later crowned 'Queen of the Sciences' – transcended mundane borders, as did the spill of the first minted coinage, from the gilded Lydia of King Croesus. The Seven Sages – the first Greek-speaking thinkers, most from Asia Minor – saluted no patron deity. Across the Aegean, mainland Hellenes elected to applaud Dionysus, divine play/boy arriviste from the Orient. Trouper forever on tour, he was Zeus' son by mortal Semele, victim of a literal *coup de foudre*. When pregnant, she demanded a divine visit. Zeus responded in the you-asked-for-it form of a lightning bolt. Divine condescension roasted Semele, extracted the embryo unharmed.

Parading as a smooth-cheeked *ephebe*, Dionysus proved resentful, very, should his beardless divinity not be saluted. The young Theban king Pentheus paid the exemplary price in Euripides' last play, *Bacchae*. Caught, in drag, while shadowing Dionysus' female devotees, the Bacchantes, on a rural rave, the regal voyeur was torn to pieces. His reeling mother Agave juggled her son's head in bloodied hands. Pentheus was but the first to crave answers to an old, old question: what do female initiates get up or down to when in exclusive, if not lubricious conclave? Ghetto and harem came to excite similar curiosity about Jews and women: lock them away, then peek through keyholes, suspect conspiracy, ascribe witchcraft, imagine Lyttonesque lubriciousness.

In Dionysus' wake, the first player-manager, Thespis, unhooked the back of a halted farm cart to declaim his heroic monologues. After static theatres had been carved in hillsides with suitable acoustics, a second masked, buskined male actor, then another, enlivened the play with iambic dialogue. Cutting and thrusting, one-line-each stichomythia added verbal duels to tragedy's melodious choruses. Theatre became a means of advancing abrasive ideas. Audiences sat in serried judgement, a popular press. No few spectators proved capable of remembering tracts of Euripides' *Elektra* after one hearing: hence Milton's lines of how their recitation saved 'Athenian walls from ruin bare' at the hands of Spartan Lysander. Anonymity lent energy to applause, verged on insolence in vocal form. The best criticism is still to write a better play.

Thebes had a bumpy ride in myth and history. In myth, the spurned Dionysus erupted in seismic rage; in history, the Theban oligarchs yielded to Xerxes while braver Greek cities got together, in 480 BCE, and defeated the Persian invaders: on sea at Salamis, led by the Athenians; on land by the Spartans, at Plataea. The victorious Hellenes regarded the concessive Thebans with disdain. A century and a half later, Thebes made fatal amends by joining the Athenians in resisting Macedonia's brazen incursion from the north. In 338, the new allies were crushed at Chaeronea by one-eyed Philip II and his eighteen-year-old son Alexander, both eyes on greatness.

The house of Pindar and a few religious shrines were alone left standing in flattened Thebes. The sixth-/fifth-century-BCE poet had been the first to confect commissioned eulogies to commemorate victors in the Olympic and other games. Reprieved by their heroic back-story, the defeated Athenians were saddled with an alliance with Macedon: favour and humiliation at a stroke. Demosthenes, the people's strong man, author of the magniloquent anti-Macedonian polemics known as *Philippics*, was driven to suicide. Three centuries later, in Rome, Marcus Tullius Cicero's no-less-brave speeches against Mark Antony adopted the same title. His latter-day *Philippics* stung Antony into delegating killers to cut the long civilian neck that Tully extended from between the curtains of his cornered litter. Democracy was again the casualty.

3

Homer's *Iliad* his warrant, newly enthroned Alexander led his Macedonians and as many mainland Greeks as he could muster in what he paraded as revenge for Xerxes' invasion of well over a century before. Asiatic Hellenes fought the pillaging invaders in greater numbers than Alexander had raised mainland auxiliaries. Aristotle's great-nephew, Callisthenes, was commissioned to play Alexander's embedded historian, as Edward Luttwak was when Anglo-American forces came to settle rigged scores with Saddam Hussein.

Callisthenes' early despatches served as laurels. They failed to save his neck after he presumed a Macedonian's entitlement to old-style free speech and spoke out against the conqueror's policy of uniting Greek and Persian courts. Hellenes were then obliged to pay grovelling obeisance, *proskynesis*, in the oriental manner. Alexander later planned to crossbreed an elite, rootless class to enforce his law and rigorous order. Like Himmler's Death's-Head SS, they were to do and die in an environment without family affinities or local allegiances. The shiny, black-helmeted rank and file of Francisco Franco's Guardia Civil, motto *Todo Por La Patria*, were barracked far from their native soil, so too Stalin's NKVD and its successors, with their sinister loyalty.

After Alexander's fevered death, in 323 BCE, when

thirty-two years old, the Middle East was fractured into kingdoms sequestered by his soon contentious marshals. Ptolemy, quickest off the mark, ensconced himself in Egypt, sea and desert its natural ramparts. The Ptolemaic dynasty, alien pharaohs, ruled for three centuries; Cleopatra, the last, was the first to be fluent in the local language. Alexandria – tradesman's corner of the Mediterranean, roundly advertised by the Pharos lighthouse – soon harboured a cosmopolitan population. Greeks and Jews, competitive Levantines, merchants, fancy poets, tricky dicks, drawn by commercial prospects, voluminous library, whores for all tastes. Prolific third-century-BCE Callimachus' verses set a showy bookman's tone. Doctus (wise guy) Gaius Valerius Catullus rehearsed its allusive wit two centuries later.

The last of the City of Love's poets, Constantine Cavafy (1863–1933), lived above a brothel in the Rue Lepsius, commonly known as the Rue Clapsius. Buy-the-hour houris pandered to tastes with no appeal to its upstairs neighbour. Alex's patchwork society lasted till the mid-1950s. Pan-Arabist pretender Gamel Abdul Nasser expelled Egypt's last king, Farouk, de luxe porno collector, and a swath of long-resident Greeks and Jews. How many Egyptians rejoiced to be collated as Arabs? The Levant's many-faceted jewel, Alexandria became a prosaic dump. Copts, a dissident sect of native Christians, were suffered to remain as odd men in. One of their churches was burnt down, congregation incinerated, in 2022, by Muslim zealots who remain unpunished.

Lawrence Durrell's Alexandrian tetralogy (1957–60) stands as polychrome obituary for the happy-for-some days when the British lorded it over the city. So what if one volume features a Coptic grandee being treated to a Muslim funeral or upgrades green to a primary colour? Justine, raven Jewess, echoes Proust's Rachel-when-from-the-lord; little Larry, a little over five feet tall, resuscitates *le petit Marcel*. Einstein's theory of relativity served to deck Durrell with a coat of philosophical chic, as Henri Bergson's *élan vital* had Proust's *A la recherche du temps perdu*. Durrell based a character called 'the poet' on a scarcely disguised Cavafy, who died before he could witness his sumptuous city of lettered love reduced to witless monotony and littered scruffiness.

Like Socrates, Cavafy – first language English (he spent early years in mercantile Liverpool) – had no affection for the countryside. Unlike Socrates, who cared for nowhere else, the poet never felt at ease in Athens. In hospital there, under treatment for terminal cancer, the Alexandrian yawned at the steep view of honeyed Hymettus. Abroad and the past served Cavafy for where and when, as for countless Greeks and Jews. 'Moiadzouni' (they're like each other), an Athenian barber told me, while littering his floor with sections of my then-copious black hair.

When did racial affinity guarantee affection? *Frères-ennemis* abound in the Mediterranean. Leopardi despised the French for their stiff treatment of Latin. James Joyce, in his Hibernian liaison between Jew and Greek, Dublin-wandering Leopold Bloom, based in part on Joyce's Triestine friend and protégé Italo Svevo (né Aron Hektor Schmitz), contracts Odysseus' ten-year trek, Homer's twenty-four-book *Odyssey*, into twenty-four stylistically variform hours. *Ulysses* (1922) was trumpeted by admirers as the *ne plus ultra* of the novel. More variform curiosity than classic revision, how many readers does it now excite, for all the long-censored entrance of Cunty Kate in those delectably soiled knickers?

4

The first clutch of Hellenic savants competed for attention, severally, near the Mediterranean's eastern littoral. Clustered and cloistered under Persian dominion, their speculations reached few ears or eyes in mainland Hellas. Alike only in discounting divine visitations, Thales and his peers proposed various, non-mythical, accounts of the material universe. Their alien speculations provoked no pious indignation among Medes and Persians. The Seven Sages, as they came to be ranked, seldom ruminated about death; nor did they toy, in public, with sex, as Diogenes came literally to do by masturbating in public. Reason and Females had an uneasy relationship from the start. Philosophers may be amorous ('Freddy' Ayer not least); they rarely dwell on Robert Graves's 'meum-tuum sense'. Socrates' wife, Xanthippe, was traditionally portrayed as a shrew. In the 1996 dialogues bearing her name, Roger Scruton, rare and scholarly master of erotic refinement, lent her a tart tongue.

Few early free spirits craved collegiate salutes. Heraclitus of Ephesus alludes to others only to disparage them. War no common topic, Heraclitus was markedly shrewd in declaring it king and father of all things. No less epigrammatic, the philosopher-poet T. E. Hulme echoed him in Edwardian England and died, a thirty-four-year-old volunteer, in the trenches in the Great War. One of the neat images in his tart verses was 'like any creeping Turk to the Bosphorus'. Major Clement Attlee, Gallipoli veteran, came to say, 'Johnny Turk isn't a bad chap.'

Long-lived Democritus (460–370 BCE) is rare in being credited with a smile. His atomic theory was more logical than scientific: if things were smaller than each other, it followed that whatever was smallest had to be fundamental. Chaptered together by tendentious scholars to fashion a plinth for understanding Plato, the thinkers grouped as pre-Socratic (not a few disparaged as needing-the-money sophists) were variously inventive, seldom in step when it came to the origin and nature of the physical world. As for the gods, Heraclitus is unusual in referring, if with small piety, to 'the power that men do, or do not, call Zeus'.

In the late fifth century, Pericles' imported guru, Anaxagoras of Clazomenae, declared the moon a bolus of molten metal larger than the Peloponnese. Outraged by what they took for blasphemy, if not lunacy, lumpen Athenians clamoured for his indictment, a hint to Pericles that in a democracy no one was immune, orthodoxy boxed with innovation; see today's Israel. Anaxagoras quit Attica with prompt discretion and set up as a freelance pundit in Lampsacus in the Troad.

5

In 1794, Antoine Lavoisier was sentenced to the guillotine, on specious charges, by Parisian judges. Capital levellers, while conceding his rare qualities as a physicist, they chose to remain too principled to have them warrant his reprieve. Revolutionaries exult in making no exception of the exceptional. Jesus complained, unless he boasted, that the Son of Man had no sure place to lay his head. Wittgenstein conceded – or was it insisted? – that the philosopher was implicitly homeless. The exaltation of vagrancy hinted at the Jewishness he long sought to evade. Those bracketing hand-gestures, chopping logic, which the faithful imitated in mimetic piety, can be read for sublime tinkering and tailoring. Any brazen dissident is wise to keep a bag packed.

Socrates advocated no theories, spoke only Attic Greek, sought no society other than chatty, unduly smug Athenians. Buzzy body, the gadfly is on record as quizzing a slave just once, to prove, by a series of leading questions, the validity of the theory of anamnesis: stored in his immortal soul, the supposed ignoramus 'remembered' more than he knew and could be re/minded of it, by leading questions. Anamnesis contributed to the Christian notion that belief, then Faith, trumps knowledge. Famous for *eironeia* – our irony, his tease – feet-on-the-ground Socrates had little time for the stilted presumption of metaphysics. He took the opinionated to mean what they said, then put them to the question until they conceded that its plausibility was flawed. Two and a half thousand years later, John Wisdom reported having had an unsatisfactory afternoon with another philosopher. 'Perhaps you made the mistake,' Wittgenstein told him, 'of disagreeing with something he said.' W's quasi-Socratic method was to coach (not to say intimidate) a speaker into realising his own inadequacy and so to repair his own flaws: psychoanalysis above the belt. W's Cambridge seminars resembled the diagnostic sessions of a physician who never affected to heal himself.

Gate-crashing Thrasymachus (Mr Fisticuffs), in *The Republic*, is alone in being recorded by Plato as having got the better of Socrates. Barging in to declare justice 'the will of the stronger', he proved rough and tough enough to rock the notion that Justice was an immutable golden measure. Doctor Johnson took a no-less-unsubtle attitude to Bishop Berkeley's 'idealism'. Kicking a stone, he said, 'Thus do I refute him.' In modern times, G. E. Moore held up a polite, policing hand to illustrate that common sense promised that reality was more solid than 'sense data'. Does the latter concept remain exemplary anywhere outside retrospective academia?

6

When the executioner handed him his fatal cup of hemlock, Socrates offered a cocky toast to Asclepius, god of healing, before draining the paralysing draught. Modern medicos are known to call the opiate offered to those in their last agony a 'terminal cocktail'. Socrates' death primed his disciple Plato to attribute all manner of theories to the silenced chatterbox, as St Paul did to Jesus; so too the conceits echoed in Stalin's verbose appropriation of Lenin's mantle. *Theaetetus* is an astronomical scheme never advanced *in propria persona* by the Athenian gadfly. Who but Saint Paul ever vaunted his native Tarsus as other than a mean city?

Provincial insolence stimulated Paul to fancies which the Jerusalem disciples lacked the gall to propound. Jesus of Nazareth came to be adorned with celestial finery by a multi-national, elaborately robed clerisy. Its pontiffs delivered *ex cathedra* ideas that were never His. During an abbreviated lifetime, before crucifixion by the Romans, he preached exclusively to the circumcised. Yes, he composed a chastening parable about the Good Samaritan, but did he ever venture into proto-methodist Samaria? As with Socrates, all sorts of ideas came to be branded under his name. Academic jokers accuse both of the same mistake: neither published.

Friedrich Nietzsche charged Socrates with blighting the

spontaneity that, he fancied, had sharpened Greek wits before second thoughts sissified it. If Nietzsche's unpruned moustache advertised a virility he scarcely exemplified when it came to the ball-breaking charm of Lou Andreas-Salomé, his genius postulated Apollonian and Dionysiac strains, proportion and disproportion, creatively at odds in the Greek psyche. *Men* and *de* – on the one hand and then on the other – recur in Hellenic counterpoised garrulity. Nietzsche, wandering Gentile, clinched his place among top aphorists with 'There can be no argument about matters of taste? All life is an argument about matters of taste.' Collapsing into madness in arcaded Turin, Zarathustra's callous spokesman fell weeping onto the neck of a sorry cab-horse as it was being flogged.

Friedrich out of the way, his sister Elisabeth twisted his prophecies to clap approval on National Socialism and its anti-Semitism. In fact, not least to needle his ex-friend Richard Wagner, Nietzsche rated Jews not unusually more intelligent than the *Herren Volk*. His proclamation of the death of God induced the philosopher's inferiors to ridicule the augur of a brutal century which Christian confidence scarcely survived.

7

Sceptics are more reliable sources than disciples. Defining 'gospel' as the highest form of truth is Christian insolence. Seven centuries later, that presumption was matched by Islam declaring the Prophet Muhammad without conceivable successor, the Koran the last word. Socrates, good and dead, has been saddled with Plato's ideas, Jesus of Nazareth with the syncretism concocted by Paul of Tarsus. He was succeeded by a train of sainted speculators, bent on embellishing ecclesiastical credentials and proto-papal vanities. The Vatican crossed Delphi with Orwell's Ministry of Truth in dogmatic kit. Images of the balding Paul were graced with saintly majesty; so too were busts of pug-faced Socrates unrumpled into images of serene sagacity.

What more surely certifies Aristophanes' genius than that the Greek colonels, in power from 1967 till 1974, banned production of his satires? In the midst of the Peloponnesian War, ancient Athenians had greeted *Lysistrata*, the playwright's ridiculing of their city's bellicose policy, with the ribaldry of the world's original democrats. The colonels dreaded derision licensed by the oldest scripted comedies in Western civilisation. The last of the '67 putschists, Dimitrios Ioannides, was pitiless, first to his friends, then to himself: after the return of democracy and of Constantine Karamanlis (from eleven years of Parisian exile), his vanity chose prison before apology. Sado-masochism, humanity's alternating current, seldom lacks brutes craving brutality.

Ancient Attica his adult play/ground, himself a closet dramatist, Plato paid sporting tribute to Aristophanes by casting him as a star participant in *The Symposium*. He was then credited with that dialogue's image of lovers resembling two halves of what was once a single person, severed at birth, each yearning for reunion with the other. Aristophanes and Socrates were the jokers in the Attic pack: odd men in. Plato later became the unsmiling monitor of the so-called 'Republic'.

In the late 1960s (as the early 1970s were called), on his return to Byron's 'tight little island' from starring on Broadway in *Beyond the Fringe*, Peter Cook affected to be dismayed by the deluge of giggling he and his Oxbridge quartet had primed. His horror was sharpened by finding David Frost in command of the TV sat/ire biz, backed by an entourage of larky scriptwriters. Kitty Muggeridge capped Frosty's captious fellow-satirists when she said of that soon-beknighted operator, 'He rose without trace.'

8

In the sixth century BCE, Thales declared water the origin of life. Said to have foretold an eclipse of the sun (a prediction probably derived from Babylonian astrologers), he had the mundane sagacity to make a fortune in olive oil futures. 'Speculation' soon acquired its two faces. Anaximander, another native of mercantile Miletus, on the receding shore of Persian-ruled Asia Minor, declared to apeiron, the unlimited, the stuff of life. In the later fifth century, Protagoras of Abdera, in Thrace, declared man to be the 'measure of things that are, that they are, and of things that are not, that they are not'. Gods did not come into it; nor would they into Thucydides' unsentimental elegy for the humiliation of Athens in the Peloponnesian War. Speeches attributed to significant players in the war were plausible approximations. 'Dramatise, dramatise,' Henry James would say. Fiction and non-fiction, affecting distinction in library catalogues, season each other's progeny. Thucydides backed his doleful history to be a *kteema es aei*, prize (and awful warning) for the ages.

Tradition's 'Father of History', Herodotus had been a product of Halicarnassus on the Asiatic littoral. Inquisitive traveller, he came back with a plethora of appetising stories. His chronicle of Xerxes' ill-fated Persian expeditions to Hellas, first published during a prolonged recital at the Olympic

Games, made him the prototypical raconteur, A.J.P. Taylor his 20th-century successor. The opinionated early Greek-speaking pundits lived on the eastern Mediterranean rim of the wide Persian Empire. Their elastic language disposed them to be snappy – not lyrical, as Hebrew did the prophets. Both languages packed portable treasure for wanderers and won-derers. Prattling like frogs, as Plato put it, around the Black Sea, as well as the Mediterranean, Greek speakers shared a Homeric culture, but no common citizenship until 1821; Jews – after the fall of Jerusalem in 70 CE – had their books but knew no homeland until 1948.

Isolation has sharpened all manner of minds, from Boethius to Sir Walter Raleigh, Bonnivard to Baruch (later Benedict) Spinoza, Antonio Gramsci to Joseph Brodsky, Adolf Hitler to Nelson Mandela. Doctor Johnson observed that the pros-pect of being hanged in a fortnight concentrated a man's mind wonderfully. It is truer, if less waggish, to say that having no prospect of reprieve liberates candour. What is there to lose when there's nothing to lose? Philosopher and solipsist are compounded in solitary.

9

Pythagoras (570-495 BCE) was born on the island of Samos when it was ruled by Polycrates, the 'much-powered'. His enlightened tyranny posed a sparkling Hellenic alternative to the near-neighbouring Great King's Persia. Lured by the prospect of mainland power, Polycrates crossed the narrow water to conspire with the local satrap (provincial viceroy). Had the latter grandee been tipped off that the Great King had his truth-telling spies, or was he a two-timing fisher of men all along? Not as empowered as he was nominated, Polycrates was crucified soon after stepping on Asiatic soil. Pythagoras, by now on his travels, attracted followers over whom he exercised mesmerising authority. As the 'reverend' Jim Jones would prove, over two millennia later, ductile gulls are never in short supply.

Samos did not lose its distinction. After Xerxes' calamitous invasion of Greece in 480 BCE, the islanders voted to join the Delian confederacy, which soon became the Athenian Empire. A few years later, its treasury was hefted from Delos to the resurrected, magnificent Parthenon, paid for in good part by the allies' involuntary subscriptions. Lazier signatories financed their own subjection by subscribing to Athens's 'protection'; the Samians elected to retain their fleet. When they voted to secede from Pericles' increasingly dictatorial Athenian Empire, he sent a force to nail their leaders to planks. After a

nine-month siege, so a latish source promises, lingering survivors were cudgelled to death. Ruthlessness abroad served
to confirm popularity at home. Karl Marx took the view that
nineteenth-century English lower orders were too proudly
Union-Jacketed ever to identify with the workers of the world.

Standard accounts promise that Pericles (Mr All-About-
Fame) was as good as president for life of democratic Athens
in its golden age. His standing was maintained by his being
repeatedly voted a member of the panel of generals. Its
incumbents could be re-elected year after year. Civil magistra-
cies, by contrast, rotated annually, from members of one of
Cleisthenes' factitious 'tribes' to the next, in order to avoid
any single man lording it over the city, as Pericles contrived to
do, not without a few bumps in his commanding path, until
his death in 429 BCE. Maurice Bowra, wag in person, prig on
the page, most fulsome of his promoters, has inflated Pericles'
fame. With the rhetorical superiority and personal wealth to
dominate the assembly, thanks to Thucydides, he imperson-
ates his city's glorious age. Early death, from the plague, has
axed his responsibility for initiating the eventually calamitous
Peloponnesian War.

10

There is a quiet case for claiming that the greatest of Athenians was the creator of its durable democratic constitution. Cleisthenes (570–507 BCE) engineered a fundamental resection of the city's dated political system, cobbled by Solon. Internal territorial antagonisms were effaced, city and rural factions healed in bold and ingenious fashion. Each previously contentious section of society was persuaded that it would profit from the reconstituted arrangement. No one accused Cleisthenes of favouritism or self-advancement. Thriving on energetic diversity, the Athenians raised their city to a century of expansive prosperity. Cleisthenes' lack of self-importance was such that he slipped from the parade of antiquity's top celebrities until Pierre Lévêque and Pierre Vidal-Naquet's *Clisthène l'Athénien* leavened his status.

Two years after the death of Pericles, in 429 BCE, the city of Mytilene on Lesbos elected to secede from the alliance that had become the Athenian Empire. Pericles' successor, the hardly-less-rich, much-less-suave Cleon, persuaded his fellow-citizens to repeat the Olympian's treatment of the Samian rebels. Following a snap vote in the Assembly, a state trireme was despatched with merciless orders to the fleet commander on the spot. Next day, according to Thucydides, the *demos* was persuaded to second thoughts. More pragmatic than humane, one Diodotus – in his sole indexed appearance on history's stage – argued that ruthlessness would offer dissident allies no alternative but to resist to the death. Votes counted, thumbs up, a trireme with a reprieve set off in pursuit of the lethal one. Good news travelled faster. In a dead heat on reaching Lesbos, number two took precedence.

Cleon achieved caddish triumph as a first-time general. Tired of his sneering at the elected generals, in 425 the Athenians – at least slightly hoping that he would look a fool? – despatched him to practise the bully measures he never stopped advocating. He was unheroic and innovative enough literally to smoke out a choking garrison of almost 120 high-born Spartiates on the island of Sphacteria. Cornered on an islet off the coast of the Peloponnese, they surrendered without having the chance of a fight. Sparta – always in dread of a shortage of elite citizens – immediately asked for terms for their release.

Teamed with Pericles' ward, glamorous, self-advancing young Alcibiades, Cleon elaborated the diplomatic end-game. Their captives were allowed to return home on the promise of a signature of peace and a formal alliance. After Cleon was killed leading a self-aggrandising expedition to Thrace in 421 BCE, Athens lost the authority to lord it, Sparta as adjutant, over the Hellenes. Corinth, Thebes and lesser cities had dreaded the prospect of a dyarchy no coalition of also-rans could have hoped to upset. They now rallied publicly to Lacedaemon less out of loyalty than self-interest. Spartiate confidence reflated, the war resumed.

11

In 415 BCE, while serving as a commander in the Athenians' Cerberus-headed Sicilian expedition, Alcibiades was impeached for sacrilege by the conservative citizens the fleet had left behind in Athens. Just before it sailed, the city's Herms – phallic stone house-minders – were found to have been mutilated overnight, erections snapped. Already at sea, Alcibiades was indicted, on a more solemn charge of profaning the Eleusinian Mysteries, by the old dogs left to chew on the issue. A posse pursued him. Almost certainly innocent as charged, if scarcely beyond suspicion (he had got away with dumping his rich bride and filching her fortune), Alcibiades was never disposed to abide other people's verdicts. Having procured leave to travel home-wards in his own flash flagship, the grandee slipped his escort and took shameless refuge in Sparta.

Repaying sanctuary with strategic advice, he suggested that his hosts establish a base at Decelea, midway between Athens and the Theban border of Attica, as a tempting way-station for fugitive slaves from the silver mines at Laurium. Duped runaways (many the property of Nikias, Alcibiades' unfriendly colleague in Sicily) were sold on elsewhere. Athens ran short of specie, diplomacy's most persuasive arm.

Alcibiades' two-facedness was not without mythical prec-edent. Did Odysseus not do his best to avoid doing his duty in the Trojan War? Out-tricked by Palamedes, Agamemnon's astute recruiting officer, Odysseus paid him back, once at Troy, by planting fake evidence that Palamedes – inventor of several letters in the alphabet – was a traitor. Palamedes tried to float oars, inscribed with telegraphic calls for help, across to his fiefdom of Euboea, without success. Vengeful Odysseus procured his execution. Does any ancient or modern commentator think ill of Homer's wandering hero? Such is charm.

Achilles was no unswerving Hellenic patriot. Denied the lovely captive Briseis, the ace in the Achaean pack jeopardised the allies' cause by sulking in his tent. The expedition's never-popular C-in-C, Agamemnon had to give way to *force majeure* and concede the crumpet. *Patriotismos*, today's Greek for patriotism, had no ancient equivalent. *Patriotes* meant only 'compatriot'; it made no abiding promise.

Themistocles is renowned for misleading Xerxes by sending a messenger from Salamis with a warning that the Greek fleet was about to escape. While the Greeks rested, the Persian oarsmen exhausted their energy patrolling the narrow waters. They were in no state for the subsequent battle. Might it be that Themistocles both tricked Xerxes and took out insurance against a Greek defeat? Themistocles was first a hero and then, when the Athenians tired of his leadership, found a welcome in the Great King's court and turned his coat into that of a provincial satrap. The Athenians failed to take a sporting view of his double-dealing and denied his body repatriation.

Single-minded patriotism was more Roman than Greek: Regulus a prime exemplar; Coriolanus the self-important Awful Warning. Regulus was captured by the Carthaginians, in the third century BCE, when they were the dominant maritime and trading power in the Mediterranean. He was sent on parole to Rome after undertaking to urge the Senate to come to terms with the North African state. Free to address the senators, he took the opportunity to urge his countrymen to soldier on for final victory. The Roman fleet that made the Med. *Mare nostrum* (our sea) came later. The Senate begged Regulus to break his word and stay to lead the fight. No Alcibiades, he declared that personal honour required his return to Carthage, where he was tortured to death.

During Alcibiades' affair with the wife of one of the Spartan kings, the ground literally moved beneath them, exposing the embedded lovers to public view. Spartiates usually took an upper-classy view of adultery (replenishing the senior genetic pool came first); royal sex with an alien gallant was a liberty too far. The glamour boy skipped the tightrope back to Athens. Military savvy and social charisma retrieved the latter-day Achilles' reputation. Given command of the Aegean fleet, his brio might yet have won the war, had his subordinate Antiochus – keen to shine in the admiral's absence on a diplomatic mission – not led the Athenian navy to defeat at Notium in 406 BCE.

When catastrophe followed at Aegospotami, in the Hellespont, in 405 BCE, Lysander, the Spartan commander, did not box clever: three thousand Athenian prisoners were slaughtered. What historian has told us how so many men could be killed without the use of automatic weapons? Did none make a run for it? Was shame their jailer? Lysander's remorselessness served notice on his compatriots not to baulk his ascent to power at home. After Athens surrendered, he had flutes play as the insolent walls between the city and Piraeus were levelled. Meanwhile, Alcibiades, like some Hellenic Sundance Kid, was surprised in his latest beautiful mistress's bed. He scampered out of his Asiatic bolthole and died like a man, wounds facing his assassins. Lysander went to war again a few years later. He was killed at the siege of Haliartus in Boeotia. How many of the thoroughbred Spartiate elite mourned the downed upstart?

12

Whether or not Pythagoras merits sole credit for the trim theorem that bears his name (a recently discovered version dates from a thousand years before his lifetime), he is mythical for maintaining that numbers, odds better than evens, encode stable and ultimate truths, as Hasidic mystics hold that Hebrew letters do. Two and a quarter millennia later, Bertrand Russell and Alfred North Whitehead devoted many years to elaborating a not-dissimilar, sophisticated presumption in their *Principia Mathematica*. When twenty-year-old Ludwig Wittgenstein arrived on pilgrimage in Edwardian Cambridge he was quick, not to say eager, to disabuse his seniors of the fancy that higher mathematics could furnish basic truths more substantial than any apotheosis. However exhilarating the pace, you got nowhere fast on a roundabout. Intellectual honour required that Russell concede the prodigy's point; vanity had him bide his time.

The bundling of all the first philosophers as 'pre-Socratic' promotes the Athenocentrism consequent on Christian apologists enlisting the metaphysics of Plato and Aristotle. Immortality of the soul and the sun's rotation around the earth served as appetisers to glorify Christian doctrine. Torturers exacted endorsement. Long resident in Athens, Aristotle was born in 384 BCE in Stageira, in Chalcidice on the borders of

Macedonia, and – extravagant dresser – lived to play gaudy eminence to Alexander the Great. Close observer of nature, the Stagirite's wizard eye for the main chance led him to classify sheepish-sounding bah-barbarians as natural slaves. Conceits of a similar order would impel Jews, Romans, Christians and European imperialists – 'Aryans' not least – to presumptions of innate superiority.

For no few native Greeks, Alexander of Macedon rated hardly better than a semi-barbarian. He had to conquer Hellas before he could parade as its leader. When Alexander's father Philip sent word to the Spartans asking whether to come as friend or enemy, the Laconic retort was 'Neither'. Grexit, it might be termed, doomed them to survive only as a sidelined curiosity. Under the Roman imperium, tourists would come to patronise the sadistic initiations of the adolescents of the once-redoubtable polis.

The Christian/heathen, saved/damned dichotomy – touted by Evelyn Waugh, derided by George Orwell – was cribbed by literate Europeans from Hellenic and Jewish notions of exceptionalism. Greeks retained wary, if not envious, respect for Judaism's fundamental role. The Romans, then the British, idealised Spartan readiness to do or die, like guardsmen of various stamps. English public schools based their discipline of corporal punishment and lumpy porridge on the Laconic model. Cold baths, oafish team games, straight bats, never passing the soccer ball backwards made neo-Spartiates of the sons of upwardly mobile Victorian bourgeois. Vanities and prejudices studded their language. Austerity kept expenses down for their ushers.

The Lacedaemonians first entered the Peloponnese, so their myth boasted, as Dorian invaders from the north. By the seventh century BCE, they had supplanted and enslaved the Messenians, original inhabitants of the green valley of the Eurotas. The degradation of the Helots (Captives), as

Messenians came to be branded, was a precedent followed by European colonisers, especially the British. As the geographers' globe reddened, 'natives' became a term of disdain for original tenants who had lacked firearms. 'The first shall be last' – literally, in the case of the Tasmanian aborigines eliminated to the last man, woman and child by English arrivistes – assumed a sardonic aptitude for Christian colonisers.

13

'The Jews' have never been forgiven since their singular tribal deity JHVH was filched and represented as head of a confected universal Trinity. 'Stiff-necked' Semitic exceptionalism led to subjection to totalitarian warrants for mass murder. Jews became the quintessential affront to Christendom. The instatement of Israel is hated, in part at least, for defying the mythology of its enemies, left and right. A Jewish state's existence, in what they take for their heartland, is an affront to Muslim conceit, Christian Catholicity, meta-Marxist vanity. When did moderation appear on ideologues' agenda?

Philosophers *de tout bord* indulge in picking and choosing the Things That Count. Hegel's notion of Reason discounted whatever failed to fit his schematics, not least the precociousness of 'the Jews'. Schopenhauer, no philo-Semite, denounced Hegel's versatile verbosity as gobbledegook; so, in time, did G. E. Moore and Bertrand Russell, thus insulating the literate Anglo-Saxon tradition, Francis Bacon at its root, David Hume, John Stuart Mill, William James its perennial garland. By contrast, continental philosophers have sought to impose schemes on history by parading a 'logic' with pre-determining content and inevitable consequences. Threat and promise, rigour and malice forever hold hands, clench fists, wring necks.

Despite his adulation of the dictatorial Julius Caesar, scholar and Nobel laureate Theodor Mommsen (1817–1903) was outstanding in opposing Heinrich von Treitschke's grim fancy that 'the Jews' were 'Germany's misfortune'. Recognition of the play of chance, character and anomaly is more marked among historians, unless ideologically predisposed, like Eric Hobsbawm, than among philosophers. Not a few of the free world's monitors elect to appease, often to honour, those who denounce what the cant calls capitalism. Never retracting support for the Stalinist purges and massacres, mostly by starvation, of millions of so-labelled counter-revolutionaries, in particular Ukrainian *kulaks* (a factitious class of 'rich peasants', some flaunting luxuries such as a brass bedstead and a cow or two), Hobsbawm (excellent tutor, they say) has not flinched from chesting the British Companion of Honour. Two into one can fit very smoothly.

14

Isaiah Berlin slipped the works of Johann Gottfried Herder (1744–1803) through Oxford's customs in order to fortify his notion of individuality. For all the promotional diligence of Henry Hardy, Berlin blended hauteur with close-to-Pnin-striped deference. Elective hybridism offered an easy chair in the deeing and dumming of incompatibles. Human intelligence was boundless, he thought, but inconclusive. In the end, there is no end, possibly. The distinction between Berlin and Wittgenstein was that the former took flower-in-his-buttonhole pleasure in the money he inherited and, in due time, married.

While Isaiah became the Jeeves of All Souls, Wittgenstein disembarrassed himself of the taint of family wealth and played the Diogenes of Moral Sciences. Metaphorically speaking, W spent a lifetime washing his hands of lucre and hoping Jewishness would come off with it. He was generous with what cash was left, not least to the adherent Miss Anscombe. Told that Iris Murdoch proposed to be a writer, he gave her a wastepaper basket. Novelistic success disposed her to make less and less use of it.

Berlin relished cushioned living and entitled eminence. Suave arrivistes have showier manners and, like Bernard Shaw's Hungarian in *Pygmalion*, fancier phrasing than native speakers. The barbed courtesies exchanged between Berlin and T. S. Eliot, over the *numerus clausus* of Jews in the latter's scheme for a Christian society, qualify both *métèques* to play Rosencrantz and Guildenstern, the bland leading the bland.

Georg Simmel, nineteenth-century German Jewish professor, prototypical analytic philosopher, was *sans complexes* in saluting the role of money in human calculations. In his lucid account, it doubled as base in the fundamental and in what Freud would declare the faecal sense. While Wittgenstein admitted no instruction from Simmel's pioneering, ambiguities of a similar order appear in his depends-how-you-look-at-it duck'n'rabbit in *Philosophical Investigations*. Berlin followed suit in his zoological pairing with the contrast of *The Hedgehog and the Fox*, cribbed, with proper acknowledgment, from the seventh-century-BCE Parian poet Archilochus' lines: 'The fox has many tricks, the hedgehog only one: but it's a beauty.' Berlin chose to be vulpine, with a Shavian metic's exquisite vocabulary.

The meta-Hegelian comeback in recent years has furnished academic playmates with a new set of balls. Hegel's Reason constitutes an alluring example of persuasive definition. Positing a distinction between essential and contingent factors, he rigged History in the guise of a vessel on a course requiring a dialectically adroit Palinurus, a steersman who knows how to stay on board in rocky seas. Sartre made a distinction between essential and contingent fucks when proposing a lax, enduring sexual relationship with Simone de Beauvoir; was this ambivalence more apologetic (if not voyeuristic) than admirers care to guess? Jean-Marie Le Pen's rating of the Holocaust as a *point de détail* was a loutish recension of Hegel's premeditated trimming. Arnold Toynbee damned Israel on categorical grounds; it was, he said, a 'fossil state'. His judgement was petrified with Arab subsidies from states confected by France and Great Britain, later by the CIA, the better to retain control of Middle Eastern oil and its revenues. Purposeful scissors snip and snap, sometimes slip, in the hands of the tailors of the world's *histoire-géo*.

15

The first Greek philosophers had one common, negative characteristic: none gave overt offence to the Great King of Persia. Caution can encode audacity. Speculation in a subordinate argot or arcane discipline excites little offence. On the other side of the Aegean, sixth- and fifth-century-BCE Hellas – Attica in particular – was vivid with dramatic genius and musical verve, including the erotic Lydian mode, imported jazz deplored by Plato. In the Great Dionysia festivals, inaugurated by Athens's benign tyrant Peisistratus, the appearance of the *deus ex machina* at the end of a tragedy could resolve matters with one arbitrary bound. Euripides' Medea, after murdering her own children by the unfaithful Jason, was abstracted from mortal justice in the swooping chariot of her grandfather, the Sun.

Tragic theatre's formality, its masked male cast looming on high-heeled buskins, was long assumed inflexible, but how a piece is rehearsed, then performed, generates nuanced interpretations and sub/versions. Euripides' Helen chooses to sit out the Trojan War in Egypt. After a solemn, often three-part programme, tragedians wagged satyric tales to send the audience home with a laugh. Magniloquent Aeschylus could be more skittish than surviving manuscripts suggest. His comedies pursed orthodox lips and sent him into discreet exile. Theatre dismantles social niceties, puts insolence on the menu. Greek comedies pursed Christian lips and were piously Vati/ canned.

Unintended hilarity distinguishes the English translation of the *Oresteia* by the great refugee scholar Eduard Fraenkel, who was renowned (and tolerated) for groping female students, after he himself had been translated to Oxford. Performed aloud, Fraenkel's text would get more laughs than A. E. Housman's parodic chunk of tragic grandiloquence. Art Spiegelman's *Maus* (1980–1991) might be a sour remake of Homer's lost wars of the Lilliputian mice, a rodent riddling of the *Iliad*. Armand D'Angour, scholar and cellist, is restoring music that accompanied tragic choruses. Tragic masks demanded precise articulation, aided by the acoustics of the amphitheatre at Epidaurus where, it is said, you can hear a pin drop, like a Pinteresque pause.

At the mortified end of Athens's glorious fifth century, it seemed that the democratic model had foundered. The righteous blamed the vacillations of the (all-male) citizen voters and their susceptibility to *peitho*, rhetorical seduction. Plato, sly practitioner of the same art, if only on the written page, postulated that Opinion should defer to Knowledge as propounded by pundits who, like himself, craved neither money nor personal advancement. Did Socrates ever propound the immutable 'Ideas' whose certificate Plato wished on him? Would Jesus recognise Saint Paul as an accurate emissary? Cooking the books which their icons neglected to write was the salvation of those who honoured the Greek, spiked the Jew. What newly arrived Martian would today guess that Jesus never preached to any but the people from whom he was excerpted? Socrates' refusal to scamper into exile certified the centrality of Athens in his life. Some two thousand years later, the Nazi collaborator, rampant anti-Semite, *pédé* and Corneille scholar Robert Brasillach faced de Gaulle's firing squad with the hardly infamous last words, '*Vive la France quand même!*'

16

The seniority of truth was not native to Hellas. Beauty came first; so did coming first. Prizes and ovations were the rewards in both sport and the arts. Apart from whoever came second; no one commemorated who came second. Fifth-century, democratic Athens pulsed with competitive rhetoric; Spartans paraded a virtue of doing and dying without question. Victory over Athens was not won without a degrading price: in return for subsidies from the Persians, the Lacedaemonians conceded control of the Aegean to the Great King. His counsellors were sworn to report the truth, however disagreeable, less a moral than a courtly obligation. Without fearless informants, how could he administer or forestall what might be going on in his disparate realm?

Philosophy spawned conceits that clashed, quietly, with the so-called immutable laws of the Medes and Persians, old enemies paraded by Darius I and his successors as forever in step. The United States, the United Kingdom, the Soviet Union all came to enforce titular unities to bond clannish divisions, justify coercive leaders. Abraham Lincoln held the Constitution of the United States to demand the bloodshed that held the schismatic Union together. Confected societies (modern Greece not least) are apt to badge themselves with reproduction antiquity. Rowdy under-languages keep divisions vivid, puncture pomposity, sharpen dialogue.

Ephesian Heraclitus made a speciality of enigmatic dicta that acolytes were left to unpack: 'One cannot step in the same river twice'; 'A man's character is his fate'; or is it, as Greek grammar allows, 'A man's fate is his character'? Celebrating duplicities harboured by language, such as Heraclitus' *panta rhei* (everything is in a state of flux – sweetly mistranslated as 'all awry'), prefigures something of Heisenberg's Uncertainty Principle. When Heraclitus dares to say that the world is the province of what 'men do or do not call Zeus', he foreshadows Spinoza's *Deus sive natura* (God or Nature). The Hellenistic epitaph 'They told me, Heraclitus, they told me you were dead' mourns a different, sociable Heraclitus: no call to weep over the same one twice.

In what Wittgenstein, no mean coiner of oblique brevities, came to call 'the game', few play doubles. That amiable Oxonian Peter Hacker, W's prime exegete, fell out with his co-author, while on the same side of the net, over whether there could be what W called a 'private language'. A matter of definition was it (if it's private, it can't be a language) or of circumstance (there will always be a Turing to decode it)? Like Orwell's Snowball in *Animal Farm*, Hacker's oppo melted away. Bertrand Russell and Alfred North Whitehead's long collaboration, before the Great War, was essentially mathematical. How much else did they have in common, apart from Whitehead's wife?

17

The craving to play ruler (and rap knuckles) was as typical of
Pythagoras in the sixth century BCE, and of Plato in the fourth,
as of Hegel in the nineteenth century CE, Heidegger in the
twentieth. Plato's curriculum for apprentice philosopher-kings
was protracted and not leavened with laughs. The attempt to
impose it on Dion, rival and successor to Dionysius II, tyrant
of Syracuse, ended with the august tutor being dumped into
slavery on independent Aegina, across from Athens in the
Saronic Gulf, whence it was convenient for friends to ransom
him. Plato set up as master of his own Academy in shriven
Athens. Anti-democratic metaphysics was incorporated in
his factitious *politeia*, the so-called Republic: blueprint for a
triple-decker society of all-but-impermeable classes, hereditary
philosopher-kings on top, their authority strutted by the *gennaion
pseudos*, often translated as 'noble lie', more accurately
'genetic fakery'.

The Nazi fancy of innate Aryan supremacy, enforced
by blond beasts all set to put their boots in, was of a piece
with Plato's ideal society ruled by pedigreed 'Guardians',
top dogs backed by meta-Spartiate enforcers. When Martin
Heidegger retreated from *Heil*ing Hitler at close quarters, colleagues
whispered, 'Back from Syracuse?' Did he crack a smile
at the Platonic reference? That curt moustache argues for a

perpetually strict face. To be taken seriously, it is wise never to laugh out loud or, as Hitler observed, having seen early film of the tsar and his family scampering in what used to be called 'the altogether' into the sea, to be caught without bossy clothes on. The cadet Charles de Gaulle was never to be seen in the common *douches* at Saint-Cyr.

The creature that Desmond Morris, in his 1967 bestseller, called the 'Naked Ape' generally prefers to be cloaked in authority; General Orde Wingate, pragmatic Zionist and commander of the Chindits, an ostentatious exception; so too, I remember, Brough Stuart Churchill Gurney-Randall when he took *adsum* in Lockites in 1945, bushy and bare-assed in toshes (Charterhouse slang for after-football baths). Tall and spo-ey enough to qualify as a Blood, specialist in the now-illicit sliding tackle, dip-pen between gleaming off-the-field teeth, BSCGR would have been ideal casting for the public schoolboy who peaked too soon in Harold Nicolson's *Some People* (1927).

Heidegger never again ventured into practical politics; nor did he concede, after Hitler's fall, that he had been duped by the swaggering swastika. His vanity, like his secreted, voluminous anti-Semitism, remained immune to shame. His domination, intellectual and sexual, of Hannah Arendt, before and after the war, illustrates the futility of seeking determinant causes for human conduct. Even in her all-but-scathing, seldom witty English, Arendt paid dues to the teacher from whom, in her New York reincarnation, she sought, somewhat, to distinguish herself. Her quondam lover lent her something of the renown of Teresa Guiccioli, whose third husband chose to introduce her as *ma femme, ancienne maîtresse de Lord Byron*.

Heidegger's claim to mastery was echoed, with enhancing post-war effect, by Jean-Paul Sartre. In the human case alone, Sartre declared, in his impenetrable *L'être et le néant*, existence precedes essence: conscious choice decides the individual to be a man, or a dupe, as in a duplicate. Installing himself as the regulator who set the terms for redemption, Sartre escaped quizzing, for some years at least, with regard to his own *attentisme* during the Occupation. The protraction of *L'être et le néant* had served as his Penelope's shroud, as did the stretched shooting of Marcel Carné's *Les Enfants du Paradis* in covering a tranche of the acting profession, Jean-Louis Barrault *en tête*.

The curtain went up on Sartre's ambitious and ambiguous play, *Les Mouches*, attended by *le tout Paris collabo*, on the third of June 1943. Its ambiguity lay in whether the *mouches* (flies) plaguing ancient Argos stood for the Jews (hence acceptable by the Nazis) or – convenient to maintain in the *après-guerre* – the same flies stood for the Germans, who had been too thick to construe the sphinx-like Sartre aright. Just over a year later, D-Day promised the end of the Occupation and the re/turning of the coats of any number of those, Coco Chanel not least, preparing to make their peace with de Gaulle, Sartre not conspicuous among them. The enemies Poulou confronted were always liable to be fellow-citizens.

In return for Sartre's voluminous devotion, Heidegger put it about that his disciple had got it all wrong. Nice that one of the sons borne by the unrepentant Nazi Frau Heidegger was not her husband's. *Tournent, tournent mes personnages...* Max Ophuls kept it light and Viennesey in his film *La Ronde*, in which Anton Walbrook, intoning that refrain, played ringmaster. Max's son Marcel was less stylish, more sombre. His documentary about collaboration in wartime Clermont-Ferrand, *Le Chagrin et la Pitié*, tore away the camouflage concealing the degree to which the French (not only Vichy) authorities seconded the Holocaust. The Ophuls' original name was Oppenheimer.

18

Pythagoras, prototypical pied-piping redeemer, was a root-and-branch vegan: even kidney-beans, which he saw as cradled in embryonic down, were deemed what Jews call *trefa*, inedible. Dietetic foibles are not unusual symptoms of presumption. The Marchesa Casati (1881–1957), beauty, muse, riches-to-rags patron of the arts and artists, ate only white food; Hitler was a vegetAryan hot to spill blood, never swallow it; King George V of England recoiled when served soup at luncheon. The Roman emperor Caligula, in genial mood, wondered what Jews had against pork. Pythagoras and his suite had the presumption to assume power in the bulky city of Croton, in south-eastern Italy. In 510 BCE, they incited the Crotoniates to flatten the neighbouring city of Sybaris. Its sole remains are underwater flagstones. Sybarites banished poultry from the city limits, less out of dietetic refinement than because cockcrow disturbed their sleep. Their adjacent hedonism seems to have kept Pythagoras awake. After a term of his hegemony, native Crotoniates tired of righteous rigidity and expelled their cranky supervisor, as the Florentines would the killjoy Savonarola.

Democratic Croton's abiding native hero was Milon. Six times a sixth-century-BCE Olympic wrestling champion, a twenty-year reign, he was defeated, in old age, by a pine tree.

The trunk he had braced himself to split apart snapped back and clamped him in a lethal vice. No young Milon – said to have toted an ox above his head into the Olympic arena and then to have made a meal of it – was at hand to spring him.

Plato came to advocate immutable legislation of a kind still to be seen, aslant on chiselled tablets, in the inland Cretan city of Gortyn. His projected 'Politeia', also plotted to be inland, flourished no egalitarian manifesto. Naval powers, with their call for citizen-oarsmen, tended to be democratic. Ships' captains have to think for themselves. Plato's key parable, in the persuasively translated *Republic*, imagines humanity benched and chained in a cave. Backs to enlightenment, they infer immutable Truths only from shadows projected on the wall by the Reality they cannot face. Did it not occur to Plato that his troglodytes – like those who made their fires and mixed mineral colours in the caverns at Lascaux – might make their own palm-printed, mineral-coloured marks on the walls, followed by bolder presentations of the natural world and so make light of bondage?

Entertaining possibilities is the human genius; speculation and humour brighten mortality's cell. The Ten Commandments, if you undo the nots, double for a wanton's menu. Then again, what other species has a tongue loose enough to flatter itself with the notion of an afterlife? Achilles' shade did not think much of Hades. Eternal life essential to their prospectus, Christians hold that saints are 'with God'.

Plato and Pythagoras promised that their ideal states would transcend existing practices. For Plato, only root-and-branch carpentry could rectify the twisted timber of humanity; hence Platonic love? No; the preconceived sexlessness of the soul entailed that females must be eligible as Guardians. The struggle to rectify humanity's double-stranded character enthrals the lofty monkey-trainers of the world. The concept of soul generates fantasies of incorporeal virtue. Infinite life promises nothing in the way of extension; duration has no place in a timeless dimension. Might it not be that eternal bliss is but a blink of *jouissance*, the ultimate big bang threatened by Tom Lehrer?

19

Gilbert Ryle's *The Concept of Mind* (1949) deplores the notion of man having any kind of higher/inner personality, composed as it were of mental phlogiston. Student (Fellow) of Christ Church, Oxford, grandson of an Anglican bishop, Ryle was a wary iconoclast. As editor of *Mind*, the principal philosophical journal, he declined even to review Ernest Gellner's *Words and Things* (1959), a continental attack on the insular post-war Oxbridge notion of intellectual pertinence. Colin Wilson's *The Outsider* (1956), parading existentialism and allied continental fads, had been too manifestly the work of a twenty-five-year-old self-taught amateur to merit so much as dismissal. Hailed as a precocious masterpiece by posh Sunday critics, it did little to impress Oxbridge pundits. Cyril Connolly and Philip Toynbee turned on Wilson when he was revealed as a turtle-necked, sleeping-in-the-open self-publicist without classy connections. *The Outsider*'s sequel was panned, as if in apology for previous enthusy-musy. Not visibly fazed, Colin – in that orange turtle-necked sweater – continued to publish books on the macabre and the outlandish between enjoying singsongs (he invited me to one) at the ungentlemanly Savage Club.

Straight-faced Ryle was by no means always unambiguous. At a lecture I attended in 1950s Cambridge, he spoke of 'the q-ness of p', and then again of the 'p-ness of q'. Might he have hoped to get a laugh? Smirks he did. When Bertrand Russell rallied to Gellner, he was deemed an 'old troublemaker'. They spared him the hemlock. Gellner served due notice on the Oxbridge aversion from examining links between ideological warrants and mass murder. At the beginning of the war, Wittgenstein was scandalised when his friend and disciple Norman Malcolm claimed that there were ruses too far below the belt for decent Englishmen to be capable of employing. W knew, first-hand, if briefly, that supposedly civilised Austrians (and Germans) after the *Anschluss* had blighted for good the illusion that some strand of humanity was incapable, genetically, of ruthless brutality. When the Shoah became public knowledge, did he ever show any symptom of outrage?

Jews who seek to detach themselves from the Semitic bind, not to say blight, are no rarity. Max von Oppenheim has been pilloried as the Nazis' would-be Max of Arabia. Keen amateur archaeologist, Middle Eastern cognoscente, he was accepted by Berlin as the man to recruit the Arabs to the Nazi cause. Hermann Goering welcomed his services and, in that connection, said that it was for him, as Reichsmarschall, to decide who was a Jew and who was not. While Himmler was a schoolmasterly follower of the rules, Goering chose to be a pot-bellied, medal-plaited drug addict and thief who gave self-indulgence a bad name. Max von Oppenheim mourned German losses in the war, never mentioned the Holocaust.

Secession from Jewishness was unremarkable in the ancient world. Tiberius Julius Alexander, born in a Jewish family in Alexandria, became Vespasian's chief of staff in the Judaean War. Wholehearted Roman, he supervised the crucifixion of countless Jews after the fall of Jerusalem in 70 CE. In the 1920s, Long Island's East Hampton was an exclusive enclave for well-heeled Wasps. The dandified gatekeeper was revealed, at the end of his life, to have been born a Jew.

20

Plato had it that political playing to the gallery resembled pastry-cookery. The brothers Churriguera combined civility and ostentation in the crusty extravagance of Salamanca's Plaza Mayor. In 1936, Miguel de Unamuno, of that city's famous university, stood up, alone, for the humanist values which fascism and communism promised to crush. After Millán Astray's infamous endorsement of death had been greeted with the cheers of Falangistas, the isolated Unamuno found the nerve to say, 'You are all hanging on my words. You know me and you know that I am unable to be silent. Sometimes to be silent is to lie…' He proceeded to denounce that 'necrophilous and senseless cry' and added, 'General Millán Astray is a cripple. Let it be said without any slighting undertone. He is a war invalid. So was Cervantes. Unfortunately, there are too many cripples in Spain just now. A cripple without the spiritual greatness of Cervantes is liable to seek ominous relief in causing mutilation around him.'

Placed under immediate house arrest, Unamuno died, broken, on the last day of 1936, hidalgo reputation intact. The Spanish Republic, deserted by the democracies, subverted by the USSR's malevolent support, fought for almost three years before it was stifled. The 1971 film *Viva la Muerte* parodies the Christian notion that this life is an entrance exam for the life to come. On the other hand, if you are killing, you are not dying: the funereally uniformed SS had death's heads on their dress caps. Gabriele d'Annunzio's precociously erotic 1894 novel *Il Trionfo della Morte* (is there anything remotely so wanton in the Victorian English novel?) supplied early mulch for fascism's lethal ambivalence. Solo high-flying – d'Annunzio's flash hobby when older – has been a recurrent element of quasi-supermanliness ever since Daedalus took off from Crete, Charles Lindbergh from St. Louis, Yuri Gagarin into space.

21

Architectural historian Sigfried Giedion (1888–1968) advocated unadorned design – Ionic, never Corinthian – as the
framework for an honest society. Wittgenstein's steel-and-glass
scheme for his sister's house in Vienna exemplified three-
dimensional rectitude. W had the precision and the budget to
disqualify a window frame three millimetres untrue to specifi-
cation. Charm, I observed, is entirely absent. Francis Bacon's
'Houses are built to live in, not to be looked on' primes Anglo-
Saxon aversion from piss-elegance. Bacon, Lord Chancellor
in 1618, carried a discreet gay streak; his twentieth-century
painter namesake dispensed with the discretion.

Jews and homosexuals came to be categorised in adjacent
files by post-war civilisation's headmistress, Hannah Arendt.
Outside the pale of Christendom, she held that disqualifica-
tion from salvation obliged them to be grateful for privileged
peonage. Robert Parker's *Miasma* (1983) stands as a handbook on the Greek notion of incurable pollution in the wake of
sacrilege. The Spartans accused Pericles of carrying an abiding
hereditary blight because his maternal great-great-great-grand-
father Megacles (the Big Famed) murdered supporters of a rival
who had sought sanctuary at an altar. Rare intelligence is most
happily trusted by Authority when its provider is known to
have something to hide. Daedalus, mythical archetype of the

craftsman and of craftiness, was a murderer on the run from Athens, grateful to find sanctuary by serving Minos, king of Crete. Duplicity doubled for freedom when he betrayed his benefactor by fashioning a frame to allow the king's lust-infected wife Pasiphae to be mounted by a bull; whence the Minotaur. Minos was a hoarder; Daedalus too inventive a traitor to be dumped. The Minotaur's maze, underground pen with no key, was his clever apology.

Subservience rendered betrayal a sly pleasure. Arms extended and winged with waxed feathers, the scoundrel took off from Crete to southern Italy. Minos was teased into fatal pursuit. Daedalus' incautious son Ikaros soared too close to the sun, melted his plumage's fixative and crashed off the island that now bears his tag. Minos was gulled by Daedalus' new patron, an Italian tyrant, into taking a shower and was scalded to death. Daedalus' art and his son's high-flying piqued the wit of Pieter Breugel the Elder, Pablo Picasso, Michael Ayrton, Maggie Hambling and Sarah Raphael (alone in depicting the infant Minotaur as a calf at Pasiphae's breast).

22

Constructed near Marseille, Le Corbusier's Unité d'habitation (1945) was advanced as the three-dimensional maquette for undifferentiated, classless post-war communities. When I first and last visited it, in 1959, its presumption of human appetite for uniformity had already inclined those filed in its steel-and-concrete cabinet to display dissentient individuality in wall colouring and balcony decoration. Marching in step is and is not a human propensity. Le Corbusier's designs appealed to grand patrons, less to those drafted to live and summoned to work in them. His League of Nations building in Geneva is a whited sepulchre for the illusion of an architecturally regulated, sharp-edged world. As his world-cultural achievements paraded, grandiose pseudonymity (the Corb was baptised Charles-Edouard Jenneret) purged him of familiar obligations. His nominal claim to singular status trumped the particule common among French toffs and tricksters. His rival for architectural supremacy, self-styled Mies van der Rohe (originally Maria Ludwig Michael) decked his 'Mies' with an umlaut and added 'van der Rohe', to clog it with an appearance more Dutch than German. Ann Sussman and Justin Hollander's *Cognitive Architecture* (2021) blows the gaff on the assertive aesthetic of post-1918 Bauhaus-inspired modernism. They see its advocates as primarily ambitious to take command of their profession.

Pseudonyms efface puerile gaucheries and often clip first names: Voltaire, Junius, Stendhal, Elia, Cassandra, Taper and who all else. Aristotle's successor as head of the Lyceum, né Tyrtamus, was nicknamed Theophrastus, 'divinely phrased', by pupils and admirers. Stall-holders in the Athenian agora (marketplace) recognised and, we may guess, mocked his Lesbian tones, for all his exquisite phrasing. Theophrastus' *Characters*, a lively deck of thirty cards, illustrates the variety, as well as the recurrence, of human types. Having lived for more than a hundred years, he complained, on his deathbed, that it had been nothing like long enough for everything he had to say.

23

Philosophers, like plain-clothed prophets, are liable to claim rare insight into the world's moral coils, unique access to follow-my-lead solutions; Michel de Montaigne (1532–93), ex-mayor of Bordeaux, was an undemanding, if not modest, exception. More mercurial than curial, he quit the Gironde only to take a long ride to Rome, Canossa never on his itinerary. His essays, serene and self-centred, resemble rambling letters to his precocious friend Étienne de la Boétie, a Sarladais, who died young. The latter's *Discours de la Servitude Volontaire* is a classic denunciation of place-seekers. Who but a denizen of *La France profonde* could have dared to compose it?

One sunny midday, I collapsed in front of La Boétie's tall, early-Renaissance diamond-paned, sandstone house in Sarlat-la-Canéda. I thought I was dying but was neither in pain nor distressed. Then again, I wasn't dying. Kind builders restoring the house called an ambulance, and I too was restored. La Boétie left his library to Montaigne, who never forgot him. To explain their ardent friendship he could say only, '*parce-que c'était lui, parce-que c'était moi*'. Montaigne's essays are a soloist's duet. Philosophers more often fall out than remain in bond to each other. Ardent disciples can give unforgiven offence: Friedrich Waismann's unassuming devotion to Wittgenstein's ideas amounted, in W's view, to plagiarism.

Having renounced a fortune, Wittgenstein remained jealous of his intellectual property. Did it ever occur to him that, had he repaired to the USSR, as he considered doing in the mid-1920s, he would have been docked of a Jew's inalienable contraband, the disposition to think for himself?

Dorothea Krook's 1962 study of Henry James, *The Ordeal of Consciousness*, analyses the pride and pain of unabridged cogitation. W's absorption into Stalin's Russia might have echoed the disappearing act of Empedocles when he kindled rumours of his immortality by leaping into the furnace mouth of Mount Etna. Winston Churchill, like Julius Caesar, was quick to compose a monumental account of his finest hour. On Churchill's retirement from the House of Commons, his portrait was commissioned as a tribute and painted by Graham Sutherland. Its puffy second-childhood face so vexed its subject and his wife Clemmy that they destroyed it, a singular case of a great man offing his own head to embellish his reputation.

Conformity was scarcely Wittgenstein's habit. In the Austrian Army, on the Italian front in the Great War, young Ludwig volunteered as lookout on a church spire with a view to the enemy lines. He was, we may guess, up there, alone, adjacent to the cross, wrestling with the same devils Russell observed him to be haunted by in pre-war Cambridge. W's elevated post, as purposeful *meteora phrontistes*, allowed him to do his duty without marching in step. Apprentice solipsist, observing no holy days, on Christmas Day 1916 he made a set of philosophical notes.

Recovered from that 1920s infatuation with the Party, Wittgenstein yielded to no subsequent ideological allegiances. Freudian analysis did, however, influence what came to be called 'therapeutic positivism'. *Philosophical Investigations*, published posthumously, as were W's brown and blue notebooks, propounded a method (shades of Sherlock Holmes), never a conclusive doctrine. What would it be to have the last word and who might pronounce it? Lucretius' image, of the man standing on '*flammantia moenia mundi*' (the flaming ramparts of the world), flinging a spear into the void, stands for an infinity of possibilities. Immeasurable in length and duration, infinity is not a very large number. Eternal life, Paul the propagandist's promise of eternal life for the faithful, likewise?

Does logic have any tight kinship with ethics? It supplies no intelligence extraneous to a proposition's premises; only false postulates or inept practice can wring novelties from its exercise; hence Wittgenstein's 'in logic there are no surprises'. In the same spirit, stunning Russell, young W perceived pure mathematics to be a tautologous construct: numbers and symbols, however elaborately ranged, cannot deliver truths that are not implicit in their rigging. On the other hand, common language's purse chinks with clipped coinage, milled counterfeits, practical currency.

But wait, possibly! Is information of a kind not conveyed by, for instance, 'It is either raining or it is not raining'? Admittedly without meteorological value, the statement posits that, in correct English, it can never rain and not rain at the same time and, more practically, that 'raining' denotes something in the world. By contrast, the Hungarian director Mike Curtiz, who said, 'You think I know fuck nothing, but you're wrong: I know fuck all', made no useful distinction, unforgettably. Logic flirts with language, but crops it of all save unambiguous consistencies. The futility of asking for the real meaning of ambivalent tropes is illustrated by Wittgenstein's image of the rabbit and the duck: audit it one way, it quacks, in another, it springs flopsy ears. What demonstrates a term's value is its use: how it plays in the concert of language.

24

The postulate of Jesus as integral intermediary can be read as an attempt to make the filial Almighty available to committed suppliants, the Holy Ghost his answer-service. Does Allah offer such facilities? Am I joking? Must I not? Why? If the advocates of faith, Christian and Muslim, were as sure of their dogmas as they insist, would they not pity or laugh at those who ignore their invitations rather than pursue them, down the centuries, with murderous indignation? The pagan shrines most often built in the Hellenistic Age were those dedicated to Tyche, Fortune or Luck. Tyche and tee-hee have a pronounced, if capricious, affinity.

Arthur Koestler became obsessed by the notion that there had to be some ulterior scheme in command of chance. He craved a non-denominational verity beyond Einstein's $E = mc^2$, which promises only that quietus is forever elusive. In the early 1980s, incurably quivering with Parkinson's disease, Koestler elected to trump resignation by making his own exit. That his lover chose to die with him has excited feminists into claiming that he coerced a healthy younger woman into a deadly duo. A counter-story claims that she had cancer. I almost dined with K at George Steiner's house in Cambridge. 'The one man sentenced to death by both the Fascists, in Spain, and Communists, in Russia. History on two legs,' George nominated him, rare dish. I wished G had not invited me at the last minute (who let him down?). I had promised Beetle I'd be home for dinner. 'You are uxorious, sir,' George said.

With a not-uncommon tincture of malice, George had invited Christopher Logue to be of the company. Until sprung by international fame, Koestler had been in the condemned cell in Málaga for a short time; Logue spent six penitential months in a British Army glasshouse, arguably a much ruder experience. To Steiner's naughty applause, Logue also wrote a lively version of the *Iliad* without knowing a word of ancient Greek. Rabid Red, it amused Logue to tote a well-used Rothschild female on his arm; so did it Joan Littlewood of the Unity Theatre to favour a French baron of that house. Glossing Proudhon's notion that property is theft, Littlewood held art not to have owners and, we are told, unhooked a valuable picture for a casual admirer. Anthony Blunt's communism was said to be fostered by indignation that several Poussins in the Queen's collection were secluded from public inspection. As keeper of Her Majesty's pictures, he had privileged access. Imagine his *à nous deux maintenant* smile.

Forty-three years before Koestler swallowed his dose of quietus, he and Walter Benjamin divided lethal quantities of a drug that Koestler always carried with him, defiance sealed with resignation. Benjamin took his helping almost immediately, in 1940 Portbou, fearing himself cornered by the Gestapo in that low-lying end-of-the-line town. Franco's Spain advertised its distinction by having uniquely gauged railway tracks. I visited Benjamin's blanched, single-flowered tomb in a marble stack overlooking the Med and snapped it for Steiner. Without the necessary papers or chutzpah to bluff his way across the border, Benjamin lacked the puff to leg it, up and over, into Spain. Steiner and Benjamin were alike in lavishing their energy on second-order commentary. Benjamin affected distaste for Joseph Roth's grub-street industry and soiled person but had to acknowledge that sorry, split figure's unblinkered, briskly inventive genius. Roth is buried in the Parisian Catholic Cimetière de Thiais. His masterpiece, *The Radetzky March*, plays on for him.

One of my earliest journalistic jobs was to ghost the memoirs of a bespectacled Anglo-Belgian church-furnisher turned Special Operations Executive agent. Jacques Doneux escaped occupied France by kicking foot-holes in the icy Pyrenees, nothing on his feet but ropey espadrilles. He lost several toes to frostbite on the way up and over. After long and painful treatment, Jacques limped in to report to the British ambassador in Madrid. Sir Samuel Hoare, the side-lined appeaser, greeted him with: 'I sometimes think you people are more trouble than you're worth.' How many of his pliable kind would not have shaken hands, as Philippe Pétain did, with a victorious Hitler had he come to enthrone Edward VIII puppet king of England? A list of the Gestapo's attendant collaborators lies secreted, beyond the usual time limit, in Whitehall's deepest vault.

Walter Benjamin's best-known essay dwells on what he promised to be the devaluing effect of the mechanical reproduction of paintings. In fact, thanks to the publicity engendered by photography, TV and AI, the art market in originals has never ceased to rise. Dr Sir Jonathan Miller wrote (almost certainly dictated) a pamphlet, in the Modern Masters series, in which he derided Marshall McLuhan's claim that the medium was the message. The evolution of TV, garrulous print journalism, tweeting, variant forms of 24/7 hustling and hazing, the iconisation of the cliché, promise that McLuhan was on the money.

25

In the *entre-deux-guerres*, high season of schisms and isms, Julien Benda's *La Trahison des Clercs* – published in 1927, the same year as Heidegger's *Sein und Zeit* (*Being and Time*) – denounced braying intellectuals who allowed their judgement to be warped, left and right, in return for billets on the facades of ideological temples. Tyrants keep happy mats for Yoricking courtiers and pliable opinonators. George Bernard Shaw applauded Mussolini, both players to the gallery among life's one-man show-offs. When a hostess asked, 'Did you enjoy yourself, Mr Shaw?' 'It's the only thing I did enjoy,' said the twinkler with the garrulous eyebrows, a penchant for political bully boys and a *faible* for leading ladies such as Mrs Patrick Campbell.

Christianity made solemnity stand for piety. It was said of the sixteenth-century Spanish mystic John of Avila that he never had a joke in his mouth. 'No hope for them as laughs,' the Aberdeen preacher said to the giggling young Byron (who had just goosed his silly mother with her own hat-pin). In Umberto Eco's *The Name of the Rose*, an implacable monk does away with the last copy of Aristotle's book on comedy. He takes it to be a deplorable appendix to the Stagirite's serviceable proto-Christian corpus. When, in 415 CE, a Christian mob came to lynch the Alexandrian pagan polymath Hypatia, she flaunted menstrual evidence of her femininity to mock the manly warrant they flashed to fuel their pious arrogance. They murdered her all the same.

The philosopher and the clown have more in common than routine distinctions allow. Impudence can find favour with power, Fool with Lear. Crowns do go to other people's heads. Liberal in Catholic France, Voltaire took pride in courting Prussia's proto-Hitlerian Frederick the Great (and railed against Jews after a German bank declined the honour of giving him an unsecured loan). More sentimental than wise, Winston Churchill played the true-blue royalist until absconding Edward VIII scuttled his own butt. In power, Churchill relished the arrogant fealty of Frederick Lindemann, first Lord Cherwell, aka 'the prof'. Forty per cent of Germany's 'Aryan' academics, Heidegger *en tête*, rallied to Hitler, Gabriele d'Annunzio, Curzio Malaparte to Mussolini. While installed in capitalism's pampered positions, no few Western intellectuals hung out their wishing on the Party line. Propriety and *méchanceté* are adjacent strangers, like crossed fingers.

Benda's *mauvaise foi* was reprised and distorted after the war, with no acknowledgment, by Jean-Paul Sartre. He applied bad faith to those who flinched from being party-lining *engagés*. Self-denying commitment to the proletarian cause supplanted honour. Louis Aragon and Elsa Triolet were exemplary in homage to Stalin; it married them, likewise Louis Althusser, who came to murder the wife who – could it be? – kept his honour clamped to dishonour. Post-war converts to *gauchiste* ideology were required to jettison the integrity which unbending Benda had advanced against the pied pipers of the 1930s.

Sartre exulted in being big enough to be cowed. In his 1948 play *Les Mains Sales*, catchily retitled *Crime Passionel*, Hugo, bourgeois convert to the Party, fails to honour his mission to assassinate the 'deviationist' Hoederer. Hoederer's forceful character – more enjoyable to create, one guesses, than any exemplary Red – disarms Hugo and seduces his wife Olga. How shall we read her? How should she be played, did Sartre imagine? Now deep, then shallow, female characters escape precise prescription. Freud never dared to conjecture what women want. I once told a clever female that I thought 'attention'. Janet agreed. Satisfaction is never enough.

How many strong women find power aphrodisiac, submission a salty tale? Few stand up to be counted *après coups*. Coco Chanel was one, Arletty another. CC got away with having had affairs with ranking Germans during the Occupation by pleading that while her heart belonged to France, what use she made of other parts was her own affair, not to say business. Evelyn Waugh's 1920s diaries refer to an Enid Raphael, whom he reports as saying, 'I don't know why they're called private parts; mine aren't private.' Provincial French girls and women who had consorted with Germans of no impressive rank had their heads shorn and were subject to abuse stemming from parochial righteousness and, in not a few cases, their chasteners' lack of comely charm. Plain women do like to speak for the sex, cuddled causes their babies.

26

Hiroshima Mon Amour (1959), directed by Alain Resnais, script by Marguerite Duras, features a heroine who had an affair with a young German during the war. Shorn by liberated moralists, she repairs to Japan and takes a lover from the city callously, never pointlessly, razed by the Americans. Duras was in the Resistance group that included her lover François Mitterrand. Vanity conflated her personal and literary lives. In a headlined case in 1980 she lent her prestige to the claim that his mother murdered 'le petit Grégory'. After many years, it was established that the mother was innocent; so much for the validity of *intimes convictions*. Duras made no audible apology. Patricia Cornwell, whose thrillers thrill many people, has taken the rich liberty of accusing Walter Sickert of having been Jack the Ripper. Some of the murders took place during Sickert's absences in London. More Watson than Holmes, Ms Cornwell's success in contriving conundrums has given her Pythian delusions.

At the end of *Les Mains Sales*, we are left with the impression that Olga has the mutability to survive. Confusion unmans Hugo. As the curtain falls, he is going out to meet the killers (shades of Hemingway's story of that name) who he knows have been deputed by the comrades to dispose of him.

Embracing ruthlessness he cannot match, he all but boasts that he is '*irrécupérable*', beyond redemption.

Michael Ayrton, too clever and too literate to fit a popular pigeon-hole, toyed with Hugo's fate. He liked to think that facing Red executioners would amount to a contribution to the Future and give his life a redemptive crown, albeit of thorns. Charles Dickens had Sidney Carton say, 'It is a far, far better thing that I do than I have ever done...' as he ascends the steps to the guillotine. One of George Steiner's I-promise-you-it's-true stories was of the French aristocrat who arrived at the same destination in a tumbril. He folded down the corner of the book he was reading, as if to resume *sa lecture* later.

Frank Leavis, untouched by Dickens's sentimental streak, unimpressed by his facility, awarded him no place in the Great Tradition. Throughout his proud ostracism by the Cambridge English Faculty, Leavis craved entry to the peerage of the academic world. Publicised walks with Wittgenstein, in open-necked outsiderdom, were as close as he came to deference. W is on record as donning a tie only once, for the purpose of presenting a respectable face to the Newnham principal, when seeking, in vain, to have his protégée Elizabeth Anscombe granted a fellowship. I once bought and still own a complete set of Leavis's house mag, *Scrutiny*. Offers?

27

Horace's 'Dulce et decorum est pro patria mori' (it is sweet and proper to die for one's fatherland) came richly from a poet who switched sides smartly after, if not during, the decisive Battle of Philippi in 42 BCE. Quintus Horatius Flaccus, briefly a republican tribune, survived to become the dutiful laureate of Augustus Caesar. In due season, he reeled off the rarely read Carmen Saeculare as well as more light-hearted, exquisite embellishments of the Augustan age. Commissioned to write the *Aeneid*, Publius Virgilius Maro – another early supporter of the eclipsed republicans – was primed with cash and kudos to supply a warrant for empire grafted on a Homeric source. In revised livery, the young man from Mantova wound up lodged in a mansion on the Palatine. Desire to root Catholicism in antiquity vested itself in Dante's vision of the supposedly prophetic Virgil playing the part of cicerone to the *Inferno*. Lope de Vega, on his deathbed, came out with, 'Now I can say it: Dante is a bore.'

The Death of Virgil (1945) by Hermann Broch, learned and lecherous Austrian refugee, imagined the dying poet, conscience-stricken by his subservience to Augustus, asking that the *Aeneid* be destroyed. He is more likely to have been ashamed of its unrevised state than of himself for composing it. The emperor made sure that the *Aeneid*, however fractured, would survive to deck his reign. As impartial in criticism as heartless in politics, the old and serene Augustus, long-established *primus inter pares*, once caught his grandson reading Cicero. When the boy stammered excuses, the emperor applauded the literary merits of 'the father of his country' whom, as the young Octavian, he himself had consigned to Mark Antony's cut-throats before rising by life's bloody and twisted stair to Francis Bacon's 'great place'.

To ignore a writer's last wish can be the happiest service a friend renders, as Max Brod did Franz Kafka when he locked his friend's manuscripts in a safe place. Byron's publisher, John Murray, and his poet friend Tom Moore ('Tommy loves a lord,' Byron said) burnt the prodigy's hot diaries, a prim turn that did no one a favour. It is reported that when Byron's body was disinterred, his genitals were well-preserved and uncommonly large. Bisexuality and buy-sexuality had kept them busy.

Julien Benda remained true to principle as Benedict Spinoza had when he disdained the false messiah Sabbatai Sevi in 1666 and the Gadarene rush of Jews who rallied to him. Both discounted Judaism while never denying Jewish origins. Benda's range was clipped by Gallic decorum and his own aptitude for detachment. His novella *Les Amants de Tibur* (1928) has as its hero the elegiac poet Sextus Propertius, whose conspicuous refusal to pander to Augustan vanity made him a 'clerk' worth honouring.

Ezra Pound's *Homage to Sextus Propertius* (1919), on the other hand, was a premature fascist salute from a writer whose treason would be literal and, save for caged months in liberated Pisa, unpunished. Pound's howler-ridden versions of the poet (*minas*, Latin for threats, rendered as 'mines', etc.) were ridiculed by Robert Graves, applauded as creative descants by my scholar contemporary John Patrick Sullivan, one of whose undergraduate works was an edition of 'Twas on the good ship Venus, / By god you should have seen us', complete with po-faced *apparatus criticus* and variant readings.

During the Occupation of France, between 1941 and 1944, Benda was forced into hiding. Perhaps mindful of the massacre of Saint Bartholomew's Day, 1572, French Protestants, descendants of its victims, were humane and resourceful when it came to hiding Jews. In *Exercice d'un enterré vif* (1945), Benda describes returning, after the Liberation, to his ransacked Parisian apartment. He discovers himself purged of concern with belongings, and of the illusion of belonging. Jean-Paul Sartre may have toyed with Benda's experience in his 1948 play *Morts Sans Sépulture*, about a clutch of resistance fighters in the condemned cell. Its production implied that its author had been in similar case. Judging and being judged quicken the imaginations of political novelists; margins run down the middle of their pages.

28

Archetypical imperialist, Alexander the Great admired Diogenes, quick wit, ostentatious pauper, public masturbator. The cynic from Sinope, on the Black Sea, Diogenes declared the earthenware *pithos* (storage jar) he made his kennel to be empire enough, insolence his game. On asking what he could do for the dogged hermit, Alexander was requested to step out of his sunlight. The restless Macedonian would later trek for two days across the Libyan desert to the oracle at Siwa where a subsidised magus was reported to have pronounced him the son of Zeus. Had it been true, why play the postulant? Then again, why do gods crave worship? Of what are they 'jealous'? Mortality and its dicey options? Almost a celebrity, Roy Strong told George Steiner, so GS told me, that he would have had more success, whatever that might have been, had he been a Jew. George himself, Heidegger's apologist, can be suspected of craving crucifixion at illustrious hands. How typical of G to come up with the names that scholiasts gave to each of the nails used to pin Jesus on the cross!

29

Plato did not inscribe himself among the company when he immortalised Socrates' last hours in *Phaedo*. Had he funked that illustrious wake? Was he already scribbling his enhanced, not to say perverted, recension of his master's ideas or was he reluctant to confess to a junior place among Socrates' intimates? In the old school of classical studies, piety presumed that worthwhile writers depicted their subjects reliably. Academics disparaged Gaius Suetonius' glittering history of a dozen caesars on account of its obsession with the bawdy. Roman erotic murals promise that scandal was more accurate, much, than prim critics cared to concede. The cutest sexy mosaics are in the baths at Piazza Armerina in Sicily where, in the twilight of the Roman Empire, bathers had slim bikinied beauties for underwater company. Not far away, below the surging black rock of Enna, is the cleft down which Minos, king of the underworld, subtracted printennial Persephone. After Demeter threatened to cancel spring unless her daughter (compromised by having tasted Minos' pomegranates) was sprung from Hades for six months in the year, the seasons settled in their quarters.

Advocates of dialectical materialism took their warrant from what they took to be history's predestined timetable; hence Wystan Auden's (later deleted) endorsement of 'the necessary murder', a copy-writer's tag-line, while paying his dues to the right (Left) side in the Spanish Civil War. Out of the library, bookish persons are liable to hanker after rough trade. Poet and cinematic maestro Pier Paolo Pasolini (1922–75) all but solicited his own martyrdom at the hands of the Ostian blades who did for him. Murderous company gave him a thrill as the East End's Kray Brothers did Bob Boothby and assorted toffs. Sado-masochistic fascism, which Pasolini denounced as abhorrent, carried mimetic allure. Giovanezza, Italian fascism's marching song, had a *dolce vita* echo in Caterina Spaak's 1960 hit '*Noi siamo giovani... l'esercito del surf*'.

Albert Speer's decor for the Nazis' Nuremberg rallies, strident avenues of light both illusory and imperious, grafted Wagnerian pretentiousness to *mise-en-scène* of the grandiose order which Max Reinhardt, booted into exile by the Nazis, had pioneered. Plagiarism comes in brazen appropriation no less than in petty pilfering. If modern art's celebration of imposture began with Jacques-Louis David's portrait of Napoleon's self-coronation, it culminated, downwards, with that painting of Hitler, in armour, as an equestrian meta-Christian crusader, unsleeping sword in hand, devil in drag. Art and kitsch go first to war, then to market. Andy Warhol's Campbell's soup cans proved that counterfeit can become more valuable than the real thing, much. The displacement of value by price marks the post-1960s obsolescence of morals and puts paid to young Wittgenstein's equivalence of ethics with aesthetics.

30

Stalin's annual parades in Red Square publicised the rocky status of however many ear-muffed apparatchiks had survived unpurged to stand beside and below him on that granitic podium. Left and right, the iconic tradition persisted in the monstrance of the Great Leader's quasi-deified person. Hitler's long, black Mercedes was a rolling pedestal. If National Socialism made little effort to recruit intellectuals, it scarcely lacked them. Dr Goebbels's loutish henchmen chucked much modern literature to the flames. Thomas Mann was envious of his brother Heinrich when the latter's books were burnt, his own not. Shades of Zero Mostel's lament in Mel Brooks's *The Producers*, 'Where did we go right?' Mann's recourse to the allied side has incurred none of the scorn visited on Flavius Josephus for retreating to Rome after risking his life in seeking to persuade the obstinate Zealots, murderers of many moderate Jews inside beleaguered Jerusalem, to come to terms with Vespasian. Being right can prove unforgivable.

Paintings deemed decadent by Hitler's follow-my-leader aesthetes resumed valuable currency in due time. Not a few were secreted by those who bet both ways, an Austrian speciality. After the war, Vienna's National Gallery sought to hold onto works confiscated from Jews. Following protracted litigation, it was ordered to return them. The Gallery then asked the owners to allow it to have them on permanent loan. David Pryce-Jones was among those who did not feel drawn to that genial concession. Hermann Göring had shown the way by pillaging Europe's great collections without affectations of Teutonic selectivity. His brother Albert collected Jews and smuggled them into Switzerland. Heidegger's brother Fritz declared Martin a straight-faced Dadaist and preserved his letters, for all their damning anti-Semitism.

Karl Marx's bookish diligence generated scholarly progeny: E. H. Carr, the Webbs, J. D. Bernal and who all else stretch – not unlike the gassed and blinded Tommies leading each other in John Singer Sargent's Great War painting – in a blinkered row to pay homage to the voluminous Stalin. While Nazism blared and stamped and had favours to bestow, it culled no shortage of treasonous clerks: Alfred Rosenberg manifestly specious, Carl Schmitt and Martin Heidegger egregiously sophisticated. Unsmiling and – even after history's misread tide had turned – unapologetic, Heidegger conceded no fault. Betraying pre-1933 friends and pupils (Husserl by Heidegger, Leo Strauss by Schmitt) furnished an earnest of ideological engagement. Deprived of bounties and bully-boy sidekicks, spiteful ravers affected to have been victimised, Céline *en tête*. Albert Speer, Hitler's slave-master, enacted the cleverest of humbug recantations. His subordinates paid his bill by being executed.

Plato's *Apologia* was what Socrates said, or is said to have said, in no apologetic spirit, in his own defence at his trial. *The Consolation of Philosophy* was written by Boethius (476-524 CE) after he had been condemned to death by the ageing Theodoric the Great, whose intellectual counsellor he had been. He had probably done nothing more treasonous than wonder where the power was going after the emperor's death and how to find favour with it. While in the tower awaiting judicial shortening at the hands of James I and Robert Cecil (whom he had addressed as 'Little Man'), that tall Devonshire man Sir Walter Raleigh set out to see how far he could get on a stylish history of the world. The sailor-poet who had singed the king of Spain's beard never apologised other than by the lines, 'Go tell the court it glows and shines like rotten wood...' James I on the throne, it was Raleigh's misfortune, according to Sellar and Yeatman's *1066 and All That*, to have been 'left over from the previous reign'. Style the man, the last words of the lover who had excited his pleasured lady, Elizabeth Throckmorton, to cry out 'swisserswatter!' were to the executioner: 'What dost thou fear? Strike, man, strike!'

In Norman Mailer's quasi-documentary *The Executioner's Song*, Gary Gilmore, approaching the electric chair, said 'Let's do it', a tribute, inadvertent or not, to Cole Porter. Mel Brooks's chain-gang, in *Blazing Saddles*, console themselves by spiritualising Cole's 'I Get a Kick Out of You'. Tragedy and farce, fact and fiction, play the same course, from different tees, on the way to much the same holes. Rallying with Walter Raleigh, another of Brooks's movies was called *History of the World, Part I*.

31

In 1951, Jean-Paul Sartre's *rive gauchissime* magazine *Les Temps Modernes* (*a clin d'oeil* to Charlie Chaplin) came out with a barbed review of Albert Camus's essay *L'Homme Révolté* (*The Rebel*). Immediately after the Liberation, Sartre had associated closely with Camus, an active member of the Resistance. Later, it was self-elevating for boss-eyed Poulou, ever the prof, to mark down Camus as a journalistic playboy. Le bon Albert was not only an agile goalkeeper but also, when it came to women, had something of Humphrey Bogart's charm (without that star's projectile spittle). Sartre promoted himself by betraying a hero. Camus's letters to Maria Casarès, resilient free-standing beauty, deliver sustained calls for attention. Reassured by a stronger character (daughter of one of the last prime ministers of Republican Spain), he cheated on her to retrieve self-assurance. Men's lives are liable to be at least doubly stranded.

One of Camus's many letters to la Casarès, none as lively as hers to him, recounts Sartre having called on him in 1950, in the south of France, where the author of *L'Étranger* (*The Outsider*) was recovering from another bout of tuberculosis. We are told only that they talked together for an hour. Who was who, who whom? Sartre was Iago enough to do down

74

a Hoederer whose *pied noir* origin denied him unequivocal partisanship in the Franco-Algerian conflict. A variant gloss can depict Sartre as the Hoederer whom Camus, like Hugo, failed to put down. Casarès (who played Death, *tout de noir vêtue*, in Jean Cocteau's 1950 showpiece movie *Orphée*) was never Sartre's Olga. Her experience of life's rough water gave her little appetite for Poulou. His desires lacked the virility to announce themselves without a mixture of coaxing and condescension (*con*/descension in Derridan section). Sex as trickery trumped passion. Consummation was among the least of Sartre's pleasures, paternity least of all.

Louis Althusser's fidelity to his communist wife was topped by his strangling her. Spared by French justice, he was left to write his sorry, less ashamed than self-pitiful *plaidoirie*. When Elsa Triolet died, Louis Aragon, the PCF's literary star, came out as homosexual, to no enlightened applause from the Party's moral officialdom. If not spurned by André Breton, Aragon might have been a happy surrealist. The Party lent him stilts, and sales, as the Roman Catholic Church did Graham Greene.

In his fat memoir *Le Lièvre de Patagonie*, Claude Lanzmann, once in Sartre's inner circle, recalled with revulsion how Poulou, having cast Lanzmann's young sister in a play, plotted her seduction, with Simone de Beauvoir's connivance. Lanzmann also reports, matter-of-factly, that his mother divorced his father rather than agree to anal intercourse. *Mains Sales/Liaisons Dangereuses*, like *l'amour/la mort*, lack seesaw play in any English equivalent, but casting can come in hard and soft forms. At the Old Vic in London in the early 1950s, the young Richard Burton and John Neville played Othello and Iago on alternate nights. Spencer Tracy did something similar, *da solo*, in the movie of *Dr. Jekyll and Mr. Hyde*. The producer explained to Somerset Maugham that Spence disdained distinctive make-up: he was acting being good and being evil. In the middle of the next take, Willie chose to whisper, 'Which one is he b-being now?'

Chaplin's *The Great Dictator* (1940) made few classy friends. The play between the gobbledegook Hitler and the nebbish Jew, both played by Chaplin, arraigned life as more two-faced than it was amusing to realise, anti-Semitism more absurd than Uncle Sam's Wasps cared to find it. In the 1930s, 'No dogs or Jews allowed' was a routine advertisement for New England country clubs' exclusivity. 'Name of father if changed' featured in election committees' inquisitions. Apart from Darryl Zanuck's *Gentleman's Agreement* (1947), the movies shunned the topic of anti-Semitism for almost a quarter of a post-war century. Mel Brooks's *The Producers* (1968) then put a fool's cap on Nazis and their addled vanities. In *Springtime for Hitler* and 'Germa/nee', singing Hitlers on one side, dancing Hitlers on the other, compete for casting as a musically comic Führer.

32

For some thirty years, until the early 1960s, Kim Philby was a paragon of British duplicities, adulterous, social, institutional, treasonous. His pin-striped performance in front of the press, when accused of being the third man in the Burgess–Maclean affair, survives as a model for actors: after what preparation – Stanislavski's term for rehearsal – did he blink symptoms of disbelief into that pallid promise of innocence? Kim's confusion procured acquittal from at-first-suspicious inquisitors. Bemused charm is the double-dealer's sweetest standby. Even his speech impediment worked for him; that tied tongue freed time to think. When inextricably rumbled, Philby's Houdiniesque flight, in 1963, to Moscow from Beirut combined swansong with curtain call. How many ex-colleagues in London were disposed to murmur, 'Trust Kim'?

Like Mountbatten, Philby had a father suspected – in the latter case with ample justice – of less-than-wholehearted devotion to British interests. Like and not like his son, Saint John Philby was attracted to The Other Side. In the course of a diplomatic career in the post-1918 carve-up of the Middle East, he was drawn to identify himself with the Arabs. Having embraced Islam, he married a Saudi second wife. There was talk of his back-pocketing a fat sum of HMG's gold with which he had been trusted in case his negotiations had to be subsidised, as had T. E. Lawrence's, in order to kindle Arab ardour. To what extent did those laundered robes, that head-dress, encourage both men to play semi-deserters? Regalia has its charms, imposture its liberties. 'Will there be cozzies?' Diana Rigg asked me, before consenting to play Klytemnestra.

Sir Richard Burton had the nerve to dress like a pilgrim and the verve to bluff his camel-backed way to Mecca. Command of Arabic avoided suspicion that he might be uncircumcised. Effrontery needs more art than authenticity. The earl of Derby offered Burton the post of British consul in Trieste. 'Six hundred a year and no noticeable duties. I thought of you at once.' Burton was a copious pornographer whose manuscripts were burnt by squeamish executors as Byron's diaries had been.

Did Kim Philby learn the joy of deception from paternal example? Propriety is a dull dog's virtue; sincerity, like fidelity, collared bondage. Is the ultimate *jouissance* to cheat opposing masters while seeming to serve both? Jesus' truest expression of mortality came when, on the crucifix, he accused his Father of deserting him. God, it seemed, had failed to believe in him. An old Jewish story tells of a boy who comes of age when his father promises to catch him if he jumps off a ladder. He jumps and his father lets him fall. Daddy's moral: never trust anyone, not even etc. In the Soviet Union, what *apparatchik* was ever reassured by a promise of come-what-may support from his peers? Ask Koestler's Rubashov. As for alien fellow-travellers, bums on plush corner-seats, they were regarded by the Kremlin as credulous dupes.

Exiled in desolate provincial surroundings among never-grateful minders, Kim Philby, urbane jungle boy, remained on the two-faced prowl. He exercised his seductive agility on his fellow-exile Melinda, comely American wife of woebegone, bisexual Donald Maclean, whose last-minute escape, along with Guy Burgess, Philby had triggered with self-interested alertness. MI5 operatives were closing on them, but had gone home for the weekend, giving the two bolters forty-eight hours to clinch their flit. Burgess might have bluffed it out; Maclean was not up to it. Sincerity has no reserves.

Anthony Blunt was not yet in danger of losing his knighthood; suave keeper of the queen's pictures, homosexuality, as covert as Burgess's was blatant, was taken to be his only secret. *Un train peut en cacher un autre* is a warning secret service men and medical diagnosticians not uncommonly fail to keep in mind. Melinda Maclean, evidently a charmer, finessed her way back to the US. Victor Kravchenko, in *I Chose Freedom* (1946), presented his own defection from the Soviet Union as a form of seeing the light. Tunnels go both ways, in various bores.

33

As the Cold War grew chillier, immigrant Edward Teller plumped for proving himself more ardent than home-grown American colleagues. The Hungarian-born physicist deplored, if he did not despise, J. R. Oppenheimer's squeamishness when it came to developing the H-bomb. Teller might lack Oppy's fastidious charisma, but he was a decidedly impressive lecturer at UC Berkeley. The defeat of Germany and Japan had, in the view of a European refugee, left the West facing a yet-more-sinister and potent enemy. Lacking Oppenheimer's polymath chic, Teller was never in two minds about manufacturing weapons of greater lethal potency.

Might it be that Oppenheimer flinched from the prospect of the Bomb being used on white men? How many Japanese had been made prisoner? Their massacre and/or self-immolation raised no humanitarian or pious objection. Two of the rare Japanese prisoners of war, on being released, went home and committed suicide; so too one of the Spartans too ill to fight with the two hundred and ninety eight who died with Leonidas at Thermopylae in 480 BCE. At Plataea, a year later, the other alleged shirker broke ranks and charged suicidally on the Persians. Showboating won no absolution for leaving his front-line neighbour unshielded on one side.

Except for flagrant Nazis, how many of the many American

citizens of German descent excited animosity after Hitler's declaration of war in 1941? My cousin Irvin Weintraub, US glider pilot killed (in fact, murdered by his captors) at Arnhem, flew for Uncle Sam. His uncle Herman had died in 1915 fighting for the Kaiser. West Coast Japanese Americans were interned en masse, without due process or redemptive prospect. China passed for being our ally. Madame Chiang Kai-shek was a celebrity-circuit star. Even after 1949, when China was 'lost', chop suey never went out of season. Greg Peck once told me, very, very slowly, that Douglas MacArthur's success in swinging Japan into step with the US and democratic habits was the least recognised one-man achievement of the post-war world. On reflection, might it be true?

In science, whatever is possible in theory is as good as achieved in practice, by somebody. That somebody, in Teller's view, had better be on our side. Science was inverted archaeology: someone was always likely to spring its crypt; sooner beat later. When it came to the evolution of species, by publishing first, Charles Darwin won a dead heat with Alfred Russel Wallace, ungrudging, all-but-unknown proponent of similar ideas. Neither had previous knowledge of the other. Wallace, a gentleman, disdained to contend for kudos. When collecting the 1962 Nobel Prize, for having cracked the helical double twist in the structure of DNA, Watson and Crick paid no tribute to the *proxime accessit* work of Rosalind Franklin, who had died of cancer a few years before. Watson had almost certainly cribbed Franklin's x-ray crystallography. S-men don't do honour. Three years earlier, under the pseudonym Mark Caine, Tom Maschler and I had confected a book entitled *The S-Man*, a forecast of greed as the creed to come.

Russia's possession of the Bomb, followed by Mao's triumph in 1949, reinforced US apprehensions. The leaders of what Karl Popper called 'the Open Society' were given reason to put coded locks on democracy's inner doors. In the optimistic years after 1945, new US embassies, such as the one I visited under construction outside Madrid in 1954, were built in Mies van der Rohe's 'international style'. Glass cladding, open and transparent offices, proclaimed that America had nothing to hide. The US embassy recently built on London's South Bank doubles for a bastion, if not a last resort.

The wisest of Gore Vidal's now-hear-this pronouncements was that Truman's 'National Security state' was the first, slippery step on a long flight towards the erosion of democracy, the rise of trumpetry and trumpery. Gore's lineage (his grandfather a blind senator for Oklahoma) was also his licence: as a young celebrity, he denounced President Eisenhower for making Guatemala a US puppet. Brief liberal hero, Gore became a non-person, so far as The *New York Times* reviewing his novels was concerned, when he came out with a homosexual (not yet 'gay') love story, *The City and the Pillar*, no title to go homo-humming, as a wittier Norman Mailer might have said.

Once the precise use made of large chunks of federal funds was classified Top Secret, unelected Washington elites were left to determine matters of life and death. Proxy wars avoided open hostilities, just, and warranted the increasing power and financial presumption of the military–industrial complex. Eisenhower, on his way out of the White House in early 1961, had the farewell wisdom to warn against ceding unsupervised authority to vested interests which, thanks not least to his debility, had already acquired it. Jack Kennedy and LBJ affected opposition to Richard Nixon while all three argued for increasing the defence budget. The Communist Menace was said to be leading in a race in which the Reds were all but lapped. Overestimating the enemy strengthened the authority of the Right-minded and, as it turned out in 1989, impelled the Russians to bankrupt themselves trying to catch up.

During the Cold War, most citizens of the Free World were persuaded to leave the elaboration of the Bomb (and the means for its delivery) to inner circles who promised no shortage of candied consolations. The hip played at hairy revolution; evangelical hedonism blended vocation and vacation. In England, earnest trudgers in the CND demanded that the nuclear genie be reinserted in her bottle; cf. toothpaste and the tube. As the myth of Eden advertised, once that clever apple was broached, science was man's serpent king.

34

The publication, in 1958, of Ian Fleming's first James Bond book, *Dr No*, a rumble for chairborne daredevils, all but coincided with the end of National Service in England. No longer called on to police a dwindling empire, conscripts were not worth the brasses they polished. Fleming delegated the keeping of the queen's peace to a monosyllabic superhero. The British were relieved to grant Meestair Bond – half sewer-rat, half lounge-lizard – licence to fight the good fight, with low blows if need be. Double-oh-seven was amusement and economy. Sentry with unexamined ways and means, soloist licensed to kill, Bond would serve like a modern Talos – Daedalus' mechanical sentry on Minoan Crete – to keep malign invaders at bay.

Despite the real-life examples of Burgess, Maclean and, in time, Kim Philby, Anthony Blunt and who all else, no Fleming villain was ever a Brit or an American. When Jack Kennedy let it be known that James Bond was his favourite reading, it ensured that Fleming's fortune was made. It also promised that White House tenants need never again admit to serious reading or affect to have written books, as JFK himself had, with or without ghostly help. His *Profiles in Courage* (1955) was calculated both to advertise his literary worthiness for the presidency and to remind voters of his active (and wet) service in wartime. Its bestselling certificate was assured by his father; the millionaire crook bought up the whole of the first edition. British Prime Minister Harold Macmillan came from a family of classy publishers. François Mitterrand, master of two-facedness, sexual and political, played the man of letters with solemn conviction, while also fiddling the books.

By the 1970s, protection of liberal democracy was held too serious a matter, at the sharp end, for its mostly unelected guardians to be subject to public scrutiny. Thucydides, the first mundane historian – unlike gossipy Herodotus, he discounted divine portents – would have recognised the leave-it-to-us nostrum as typical of oligarchy, to which he was by no means dogmatically opposed. His 'Melian Dialogue' was tradition-ally construed as a salute to the Cycladic islanders' gallant retort, in 416 BCE, to the ultimatum 'Surrender or die' deliv-ered by democratic Athenian imperialists, during an interlude of peace between Peloponnesian Wars. Until the advent of the liberal historian George Grote (1794–1871), this callousness, like the trial and execution of Socrates, was presumed to illus-trate the unreliable nature of democracy.

More recently, the Melian oligarchs' obduracy has been con-strued as self-interest. The sovereignty of the few determined the fate of the unconsulted many others. After a brave siege, the island's men were slaughtered, women and children sold into slavery. Had the mass of male inhabitants been granted a vote, the oligarchs might have been ousted and the majority of Melians have survived. Led by the persuasive diplomacy of Brasidas, the Spartans delivered no-less-abrupt ultimata to the Greek cities of Thrace allied with their enemies. Posterity was supplied no occasion for moralising.

Winston Churchill's defiance of Hitler and of the odds in 1940 was ennobled by the outcome. Islands sometimes beat the odds. Malta did in 1565 against the Ottomans and, almost four centuries later, against the Axis. Winston's well-chewed rhetoric and the 1945 British victory, with a little help from trans-Atlantic and Russian allies, rendered him mythical. Unwavering Britannia, it seemed, still ruled. 'Three cheers for king and emperor' was the cry raised, after the Japanese surrender, by Lord Louis Mountbatten, grandee with more decorations than all but the tallest Christmas tree.

Mountbatten's personal history was braided with gilt. Lofty and laundered patriotism doubled with revenge on and alliance with the Windsors, as the British royal family had been inventively renamed during the Great War. In 1914, Germanic origins (much like George V's) served to disgrace Mountbatten's Battenberg father, at the time the First Sea Lord. His son's five-gold-ringed naval career closed the breach and exaggerated his qualities. That haughty face supplied a fulcrum for snobs. E. Arnot Robertson paid salty tribute in verses beginning, 'As I said to Dickie Mountbatten...' Lord Louis was the apt last viceroy of an empire sustained by vanity. The 1947 scuttle from India, which he supervised, leaving more than a million Muslims and Hindus to celebrate liberation by slaughtering each other, was a resignation of imperial tutelage close to 'You asked for it.' Mountbatten's wife Edwina's closeness to Pandit Nehru and later carnal connections with a suite of men, two black, rendered him a gilded cuckold with a discreet preference for young men.

Max Beaverbrook never forgot or forgave Mountbatten after the 1942 Dieppe commando raid. A large number of the Beaver's Canadian compatriots were lost or taken in chains into captivity, as a result of hurried planning, inept execution. The raid's main purpose had been to reassure the Russians that the Second Front was imminent, when it was not. Max suspected Mountbatten of casting the show so that no one of social consequence was likely to perish. Had not the same been true at Gallipoli? In Thomas Mann's novel *The Holy Sinner*, recurrent casualties are said to be low-class people none of whom would be missed. Noel Coward's film *In Which We Serve* further decorated the grandee who heard more shots fired in salutes than in anger. Working on the *Sunday Express* in 1949, I assimilated the unspoken rule that nothing good was to be said about Mountbatten.

In 1955, in the *New Statesman*, Malcolm Muggeridge coined 'royal soap opera' to describe the drama of Princess Margaret's enforced renunciation of Group-Captain Peter Townsend. The royal crisis was a tear-jerking rehash of the abdication of Edward VIII a score of years earlier. In a country where scarcely five per cent of the population were now churchgoers, the Church of England's leading primate, Geoffrey Fisher, notorious flogger as a public school headmaster, again struck pious attitudes. The factitious outrage that greeted Muggeridge's apt coinage has been followed by the recognition, now merchandised on Netflix, that Buckingham Palace might serve as a peep-show adjunct of the National Theatre. After a career of social and sexual climbing, Malcolm repaired, as had that low-life Trasteverine sonneteer Giuseppe Belli (1791–1863), to commodiously bosomed Mother Church. Blaise Pascal might have bet on it.

35

After 1945, the right to differ was inhibited in the US and throttled in the USSR by a sustained state of international crisis. The Great Powers' prolonged mutual intimidation, to the advantage of rulers and arms dealers on all sides, was satirised, with scant humour, by George Orwell's *Nineteen Eighty-Four*, first published in 1949. Charmless Winston Smith lives in a glum urban enclave threatened by implacable, imprecise external powers. A repressive state of emergency is justified by irregular explosions, their authors never caught (a situation made art by Luis Buñuel in *That Obscure Object of Desire*). The threat to 1984 society within its own borders is attributed by its ruling cabal to bogeymen led by Emmanuel Goldstein, Judas-cum-Trotsky. Orwell (né Blair) relied on a revulsion rooted in the British psyche. In *Shooting an Elephant*, he recorded his surprise when an Indian admitted that he was 'a Joo, sir'. Goldstein, fiction within a fiction, depended on a reflex of revulsion. So too Harold Pinter's bully-boy Goldberg in *The Birthday Party*? In the nicest possible sense, Harold picked his own nose.

'We've got to get rid of the yids' was ever a popular chorus, whether as a 1930s Mosleyite war-cry or as a larky post-war provocation, for local instance to put down Tottenham Hotspur supporters, of whom A. J. Ayer advertised himself

one. Calling themselves 'The Yids', Spurs supporters trans-
posed pariahdom into local distinction. Dickens's archetypal
Jew, Fagin, continues to be generic, a twister with no amiable
gloss. Today his name is generalised to designate non-Jewish, often Asiatic organisers of child thieves. While quite the
philo-Semite, Byron had the Regency buck's style to brand all
moneylenders 'Jews'.

George Orwell, a figurehead without a childhood, rarely
washed but never, it seems, caught in any unworthy act, now
stands for the ideal post-imperialist writer. At once some kind
of a toff – as Eric Blair, Old Etonian – and all but a tramp, in
Down and Out in London and Paris, Orwell was scarcely a
novelist of quality. People, it seems, did not greatly interest
him. Its one human character, the farmer, banished within a
few pages, his masterpiece, *Animal Farm* (1945), owes something to Jonathan Swift and sits alone among his books as a
work of art. Orwell was scarcely alone in seeing no market
when it came to the abandonment and murder of Europe's
Jews.

The not necessarily, but probably, malevolent English
General Evelyn Barker, C-in-C Palestine, asked Golda Meir
what the Jews had done to incur (he did not, it is nice to
presume, quite say 'deserve') their treatment. They couldn't
have been murdered *en masse* for no reason, could they?
Kafka's *The Trial* was not, we may guess, on the general's
reading list. Sufferance never Golda's badge, her disgust made
it clear that Zionists were not like the old Jewy Jews. The
explosion in the King David Hotel in Jerusalem in 1946, triggered by Irgun Zvai Leumi, outraged the British more than
the Holocaust ever did. What was the world coming to when
worms turned? A warning is said to have been given, but
ignored; idleness or *realpolitik*?

The flat accountancy of Raul Hilberg's *The Destruction of
the European Jews* (1961) had a dismissive reception from

Hannah Arendt. Translated into a New York intellectual, *bras dessus bras dessous* with Mary McCarthy, Arendt was too grand to be impressed by a largely statistical register of what had happened in the Europe she had skipped. Hilberg's want of philosophical elaboration denied metaphysical significance to systematic butchery and (often ignored) wholesale theft. Heidegger continued to stand for the German in her, abstruse emblem of what she had over him, not to mention vice versa. Arendt all but subscribed to the canard which held Jewish 'leaders' *de facto* collaborators in the slaughter. This view was seconded, with regard to the Zionists, in a play directed by the British left-wing film director Ken Loach. It condoned the myth that the Jews as good as massacred themselves, a political revision of Christian anathema. 'Good riddance' keeps blowing in the wind. Lady Macbeths of both sexes never cease to wash their hands.

The small truth is that Zionists did indeed try to persuade the Nazis, in the early years of their ascendancy, to allow them to arrange for Jews to leave Germany for Palestine. Where was the scandal? Persecution was already a German national sport, the Holocaust as yet unthinkable, at least out loud. In the late 1930s, on neutral ground in Switzerland, Wittgenstein – now a Cambridge resident – negotiated with Nazi quasi-diplomats in order to ransom his sisters. No Regulus, he conceded the huge family fortune in return for their exemption from the common lot. What complex of reasons, fears and vanities led to his supine performance? Flavius Josephus has been more harshly judged for saving his skin by surrendering to the Romans in 67 CE, at no one's expense. Who will say what Wittgenstein should have done? By divesting the family of its gelt, did he hope to purge them of Jewishness?

Relegating Eichmann's evil to banality, thus of small intellectual interest, Arendt filed the Nazi psyche as unworthy of prolonged diagnosis. That reduction was the closest she could come to both sniping at and acquitting her ex-lover who had, in 1933, rallied to Germany's man of destiny. In 1962, having stayed in garrulous Jerusalem just long enough to file a fatly commissioned quota of words for the *New Yorker* on the Eichmann trial, Arendt stopped by in Germany for a rapprochement with Heidegger. He was more her kind of person than those shrill, gesticulating *Ost-Juden*.

Arendt deplored Eichmann's abduction from Argentina and, in particular, his trial being sited in Jerusalem. She held that he should have been judged in Germany, presumably in the interests of impartiality. Did her clipped coinage 'the banality of evil' derive from Heidegger's notion of the 'thoughtlessness' typical, in his view, of science, hence its lack of philosophical *profondeur*? Karl Kraus had said, in 1933, that when he tried to think about Hitler, nothing came to mind (echoing Gertrude Stein's on her native Oakland, California: 'There's no there there'). Heidegger took a similar view of Jews, alive or dead, until he saw Arendt again, exceptional proof of his rule.

Hegel had promoted the notion of 'world-historical' men, Napoleon *en tête*, who twitch the tiller of civilisation. In 1934, in his inaugural lecture as rector of Freiburg University, Heidegger named Adolf Hitler another such. Sufficiently disempowered soon to resign his rectorship, Heidegger never quit the Nazi Party; it sank under him in 1945, leaving no end of mutually supportive floaters. The Master offered no apology to colleagues whom he had abused. In 1941, under pressure from his publisher, he had deleted the dedication to Husserl of his magnum opus *Sein und Zeit*. Thenceforth he referred to his old tutor as 'the Jew Husserl', an act of abiding ignominy. He never acknowledged that the Holocaust ever occurred or, if it had, that it was regrettable. He and his unrepentant Nazi wife lumbered Arendt with hawking his manuscripts in the US. 'You people', they implied, are good at that sort of thing.

Cossetted by post-war admirers, perversity close to pride, Heidegger answered no unpremeditated questions at any of their symposia. Recently discovered papers confirm sustained, logorrheic hostility to Jews and suggest how, in various registers, he may have enjoyed punishing Arendt with stiff favours. What quiver of motives impelled a smart nineteen-year-old to fuck a married professor? Fiction could play with a mixture of vanity and masochism. Source-ridden biography is too chaste to guess.

36

In the immediate *après-guerre*, Jean-Paul Sartre led the *peloton de tête* to restore Heidegger's reputation. Poulou's reward was to be accused by the Master of misrepresenting the ideas which lay, so he thought, at the root of his version of existentialism (Søren Kierkegaard its pioneer). As for Sartre's protracted masterwork, *L'être et le néant*, Heidegger accepted the salute only by observing that his disciple had failed to plagiarise accurately. A. J. Ayer kept his verdict short: Sartre's portentous prolixity was based on a misunderstanding of the meaning, i.e. the proper use, of the verb 'to be'. Matching the Oxonian's brevity, for once, Sartre said that Ayer was a con. The Channel grew wider. Continental topics seldom pass Anglo-Saxon customs.

William James's pragmatism, grudgingly celebrated in the UK, was of a piece with the empirical tradition. Mutual gracelessness is an old habit among philosophers in pursuit of the grail. Heraclitus dismissed contemporary know-alls as knowing nothing in particular. That snappy misogynist Schopenhauer ridiculed verbose Hegel. Virgin all his life, was he, as Gilbert Ryle seems to have been? Wittgenstein capped them all by his exit line on a legendary Cambridge occasion: 'What do you know about philosophy, Russell, what have you ever known?'

In a late, skimpy book, Ayer filleted Wittgenstein as a man of more mystery than substance. It is tempting to find some affinity between Ryle's virginity and the closed province in which he practised his chaste philosophy. Casimir Lewy, a contemporary Cambridge philosopher, excluded the Holocaust from the logical field in which he specialised. The continent was so alien to him that he advised the postulant Anthony Rudolf to read Descartes in an English translation castrated of Gallic enchantment.

Arendt's dollar-a-word account of the Eichmann trial launched the process by which the Holocaust became the fate, if not the fault, of spineless Jews. Isaiah Berlin never forgave her for implying that his elderly parents should have taken up arms. Given to paradox, Arendt spent more time slating the Israeli prosecutor, Gideon Hausner, than in dwelling on the horror, the horror over which the man in the transparent bulletproof dock had officiated.

David Irving and others, including British-born Robert Faurisson, came to claim that the Jews were guilty of retailing their woes, if not of fabricating and profiting from them. The duke of Portland, direct descendant of Disraeli's great friend Cavendish-Bentinck, had said as much during the busiest period of the Nazis' murderous industry. Foreign Office grandee, he discounted the evidence of 'whining Jews'. Did Jesus not warn that, if a man came back from the dead, he would not be believed? Houston Stewart Chamberlain (1855–1927), an Englishman translated into a German, was a strident early advocate of political racism. *En bon antisémite*, he pilfered the notion of *élan vital* from Henri Bergson, Marcel Proust's *maître-à-penser*.

37

For not a few nice people, the Shoah – as Claude Lanzmann's landmark nine-hour film conclusively labelled it – was insufferable less because millions of Jews were done to death than because it primed accusatory charges against Christendom. Survivors, never the dead, were the big embarrassment; America and Great Britain had offered haven to no more than a token, well-connected few. Had all Europe's Jews been eliminated, their disappearance might well have been sighed away as good riddance. The Walrus and the Carpenter showed the way; so did the weeping crocodile. Ernest Bevin, Britain's post-war socialist foreign secretary, accused Jewish survivors of pushing to the front of the queue. For all his lapsed aitches, Bevin was a Foreign Office favourite: Arabists abounded in Anthony Eden's wake. He called Ike 'my dear', without evoking any reciprocal gush. With small British assistance, Palestine became a post-war dump for unwanted Jews. If it landed them in trouble, they had asked for it.

The British had followed the Romans in dividing and ruling, not least in India, not last in Palestine, first in Cromwell's Ireland. Other colonial powers followed suit. Hutu and Tutsi were rivalrous, never murderous, inhabitants of Rwanda until Belgian colonists encouraged quasi-racial discrimination, the better to divide 'natives' against each other. The richer Tutsi were awarded a privileged interest in European ruthlessness. When the Belgians left, opportunists moved in. Fabricated hostility licensed massacre and the appropriation of spoils. In Syria, the French promoted a despised minority, the Alawites, to be their colonial *milice*. The rise of the dictatorial Assad family was the legacy of their abandoned *mission civilisatrice*.

Keeping local wounds open is a staple exercise in Great Power operations. After they had been brought, not to say bought, into the Great War, the Arab elite, all blanched laundry, lucky oil under the hoofs of their big-toed mounts, were tipped to dispute any exclusive Zionist/Palestinian compromise. The exceptional King Abdullah of Jordan, who favoured fruitful co-existence, was assassinated in 1951 to encourage the others. Glubb Pasha, British leader of the Arab Legion, stayed in office long enough to lead his men into fruitless battle.

Britain's posture of impartial adjudicator served, for a while, to procure favourable deals from Middle Eastern oil producers. Jon Kimche's *Seven Fallen Pillars* (1953) proves how little wisdom Whitehall showed in its last spasm of imperious authority. If the state of Israel, established in 1948, has turned out to be little more gracious than its neighbours, it does not constantly announce its wish to kill everybody in them. What country surrounded by implacable enemies sets a better example?

The anti-Semite appears again and again to fear that the Jew will outsmart him. Gauleiter Julius Streicher, ranting editor of *Der Stürmer*, conceded as much on the eve of his execution, when he requested leave to switch sides. He was deemed to have left second thoughts a bit late. Father Bauer, a German Jesuit working in Rome in 1943, wondered, quietly, whether God might not want the Jews to be converted or destroyed.

The resurgent Jewish state serves as sore thumb to European civilisation. Anything that allows Israel to be rated a Bad Thing suits the uneasy conscience of meta-Christendom. It also arms the anti-nationalist (unless pro-Chinese) affectations of Stalinist Left-overs. The notion of an idea being 'over-determined' might well be reserved for anti-Jewish sentiment. Diabolisation of 'Israel' is innate in the language of Christianity and of meta-Marxism. Philosophy and theology recycled, 'The Jews' are still there to be broken, again and again, on their enemies' wheels within wheels.

Arnold Toynbee wished the Arabs well in 1973 not least because their victory would vindicate his affectations of access to history's irrevocable process. It is also said that there was a fat honorarium in it for him. Hugh Trevor-Roper favoured Israel, not least, it is tempting to think, to pique his sententious fellow-historian. In an adjacent case, the Nobel Prize-winning zoologist Peter Medawar took accurate pleasure in lancing Teilhard de Chardin's pretentious synthesis of science with Roman Catholicism.

38

In Orwell's *Nineteen Eighty-Four*, the party-lining patois of the official media docks the population of linguistic resource. Repeated slogans deprive the proles of capacity to express, or even to recognise, the truth. The limits of their world are ruled by the limitation of their language. Modern audiences find it difficult to think outside the box of clichés that outstares and outblares them in their living rooms. Orwell took his cue from **Pravda**, from the BBC (his employer) and from C. K. Ogden's well-meaning 'Basic English'. Evangelical pidgin, it was to render post-war humanity as reasonable as the triumphant Anglo-Saxons and also, coincidentally, to underwrite their cultural dominion. It did not catch on. Cultures have unkempt resistances of their own. What could be less interesting than a completed Tower of Babel, the same tongue spoken on every floor? It might as well be a bungalow. Might solitary JHVH have dreaded the tedium of listening to the imprecatory clichés of monoglot humanity? I never found Agatha Christie worth a glance until I read her in Spanish; that way, *desde luego*, one learns something. Richmal Crompton's William stories carry satirical undertones of a much higher quality. What is the French for Violet Elizabeth Bott's lisp?

Vladimir Nabokov forecast the fall of the Soviet regime on the grounds not of economic overreach or popular indignation, but because the great Russian language was sure to confound those who had abused it so sorely. Edmund Wilson affected to be a better Russian scholar than his one-time protégé. Ridiculing Nabokov's translation of Pushkin into English (a high-stepping 'pony') was a displacement sideways both of Wilson's conviction that Marxism had irrefutable validity and of his envy of *Lolita*'s bestsellerdom. Wilson's novel *I Thought of Daisy*, all lacklustre sadism and witless prose, dismayed highbrow admirers without recruiting any regiment of wantons as *Lo* did. Neither Wilson nor Volodya lived to see the disintegration of the Soviet Union. In 1988, dining in the hilltop restaurant in Domme, in the Périgord, we were advised by a young US academic who had been in Moscow trying to be helpful, that Russia's leaders were incapable of thinking how to save it other than in the delusive terms that had brought it low. Was it as simple as that? Somewhat.

Russia's afterlife has been read under vari-coloured lights. Early in his progress to autocracy, ex-KGB operative Vladimir Putin was accused of staging or making exemplary use of incidents such as the deaths in the Moscow theatre where official rescuers killed more people, with gas, than the allegedly Chechen terrorists had with bullets. Something similar happened in Beslan, near the Chechen border. Hundreds of children died when Russian security forces stormed the school in which the pupils had been taken hostage. The number of deaths, in both cases, was due to the clumsiness, if not corruption, of the 'security' services. Putin's supremacy was fortified by its own ineptitude. Ruthlessness paraded as a just response to carnage which, objectively speaking, ex-comrades, did him a favour.

The generalised bogey term 'Terrorism' renews the lease and rearms the mandate of the National Security state and its shameless parodies. The Chechens, already deported in large numbers by Putin's model, Joseph Stalin, served Putin in the role of Emmanuel Goldstein and his gang. Surviving Chechen opportunists have been translated into Putin's punitive thugs in the elimination of Ukrainian civilians from their rich native soil. Syrian auxiliaries are enrolled as cannon-fodder and expendable killers; so were Moroccan Moors ferried across the straits of Gibraltar, in 1936, to do the dirty work for Francisco Franco. Henry Kissinger hoped that both sides would lose the Iran–Iraq War.

Conrad's Mr Verloc, in *The Secret Agent*, has countless real or imaginary descendants. Nihilism is without programme or headquarters. There is always some bogey we can do little about; that is its recurrent utility. Invisible devils justify perpetual states of emergency. In Luis Buñuel's masterpiece, *That Obscure Object of Desire*, the 'Revolutionary Army of the Infant Jesus' sets off random explosions. Survivors are seen to shrug; life goes on, as it does as long as it does. Buñuel's groupuscule's name was pirated by a 1980s pop of small percussive impact.

39

Jews will be Jews. Tautologies can be aggressive. Straight-faced under Lenin's piqued cap, Jeremy Corbyn, imposed for a giggle as leader of Britain's Labour Party, announced that Zionists, even when British citizens, 'don't understand English irony'. Is not all Jewish literature, *y compris* Marcel Proust, a demonstration of irony? Jeremy's point? *Vous croyez?* Further evidence of parodic meta-Stalinism came when Corbyn ordered an inquiry into anti-Semitism in the Labour Party. What Tiresias stood up to say, 'Thou art the man'? In *Working Class Anti-Semite* (1954), James Robb had long ago established that hostility to Jews has deep roots in the British working class. Employing Mátyás Rákosi's 'salami tactics', Labour's 2015 republican leader procured the ennoblement of the bearer of the whitewash, herself a member of a minority. Irony anyone? Anti-Semitism has been a centuries-old religious, linguistic and social habit in notoriously tolerant England. Enoch Powell was not given to it, but the London dockers who paraded in his favour made no secret of their favourite xenophobia. It has become something a disparate and immigrant population can enjoy in common. Dare we say, as politely as may be, that every boatload of Muslim refugees (from other Muslims) admitted into England makes anti-Semitism a more paying bet for the Labour Party?

Sentimentalisation of 'The Palestinians' resurrects 'The Jews' as cruel and persecutory. The *bien-pensant* campaign to equate 'Islamophobia' and anti-Semitism is chimerical humbug. Judaism does not advocate, or dream of, the forcible enrolment of any category of humanity, let alone its elimination. Exclusivity breeds indifference. In the 1949 film of Ayn Rand's hyperbolic masterpiece *The Fountainhead*, Gary Cooper, as the ostracised architectural genius Howard Roark, finds himself alone with Ellsworth Toohey, the critic who has destroyed his career. Toohey says, 'You can tell me exactly what you think of me.' Roark says, 'But I don't think of you.'

In the early 1960s, Norman Podhoretz wrote a promptly infamous article entitled 'My Negro Problem – and Ours'. In it he confessed to illiberal, if civilised, apprehensions. One would incur more odium, in today's England, if he were to admit dread of the growing Islamic population or the monomanic malice harboured by no few sections of it. Max Frisch's *The Fire Raisers* (1960) made precocious play with similar not-in-our-house complacency. Tolerance and appeasement are easily twin-bedded. Rowan Williams, Emeritus Archbishop of Canterbury, favoured embracing elements of Sharia law in the law of the land. Must we look forward to that? Hands up for hands off.

By equating criticism of Mohammed with sacrilege, loudly in the case of *Le Canard enchaîné*, Muslim pietists (not to mention gangsters) have intimidated liberal society into exempting them from caricatural scepticism. Rendering themselves piously incorrigible, as well as traditionally mutually murderous, Shiite and Sunni faithful unite only in making Jews archetypal villains. Mohammed, as would Martin Luther, first tried to convert local Jews; reluctance to kneel sanctioned their massacre in both camps. Principle is signatory to murders beyond the scope of individual malice. 'Nothing personal' has no conscience. Will state-run AI have an apology button?

Genocide will be labelled self-defence. Pillage is the gangster's connoisseurship; so were the treasures of Constantinople for the faithful of Mehmet II. No few works of art, pillaged by the Nazis, often secreted, sometimes displayed, after the war, by well-heeled above-the-battle bankers and galleries, have yet to be restored to their legitimate owners.

Carl Gustav Jung argued that the Devil should be admitted as an indispensable element of the Trinity: has He not been central in keeping Them united? Pontius Pilate's advocates would have him elevated to sainthood on the grounds that his part in the crucifixion was essential to the divine scheme. Common enmities are a regular, if rarely reliable, adhesive. Catholics and Protestants goose-stepped in unison. Hitler and his admirers rated Jews bacilli, thus qualifying them for sanitary extermination. The ingenuity of German plumbing and obsession with cleanliness were aspects of a fantasy of purity, of blood and bowels; its correlative the dread of alien toxicity. Faith carries a sliver of doubt; otherwise, it would be knowledge.

40

In *Homo Ludens* (1955), Johan Huizinga embraces all sorts of sportsmanlike activities in usually limited arenas. Agreements to differ and then shake hands, once time is called, abate hostilities. Wars between Hellenes – as common as they were deplored – were suspended to allow contestants safe passage to and from the ancient Olympic Games. Conventional civilities flouted, the consequences can become bloody beyond whistled recall. Social tensions in sixth-century Byzantium were expressed in bagarres between racing fans sporting rival colours, the Greens and the Blues, adjacency in the spectrum an incidental irony. In vexed circumstances, colourful loyalties – however casually adopted – sour into murderous factionalism. Cheer- and jeer-leaders accumulate power and wealth from the dividends of division. Legislation to ban distinctions of race, class and sex serves to bank hostilities. Jesus' prescription for neighbours to love each other is as good as advice to take care in choosing one's neighbourhood.

41

Immediately after the defeat of Nazi Germany, and the demonstration of unmatched American power over Hiroshima and Nagasaki, the Soviet Union appeared to be the only surviving threat to Western supremacy. The menace with which the USSR eye-balled the US, and vice versa, fostered what Gore Vidal denounced as 'the National Security state'. Inaugurated by Harry Truman, its inner circle, mostly unelected, became democracy's oligarchs. Fortified by his successors, except for provincial Jimmy Carter, as well-intentioned as he was ill-advised, the CIA's heavy hand displaced diplomatic subtlety. The subversive installation of the Shah of Persia in 1953 in the place of the populist Mossadeq was a short-term success, ended by a reactionary revolution and the installation, in 1979, of the vindictive and autocratic Ayatollahs. Hostility between leaders in the 'Socialist' and the 'Free' world grew implacable while the appetites of their young converged in pop and pot, jeans and trainers a common uniform without abating antagonisms. In Yoko Ono's chess set both sides played white. Monotony promises no durable truce. Players of quality clash without board or distinctly coloured pieces.

Tacitus said of the briefly laurelled Roman Emperor Galba that he was '*consensu omnium capax imperii nisi imperasset*' (by general consent, competent to be an emperor, had he not become one). Harry Truman was the reverse. Why did FDR select a Midwestern *apparatchik* to replace the eloquent populist Henry Wallace as vice president other than to make his replacement no new broom to look forward to? With small wish to be outshone by his successor, the waning Roosevelt reverted to mandarin caution. Middle-Westerners rarely rock boats. Pitched into the White House in 1945, Truman proved himself, in a majority of American eyes, eligible to be returned as president in 1948. His unsubtle diplomacy surprised Stalin and his *nyet*-saying Foreign Minister Molotov. Truman's strength was lack of the patrician vanity that made Roosevelt's charm, as it would Obama's, at once political strength and diplomatic weakness. Charmers mistake being winning for having won.

The ideological face-off of the Cold War promoted power struggles within both sides of the Iron Curtain. In the 1950s, President Eisenhower's failure to denounce Senator McCarthy's attacks on freedom, in Freedom's name, was held to be the result of physical enfeeblement. 'This would never have happened,' some joker said, 'if Ike had been alive.' In Marxist terms, Eisenhower was the objective ally of those out to lame the progressive wing of American political thinkers and to depict contrarian liberals as traitors. No one did nothing quite like him. The conviction for perjury of Alger Hiss had exemplary uses for enemies of East Coast culture. With his apt onomatopoeic name and friendship with his accuser, the previously unreformed communist Whittaker Chambers, well-tailored Hiss was cast as surrogate for J. R. Oppenheimer, whose dated scruples the new right was eager to besmirch but had no legal case to prosecute.

Charged with treason, Julius and Ethel Rosenberg were said to have transmitted formulae and equations beyond their competence to understand or, knowledgeable sources claim, even to copy correctly. Couriers no doubt, they were scarcely spies eligible for exemplary punishment. Their guilt was service-able, left and right. Who was keener to see them martyred by McCarthy than their communist friends? The judge selected to try the case and pronounce the death sentences was called Kaufman.

42

In 1996, the British Chief Rabbi, the late Jonathan Sacks, was censured by his orthodox caucus for planning to attend the funeral of Hugo Gryn, a rabbi of a slightly different stripe. Gryn had been in a Nazi concentration camp for several years, during which he conducted himself with exemplary distinction. While Jewish zealotry is no more tolerant, in doctrinal matters, than all-embracing (and often coercing) Christianity, Tertullian's remark that the death and resurrection of God's Son was 'credibile quia absurdum est' (to be believed because it's absurd) had no relevance to Mosaic monotheism. Judaism is less faith than compact. Its precepts, however demanding, left space, as Christianity did not and the pre-Socratics had, for scientific examination of the natural world without the imposition of a priori 'truths'. Not a few items of dogma, including the notion that the sun rotated around the earth, were derived from Aristotle before being certified sacrosanct. The Ten Commandments have more to do with communal piety than with individual salvation. A single Jew at prayer lacks the call on divine attention credited to a minyan of at least ten male postulants.

Like ancient Greek polytheism, Judaism left middle ground, to meson, uncluttered by predetermined dogma. Rituals and superstitions had their places; they failed to circumscribe diurnal intelligence. Greek priesthoods were allotted occasional honours, never in the light of spiritual vocation. Rabbis are teachers, not dispensers of forgiveness or tickets to salvation. The Talmud testifies to the scope of countless conjectures among generations of pious disputants. Despite those 603 admonitory ordinances devised by rabbis, in amplification of the Sinaitic commandments and their own authority, Jews remain free to exercise what D. H. Lawrence called, with no loud irony, their genius for 'disinterested speculation'.

The hero of DHL's *Kangaroo* was based on the Anzac Jew General Monash who led his do-and-die men at Gallipoli (and who claimed to have met Ned Kelly, the Aussie outlaw made iconic by Sidney Nolan). Although no one much said so, were Anzacs not dispensable because their names on casualty lists would excite no loud indignation in London or anguish in Great Houses? Anzac bitterness was a stimulating ingredient of the heterodoxy of Bob Hughes, as of Clive James's caustic geniality.

As for what my friend Simon Raven – note the ambivalent name – called 'Jewy Jews', pinched in the ghetto by Christians who could never be wrong, they enjoyed a reservation, however bleak, in which minds were free to play. Folklore has a story in which God is late for a meeting. The assembled rabbis had already voted for a reading which the Holy One had intended to oppose. He has the grace to smile and say, 'My children have overruled me.' What pope ever make such a concession?

43

What the baptised Karl Popper called *Logik der Forschung* (*The Logic of Scientific Thought* – better 'Investigation' or 'Research') did not spring from the ghetto, but no few Jews contributed to it. A. C. Grayling holds that Popper's allegedly scientific principles were of negligible practical significance. They do, however, embody ideals of public scrutiny and scholarly honour. Honest conclusions depend on scrupulous consideration of what might be wrong with them or with the arguments strutting them. Einstein's verification of his own prediction that rays of light could be bent by astral gravity is exemplary in that regard.

Before 1914, science was a subject without territorial boundaries. Discoveries were presumed available for the profit of all. Innovative machinery was the mark of advanced societies. Hiram Maxim was never reproached for peddling his machine-gun on the international market. The presumption was that it would be used by civilised states, which could afford it, against 'natives', who could not. The law of unforeseen consequences had it that machine-guns were cardinal in the mechanised slaughter of the Great War. After the Versailles Treaty of 1919, President Woodrow Wilson's seemingly unarguable doctrine of 'self-determination' served to fracture Europe's heterogeneous miscellanies into distinct nations and authorise the righteous persecution of minorities. A new brand of upstarts advertised furious grievances and set out to exercise the supposedly licensed right to bully and brutalise. Puppet kings were manipulated by praetorian guards and one-party henchmen. Democracy was denounced, left and right, for fear of majorities terminating the lease of self-determined swaggerers. Parades displaced civilised argument.

Science and armaments became inseparable. In 1948, accused of supplying the USSR with classified material relating to the development of the atomic bomb, Klaus Fuchs claimed to hold it immoral for scientists not to share their discoveries. Might he have believed what he said? Seen through aptly tinted spectacles, the space programme passed for the next stage in human scientific progress. Closer to, it has been linked with domination of the world, if not the universe, by devious elites. Leading lights emerge from under bushels. Bosses of multi-national enterprises beyond voters' control now collude with gangster oligarchies which, since the implosion of the Soviet Union, need affect small high-mindedness. In any future Armageddon, no adventurer will have to sport a salvationary creed. Humbug has lost its braid, the Book its warrant. Tendentious patriotism, as in Brexit, arms the humbug of cliquish opportunists.

As for the Bomb and allied devices, would a successful attempt to keep them secret, as Greek fire was for so long by Christian Constantinople, have made the world safer, or less safe (for some), than it has turned out? History neither licenses predictions nor exemplifies regularity. Hugh Trevor-Roper pricked out the megalomania behind Arnold Toynbee's scheme of meta-Hegelian human progress. TR himself later propounded the modest rule that powers – he was thinking of Germany – might fight two losing wars for continental or world domination, but never undertake a third. There was all the difference in the world, he argued, between case-by-case observation as against the presumption of regent access to the irrevocable scheme of things. Vanity and Rupert Murdoch's easy money led the older, no wiser, Trevor-Roper to validate forged diaries attributed to Adolf Hitler and so besmirch his own pedestal.

As Benedict (né Baruch) Spinoza argued, *sub specie aeternitatis* everything is inevitable; meanwhile we have wanton comedy. The H-bomb and even more annihilatory machinery and delivery systems render their possessors both unconscionably powerful and helpless in the face of whoever also has them. The new colonies, whatever their native riches, are client states whose leaders cannot retaliate against domineering powers. Supplied with whatever obsolescent weaponry, they are clamped under the aegis of their nuclear masters.

44

Senator Joe McCarthy's televised disparagement of liberals, not least in Hollywood, disposed movie studios to become play-safe confectioners. In his whiskered and whiskied wake, political arrivistes – Richard Nixon the least subtle, Robert Kennedy the most adroit – and military men of various degrees of callousness or absurdity, caricatured as General Jack D. Ripper in Kubrick's *Dr. Strangelove*, set out to evict East Coast fancy-pants from seats of power. There followed the collapse of quasi-Fabian benevolence that had graced and limited the Democrats' ruthlessness. FDR's progressive wing had been not inconveniently braked by the Dixiecrats. Reaganite Republicans, for whom freedom was liberty to purchase privilege, made sure that whatever was good for the defence of the Union was good for business. The Land of the Free now doubles with the land of the freebooters and all the voters they can rent, dupe or intimidate.

In 1960s Europe, the fracture of traditional loyalties and the disintegration of the educated class began, loudly, with the *événements de Mai Soixante-Huit*. Free of the republican tradition of military service and the danger of being drafted to go to war in Algeria, students at the Sorbonne parodied Jacobin ruthlessness. Their chant of '*Le giraffe à la lanterne*' called, naughty-boyishly, for de Gaulle to be strung up by his long neck. How many of the bold company had denounced the 'police riot' of 1962 which resulted in hundreds of Parisian Algerians being killed and dumped in the Seine?

Raymond Aron made few friends among the *jeunes* when he described their antics as '*psychodrame*', parodic revolution. It emboldened them to parade, mock-militants, on Daniel Cohn-Bendit's behalf, under the rubric '*Nous sommes tous des juifs allemands*'. Alain Finkielkraut was unsporting enough to read their bravado as contemptible appropriation. Slogans are no more beliefs than recipes are food.

In the US, the good fight for a colour-blind society has both closed ranks and widened regimental divisions. The compact which once joined Jews and Blacks in the fight for civil rights was sundered after Blacks discovered the risk-free pleasure of flexing muscles against one-time allies. The Reverend Louis Farrakhan called his red-bow-tied followers – bandsmen all beating the same invisible drum – 'The Nation of Islam'. Tax-free religiosity has fabricated innumerable cults and culls of resentment. Feminism abrogated the civility which had married white society and denounced it as a phallocratic conspiracy. Women, so Kate Millett and others advertised, no longer had to beware women, as Thomas Midleton advised his Jacobean audience; better embrace their sisters, handle their own orgasms, raise fatherless children.

Single-issue campaigning can be neatly packaged for TV. David Attenborough has become a lay saint in England by crooning insistence that we must redeem the world by preserving endangered species and fencing wildernesses. Nature has a moral call on human penitence and the redemption of – what else? – the planet. Jonathan Swift might propose that the best chance of verdant resurrection would be for humanity to be reduced to something like a quarter of its increasing numbers. Why not allow COVID-19 and its derivatives to carry out an unopposed, eco-friendly cull? That suave on-the-maker Boris Johnson hinted at such a policy and was hounded from office.

In humane practice, civilised people have small inclination to embrace any unprofitable programme that goes much further than dispensing with indestructible plastic. Mass murder by increasingly lethal machinery is the closest we are likely to come to incidental collaboration with natural selection. Flanders' fields were never so green as after 1918. As it happens, the colour-blind commonly fail to distinguish red from green. The surest way to save the planet is to rid it of boss-eyed man. Mass-murderous weaponry, chatty as Kubrick's HAL, Daedalus' Talos in mechanical dress, is the likeliest implement of redemption. Will machines find ways to proceed to mutual obliteration after they have done with man? 'You betcha', did HAL say?

45

Liberal education has been riven by the notion that nothing can be taught or said in a neutral language. This chimes, left and right, with the meta-Marxist notion that objectivity is humbug; in the humanities, nothing can escape being political. Opinion rules; cant conquers. The degeneration of culture is accelerated by distribution of awards and prizes in accordance with political rectitude, social pressures. Reliably second-rate fixers square every circle. Wishful equalities become mandatory in the programmes of Our Betters.

After May '68, General de Gaulle defused student menace to the authority of the old Right by means similar to those deployed in his rise to power in 1958. By telling Algerian *pieds noirs 'Je vous ai compris'*, he procured a pause. Having understood them too well for their own good, he devised means to sap their cohesion. When a winning general grants a truce, it is likely to be in order to give him time to reinforce his own position. De Gaulle appointed Edgar Faure, a scholarly centrist politician, to revise the academic curriculum in a way that would both seem concessive to the radicals and sever the cleverest sons and daughters from the lumpen-extremists.

Offering easier access to state-sponsored emoluments, Faure dismantled the source of his own eminence. Independent minds were left with small prospect of economic subsidy. Informed rumour has it that Faure was deputed to work undisturbed not least because he was notorious for pungent farts. His foregone conclusions weakened the prestige, hence the influence, of liberal arts graduates such as himself. Efficiency before morality paved the likeliest road to plump salvation. Science doesn't do conscience. Archimedes was the historical archetype of the rented sage, Daedalus the mythical. Both lent their wits to the defence of tyranny. The moral mutability of modern scientists was exemplified by Werner von Braun's translation from Hitler's rocket genius to overseer of America's ballistic programme. The money of project-masters has no smell.

The Nazi claim that Albert Einstein's now-canonical theories could be dismissed as 'Jewish physics' proved the inanity of attaching ideological or racial labels to scientific discoveries. Stalin's embrace of Lysenko's charlatan notion of characteristics acquired, contagiously as it were, thanks to a 'socialist' environment, was only one example of ideologically imposed 'truths'. In secular creeds, as in Catholicism, doctrine blinkers intelligence and bans dissent, that regular source of progress. Constantine the Great's deployment of his version of Christianity to serve as a socially unifying doctrine was an early instance of the adaptation of ideas to hobble mankind in a faith that was then called Truth. Jesting Pilate had the last pagan laugh. Unsmiling belief became society's supervisor. Christian clergy were the cops of knowledge, unless dissent was sly and refined enough, like Renaissance art and literature, to secrete ambiguity.

46

In ancient Rome, the gates of the temple of two-faced Janus were closed only in times of peace, hence rarely. Augustus claimed to have had them shut three times, but war remained Rome's business, the gates usually open for it. The Capitol in Washington, DC is a parody of ancient Roman architecture; while, briefly, National Security Advisor to President Trump John Bolton retrieved the old Latin slogan '*Si pacem* vis, para bellum' (if you want peace, prepare (for) war). First Hebrew, then Greek, then Latin articulated the fundamentals of Western civilisation. In tailored quotation, they append kudos to what is often mistranslated.

Science and mathematics have notations, not languages; grammar yes, ethics no. A theorem or a proof may be 'beautiful'; never good, or bad, it has no room for metaphor, no hook for wit. Whoever formulates it has neither the right nor the power to prescribe its application. Might a metaphysician be tempted to read God's omnipotence in the same spirit? Whoever can do absolutely anything is bound to do nothing specific. If He could have chosen otherwise, He would then be open to criticism. Spinoza implies as much when he equates Nature and Deity. Can Leibniz's straight-faced notion that all is for the best in the best of all possible worlds, mocked to scorn in Voltaire's *Candide*, be taken for a gloss on his correspondent the Jew Spinoza's un-Jewish determinism?

47

A cyclic change in the cerebral attitudes in the US command structure was sealed by the 'logic' of Robert McNamara (middle name Strange), Secretary of Defense during Lyndon Johnson's presidency. The Vietnam War had been primed, discreetly, by Jack Kennedy. How far was JFK's fistic stance provoked by Nikita Khrushchev's gangster challenge to the new boy's arrival in the world's playground? Conforming with the Harvard Business School's double-entry ethos, McNamara saw war as an exercise susceptible to cost-efficient control. Losses were relative to dividends, casualties collateral, blood discounted. Hypocrisy hung up its high hat.

In accordance with his father's commercial-cum-criminal tactics, John Fitzgerald Kennedy engaged the US in calculated puppetry in Vietnam. The family's connections with finance and organised crime fostered deniability, a tactic common to employers of Secret Service agents, tax planners and hit-men. Undeclared wars and secreted revenue share devious facilities. After his death, JFK was ennobled as a martyr to the system which bought him to power. Remember that hat-off, sweeping bow to his father, before the inauguration, honouring debts, literal and metaphorical, to higher racketeering? Who will deny Faustian irony in that overdose of courtesy?

Both handsome and murdered before his reputation could

be tainted or his chin doubled, J. F. K. has been configured as the good guy who would never have allowed the US to become snared and bloodied in South-East Asia. In truth (philosopher Richard Rorty's essential variable), his successor Lyndon Johnson was saddled with a Kennedy policy. Having honoured it with self-destructive piety, it was hung around his neck by Jack's born-again, suddenly liberal brother. Previously the mean political machine man, Robert Kennedy was transformed into imminent redeemer by assuming his brother's well-lined mantle. He then sought to disassociate the family from the Vietnam involvement Jack had primed. Opposing Lyndon Johnson in the run-up to the 1968 presidential election, he rendered populism and plutocracy hand in glove. In the months before his own assassination, RFK campaigned as the honest-to-God multi-millionaire, tribune of the ill-used and underpaid. The accumulation of wealth, primed by bootlegging during Prohibition, gave the Kennedys the means to affect hostility to the Mob, with which Joe Kennedy had been allied, and to Wall Street, where their money continued to fatten. The compact between decorated military and moneyed surrogates was sealed under Nixon and Kissinger. With the advent of Ronald Reagan, the Cold War was won for long enough for Francis Fukuyama to claim that liberal democracy would henceforth be the universal measure of political achievement. Now we know.

It had become amusing to portray LBJ as Macbeth, JFK as his noble victim. Kennedy and Jackie had the modern advantage of being photogenic; acted closeness became the real thing. Like veteran wrinkles, reason has limited appeal. When in 1992 Bill Clinton came to defeat the too-experienced George Bush, he would prove that, for a post-McLuhan electorate, youth became an argument, insolence achievement, wrinkles a downer. Athletes and sportspeople alone continue to be judged solely on their merits. The advantages a multi-millionaire can derive from playing the tribune of blue-collared rednecks may have been the only history lesson Donald Trump ever learnt. He won election by reiterated sloganeering. Hillary Clinton's allusion to 'deplorables' lost her the 2016 election in one word.

48

The collapse of the USSR and its glacial – hence slow-moving – hostility required a new bogey to justify the continued domination of uniformed experts and plutocrats in societies allegedly controlled, every so often, by popular votes and honest accountancy. This tradition was breached, with insolent flagrancy, when the old-moneyed Bush family and its backers were suffered to rig the election of George W. as president. For the sorry sake of prompt continuity, the Supreme Court voted to overlook fraud in the framing of ballot papers, if not (as is likely) in filling them out, in the pivotal state of Florida. Its governor, Jeb Bush, was the brother of Al Gore's opponent. Franklin D. Roosevelt had been the first president to make it politic to stuff the Supreme Court with justices favourable to his New Deal. *On le lui a bien rendu.*

Less than a year after Bush Jr's inauguration, federal security services with divergent, competitive agenda neglected to head off recognised alien terrorists before they acquired the competence to fly (but not to land) the planes which, on 9/11, delivered death to New York City and Washington, DC (not forgetting, as people often do, the passengers and crew who happened to be in them). A further curtailment of liberty and another bout of authoritarian rule were, it seemed, forced on G. W. Bush, as it had been on Putin by Beslan. Professor Mary

Beard is reported as saying that the Americans 'had it coming to them'. Not long afterwards, she went on an enriching lecture tour of American universities. Women, she regularly implies, behave better than men. She wears don't-look-now trousers to prove it. The cult of the Virgin Mary lingers *en revers*.

No Orwellian paranoia is needed to conceive that the incompetence of the security services before 9/11 was a tactical device by an agency bent on strengthening G. W. Bush's questionable authority. Outrage at the fall of the Twin Towers retrieved national solidarity, for a time. As mayor of New York, Rudy Giuliani appeared a sudden hero; false colours more gallant than have since come true. It remained tempting for many people, not only the actual conspirators, to wish guilt on the victims. Paranoia parodies science in the sense that it holds nothing accidental; everything has to have a furtive, if unproved, cause. Arab propagandists claimed that 9/11 was a Mossad plot. Why else were there no Jews in NYC's Twin Towers on the fatal day? That might indeed have been sinister, had it been true; it was not.

Perhaps taking a lesson from the dividend Margaret Thatcher drew from her own government's ineptitude, once the Falklands War had redeemed Britannia's vanity, G. W. Bush proceeded from victorious vengeance in Iraq to all-but-unopposed re-election. Al Gore, cheated of the presidency – which by no means implies that he merited it – retired to the moral high ground. Votes were not needed to elect him the Green Man, pedestalled to prophesy the desolation of the planet. Mankind is now being urged to unite in apology for hedonistic sins and plastic wrappings. Plutocratic Savonarola of conservationists, Gore, bloody by name, calls on mankind to repent while there is still a sliver of time by his expensive watch. Whether or not *Homo sapiens* becomes extinct, the butterfly will come through, in accordance with lepidopterist Vladimir Nabokov's first law of nature, survival of the frailest.

Victory over Saddam Hussein's Iraq, deemed complicit with what happened to the Twin Towers, passed for a triumph for the good guys. Accelerated destabilisation of the splintered Middle East, due to lack of any practical Anglo-American scheme for its political redemption, procured a shoo-in second term for the born-again pseudo-cowboy. GWB showed Tony Blair how to walk like J. R. Ewing in Dallas; swagger too imitates art, of a kind. The twenty-first century began with fabricated excuses for Great Power opportunism. Russia's invasion of Ukraine, like its earlier reinforcement of Bashar al-Assad's war on his own people, has outraged those who set a precedent with the 2003 bombardment of Baghdad, justified by decidedly misinterpreted evidence on the part of the Bush administration's honest-to-God diplomacy.

49

Literacy as a qualification for office incited Jack Kennedy to write, or to have written, his 1957 book *Profiles in Courage*. Proof of Harvard-educated competence, it also served to mind electors of his wartime gallantry. In the twenty-first century, such a publication, for electioneering purposes, would be a waste of money. Twittering requires less effort; instant banality fortifies the prejudices and conceit of those to whom it is addressed. What affects to unite men has every prospect of dividing them. The planet will endure; man may not. Must it matter *sub specie aeternitatis*? Eternity seals the accounts. Hans Vaihinger's prescient 1911 *The Philosophy of 'As If'* refurbished values without celestial certification. Language embraces what logic excludes. Humanity's shoes are laced with imposture. Truth may be stranger than fiction; fiction is truer.

While Donald Trump has never been accused of opening any books, his frequently replaced kitchen cabinet was never averse to cooking them. Scorn for intelligence adds lustre to his appeal. Moneyed megalomania offers the semblance of solidarity with an ill-educated public for whom prejudices and malevolence are reliable adhesives. The military–industrial–criminal complex has no interest in increasing the literacy of the proles; nor do single-issue politicians and their trumpeters care to dispense anything but monotonous vanities. One of Wittgenstein's parables was of the man who read something in the newspaper and, to confirm that it was true, went out and bought another copy of the same paper. Readers of the *Daily Mail*, like viewers of Fox News, might ask, 'What's your point?'

The merchandising of sentiment follows from the media's pseudo-crusading temper: proprietorial interests parade as indignant purpose. Herbert Marcuse's accusation that bourgeois society was one of 'repressive tolerance' has been trumped by political correctness. Cant ranks repetition as integrity. The modern world, from as far back as Harry Truman's 'innocent' institution of the National Security Council, has placed key decisions in the hands of an Inner Circle sealed away from unreliable, elected politicians. A surreptitious revolution, with no practical programme except the monopoly of power, lifted decision from the people in the name of taking care of them. The terrible beauty of this subversion is that it needs no articulate engineer, no supervising Soviet. The waning of Christianity exempts presumption from the cover story of hypocrisy. Left and right shed moral camouflage.

What François Mitterrand called '*le coup d'état permanent*', when describing the means and style of de Gaulle's resumption of power in 1958, has been matched in the US, without the use of military strength or overt breach of constitutional propriety. There has followed a series of crises which, we are promised, were it not for measures argued and sealed in secret, would have ended in catastrophe. Science gave first the president of the USA, then leaders of other nuclear powers, a red button that would, if pressed, usher in the world of *Mad Max*, if Max was lucky. Permanent emergencies warrant the suspension of civility. Military considerations dispense with civil explanations. Fortified war rooms promise to deliver a select company from thermonuclear dissolution. The few will emerge, they presume, to take possession of an Eden roasted and poisoned by their own recipes.

50

Vladimir Putin's ostentatious investment in Russian military power promised that he has no project for the internal welfare, unbent justice or democratisation of Russia. Ukraine? Before denouncing its instigator, Stalin, in 1956, when he was well dead, Nikita Khruschev officiated, in the 1930s, over the deliberate starvation of some 5 million of the citizens of the greatest grain-producer in the world. The Mother Russia card was played, *in extremis*, by Putin's paragon, Joseph Vissarionovich, a sudden self-promoted marshal, in 1941. Eighty years on, Putin has replaced etiolated democracy with nostalgia for Soviet-cum-tsarist ruthlessness and dominion. He sustains his solo strut (mark of the little man), when not stripped to the waist for a virile gallop, by shooting his cuffs while parading, solo, Russia as a Great Power *redidivus*.

The year 1989 came, with textbook neatness, seventy years after the Treaty of Versailles and its role in prolonging what it affected to end. By comparison with Putin, Stalin was Moloch with principles. Whatever their mass-murderous policies, he and his Supreme Soviet accomplices, dachas to one side, were never accused of personal enrichment on a grandiose scale or lack of some show of perverted idealism. Incapable of rising to hypocrisy, Putin and his plutocratic accomplices advertise no manifesto for the improvement or happiness of Russian society. Multi-decked yachts stand ready for sumptuous get-aways, provided the plunderers survive long enough to reach them from their exaggerated mansions. Who has ever stayed in all those bedrooms?

51

T. S. Eliot's clerically cut assimilation to an English gentleman rigged him as a striped-trousered, umbrella-toting churchwarden, at ease among those averse to modern life. Although he regarded the world with a dated Christian wince, somewhat mimicked by Geoffrey Hill, a recent survey named Eliot the most popular modern English poet. Need this mean more than that his was the first name people came up with or recognised? Eliot's hankering for a mandarin society had little influence on the post-war US. It retained its appeal for British devotees for whom science belonged in another park. Eliot's list of principles seemed to promise the new subject's adhesion to the British Crown. In truth, his monarchical craving derived from the thinking of Charles Maurras, who – despite previously loud anti-German feelings – greeted the French capitulation, and Pétain's dismantling of the Republic, as a 'divine surprise'.

Did anyone in the House of Windsor possess the qualities of the ideal sovereign whose image Maurras and his *Action Française* impressed on Eliot's mind? In his urge to muster with the Parisian reactionary world, young Tom composed verses in French. He too did voices. Love of cats added an endearing nursery volume (never as good as *Winnie-the-Pooh*) to his works and furred his claws. George Steiner had it that children's books – *Gulliver's Travels, Treasure Island, Alice in Wonderland, Lord of the Flies* – were at the artful apex of English-language literature.

The redemption of Eliot's *'miglior fabbro'* Ezra Pound (Derridans might cut in 'fab/bro') was signalled by ole Ez being awarded the first Bollingen Prize in 1949. Did his selection not have more than a little to do with the desire of Eliot and his friends to be done with memories of the Nazi and Fascist eras? Those who deny it give us reason to believe it. At the same time, communist affiliations, genuine, dated or confected, led to the pillorying of all manner of people, in particular celebrities and office-holders, whose pursuit might attract most publicity. Hollywood supplied headline prey and right-wing beaters. Stanley Donen played rueful at not being made famous by being targeted. 'I guess they had enough directors,' he told me. Stars were the movie world's prime celebrities until the New Wave, Jean-Luc Godard and his *frère-ennemi* François Truffaut *en tête*, served their own conceit by jacking up the director as *auteur*.

Ezra Pound's absolution signified the determination of the literary establishment to discount Nazism's freight of corpses and ashes and ole Ez's delight in it. Karl Shapiro's vote against Pound getting the Bollingen Prize led to banishment from the anthological rota. Shapiro's active war service was good reason for stay-at-home in-groupers to club together to procure his ostracism. Pound's resurrection was a first step towards the relegation of the Holocaust from a capital charge against Christendom to a gangster aberration. What right-wing intellectual has yet attempted to dissect what madness or badness impelled acquiescence in witless tyranny and mass murder? Gregor von Rezzori stands skittishly alone with *Memoirs of an Anti-Semite*.

At the Nuremberg trials, Albert Speer distinguished himself from the killer crew by playing the well-groomed technocrat going gallantly out of his way to volunteer guilt. Clever stuff was his tailored speciality. Penitential humbug dressed him as an exception to the mass-murderous brutality which his own organisation demanded of subordinates. Not a few of his direct, less plausible, legates went to the scaffold.

French Protestant communities were exceptional in harbouring Jews. So, in rare particular, were some of the Catholic clergy in south-western France where, six hundred years earlier, Albigensian heretics had been hunted down by the Papacy. The Archbishop of Toulouse was exceptional among Catholic hierarchs in denouncing the anti-Semitism sanctified by the French episcopate after the defeat of 1940. In 1945, it became politic to camouflage the fellow-travelling Pius XII as a saint and to excuse those who took their callous cue from him.

During the inter-war years of competitive tyrannies, left and right, and during the war until 1943, intellectuals were conspicuous, in France especially, for deference to the strutting masters of the New Europe. André Malraux advised Sartre and Simone de Beauvoir to bide their time before joining the Anglo-Saxons' victory parade. Quondam Red pilot, then latter-day Talleyrand, Malraux emerged in regular colonel's uniform in order to become General de Gaulle's virtuous and voluble *aide de camp*. Who among its audience cannot remember that warbling eulogy of Jean Moulin, rendered windier by the outdoor venue, that obliged de Gaulle to listen in protracted, all but sullen, silence?

Among academics, a no-more-than-methodical trick was played by Fernand Braudel, of the Annales school. His proposal that history should concern itself with the *longue durée* *rendered* aberrations such as the round-up of Jews in the Vel' d'Hiv, preparatory to being railroaded to their deaths, of merely incidental significance. Making his speciality the Mediterranean world, he marginalised a topic which might have engaged him, Jew of a kind, in academic in-fighting. Principles not in question, his nerve perhaps, Lewis Namier, stamped true blue by his knighthood, vanished into meticulous study of particular politicians, and their interests, in the time of the Four Georges. Self-effacement and modesty are by no means synonymous.

52

Britain's posture of unflinching righteousness was merited more by the convenience of maritime geography and her allies' fire-power than by shoulder-to-shoulder nobility. The process of advancing Clement Attlee as a modest paragon has been decorated, recently, by the revelation that he gave brief shelter to a child refugee from the Nazis. You are taken to have been exceptionally nice to care about a single small child if it happened to be Jewish. In muffled fact, Attlee presided over a government which, in the immediate post-war years, made it as difficult as possible for 'displaced persons' to enter Palestine or to come to England. No searching questions were asked in 1946 when he imported a regiment of Ukrainian SS men to work in the coal mines. David Cesarani's *Delayed Justice* (1992) carries a detailed account of that pragmatic smuggle. Guilty men can be relied on to keep their heads down, literally in the case of killers secreted at the coal face.

With Eliotesque finesse, Christopher Ricks came, in time, to deplore the Jewish appropriation of 'our' word 'holocaust' and the insolence of clapping a capital letter on it, as if it belonged only to a single Hebrew case. With prissy precision, Ricks misconstrued 'holocaust' when he claimed that, since not all Jews had been burnt, it was ungrammatical to apply it to their case. In fact, 'holocaust' means 'wholly burnt'.

If a sacrificial herd of oxen were burnt in sacrifice, it could properly be said to be a holocaust; not all the oxen in the world have to have been so consumed. Ricks is a reverential embalmer of Eliot's Christian virtues. Did he ever allude to, let alone smile at, Eliot's correspondent Groucho Marx's remark on a restricted beach, 'My son is only half-Jewish, can he go in up to his knees'? Who considered himself more privileged, during their correspondence, to receive a letter, Groucho or the great Tom?

Anglo-Saxon intellectuals were never put to the divisive question, as was the French *gratin*, of whether or not to collaborate with Nazism. Pierre Drieu la Rochelle, Louis-Ferdinand Céline, Lucien Rebatet and Robert Brasillach did so, gleefully. The readiness of the aged David Lloyd-George, heroic victor in 1918, to step up and play the Pétain part, unless the duke of Windsor beat him to it, suggests that, had things gone badly, British solidarity might have been less firm than sentiment insists. Ballsy 'Tom' Mosley, with his tight belt, knitted shoulders, never lost admirers, right and left, from Enoch Powell to Michael Foot. In the early 1950s, I lunched adjacent to him, in Overton's restaurant, islanded near Victoria Station. He bragged, to be overheard, of his swagger acquaintances and wait-and-see perspicacity.

In *Not Their Finest Hour* (1977), David Pryce-Jones is ruthlessly civil in itemising a range of all-but-signed-up collaborators, had Hitler successfully invaded Britain. Long after the usual obligatory period, HMG continues to refuse publication of the Home Office's crypt of latent swivellers. The Occupation had put the French to an abrupt, practical test. After the Liberation, France remained divided in two in a fashion which Anglo-Saxons were spared until Brexit, which Mrs May came to lead, after splitting herself in two. Remainer before fifty-two per cent of the voters decided to leave, with the prospect of Number 10 on her front door, she became an anglicised version of Ledru-Rollin (1807–74), the French politician who, observing a march in favour of his supposed cause, said,' 'I am their leader. I must follow them.' To establish her narrowed notion of people who mattered, Mrs May denounced 'cosmopolitans' who favoured European Union. Sovietologists will recall a frequently used quasi-meiotic term for Jews. *Point de détail*?

The post-war resuscitation of Anglicanism and its God, the convenient remarriage of religion and art, was advertised by Graham Sutherland's prompt, by-the-yard backdrop for the altar of not-yet-rebuilt Coventry Cathedral, lofty reproach to the enemy which had bombed a sacred place. In fact, wartime Coventry was both a cathedral city and another thing: an industrial hub largely devoted to the armament industry. Pious reconstruction was a way of obliterating memory of the pre-war Anglican hierarchy cringing in the face of malignant inhumanity.

The image of the cross on the dome of St Paul's, silhouetted against the flames of the burning London docks and East End, had served as promise that God was on the right side and, like the royal family – some of it – had been through it with the rest of us. The conspicuously absent Duke of Windsor, imploding with self-pity, may have advised the Nazis to switch their attack from the RAF's airfields to London. Buckingham Palace in particular received a bomb which proved a godsend: the royal family could, as the queen put it, 'look the East End in the eye'. The switch of targets was literally ill-advised. The RAF survived to win the Battle of Britain. It's a wonder that ex-Edward VIII, like some Themistocles *redivivus*, never had the gall to claim credit for misleading the Krauts.

Anglican gratitude to the Almighty served to prove that He was still there as well as to obscure the fact that, in 1935, the Church of England Assembly had voted, unanimously but for the Archbishop of York, against admitting any Jewish refugees into Britain. Politically, such an attitude was defensible: Britain was suffering from mass unemployment. Morally, it stands unforgivable. Members of the British House of Commons continued to be fastidious, well into the war, when it came to room at the inn. One MP alleged, with callous ignorance, that the Germans would be obliged to feed the Jews if they were left where they were. The myth of British magnanimity centres on the *Kindertransport*, in which ten thousand children were admitted into the country between late 1938 and 1940. HMG had small part in the rescue, except not to oppose it. The evacuation was instigated by Nicholas Winton. He received no British recognition until very late in a long life. His knighthood was less honour for him than cover-up for a callous establishment.

53

America's post-war development of advanced space explo-
ration, iced for MacNamara-esque 'cost-efficiency' reasons,
reads like the synopsis of a story better narrated by strip-
cartoon than by prosaic journalism. Clever young men were
drawn into a programme which procured deferment from
the draft. Desire for applause supplanted conscience. 'How?'
was a proper scientific question; 'Why?' not. The call for anti-
communist zeal was a modernisation of the British Navy's old
requirement of commissioned officers that they be 'ambitious'
for promotion, implying that they would be wise never to
be critical of strategic or political objectives. An occasional
modern naval officer had the nerve to mimic Horatio Nelson,
when he clapped his telescope to his blind eye at the battle
of Copenhagen, and rely on success to gild his gall. Some ten
years after the war, I met a submarine commander who had
been conspicuously and gloriously disobedient in penetrating
a U-boat base. Intrepid impudence won him the DSO and
DSC. In the early 1960s, he diddled a friend of mine out of
£400,000.

Salutes for independent initiative seldom greet army com-
manders. Pistol-packing General George Patton was an
exception after his dash for Paris in 1944. Ever since the
common people of Athens, the *demos,* supplied the motor

energy needed to save the city in 480 BCE, naval officers and men have been more likely to stand out against central authority. In 1967, after the Colonels' seizure of power, ships of the Greek Navy awaited the call of the young (now late) king Constantine to oppose the coup. It never came. Until recently the Hellenic fleet was composed in no small part by ships donated by rich (and competitive) benefactors such as Aristotle Onassis and Stavros Niarchos. No few Athenian triremes had been similarly funded by so-called liturgies two millennia earlier. Rich Athenians were expected to strengthen the city; unlike triumphal Romans, they built no mansions to advertise personal wealth.

Eisenstein celebrated an early, emblematic twentieth-century naval occasion in his film *Battleship Potemkin*. Memorable footage saluted the proletarian crew that rebelled against rotten food and conditions in 1905. In 1921, one of the few acknowledged 'proletarian' objections to the assumption of power of the Bolsheviks came from the Baltic fleet at Kronstadt. Trotsky had no compunction in ordering the summary repression warranted, in Marxist terms, by their insolence as enemies of History. What film commemorates them?

54

The discoveries of one scientific mind are liable to be matched or amplified, with whatever delay, by another. Modern researchers are rendered compliant with power by the near impossibility of pursuing applied science without government funding. Mechanisation of the arts, relegated to the status of entertainment, leads to the dependence of 'artists' on institutions devoted to serving ever-greater audiences with tendentious placebos. Larger salaries than they could hope to earn elsewhere render commissioning custodians (of their own offices) in fashionable line. Mary may still be contrary, but she is liable to be denied funding or facilities on account of it. Curators dominate the visual arts; publishers abide the verdict of sales managers; TV executives think that they know what will keep them out of trouble and in their jobs. Prizes are allocated by celebrity judges primed to placate candidates whose ancestors were unfavoured. Books by promoted authors are gilded with hyperbole like the fizz touted by Thomas Mann's Felix Krull, confidence trickster.

55

The Vienna Circle's Logical Positivism codified the truncation of philosophy. Truth, it claimed, was based on objective evidence and peer review; any other postulate was 'metaphysics': egotistic fancy. The English have an aversion from rigid schemes propounded by foreigners, hence abiding affection for the murderous Henry VIII, after his breach with Rome. (What prize-seeking novelist will furnish us with Cardinal Wolsey's *apologia pro vita sua*?) When they fell on A. J. Ayer's anglicised version of Logical Positivism, Oxford colleagues, rivals rarely friends, relished pointing out that the principle of verifiability could not itself be verified. J. L. Austin, ex-colonel in the Intelligence Corps, combined testiness with trenchancy by observing that Germanic insistence that what was said should conform with verifiable truth was at odds with the jagged and jazzy range of, in particular, English expletives and linguistic subtlety.

Might it be that Ayer agreed too readily to be outranked? Because umpteen looks like a number but is not, does that mean that London Bridge is not safe to cross? A *proposito*, somewhat, the great bridge player and wit S. J. Simon (né Skidelsky) was never more naturalised as a Londoner than in his pragmatic demolition of the elaborate Vienna System of bidding in contract bridge. His (and Jack Marx's) trim system, Acol, named after a road and club in North London, was flexible and irregular, like English grammar. In 1936, the aristocratic German team captain applauded Skid's remark-able sportsmanship. If only he could introduce him to Hitler, he dared to say, the Führer might drop his manic racism. Despite professional quibblers, Ayer's *Language, Truth and Logic* (1936) retains popular appeal; forty years later he told me, in the tone of Saint Paul declaring that he had sold the paperback rights to the *Epistles*, that it still brought him in a thousand a year. Despite and because of their assault on intellectual pretentiousness, Ayer encouraged the contraction of the humanities: ethics and aesthetics were both out. He proclaimed the obsolescence of punditry: sentences beginning 'I' were 'mere autobiography'. His bumptious conceit was to play the 'journeyman', not yet the pundit.

Later in his professorial life, it amused him to side with his early critics and denounce his own polemic as no more than the *jeu d'un esprit jeune*. Might it be that young Ayer's notion that everything not subject to empirical verification was 'literal non/sense' was an overstated reading of what the Logical Positivists had sought to establish? Science, in their view, should admit a canon of propositions whose veracity, unless and until disproved, it was senseless for any intelligence to dispute. Did it follow that, as Austin read it, they denied the vernacular a place in civilised coffee-shopping?

In *Language, Truth and Logic*, Ayer affected to junk what-ever lay outside the Viennese rota. Might it be that the urge to be done with religion (i.e. Jewishness) led him to stiffen a doctrine rather than read it as a way of classifying, never sanctifying, scientific propositions? If so, he can be accused of what his master, Gilbert Ryle, called '*ignoratio elenchi* by higher re-definition'. After taking a formal filing system as banishing the demotic, and so painting himself into an unnecessarily tight corner, Ayer embraced relegation upwards into the meta-Anglican role of playboy professor.

John Gray has it that individual human characters are really (ah, really!) composites, without central agent or – key word – singular consciousness. How dismaying is this? To be articulate, literally or metaphorically, does not rule out the capacity for surprising oneself. Versatility does nothing to dis-establish personal identity. Human anatomy – head and other parts – engenders contradictory schemes, tendencies, ambitions. Allegedly immutable personality is often breached, in resourceful minds, by irregular, capricious possibilities. That is its strength, never its flaw.

The disparagement of Descartes, encapsulated in Ryle's *The Concept of Mind*, has been taken to be conclusive. What Ryle called 'the systematic elusiveness of "I"' eliminates 'I' from any logical system; so much for *ergo sum*. Nimbleness and muta-bility render logic a necessarily partial – only thus acceptable – account of human mentality. Lived life needs no self-denying rigidity. Ideology draws its murderous licence from a show of rigged certainties. Read as a metaphor, the mind/body duality recovers plausibility: head and heart are old duellists; human anatomy, above and below the belt, embodies the play-off of reason and desire. Home-spinning spiders are never in two minds. Ravelled in her own silk, for all her longevity Arachne is bound not to change in any ingenious regard. To be creative requires duplicity.

Shorn of an unquestionable deity, pious notions of fidelity, sexual and personal, yield to a morality derived from positiv-ism, with little of its bony propriety. Anglo-Saxon pragmatism promotes the superiority of the informal, if not the lazy. Wittgenstein recommended: 'Don't ask for the meaning, ask for the use.' Scorn for metaphysical trappings found an objec-tive correlative in architectural functionalism. Basil Spence's meta-Puritan concrete post-war complex on London's South

Bank stands as a monument to a cropped austerity that dates but is failing to age.

Moral and aesthetic traffic rarely flows in one direction for long. Affectations of nostalgia for defiant Protestantism sponsored the British retreat from the meta-Catholicism of post-modern Europe. Self-inflating insularity lay at the heart of the UK's secession from the Treaty of Rome. Docked of imperial reach, John of Gaunt's Scept'red Isle doubles for a self-determining and moated fortress. Its vanity rests on a special relationship with the USA which Washington is unlikely to honour again. As Christopher Thorne showed, in *Allies of a Kind* (1979), even during the supposedly tight alliance of the Second World War, FDR regarded the British Empire with small loyalty. The historical John of Gaunt did not hesitate to venture into Europe in pursuit of a throne in Castile. He returned to serve Shakespeare as a spokesman for 'this England'. Has his dying speech ever been delivered with a hint of sarcastic resignation?

56

Adhesion to the scientific elite has long involved combining rare qualities with submission to the impersonal logic of scientific method. Hence Heidegger, who thought Adolf Hitler the Messiah, was prompted to say: 'Science can't think.' One result of the discoveries attendant upon nuclear physics – science linked with the accelerated incineration of unspecified numbers – has been the subjection of the world's population to powers without ethical affectations. Science has a non-territorial empire, terrorist organisations its parodies; nothing is morally unthinkable, no possibility, vile or fanciful, beyond consideration. Once unearthed, nothing can be returned to oblivion.

In a piecemeal, need-to-know environment, the central machinery, like Stanley Kubrick's robotic HAL (first cousin to ICI) sports a coaxing voice, wit never; memory, yes; conscience, no. With programmed aptitude for callousness, it lacks hopes or ideas. Kubrick had the skittish idea of asking Jackie Mason to be the voice of HAL. The CND (Campaign for Nuclear Disarmament) sought to inject moral scruples into an activity in which peer review and confirmation are the sole forms of rectitude. The end of humanity and of the humanities lie adjacent.

'Imagine,' said John Lennon, unless it was Yoko Ono.

Science cannot; private sentiments, fears, hopes are irrelevant. However refined an individual scientist, scientific rectitude concerns procedures, never consequences: the wish to cure cancer is as much a prestigious ambition as humane mission. The more a surgeon sympathises, the less reliable his hand. The prize culture is a way of controlling the arts. Laurels, allotted by safe pairs of hands to people who are then held to merit them, are liable to be as much millstones as milestones. In sport alone, eligibility is determined by excellence or its promise; add 'almost' in honour of the cruelly misjudged Mark Ramprakash.

Sinclair Lewis was outspoken in saying he feared that, after receiving the Nobel Prize for Literature in 1930, he would be unable to write another book. Ernest Hemingway was elevated into impotence after being honoured for one of his several least-good novels. Recent English-language laureates, Harold Pinter and Doris Lessing, were more regularly applauded for moral pretentiousness than for literary virtuosity. Pinter's renown depended on admirers' ignorance not only of Ionescu, but also of Adamov and other absurdists in the tradition of Jarry's 1896 play *Ubu Roi*. Harold's conceit became his surrogate foreskin. Did Doris Lessing ever write a witty word? Want of humour doubles with didactic self-importance.

It is part of the trust-me-chums 'criticism' promoted by Oxford professor John Carey, when playing his protracted innings as top-of-the-page journalist, to claim that in literature there can be no objective measure of quality. Who says as much when it comes to music, dance or architecture? Painting seems a vexed case; the distribution of honours (the Turner Prize in particular) is likely to be based on capricious categories and attention-seeking judges. Specious innovation is the quality most lauded by committees and pushy advocates. Drawing remains an art in which bluff, like that of Damien Hirst with his bottled beasts, cannot prevail, hence its price can be less easily rigged and its lack of juggling hustlers. No few English art schools classify drawing as undemocratic and elitist. Follow that bandwagon, some say; head for them hills, say others. Pastoral is a version of escape in which no one gets very far.

57

The novel and movie of *The Remains of the Day* furnish a random instance of the calculated post-modern masterpiece; scandal doubles with snobbery. Sentimentalising Cliveden's toffs and its below-stairs staff flatters Old England while seeming to satirise it. Confected by a nicely spoken person of foreign provenance, the duly beknighted Kazuo Ishiguro's work supplied a perfect prize-winning number. Partiality and impartiality dead heat on the same mount. The American dinner guest at the cinematic Cliveden combines a few away-from-home truths with gaucherie that lames his rhetoric. The servants, in the Figaro tradition, appear keener than their masters, and more appealing; freer too, the cant (and the casting) has it. Below-stairs stars.

The arts in general have been relegated to the status of entertainment, to be savoured in the intervals of BREAKING NEWS: consolation for lost leisure, crumbling civility. Writers have been downgraded to employees, pampered, promoted or dumped. Today's dominance of executives in the movie business, however venal or commercial it once was, relegates the creative to lackeydom. Dialogue, in movies and TV, has been trimmed to clichés and code-words. Wit is no longer marketable, allusion lost on most audiences. In what used to be literature, prizes are rigged to placate pressure groups and to prove the eligibility of judges for reappointment. Robert Graves and Karl Shapiro stand as early instance of what happens to those who take exception.

In neo-Platonist mode, Geoffrey Hill has persuaded himself, never everyone, that 'difficult' poetry is 'democratic' because it fosters the belief that nothing is beyond the common intelligence; stretching is good mental exercise. In truth, literature is what pundits and pushers – can you get a Noël Cowardly pin between them? – think will earn them the gratitude, and specie, of readers. The show of different labels on all-but-indistinguishable products applies to electronic grocers, such as Amazon and Netflix, as well as to the dwindling parade of high street supermarkets. Ready-when-you-are literature, conceived without passion, claims no permanent house-room.

58

The super-rich hope to avoid the common fate by escaping as space-yachtsmen. The desiccation of the earth, with its superfluity of people and their implacable thirsts, is said to be imminent unless science saves the planet which its discoveries, benign no less than murderous, have brought to the verge of disaster. Heraclitus of Ephesus 540–480 BCE 540–480 bce remarked that the road up and the road down were the same road. This is of a piece with the notion of the alternation of war and peace, coming together and pulling apart, epitomised by Empedocles of many-templed Sicilian Acragas (Agrigento). Man vacillates between fraternity and fratricide. Science kills, with more and more refined weaponry; death-dealing at a distance requires no courage. Laboratories both refine the means of postponing death, by cancers not least, and generate lethal germs to deliver it.

How could the extension of life on earth, or outside it, not lead to even more savagery? Science might furnish Jacob with a heavenly ladder, but if space colonisation is to involve a human crew, however A-listed, the flight of humanity must carry antagonisms with it. Any stellar pantisocracy, choice as it may be, cannot do without a Prometheus to confound expectations. The way out of one maze is the way into another.

Genet's '*Nous ne sortirons jamais de ce bordel*' will loop any human society.

J. Robert Oppenheimer's exclusion from the further development of the powers whose unbottling he had supervised makes it clear how scientific progress is independent of particular individuals. 'Genius' is a romantic label. No valid science is not assimilable to other scientific schemes, unless it renders them obsolete; there can be nominal attribution, no possessive rights. Great art is what no one else could have produced. All science was 'always there', like whatever a miner, brave or lucky, may unearth. Art is invaluable and unnecessary, what god is capable of it?

59

First convened in what seemed the durable civility of pre-Great War Europe, the coffee-housing set of 'Logical Positivists' known as the Vienna Circle encompassed Jews and Gentiles. Under Moritz Schlick's chairmanship, it foresaw a world purged of metaphysical vanities. A reasonable future was to be based on a common corpus of valid propositions. After 1918, affectations of impartiality were alien to the jigsawn new world of grasping winners, snarling losers, uneasy in-betweeners. Vanities and grudges dug trenches in what had seemed secure common ground.

The enthronement of Eugenio Pacelli, Pius XII, in the Vatican in March 1939 promised the abdication of Roman Catholic moral authority in return for the exemption of the Church from the ideological malice of Hitler's Germany. With Pacelli's connivance, Hitler exalted Bismarck's *Kulturkampf* by making a domestic pet of Germany's Catholic press. Pius connived with the Führer, provided the Church's capital remained untouched. Christ's vicar licensed Mammon and so retained his lease on the pinnacle of the Temple.

Once salvation services quackery, moral chaos passes for liberation. Hence the collapse of the US into a babel of trumpery, the UK into a parody of Churchillian vanities. In societies less prone to fight on beaches than to laze on them, cashiered elites escape responsibility for the consequences of their vanities. The next stop is a society which, as Caligula wished for the Roman people, has a single neck. When it can be wrung with impunity, science will have a button for it. If pressed deliberately, it will be after a self-selected super-rich coven has the means to rocket off to a new world.

The question remains: what consignment of crew/personnel, chosen by whatever 'impersonal, independent' selective instrument, will not carry with it the toxins which will reproduce, in whatever galaxy, the schisms and malice from which the new Pilgrims had presumed to be delivering themselves? No selection of those who are to be saved can excise the doubleness implicit in the forked species. Even the promise of a static life, indefinitely prolonged, this time by science, not by divine favour, cannot be kept. Those with no hopeful use for the future tense have no future. The flaw in Plato's recommended society was that it was to turn its back on the world, by having no fleet, and contain a population which was neither to grow nor to diminish. Stability and decline are inseparable. A society jacketed in rectitude, with zero emissions, no sanction for improvement, no questionable programme, is bound to double Dante's inferno.

A vision for 2020: as the world rolled on into the third Christian millennium, the Pope could be seen delivering blessings to an empty St Peter's Square. The Archbishop of York talked with lengthy admiration about a rabbi who had said something worth listening to. As AD yields to CE, churches are closed; no pontiff promises the pious a priority channel through the strait gate. Communion wine does not figure among prescribed *materia medica*. Before science became the measurer of all things, the Black Death could be blamed on the you-know-whos who poisoned the wells, thus redeeming Saint Augustine's claim that, thanks to Jesus, God could be relied on to favour Christians. Hate/dread of the Jews united good conscience with bad medicine. Theology stiffened, in the early Middle Ages, into hierarchical orthodoxy. As the Roman Church made claim to universal reach, the Vatican's exemplary extinction of the Albigensians in the early thirteenth century promised that hell had no waiting room. Torture abbreviated argument. The Holy Inquisition braced the Church with righteous brutality; blackmail enriched its coffers. The *auto-da-fé* drummed up a Holyday audience; Christian sadism reprised the Roman circus. Down with the down is an undying nostrum.

60

Sequestered in his Girondin *château*, Michel de Montaigne advanced outlandish notions of tolerance while the plague decimated sixteenth-century Bordeaux. Since he had just ceased to be the city's mayor, the Church accused him of cowardice, if not complicity, in locking himself away outside the city's walls. Reluctance to endorse the incineration of dissenters was held heretical. A century later, Blaise Pascal recommended betting on Christ while you still had time; he also invented a prototypical wristwatch so that you could always have it on you. His contemporary René Descartes evaded papal sanction by an appendix to his *cogito* which made God the certifier of appearances, thus proving the necessity of His existence. Genius and accommodation with power are recurrent associates. Descartes made a sage retreat from France to the off-centre court of Queen Christina of Sweden, where he was smothered in his sleep by fumes from a defective stove. To each his own Samarra.

The slogan carved on the beam above Montaigne's worktable, *NIHIL HUMANUM A ME ALIENUM PUTO* (I rate nothing human foreign to me), advertised insolent modesty. God and His Trinity are not saluted among its author's familiars. Montaigne's observation that one had better be very sure of being right before burning human beings alive smacked of *lèse-majesté*. His wife (whom he probably never saw naked) is said to have been from a family of *conversos*, converted Jews. Aha, said the pious. Women and Jews are recurrent European scapegoats: worldly weaklings, averse to killing, apt victims. Sufferance becomes suspect: deceivers all, how can they or their kin not be planning revenge? The worse Jews and women are treated, the more duplicitous they are taken to be, the more warranted their prophylactic sequestration, if not incineration. Father, Son and Holy Ghost have never lacked vigilantes, often in mutually murderous rig as Protestant and Catholic, until rendered altogether boys by Nazi conscription. God protect us, some say, from Supreme Leaders and the vessels of His/Her Word.

61

COVID excited no pious response. The British now venerate a trinity of initials. The NHS enjoys the credulity once attached to the king's touch. No one, unless cracked, has suggested that COVID-19 is a premonitory sign of things to come; it came, pointless and pitiless. Holding everything, stalling everyone until laboratories distilled the right medicine, implied the irrelevance of prayer. Meanwhile the sick were consigned to attendance for attention or, if past it, binned in don't-care-homes. Anthropologists will remember which primitive tribe, without sentiment or employment for the aged, put seniors out like garbage. For today's lumpen laity, television pumps reminders of the way we were; the present is dosed with crowned yesterdays, crash-bang-wallop tomorrows. Killing, staged or documentary, reminds us, on several channels, of how lucky we are to be sequestered in the padded kennels Morgan Forster had the wit to foresee replacing common ground and personal contact.

'*Tout passe,*' Théophile Gautier declared; that it is liable to return, rebranded, he did not say. Gods, like Bottom, can be translated; His central Temple burnt, the Trinity its Phoenix; up Jehovah went, to be universalised as God Almighty. Stripped of its traditionally reverential custodians, the Covenant tilted into grabbing hands. Edited by the Evangelists, gentle Jesus, once meek and mild, was refigured in coalition with Augustus Caesar. The Roman emperor, then the Roman pope, became the deity's watchman. Robert Graves's disappointed zealot Judas Iscariot was declared the agent of the anti-Christ. Gospel truth, like the elevation of the Virgin, was propagated by an Orwellian ministry. Christianity grew to be a construct for ecclesiastic intimidation; petrified Peter hardened into the rock on which free speech was booked to founder.

In our time, the Redeemer's establishment was bent on surviving the Nazis. Pius XII neither endorsed the extinction of the Jews nor deplored it. His private correspondence records revulsion from the once-Chosen. After the war, the Polish Cardinal Glemp raised a triumphant cross at Auschwitz. Its removal was as close as Poles came to remorse, the Church to shame. Christianity edited itself in very slightly penitent form: the Faithful were no longer to be reminded aloud, in the Mass, of the perfidy of the Jews. Abolition of the Latin version, in the hope of an enlightened congregation, precipitated a steep fall in churchgoing (and in the number christened Mary, as tabulated in *L'archipel français* by Jérôme Fourquet).

There followed a rash of reactionary piety exemplified by Monseigneur Lefebvre and his Old Religionists. Tolerant sects make few converts: how many Muslims have ever joined the all-embracing Baha'i with their reproduction Garden of Eden terraced on Mount Hebron, above Haifa? Servants of the Truth prefer to kill each other and dispossess infidels. If Jews have proved hardly less schismatic, have they ever, since the competition between Saul and David, been mutually bloodthirsty? Then again, where did those ten tribes go, and how?

62

COVID-19 and its derivatives cull the unlucky without regard for religious affiliations. So did all previous plagues? Ah, but they were not read in a common light! The Egyptians were said to be plague-ridden for maltreating the Hebrews; the Athenians to be paying the price for being led by Pericles, of a family contaminated by miasma (pollution through sacrilege). For all but two millennia, Christianity promised death to be a junction for select celestial transport. It is now a terminus: COVID-19 delivers people to the morgue as if to the rubbish dump. Abbreviation of rites of passage implies that we are going nowhere.

Greeting Colonel Stanhope (and his biblical ammunition) at Missolonghi, Byron reached out to take 'that honest right hand'. In the modern plague knocking elbows at once salutes and fends off the other. The French suspended exchanging *bises*. Self-preservation disjoins society. Singular stoicism and rampant hedonism are alike without celestial prospect. Salvation in today's England is with the NHS, a worldly institution of noble intent, questionable efficiency. To criticise it has become secular blasphemy. '*Il faut ne pas désespérer Boulogne-Billancourt*' is translated in prescription form. The Christian God survived the Holocaust, just.

When was there anything unholy about murdering Jews?

In the 1930s, G. B. Shaw, old dog whose tales wagged for Britain, deemed governments entitled arbiters of who should live or die within their boundaries. Mass murder enhances the self-esteem of ideologues, warns off dissenters. The heathen can be dispossessed under pious licence or regal fiat. The Church itself has not escaped pillage by the pious and the Puritan. Defender of the Faith Henry VIII, murderer, thief and moral solipsist, is the most popular royal for dramatic resuscitation. Robert Bolt's *A Man For All Seasons* put Henry's principled adviser Sir Thomas More centre stage, but how often and for how long does a moral paragon excite affection? Aristides the Just became so obnoxiously virtuous that the ancient Athenians ostracised him. As Hilary Mantel's *Wolf Hall* signalled, scoundrel aberration is likelier to become folkloric than principled rectitude.

Christianity has rare digestive powers. Cynic and martyr are cards in the same pack. Carl Gustav Jung thought the Church missed a trick by not incorporating the Devil in a four-sided Trinity. The vocabulary of Christendom soon embraced what reason ruled out: Tertullian's bravado '*Certum est quia impossibile est*' (it's certain because it's impossible) chimes with Pascal's conceit '*Le coeur a ses raisons, que la raison ne connaît point*'. Century after century, Christian factions jostle for primacy more than for harmony. They share only the presumption that God is on their side. He just might intervene, if worthily implored or palm amply gilded, but that irreversible grant of free will dispensed Him from responsibility for human choices. Mammon reciprocated by having 'acts of God' exempt insurers from paying out.

Saints continue to be sanctified in Roman Catholicism only if shown to have intervened against nature on at least three occasions. Spinoza's *deus sive natura* declared such acts self-contradictory in the snappiest possible manner. Theologians sigh at sceptics' quibbles and jibes. Their own Jesuitries have been devised to preserve the machinery of the sacraments and shore up the vanity that God will, in His own good time, recognise His own and roast the rest. The Christian God cannot take a joke, as JHVH supposedly did when, according to some Talmudic sidebar, He allowed, with a smile, after arriving late for a meeting, that His children had outvoted Him. How might He respond to a scholiast's pun, 'Deus/CV/Natura'?

63

Co-opted from Plato, the incorporeal, sexless soul, sprung from mortal moorings, was deemed to qualify for a celestial school of pure spirits, provided baptism had put them down for it and no mortal sin sprang a veto. In Graham Greene's *The Heart of the Matter*, the character of Scobie trumps God and disqualifies himself from having a heavenly mansion by laying down his soul for another. 'Grim Grin' the French called the novelist who contrived to have his faith and tease it too.

Each new European generation has been recruited to Christian soldiering until scandalous appetite or incidental misfortune fractures faith. Clergypersons, in waning numbers, continue to be primed to welcome back the prodigal. God will once again be thanked when, panic over, antidote or palliative in good supply, survivors are convoked to hear cross-patched spokespersons incite them to gratitude. The divinity's absence, during COVID's parody of the lethal statistics of the Second World War, has proved more damaging to Christendom for want of credible diabolical agents, other than the Chinese, to take the rap.

Veneration of Nature, advocated by whatever soft-spoken televised pundit, virgin prophetess, knighted *souffleur*, seems green indeed. Playing Nature's friend makes no promise of humane politics: loving dogs, Hitler was a vegetarian who consigned only human beings, by the million, to the abattoir; Henry Williamson was at one with otters and Heiled the Führer, whose emblem, he said, was 'the happy child'. Ingenious as she is callous, man is an expendable form of Nature's progeny. As if monkeying about were not part of our machinery, we are incited to respect and conserve our indifferent mother as dispenser of terrestrial blessings. The green and the red, bud and bloodshed, fire and water, are Nature's Empedoclean stop and go.

The young are happy to accuse their elders of greed for having preceded them to the drying trough. Somerset Maugham, in his eighties, was advised by his doctor that the best thing to do about some affliction was to 'let nature take its course'. The Maughamian reply? 'At my age, that's the last thing I want.' In unwanted truth, Nature will consume and recycle man without pity or intention. All sorts of animals and plants will be extinct if we go on as we are; if we do not, others will. *Cornucopiae* are made for spillage. Man may be supplanted, but any rectified model will perish (or not) before it can exhaust the earth's resources. If humanity fails to save itself, some rough beast will be sure to slouch somewhere to be born in its superannuated stead.

64

Theology's retreat, from doctrinal ordinance to historiography, goes along with the degradation of language, though neither causes the other. All proofs of God are circular? Then blessed be the circle we are squared in, some say. Under popular revision, language leaps and bounds into cliché; literature is suffocated by journalism. 'Difficult time', 'decade', 'tragic death', 'sadly died' and the like supplant specific obituary or discrete eloquence. Unforgettable is synonymous with soon forgotten. Incredible? You'd better believe it. Previous ladders to heaven or to hell have been renamed with mollifying banality. Relieved of dictatorial or alien landlords, cities revert to antique nomenclature or are vested with modern camouflage: Leningrad to St Petersburg, Stalingrad to who knows what, without either being purged of ideological ghosts and courageous defenders. Belsen is forever Belsen.

The eclipse of a deity or religious system summons its replacement, seven devils for previous ones. In decree-dominated societies, religious 'communities' dedicated to antique conceits flout medical edicts to refrain from close contact. Contagion all their style, faith in death stamps mortal caution as cowardice. Liberal education is banned from questioning (labelled 'judging') outlandish beliefs and ordinances. Multiculturalism makes a privilege of ignorance. Robed leaders are aggrandised by the masses whose self-serving thuggery they license. The young H. G. Wells said, 'Grown men don't need leaders.' Nor do leaders, he might have added, need grown men, still less educated women. Later, with the rise of fascism, Wells held civilisation to be 'at the end of its tether'. There it swings.

Superstition encourages human beings *tenter le grand peut-être*, to which the non-swimmer Shelley resigned himself when caught in a storm while boating on Lake Leman. Byron, more nimble in water than on land, proposed to save him. Shelley said, 'Better save yourself.' Both survived, for a while. Britain's minorities, however marginal, if not because marginal, declare their faiths by declining to exercise civil caution, or honour common decencies.

65

Language cannot promise a destination beyond itself. However many stations of elegant construction he may position along a line alleged to lead to a terminus beyond oblivion, man's train of thought will go round in Hornby oo circles, tunnels and loops. If theology were a genuine queen of the sciences, as it may be some kind of art, or aesthetic, it would by now, as would its lay cousin philosophy, have come to unarguable, rather than coercive, truths or rhetorical prospects, as in Jeremy Taylor's *Holy Dying*. It may edify; it never proves. Hence the Inquisition's putting men to the question as answer. '*Eppur si muove*,' muttered Galileo, as little boys once crossed their fingers in furtive disclaimer. The Church's secret police set the fashion for ideological terror, not least in its zeal for tabulating its own mercilessness. The Gestapo filed its murders, as narcissists their nails.

Christendom's evaporating hegemony, St Peter's emptiness its foretaste, offers small prospect of drawing a durable moral from that old triple crown. Insolence may amuse or appal; it is seldom constructive. Satire, like prejudice, flatters what it derides, deconstruction its unamusing cousin. Victoria's first prime minister, Lord Melbourne, speaking of the Church of England, said that he was not so much a pillar as a buttress; he supported it from outside. On what should satire rely without a firm establishment? It is always liable to affect a loftier style than the culture it mocks and depends upon; cf. Junius, Bernard Levin, Tacitus and other stylish tailors close to the wind.

66

The applause of the British for the NHS at a set time of day made Boris Johnson, mimicking pious modesty, a grounded caricature of the Muezzin. Criticism of inept administration could then be scored as apostasy – convenient for operators who had made Brexit a form of lay Protestantism; 'Remoaners' were analogous to Catholic recusants. Who but arrivistes benefit from referenda? The greatest, if not the only, inspiration for Johnson and Gove to play big little-Englanders was that hot air was enough to inflate their windbag.

The royal broadcast to the nation in the face of COVID was greeted, in public at least, as a bold recension of the bulldog spirit as poured in backbone-stiffening doses in 1940. Winston Churchill's masticated defiance became the patriotic mixture-as-before until, with a little help from unappetising allies, the British won the war. The electors' appetite for socialism in 1945 doubled for resignation from Great Power pretensions. Francisco Franco, the *fascisant* devil we knew, was left where he was, lest exiled democrats spring embarrassing secrets. The incorruptible are never to be trusted.

In post-war Britain, chintzy curtains were drawn in pre-fabricated housing; familiar spites resumed parliamentary business as usual. The idealism of Sir Richard Acland's radical

Commonwealth Party won small public support. With Attlee as headmaster, Nye Bevan took on the lay chaplain's role, health his salvation, specs and teeth for bread and wine. Its topsy budget growed and growed.

The analogy drawn by the late queen, never without political licence, between now and our Finest Hour flatters today's population, as if it were sheltering in a brave Blitz, waiting for Henry Moore to sanctify its blanketed dormition. Dependence makes criticism unpatriotic. The garrison on the medical front line is saluted in lieu of having been properly equipped or efficiently organised. The old story has it that the Tommies at Mons opposed machine-gunners with such rapid fire that the Germans took the guardsmen's Lee Enfield .303s for machine-guns as good as their own. Retreat became angelic. Today's sufferers from cancer are habitually said to be 'battling' what lays them low.

Elizabeth II, dignified and well-spoken, displayed something of the durability of Franz Josef. In 1914, taken to be the immovable father of the empire, in his last of very many years, he deemed it patriotic to issue a call to arms indistinguishable from national suicide. The dissolution of Austria-Hungary was accelerated by a parade of unity. In 2020 England, Her Majesty sought, gallantly, to turn coronavirus into a means to keep the Crown in its place, her kingdom united while perforated with dotted lines.

Citizens of the disunited US and subjects of the fragile UK consigned themselves to egotists with improbable hair and parodic heroism. Calls for unity with a dash of intolerance are a feature of division; punters are urged to consign themselves to the good offices of mountebanks. The ethics of modern public life are akin to the aesthetics of Andy Warhol. What sells determines merit. Publishers care only to discover another Dr Campbell, Thomas, whom Doctor Johnson

described as the richest writer to graze the meadow of literature. In politics, what voters will buy constitutes our policy,
whoever we are.

67

What is left of Walter Benjamin's view of photographic reproduction? Tease supplants aesthetics: a sectioned carcass in formaldehyde, encased in a museum, provokes as many visitors as any Rodin. David Hockney's hand-made reiteration – oh all those flowering paths to nowhere! – has classic merit when compared with Tracy Emin's ready-mades. The integrity of painting is that it cannot be denied significance but defies translation, even in pony form. W. B. Yeats's brother Jack refused to have any of his paintings reproduced for fear of distortion. An icon may flag its meaning, but what it implies, in Russian, Greek or any other culture, is likely to be more than the punctilious historian is right to spell out. What things are held no longer to mean remains part of their meaning.

Mountebanks hustle placebos, journalists append five stars; humbug effaces distinction between busking and expertise. Pseudo-belligerence is the mark of the dodgy columnist. It is never wrong and never dangerous to mock 'the bourgeoisie', a category to which nearly all readers belong, though few own up to it as they open their specially offered *Daily Telegraph*. Royalty, shorn of ifs, supplies butts.

Simon Schama's account of the golden age of the Dutch Republic was spelt out on the basis of objective evidence. When paintings are read as documents, might there be merit, given today's fractured civilisations, in regarding their imagery with both accuracy and suspicion? The Dutch sensibility is not necessarily translatable because the Dutch were, for a marked period, similar to the British, hence their mutual antagonism; competitive appetite for gold and hostility to Rome and Spain left them rivals, never allies. The distinction is clear when it comes to aesthetics. Is there any such sucrose vanity among the Dutch as British portraiture has framed? Their long, low fight for independence, without John of Gaunt's moat, generated none of the high-chinned insularity which disposed the British to poetic elaboration, social distinctions, presumption of divine election. The English Channel, narrow *mare nostrum*, prompted the lucky conquerors of the Spanish Armada to ditch continental ambitions and affect to be subject only to an Anglican deity, Shakespeare their unparalleled prophet.

The perfidy ascribed to Albion is a symptom of vanity rather than a vice. The complacency with which a stock-exchanging gentleman made his word his bond distinguished traders from billing, never mind cooing, tradesmen. Hands shaken on a deal, in the stock exchange, it was a matter of honour, never patriotism, to respect it, as long as a man hoped to remain credible and creditable in a tight community.

Islanders tend to keep their word and, in the Cyclades at least, make a habit of returning lost property. Continental compacts carried no such obligation. Bismarck's promotion of Prussia had the probity of the huckster. How smart of Marx to displace this characteristic onto 'the Jews'! Mr Eliot, the spirit of Saint Louis in his quasi-Bostonian wings, did the same. His idea of a Christian society made a point of barring more than a few 'free-thinking' Jews. The kits that affect to make men free come complete with censors and manacles.

68

In 1737, in the modest German state of Baden-Württemberg, an ambitious young official who, as financial adviser and logistical expert, had grown rich in the service of the suddenly deceased duke, Carl Alexander, was arrested one day and put on trial for 'detestable abuses on gentlemen and people', although, like Kafka's K almost two centuries later, he had done nothing wrong. Joseph Süß Oppenheimer had been commissioned to organise the finances of the duchy's largely Lutheran subjects. The duke, a Roman Catholic, not only trusted Oppenheimer's administrative competence; he treated him as a personal friend, addressing him as 'My especially dear Herr Resident'. When Carl Alexander put a small tax on his officials' emoluments, it was known as 'the Jew's penny', as if Oppenheimer had been picking pockets for his own benefit. The proceeds went directly into the ducal coffers. During his lifetime, Carl Alexander was too potent to be attacked in person. He was lynched, posthumously, in the person of Joseph Süß. Cosmopolitan, well-read, with a remarkable library, and attractive to Christian females, Süß's crimes were alleged to include extortion and rape. His mistress, Luciana Fischer, who concealed her pregnancy from examining officers, was one of the few people to remain loyal to him.

There is a history of Gentile women more faithful to Jewish

husbands than many 'Aryan' male friends dared to be; Fred Uhlman's novella/memoir *Reunion* (1971) exemplifies the author's betrayal, in the 1930s, by a nice German friend suddenly infatuated with National Socialism. In that case, the dog it was that died: after the war Uhlman survives, he finds that his one-time friend was executed for his part in an anti-Hitler plot. In 1941 Berlin, Jews were threatened with arrest and deportation. Gentile wives banded together in front of Gestapo headquarters in noisy demonstration. Berliners were by no means unanimously or ardently anti-Semitic. Nazi authorities were embarrassed by the outspoken female opposition. To avert a public breach in Aryan solidarity, Goebbels ordered that the Jewish husbands be set free, temporarily. Later, he would boast that Berlin was *Judenrein*. Decorated veterans of the Great War were allowed to pay for first-class rail travel to the places where they would be done to death.

Are women less susceptible to ideological seduction than men? It would be nice to think so. As he shows in his diaries, Victor Klemperer's hundred-per-cent 'Aryan' wife, a woman of enduring courage, for a long while exempted her husband, a convert to Protestantism (as if that counted with racist fanatics), from deportation from Dresden to Auschwitz. Towards the end of the war, Klemperer's 'mixed' marriage ceased to cover him. He received an order to report to the railway station the following morning, 16 February 1945. That night an Allied fire raid on Dresden destroyed most of the ancient city, including the railway station and Gestapo headquarters and its records. Klemperer survived the war, became a professor in communist East Germany and published both his diaries and several books on the Third Reich.

Klemperer's escape presents those who make statistics their measure with an inextricable crux. Had Dresden not been bombed, he and who all else would have been entrained and sent to their deaths. So? 'Instead', thousands died in the bombing. Numbers have no morals. Pythagoras, however, regarded odd as 'better' than even (because less trimly divisible?). Jeremy Bentham's notion of the happiness of the greatest number ratifies callous ethical accountancy. It passes no judgement on the quality of anyone's happiness, which some might say determines its quantity. Andrew Marr has suggested, with glib superficiality, that the Allies were criminal in the 'unnecessary' bombing of a historic city and causing so many civilian casualties when the war was as good as won. The presumed innocence of 'ordinary Germans' prompts the schoolboy question, 'Who started it?' Marr did not mention Victor Klemperer.

Süß's Lutheran judges had hated the late duke's Catholicism as much as his mild extortions. After a travesty of a trial, his Jewish surrogate was sentenced to death. The hanging was carried out for Württembergers' holiday edification. There is a long tradition that an audience may enjoy, but is not responsible for, what is legally supplied to gratify and intimidate it. After he had been entertainingly throttled for fifteen minutes, Süß's corpse was left dangling in a high, red-and-gold-striped cage. It remained there for six years, the gallows for fifty.

A contemporary Christian lawyer conceded that there was no valid evidence for the conviction. Even in the Age of Enlightenment, a Jew's intelligence and the favour he enjoyed in high quarters were enough to warrant lynching. Catholics and Lutheran Protestants were reconciled in diabolising the Jew. Two hundred years later, the 1940 film *Jud Süß*, directed by Veit Harlan, green-lit by Josef Goebbels, gloated over the bent verdict and gloried in its enactment. Süß was portrayed as a peculating operator who deserved his fate. Harlan's movie was held to be a cinematic masterpiece by the young Michelangelo Antonioni. The latter was a citizen of Ferrara, from which, as a plaque on the schoolhouse confirms, more than seventy Jewish pupils, a few years younger than himself, were deported to be murdered in 1944. Did Harlan's black-and-white film not have a certain formal grace? Grant as much and it punctures the vacuous terseness of Wittgenstein's equation, in the *Tractatus Logico-Philosophicus*, of aesthetics with ethics. What has art to do with morals? It depends, hence mocks logic.

After the war, Harlan was quizzed by Stanley Kubrick whether he had been pressured to direct the film. Harlan was honest enough to deny it. Business was business. Kubrick told me the story. Stanley's third wife, Christiane, was Harlan's niece. She played the frail blonde German girl who sang a wavering song to a café full of doomed *poilus* at the end of *Paths of Glory*. *Jud Süß* was a gloating celebration of Süß's martyrdom. The story was rendered famous by a bestselling 1935 novel by Lion Feuchtwanger, which denounced the treatment of the Jew. Asked on some Hollywood occasion whether, to catch a green light, he would object to claiming credit for a script he had not written, Stanley Kubrick said that he would not. Business is still business.

When we were last in Ferrara, the Antonioni Museum was closed for want of visitors. *L'Avventura* is one of the great movies. When Antonioni was a very small boy in Mussolini's Ferrara, his nanny disciplined him by swinging him as if to throw the speechless child out of the window. Michelangelo stammered for the rest of his life; panned, slowly, more often than he cut. Veit Harlan's producers, if pressed for time, had Jewish babies thrown directly into the furnaces.

69

In 1870, the project of sealing German unity, from an agglomeration of minor states and in the face of the centuries-old schism between Protestant and Roman Catholic, was treated in practical and in mythologising ways. Otto von Bismarck's *Kulturkampf* set out to reduce Vatican influence on education and to nationalise the appointment of bishops. Nationalism fashioned German Christianity, as Henry VIII's Reformation did the Church of England, for politic purposes. Richard Wagner's 'total artwork' (*Gesamtkunstwerk*) composed a fanfare for chauvinism, Bayreuth its blaring epicentre. The composer's conceit was seasoned with scorn for Jewish virtuosity and ingratitude to his favourite conductor, Hermann Levi, who continued to work for him. Loyalty can be a form of revenge. Straight face, secret smile dress devoted dissidence.

In *An Uncommon Woman: The Life of Princess Vicky* (2006), Hannah Pakula tells how Bismarck and his patron, King Wilhelm I, blighted the incipient liberalism of Prussia's voters. During the early 1860s, obsessed by traditional Prussian militarism, the king joined with his unelected Junker chancellor in clamping reactionary autocracy on the German people. At the same time, Bismarck – given to tearful rant when baulked in the Reichstag – created the lineaments of the welfare state. In prototypical National Socialism, provincial fractiousness was bundled into patriotic unity by benevolence at home, aggression abroad. The fairy tales of the Brothers Grimm (academics both) stirred sadism and sugar into a brew suitable for cadets' bed-time.

Having humbled Austria-Hungary in 1866, Bismarck clinched Prussia's pan-Germanic supremacy with victory in the 1870 Franco-Prussian War. Triumph subsumed Bavarians and other distinct provincial entities under the now-imperial Wilhelm's eagled hegemony. Denial of difference, especially when manifest, called for a necessary Other, from whom German-speakers were at once distinct and indistinguishable. Anti-Semitism confirmed them *Ein Volk*, the single folk they had never been. Bismarck's observation about Benjamin Disraeli at the 1879 Congress of Berlin, '*Der alte Jude, das ist der Mann*' (the old Jew, that's the man!), was at once genuine compliment and implicit jibe. Disraeli had had the rich swagger to order that his private train get up steam when a proposed agreement was not in conformity with British interests. To avoid Emperor Wilhelm from taking precedence over Queen Victoria, Disraeli had her declared empress of India, an abruptly innovative dignity.

As domestic politician, Bismarck initiated the process whereby the electorate looks to aspiring governors to promise benefits of one kind or another. The result has been to make clients of the voters; doses of not-very-great expectations narcotise dissent. F. A. Hayek's *The Road to Serfdom*, written shortly before the end of the Second World War, spelt out the dangers of a population willing to exchange freedom for cradle-to-grave (some read 'gravy') security of a kind indistinguishable, ultimately, from docility. It has become fashionable to discredit Hayek as unduly schematic in opposing scheme.

Hitler's promise of a Volkswagen for every family was in the Bismarck style. Safety belts and straitjackets can be buckled with much the same click. Martin Kitchen's biography of

Albert Speer makes the case for believing that Hitler's war effort was systematically hobbled, despite Goebbels's hectoring about 'total war', because of the Nazi need for the civilians of the Master Race to be sufficiently pampered not to unseal their allegiance. Even Hitler had to keep, or seem about to keep, some of his promises. Totalitarianism is never total. Michel Houellebecq's 2016 novel *Soumission* plays at replacing Hayek's anti-Communism with acquiescence in seemingly benign Islamic domination: anything for a quiet life makes slaves of voters. The trick is to pamper the electorate with favours which the punters fear another party will rescind. Expectations supply better lassoes than duties.

Bismarck had his own equivalent to Joseph Süß Oppenheimer. The banker Gerson von Bleichröder both organised the state's economy and absorbed the odium generated by the chancellor's exigency. If Bleichröder was ennobled, not hanged, his grey eminence attracted hostility which his master did nothing to deplore. 'Art,' said Ivan Turgenev, 'is one of the four things which unite men.' Anti-Semitism was the one most apt to align disparate Germans.

70

The notion that they were either flippant or 'had a point at the time' has been used to excuse a swath of ranters and opportunists, left and right, high and low, from Hegel to Heidegger, Georges Sorel to Thomas Carlyle, Charles Dickens to Hilaire Belloc to J. B. Priestley and Graham Greene. Outsiders of various stripes seek membership of the in-group by flattering its prejudices and aping its vanities. The Canadian war-veteran Percy Wyndham Lewis chose to proclaim himself 'The Enemy' vis-à-vis Bloomsbury. His book in praise of Hitler was published in 1931. Affecting to take Adolf seriously, he mocked 'Yiddle Zangwill', the better to amuse his fellow-Vorticist Ezra Pound and scandalise naice people. He made being out a way of getting in.

Clichés, styled or revised, have long lives. While pandering to his readers' ready aversion to Fagins and their kind, Graham Greene had a close friend who was a Jew. The elegant John Sutro was a British equivalent to Proust's Swann. He and Greene formed the John Gordon Society in mockery of the prudish editor of the *Sunday Express*. I once had a friendly letter from him, on deckled writing paper sleeved in an envelope with purple tissue lining. My cousin, Rabbi Roderick Young, wrote to Greene questioning him about the unpleasant Jewish characters in his pre-war novels, *Brighton Rock* not least. Greene replied that he had decided to delete the anti-Semitic slurs in future editions. No longer to the public's taste, they had lost their literary lure, for the time being. Greene once accuse me of claiming, falsely, in a review that he used 'fly-buttons' in one of his skimpy 'entertainments'. One of Our Readers was good enough to write and render him undone.

By licensing efficient murder and profitable extortion, the Nazis converted people who might have been mundane bourgeois into butchers' accomplices. As can be seen, in detail, in Christopher R. Browning's *Ordinary Men* (1992), the blood on their hands christened Protestants and Catholics equally callous crusaders. Candidates for enrolment in the Sicilian mafia could not belong to Cosa Nostra, and so gain access to its dividends, until they had killed a victim whom they may well never have known, but who had incurred the displeasure of their capo. Killing without personal motive or acquaintance is a regular proof of manliness. In Alexander the Great's Macedonia, battle-blooded hands alone sanctioned reclining at table.

Arthur Koestler had it that men will rally to almost any cause that promises comradeship and kudos (and belted kit?); if there's a common bear to bait, so much the better. Koestler became a rendezvous for righteously indignant feminists, after the disclosure, on skimpy evidence, that he once sought to rape Michael Foot's wife, Jill Craigie. An experienced and sophisticated screenwriter, Craigie ('craggy Jill', as one admirer called her) was said to have escaped Koestler's unsubtle clutches by running out of her house. No one has explained why Koestler had been invited, while Michael was at what he called 'the boys' club', aka the House of Commons, nor why Jill, who had been around, went back inside while the menace was still lurking there.

Nothing was said about the matter, in public at least, until fifty years after the event. David Cesarani then featured it in a book on Koestler after he had been denied access to the Koestler archives. On hearing of his lascivious history, scarcely untypical of macho Central Europeans, righteous Glaswegian students evicted Koestler's bronze bust from a place of honour in the university. How many of them know, or would care to be told, that Koestler was the first writer to expose the ongoing extermination of European Jewry, in Cyril Connolly's classy *Horizon* in 1943? In today's student world, not a few would hold it against him. Koestler's 1940 novel *Darkness at Noon* dramatised the process by which Old Bolsheviks were coerced into confessing to crimes they had never committed, for the good of the party. Koestler became a lifelong target for Stalinist malice. Cesarani's father, to whom his Koestler book was dedicated, was a long-time member of the Communist Party, an old school with adhesive ties.

There are Jews and Jews. The Gospels tell a propagandist story of their unanimous call for the execution of Jesus of Nazareth. Unanimity has never been Jews' first characteristic. Ritualised bloodshed was a prescription for restoring communal tranquillity long before Christianity's sacraments. Walter Burkert's *Homo Necans* (1972) was at once a respectable contribution to anthropology and an inadvertent banalisation of the Shoah. The similarity of Burkert's title to Johan Huizinga's 1938 *Homo Ludens* suggests that playing and killing have much in common.

Stanley Kubrick began his movie *2001* with a scene in which a pack of agile actors aping gorillas discover the team thrill attendant on the kill; murder and the conquest of space, it is visually suggested, have an exhilarating affinity. The observatory of El Caracol at Chichen Itza proves that the pre-Columbian Maya of Yucatán were advanced astronomic observers as well as conductors of mass human sacrifices. In Kubrick's movie, a flung bone morphs into a spaceship. What animal before man established hegemony by killing its own kind? Most higher animals concede priority to alpha males rather than hang in and suffer serious wounds or death.

For many years, in a measure of accord with sacrificial logic, physicians believed that bleeding a patient calmed feverish demons. Byron's Missolonghi 'butchers' (inept English physicians) were among them. Holy Communion can be deconstructed as a sublime way of uniting, if not blooding, participants who, by the grace of God, consume the body of Christ. Bernard Richards has noted that A. J. 'Freddie' Ayer was 'shocked by this quasi-cannibalism'. In *Things Hidden Since the Foundation of the World* (1978), René Girard argued with convincing detail, if with an excess of comprehensive scheme, that human sacrifice lies at the root of civilisation. Violence, he insists, is integral to the sacred, art its camouflage and its advertisement.

71

The traditional English hunt is a rural ritual which, as Anthony Powell reminded his admirers, as well as the rest of us, goes 'from a view to a death'. The blooding of the cheeks of first-time hunters with the fox's severed 'brush' is a county version of Bacchic initiation. No longer limited to the upper classes and their entourages, hunting attracts scowls from moralists. Concern for foxes or hares justifies frightening the horses. Arthur Conan Doyle's Napoleonic Brigadier Gérard, while a visitor to England, accelerates to the front of the hunt, overtakes the hounds and despatches the fox with one gallant, Gallic stroke of his sword, so severing himself from insular respect.

Anthony Powell took his opinions seriously; that was his comedy. He was the last (short) man known to have availed himself of the Travellers Club tradition allowing members to wear hats in the dining room, quite as if their barouches were waiting, like Byron's unpaid-for carriage, to whisk them to Dover. Powell imitated being a rarity, thus establishing that he was not one. He married a duke's daughter who loved someone else. Her aristocratic allure sanctioned him to play the gentleman. Genuine impostor, he required that his name not be pronounced in the Welsh fashion.

72

Sentimentalisation of the National Health Service, rendered hectic by the COVID-19 pandemic, certifies the displacement of human hope from the supernatural to the scientific. The British government's yoking of medical research to play both (Chinese) scapegoat and the public's saviour racked up a revised metaphor for human salvation. Science becomes sacrosanct, because omnipotent and impersonal; as Catholic theology recedes, Aristotle's deity, the unmoved mover, returns, void of promises. Nature pulls rank on civilisation; meta-Marxism deplores the pleasure principle: 'we' must concede governance to a green regency for the future of the planet. Does is not occur to the righteous that the shameless with fire power will then rule it?

Christianity flatters itself, often, by taking it that the magnificence of the art which decorates its buildings promises the veracity of its doctrines. Any number of faiths, sublime or barbaric, have sponsored no-less-theatrical magnificence. Aztec and Mayan monuments, underlined with regiments of sculpted skulls, offer lapidary evidence of sanguinary staging; ritual and entertainment have adjacent quarters. Rarely depicting bloodshed, habitually reporting it (the Messenger preceded the Press), Athenian tragic theatre was distinct from piety; it both hymned and subverted routine credulities, as would Renaissance arts and craftiness.

René Girard has it that religious myths are cover-stories: they sublimate the selection of victims, often in accordance with a sacred calendar and diet sheet. Scapegoats are likely to be either condemned criminals, preserved for the red-lettered date, or selected from anathematised sub-sets of humanity. Prior to immolation, victims can be pampered with food and comforts; fatted calves recompensed for the service their blood will render the community. The condemned man's breakfast mimics the saviour's last supper. Brendan Behan's *The Quare Fellow* takes on magic distinction.

Anathematised sets or sects often appear arbitrary: in the western Pyrenees, the Basques and their clergy took cruel, not murderous, exception to a clan of families with blue eyes and without earlobes (like Byron in the latter regard). Designated 'Cagotes' or 'Cagots', their Catholicism beyond question, Basque priests were unwilling to minister to these 'racial' aliens *intra ecclesiam*. While not denied Holy Communion, the Cagots received it only through holes in the walls of churches. Branded with no specific sin or misdemeanour, barely tolerated, they spoke no different language, lived (and, to a degree, live) in quasi-ghettos. They still tend to be employed in specialised skills, such as silversmithing, which require little personal contact with graceless customers. The Cagot villages I visited had no cafés or bars. First excluded, the sect became exclusive, a charge also levelled against Jews. Since Basque priests sided with the Republic, they figure as heroes in histories of the Spanish Civil War. What was and is wrong with Cagots is that they are not Basques. Pride and exclusivity are antique mates.

In 1939, when the brave Basques, post-Guernica, had been routed by Franco and his fascist allies and were crowding across the border into France, Ben Hecht remarked on the danger of putting all your Basques in one exit. Shame on him for a Jewish joke at someone else's expense! Among the best, most prolific screenwriters of Hollywood's Golden Age, Hecht was anathematised in the United Kingdom, after the war, for declaring that there was 'a song in my heart' whenever a British soldier was killed in Palestine. In English eyes, he became *The Scoundrel*, title of a 1935 film he wrote and directed with Charles MacArthur. Noel Coward played the wicked hero. I saw most of it in New York City in 1949, on the eve of the devaluation of the pound from $4 to $2.80. What I did not see was effaced by the proximity of my delectable sweetheart Mary Jane.

73

Domestic animals are the likeliest surrogates for human victims; the sacrificial ox's nod when he lowers his head to a plate of grain was taken by ancient Athenians for acquiescence; so too the sheep's sheepishness. Wild beasts are liable to be hunted to establish their killers' virility, hence the brief happiness of Hemingway's Francis Macomber. Since they cannot be relied on to seem to consent to ritual slaughter with domesticated docility, they are rarely paraded for sacrifice, though baited often enough in the Roman amphitheatre. For fear that snarling resistance too might disconcert prescribed ritual, dogs were seldom victims. There is evidence of dog sacrifice in Sparta. I have seen canine remains in a cave near Pozzuoli, south-west of Naples, where infant skeletons were also interred. The infants may have died as the result of still-births which the dogs' sacrifice (if they came first) failed to avert or (if later) served to expiate.

Social rifts are closed, worship vindicated, consanguinity – genuine or wished for – sealed by choreographed public bloodshed. In Veit Harlan's film, Jud Süß's last words are both plea and confession: in winched suspense, he is, he cries, 'nothing but a poor little Jew'. Given the abject cue he was waiting for, the officiating magistrate drops his chin. The cage floor clicks open. Süß dangles and strangles, slowly. And that's a wrap.

Abraham's substitution of the snagged ram for his son Isaac is said to stand as proof that JHVH (Jehovah) abhorred human sacrifice. Might it be that the patriarch was about to honour a rite practised before the inception of the Covenant? Blood served recurrently as the divinity's portion. Minoan Crete and the Mithraic Middle East offer historic instances, the Hispanic bullfight a commercialised derivative. Gods are presumed to crave blood, likewise their followers, as if to mimic the divine diet. After their disastrous encirclement and quasi-annihilation by Hannibal's Carthaginian Arabs at Cannae in 216 BCE, the Romans resorted to human sacrifice to recover the favour of their pantheon of deities. In the days of Herod's Second Temple's sacrificial rites, kosher abstention rendered blood God's portion alone. Hence the rumour that Christian children and their blood were consumed in latter-day Jewish feasts. If evidence was never produced of such a dish being consumed, what did that prove but the diabolical cunning of the Semites?

74

The killing of (often favourite and female) offspring, sometimes seemingly accidental, in order to honour an oracular
injunction, is a common mythical theme. There are cases in
Greek mythology of a god promising success to human belligerence, but only after the sacrifice of an innocent, that of
Agamemnon's daughter a tragic instance. She was dubbed
Iphigeneia by Aeschylus in order to personalise the pathos as
the result of her father's trade-off for a favourable wind to
take the Greek fleet to Ilium.

Anticipating René Girard, without his claim to historical plausibility, Freud's *Moses and Monotheism* postulated
a primal horde of brothers who, by murdering their father,
liberate themselves from subjection to his monopoly of nubile
females. Similar episodes – involving expulsion, not killing –
are recorded in monkey communities. The displacement of
an aging alpha male makes way for the next generation. In
Freud's fable, human patricides were bonded by what stained
and emancipated them.

Greek theogony has an analogous story: with the complicity of Gaia, the earth-mother, who hid her latest infant in a
Cretan cave, Zeus grew up to dislodge his father Kronos. The
latter had already gobbled several of his own newborn offspring, in consequence of an oracular warning that one of

them would usurp his throne. The secreted Zeus grew up to become the leader of his regurgitated siblings, and then of his own divine offspring, empanelled on Mount Olympus where, as Louis XIV did with his courtiers at Versailles, he kept them under luxurious surveillance.

Peter Levi's *The Hill of Kronos* (1981) honours the dethroned supremo's grandstand view of Olympia, Peloponnesian site of the Olympic Games. Logic making it impossible to kill immortals, it remained only to bury them. Downed deities, like the dejected Lucifer, bringer of light, Prometheus' successor as man's best divine friend, were then feared to lead seditious subterranean lives, volcanic eruptions the evidence. Men still placate the dead by a floral show and the *nil nisi bonum* rule, tribute and appeasement. Carl Gustav Jung argued for embracing the Devil in the Christian Godhead; Satan was essential to the coherence of the Christian message; without bad, what's good? Jung's four-sided Trinity would have furnished a pretty subject for Escher's ingenious pen.

Jane Harrison's *Prolegomena to the Study of Greek Religion* (1903) was a prime text in deconstructing the Olympian deities and alerting classicists to Zeus and company's uneasy majesty after they had dethroned Kronos. The old king and his chthonic cronies, the Titans, are said to have been bundled below the earth's surface. The blood of sacrificial victims was delivered to placate them. Harrison's obsolete work still makes seductive reading. It was inspired and applauded by Gilbert Murray, a scholarly pundit whose florid versions of Euripides excited the severe displeasure of T. S. Eliot. Harrison was the subject of a 2002 put-down by the as-seen-on-and-on television classicist Mary Beard. The latter has it, in *The Roman Triumph*, that Roman males alone took pride, profit and pleasure in the conquests celebrated in the parades attending a Triumph and the subsequent distribution of goodies. The number of scheming females in Roman imperial history hardly confirms the sexual dichotomy.

The triumph enjoyed by Vespasian, after the subjection of Judaea in 70 CE, was the first to trumpet a Roman victory over a rebel province rather than an external enemy. Protracted festivities celebrating the humiliation of the Judaeans had nothing to do with the Judaeophobia which came to be promoted by systematic Christianity. The signal importance of the fall of Jerusalem was exaggerated to deck the advent of an upstart emperor. Flavius Josephus pointed out that the myth that the Judaeans were cowards scarcely chimed with protracted celebration of Roman prowess in defeating them. Last, and longest-lasting, of the four emperors who held the throne in the year 69 CE, Vespasian was a master of biding his time. Before moving on Rome, he established a power base in the Middle East with a victorious, well-trophied, booty-laden army. The Colosseum was an overstatement in stone of the outsider's accession to Nero's throne.

75

In *An Intimate History of Humanity* (1995), Theodore Zeldin claimed that the annual reprise of fraternal bonds, by a literal mingling of blood, proved how close Balkan friendships were. It was not a timely publication. Judging by what was going on in the former Yugoslavia, reiterated compacts offered small evidence of trust. Literal blood-brotherhood may still be practised in the Balkans; as the world witnessed in the later 1990s, so is something close to fratricide. Rituals of renewal suggest repeated need to avert rupture more than they supply proof of confident bonding. Hugs and handshakes promise that sword-arms are reciprocally occupied. Al Capone's gunmen held so tight to Diamond Joe Esposito's outstretched hand, when he greeted their visit, that he was powerless to defend himself as he was shot to death.

In religious ceremonial, immutable formulae are taken to be essential to divine endorsement. In ancient Rome, any *lapsus linguae* – slip of the tongue – by an officiating magistrate demanded *instauratio*: the whole routine had to be started again, from the top, as theatricals say; correct spelling belongs both to magic and to grammar. Passwords and their ritual exchange parody religious responses. The greater the number of apparently confident castles in any region of the world, the more likely a history of local clan or national antagonism. The Dordogne department of France offers many fortified instances. Castles were not only the high redoubts of French and English barons in the Hundred Years' War; valley towns such as Sarlat were thickly walled, well inland from the river, for fear of the incursions of Norman sailors who came up the Dordogne in search of booty. I knew an excellent Sarladais optician of Norman descent whose name was Monsieur Prentout; his ancestors took the lot.

76

The early ritual of mortal challenge for supremacy was described, in classic form, by James Frazer in *The Golden Bough*. In historical times, orderly succession by the first-born son became a widespread variant of the killing of an ageing king by a virile contender. It also elevated royal families into a more-or-less mutually reliable enclave. In jostling practice, accession to a throne was not infrequently disputed, especially if the current king had had male children by different wives. When Philip II of Macedon was assassinated, in 336 BCE, Alexander – Philip's son by the discarded, by-no-means-resigned Olympias, a reputed sorceress – moved swiftly to kill half-brother rivals to the throne. Victory signed its own warrant. Similar ruthlessness came to be practised by Ottoman sultans, some fraternal enough merely to blind potential sibling rivals.

Nero's mother, Agrippina, no less scheming than Olympias, made sure that her late husband Claudius' son by his first wife Messalina, the personable Britannicus, did not survive to challenge her own son by the same emperor. Nero later disposed of the domineering Agrippina. Racine's *Britannicus* brought Claudius' doomed son to dramatic life. Innocence, like virginity, can be a dangerous condition. Might the Virgin Mary not be said to have been raped by God, like so many of the females 'loved' by Zeus and other Olympians? Is she ever held to have consented to divine impregnation?

Even in orderly circumstances, more-or-less-mythical sons are known to have accelerated their own coronation 'by accident'. Theseus finds no place in psychoanalytic jargon, but that hero caused his father's death by self-serving, if not calculated, inadvertence. On the watch at Sounion, on the eastern wing of Attica, King Aigeus read the black sails on Theseus' returning ship for the pre-arranged signal that his son had died in the attempt to kill the Minotaur. Aigeus threw himself off the cliff into the sea. In a hurry with the good news, Theseus had 'forgotten' to raise the pre-arranged signal of happy white sails. He mourned, briefly, and proceeded to unify Attica with Athens as its capital and so render himself historical. The hulls of Athenian triremes were always dyed red, using *miltos* (ruddle). That very grand tourist young Lord Byron scored his own name in a column of the temple to Poseidon at Sounion.

In ancient Greek theatre, ordered words regulated disorderly deeds. Retailing scenes of horror, tragic messengers, iambic reporters, excited the audience's imagination without obliging them to bloody witness. Whatever the playwright's intentions (winning prizes not the least), Aristotle claimed that *catharsis* (purging through pity and terror) retrieved social solidarity by the audience's common recoil from pollution. Killing was seldom enacted on stage; the hero's suicide in Sophocles' *Aias* (Ajax) a rare exception. The mythical past offered a play/ground for revision of old rites and wrongs. Today, war films pacify and pander to the blood lust of the sedentary.

The tragedians' aesthetic delicacy contrasted with the sanguinary rites of Athenian religion. At the city's altars, bloody sacrifice paid expensive tribute to the gods and bonded the community. Tactful time has erased adjacent stepped pyramids composed of the remnants of incinerated victims. By 'unpacking' ritual events, theatre generated scepticism which, in Euripides' devious glosses on antique stories, verged on ridicule as did the satyr plays, all but one censored into oblivion by Christian prudes; hence Plato's opinion, that an ideal, hieratic society should dispense with art and its seductive, parodic or facetious rescripts of canonical creeds.

Biblical fundamentalists, Sadducees among the first, deplore all commentary, including that implicit in translation into the vernacular. In the swagger years of Herod the Great's Temple in Jerusalem, few of the Aramaic-speaking congregation were fluent in the hieratic Hebrew in which the ceremonies were conducted. Obscurity arms the clerisy. Translation into the vernacular familiarises sacred texts and prompts revision.

In *The Eumenides*, the third of the *Oresteia* trilogy which begins with *Agamemnon*, Aeschylus had the Erinyes, the so-called Furies, revealed on the stage, their masks drooling blood. The Attic audience is said to have been panicked by the ghoulish sight. Aeschylus narrowly escaped prosecution. The vision of the Furies seemed to promise that they really existed and had better be appeased. The play's title *The Eumenides* (The Kindly Ones) bills an obsequious irony. Statues and stained glass are no less intimidating or sublime in Christian churches and cathedrals; gargoyles drool outside.

Did Aeschylus smile, secretly, at the outrage he provoked? Belief and sincerity have less to do with art than prim critics care to imagine. European artists dwelt, with meticulous, often ghoulish piety, on the crucifixion until no longer commissioned to do so. Furtive heresy persisted in the revision of antique themes, especially in the delight taken in more or, as often, less veiled female forms. Pious Velazquez surely took carnal pleasure in depicting the delectable, self-regarding *Rokeby Venus*, said to derive from the hermaphroditic sculpture in the museum in the Borghese Gardens in Rome. A rare overt, lank adult penis is to be seen on the lolling Noah, a notorious drunkard, in the Barna da Siena mural in San Gimignano. As shown by Ruskin's umanning shock on his wedding night, female pubic hair had little artistic display until Gustave Courbet's *L'origine du monde* and Pablo Picasso's nudes.

77

By schooling human beings, his sometime clay toys, to burn the fat and bones of sacrificial victims, Prometheus coached them to deceive the gods. Incense-laden smoke rose to the heavens in appetising deception, enabling mortals to hoard prime cuts for their own consumption. To trump the Olympians was an existential liberty. Prometheus' impudent tampering sentenced him to 30,000 years of having his liver pecked daily by a hungry eagle. In due timelessness, Zeus was obliged to make a deal with the wily Titan, in exchange for the secret he harboured concerning a pretender for the Olympian's throne. As the story of forbidden fruit on the tree of knowledge implies, human appetites can breach divine interdictions and survive. Cain killed his brother Abel but flourished thereafter. What did Marks do to eclipse Spencer?

Science recognises no higher court or red lines. If vivisection is deplored, it is for humane and legal, not scientific, reasons. Licensed by Nazism, German researchers had no inhibitions when using 'sub-humans', including seven- and eight-year-old Jewish children, as guinea pigs for prolonged, pitiless 'research'. Arms and legs were broken and then broken again to test how many times nature would repair them. The so-called Judaeo-Christian God's grant of free will to mankind concedes divine recognition (and envy?) of the human ability to transgress; God cannot help being good, hence He is inhuman. Ethical logic promises that choice determines the merit of human rectitude; if men were not free to sin, virtue would have no meaning. What God or gods do is thus beyond moral evaluation or censure. In English law, the king or queen initiates criminal proceedings but is, by definition, exempt from arraignment. Royalists would have it that Charles I was a 'martyr'. He bore witness above all to the self-righteousness of his Puritan executioners and their less-principled accomplices.

Freedom to choose is at the heart of human initiative. In the fifth century BCE, the so-called Old Oligarch (expectation of life being in the forties, ancient Greeks could be fogeys by thirty) denounced Athenian democracy as a form of 'ochlocracy' (mob rule) but conceded that, before all the (male) citizens received the vote, the men of Athens had not excelled all other Greeks. Once able to elect whether or not to exercise individual energy in enriching themselves and embellishing their city, they became superior in daring and ingenuity. The key moment, came after the discovery of rich silver mines at Laurium in rural Attica. The question was put to the assembly whether the new wealth should be distributed among the citizens or used to construct a fleet. The oratory of Themistocles, his power base in Piraeus, the port of Athens, persuaded the citizens to vest the lode in making their city a naval power.

In 480 bce, Xerxes reviewed his reportedly million-strong conscript army (probably a fifth of that number of effectives) on the way to invade Greece. The deposed and renegade Spartan king Demaratus, now the Persian's courtier, warned the Great King that he had no idea with what quality of resistance free men would face minions who had to be whipped into battle. Xerxes met the Athenian answer at Salamis, the Spartan at Plataea. With gloating empathy, Aeschylus' *Persae* made a clever play of the Persians' humiliation, as if from their ruler's point of view. Phrynichus was first in dramatising the subject, but had no luck when it came to production of what might be regarded as the first documentary, had the text survived.

78

Traditional rites first articulate then rigidify societies' postures before their gods. Respect for the deity is inseparable from fear, hope from dread. The wine and the bread of Holy Communion represent, if not duplicate, the Saviour's sacrificed body. Human piety is boosted, not to say purchased, by a sip and symbolic slip of immortality. Theatre and worship, royalty and imposture converge. A congregation lends force to supplication. Individual prayer smacks of self-interest. Ancient Jerusalem had no theatre, only ritually costumed ceremonial in the temple. The sack of Herod's Temple decentralised Jewish worship, turned sumptuously housed and robed priests into mendicant rabbis who conducted services and classes but abandoned sacrificial show.

Jewish writers living in the hybrid culture of Hellenistic Alexandria were liable to veer towards alien or adjacent forms. A deutero-Ezekiel wrote cross-bred tragedy in the Greek style. The modern Greek poet Iossif Ventouras was one of the few Cretan Jewish children to escape before all Cretan Jews were rounded up and deported by the Germans in 1943, destination Auschwitz. The ferry was sunk by a British submarine and all on board, including more than three hundred children, were drowned. Ventouras, born in 1938, is now the only Cretan Jew still alive. His poems are as unmistakably in the Greek style as they are certainly Jewish (as with Joseph Roth, Job is a recurrent alter ego). One of the children drowned in the Aegean is listed as 'Raphael, aged 6'.

79

With its parade of voices and impostures, the theatre has attracted a rich retinue of Jews. So has boxing, from Byron's sparring partner Jew Mendoza ('Mill away right and left' his slogan) to the twentieth-century heavyweight Max Baer, who wore trunks with a Star of David on them when he beat Hitler's champion, Max Schmeling (never a Nazi, cousin to the American Petronius scholar Gareth Schmeling). Slapsy Maxie Rosenbloom brought vaudeville to the ring. His harmless blows made his opponent his patsy. Broadway and Hollywood became havens for Jewish talent. Movie actors found it prudent to adopt Christian-sounding names: Garfield, Douglas, Robinson. Quick wits and brains of Semitic origin were often denied entry to other professions. According to who 'we' are, associations such as Cosa Nostra have culled a variety of Italian, often Sicilian, adherents, expressions and outlets. There is pretty well every kind of cuisine in the USA, except Irish, but no shortage of Irish pubs, no few New York cops, often cinematically headed by Barry Fitzgerald.

Stanley Kubrick's childhood friend Irwin Mazursky, whom he cast in an unpaid role in one of his early movies, had ambitions to be a professional actor. His friends told him that he was more likely to get work if his name did not so flagrantly announce him to be a Jew. One day, he came and told them that he had taken their advice and changed it, to Paul Mazursky. He developed into a successful screenwriter and director, including of the script from my novel *Coast to Coast*. Kubrick told me, with a straightish face, that he himself was not a Jew; he just happened to have two Jewish parents.

In *Aphrodite and the Rabbis* (2016), Burton L. Visotzky argues, with persuasive garrulity, that the reluctance of Jews to participate in Greco-Roman society has been exaggerated: they were different but not that different from other Romanised outsiders. The Romans had the shrewd pride not to stigmatise anyone who went along with their authority. Christians provoked persecution until they were powerful enough to tip the balance and enjoy centuries of vindictive revenge. Christians in Moorish Cordoba refused to be pardoned for the trouble they were taking (brandishing pork to provoke Jews and Muslims alike) to upset the *Convivencia* which, before the twelfth century, made tolerance a civilised given. The ascent to the divinity was by one of the three faces of the same mountain. Christian refusal to be tolerable gave way, three centuries later, to the root-and-branch ejection of Spain's antecedent Moors and Jews by the Catholic monarchs Ferdinand and Isabella.

Linguistic versatility declares itself in the number of Jewish or semi-Jewish writers who have become masters of European literatures: Proust, Heine, Italo Svevo (né Aron Schmitz), Joseph Roth and who all else. Céline was so enraged by Proust's literary supremacy (even rabid Lucien Rebatet conceded his genius) that he accused him of writing pretentious pseudo-French. Was he wholly wrong? Who other than Proust is so rigorously grammatical when it comes to the imperfect subjunctive? Claiming, with dubious genealogical warrant, to be a Breton Aryan, Céline followed Paul Morand, a *fascisant* novelist, who was the first (if we discount Rabelais) '*jazzer le français* with louche diction and twittering slang. Céline escaped post-war sanction by going to Denmark, the one state in occupied Europe which had found a way of evacuating its Jews before the Nazis could get at them. When the Germans marched into his realm, the Danish king wore a Yellow Star as a decoration. Licensed to return to France in the early 1950s, Céline settled in a victimised sulk in cobbled suburban Meudon. Morand was elevated to the Académie Française in 1968, not least because Charles de Gaulle had opposed his admission to that eminent and reactionary body.

Céline's admirers have had to wait until very recently for his *sacre* in the form of a Pléiade edition. The publishers at first proposed to include the anti-Semitic pamphlets which he composed during the Occupation. His paranoid penning waxed more and more venomous as the defeat of the Nazis and their friends became a certainty. Outraged comment, led by Serge Klarsfeld, impelled the publishers to cancel, or bide their time, when it came to the (hasty, often quasi-plagiarised) anti-Semitic texts.

80

For the faithful, abasement of the heretic is spectacular validation; the Other's public pain a common pleasure. The Inquisition's *auto-da-fé* attracted family crowds and intoxicant drum-beating. The suffering of heretics proves that God exists. Ritual repetition confirms myth; faith supersedes evidence. Habit passes predictable sentence; what is paraded as unalterable becomes the wishful promise that things cannot, will not, must not ever be other than the key-holders of the future proclaim. False accusations are sticky on both sides: ideologists are haunted, or should be, by dread that their brutalities might lack the divine warrant of inevitability. Hegel's Reason and Marx's dialectic both affect to grant, if not demand, exemption from humane sentiment.

If political murders were not 'necessary', as W. H. Auden scribbled in 1937, they would be savage crimes. Auden was paying urgent dues for fellow-travelling with the Communists, on whom any number of smart people were putting their money: political futures are a market like any other. Auden's tum-te-tum commentary for Basil Wright's 1936 *Night Train* hinted that, accompanied by Benjamin Britten, he was at one with the nocturnal toilers. It has become indelicate to mention Wystan's candidate membership of what used to be called 'the homintern'. Guy Burgess, despite bad breath and grimy laundry, was its seductive cheerleader in 1930s London. Auden (who skipped underpants and used toilet paper sparingly) later revised his poem, without improving it, to conform with bourgeois niceties. So did Ovid emend his *Remedia Amoris*, after Augustus had scowled at the *Ars Amatoria*, a skittish manual for wantonness taken literally by the emperor's sole daughter, Julia.

In pagan Rome, the demi-god Hercules was said to have put a stop to human sacrifice to the ancient god Saturn. He substituted an annual ritual of throwing straw effigies into the Tiber. How many who warm themselves at November bonfires now remember Guido Fawkes's prolonged torture, disembowelment and incineration? Today, newspapers and television are apt to single out a suitable hangdog figure – banker, policeman, politician, entertainer, film mogul, naughty duchess – for drawing and quartering. Scapegoats whose hard fall will gratify Our Readers are, like Lucifer and Prometheus, apt for ejection from high places. The Romans flung convicted traitors from the Tarpeian rock. Joseph Süß Oppenheimer was an exemplary eighteenth-century instance, in modern times J. Robert Oppenheimer furnished another.

81

It took almost four centuries for more-or-less-uniform Christianity to become the official, never the only, religion of imperial Rome. Ten per cent of the population of the early Empire are said to have been Jews, conversant with the genealogy of ancient Israel, its messianic hopes and garnish of tales. No few Gentiles liked to visit synagogues; Roman women, sequestered spectators and slaves were welcome; exotic stories were told, morals drawn (hairs split came later). Alone of ancient worshippers, Jews overtly identified with slaves. Celebrants were reminded annually, at Passover, that their ancestors had been slaves in Egypt, a demeaning boast in Greco-Roman eyes.

Nero's first wife, Poppaea Sabina, is said to have been a Judaiser. She befriended Yoseph ben-Matityahu (later Flavius Josephus) when he first went to Rome. Nero kicked her to death when she was pregnant. He also had his mother murdered. His poetic coterie, Petronius, Seneca and Lucan, were ordered to commit suicide. His best general, Gnaeus Domitius Corbulo, suffered the same fate. In some circumstances nothing fails like success. Nero's popularity with the urban rabble was little affected. The gratin took fright and saw him off. He is said, by my scholar friend the late professor J. P. Sullivan, to have been much misunderstood.

Saint Paul's invitation to Gentiles to become Christians, without the forfeit of circumcision, was issued not least to Judaisers. They were likely to be alert to the monotheism in which deification of Jesus Christ came to be incorporated in a triune Godhead, along with the so-called Holy Ghost/Spirit. This elevation was due in good part to a stretched reading of Jesus' conventional Jewish description of himself as a child (son?) of God. Slaves and females, a good percentage illiterate, were drawn to the new egalitarian faith and the prospectus of another world in which there would be neither marrying nor giving in marriage, neither bond nor free. Pauline Christianity bore traces of its author's provincial origins. His readiest converts were alien to metropolitan sophistication. Of the many letters he despatched to early churchmen, none was ever addressed to Jerusalem or to Athens, where audiences had listened to the great apostle's pitch with unflattering curiosity, if not open amusement.

After the fall of Jerusalem to Vespasian and his son Titus in 70 CE, Judaism was docked of the centralised, tribute-gilded magnificence to be observed in Herod's Temple. Grandiose ceremonial yielded to modest services in unsubsidised settings. Animal sacrifice ceased to have a part in the proceedings. René Girard claims that the martyrdom of Jesus, whom he holds to have been manifestly innocent, put an end to the efficacy of the 'scapegoat mechanism'. Did it? Before very long, the Jew would become the ritual beast; his abject life and, in the second millennium, his sacrificial roasting were held to be proof, Saint Augustine gloated, of Christian doctrinal veracity.

The great passion of Titus' life was the Jewish princess Berenice, sister (perhaps wife) of Agrippa II, king of Judaea and a Roman puppet ally. He took her back to Rome with him. On accession as emperor, he was alert to the risk of imposing an alien empress on the Roman people. He chose, with whatever regret, to dump her. Her last word to him, in Racine's play, was '*Adieu*', its definitive use. Berenice came off at one of history's dangerous corners. What if Titus had married her and Rome had had a Jewish empress, and perhaps, in time, a Jewish emperor?

The Judaean general Yoseph ben-Matityahu, who had surrendered to Vespasian, in circumstances of which he is the sole narrator, was pensioned in Rome and became the historian Flavius Josephus, first in a long line of alienated Jewish chroniclers. Turncoat to some, far-sighted – if repudiated – go-between to others, Josephus interprets Titus' and his legions' sack of the sacred city as God's punishment for the (mostly young) Zealots' pollution of the Temple with fraternal blood. Christian apostles read the same events as proof that God had withdrawn His favour from His once Chosen People. On their account, the Jews had failed to honour the divine provenance of His son (later hymned as 'meek and mild'), somewhat as Pentheus had disdained Dionysus.

For the sake of mythical scheme, all Jews became damnable. They were said, for dogmatic purposes, to have bayed unanimously for Jesus' blood, regardless of the blight that would fall on their children. Who but the indoctrinated can believe such a story? Unanimity is hardly a Jewish characteristic, in religious or intellectual circumstances. 'Don't ask for the meaning, ask for the use,' said Wittgenstein. What is said of Jews, tendentiously, in one doctrinal manipulation or another, becomes their indelible, universal character, what 'the Jews' is held to mean; individuality is lost first in self-righteous Christian piety, then in common abuse. Argot confirms what tendentious elders concoct. Jewish tightness comes of not putting a penny in the collective box.

82

I once heard a Christian preacher describe the symbol of the Cross as an 'I' crossed out: baptism transformed the self into unselfishness. Does it? Christian salvation is reserved for the individual soul. The dilemma facing Scobie, in Graham Greene's *The Heart of the Matter*, loses paradoxical poignancy if God can forgive a man who perjures himself for the sake of another. Like Zeus, who would have stopped the Trojan War if *moira* (fate) had not overridden him, the allegedly omnipotent Christian God appears constrained by the logic of His own laws. Hence Greene's quasi-heretical Scobie's decision to sacrifice his soul for another renders him more moral, damnably freer, than the deity. Lawrence Durrell has a transvestite Scobie, the police chief in his *Alexandria Quartet*, who revels in the panoply of imperialism. His favourite phrase, of imperishable utility, is '*C'est de la grande bogue*, old man.' Greene often rates higher than Durrell in British eyes; his *grande bogue* carries a holy-water mark.

Gilbert Ryle proclaimed 'the systematic elusiveness of "I"'; the protean First Person becomes suspect, indicative but imprecise, in theology and philosophy alike. How could 'I' have any place in science and mathematics? All first-personal declarations become, in positivist terms, without definitive sense. William Lyons has alerted me to the key passage in *The*

Concept of Mind: 'When a child asks...Who or What am I?, he's not asking about his name or nationality or sex, but "He feels that there is something in the background for which his 'I' stands, a something which still has to be described after all his ordinary personalia have been listed".' According to Ryle, the child's questions are natural, but misconceived: 'I' does not promise some internal mental organ accessible solely to discreet private observation.

We learn about ourselves, Ryle claimed, as we do about others, by observing a character's conduct and listening to his or her conversation. What 'we' designates here is difficult to divine, but the elimination of privileged access has a logical sweetness and does, incidentally, for the soul. Wittgenstein said that 'I' made no appearance in his book *The World as I Found It*, since he, as a first-person self, would not be a describable object in it. Hence the enigmatic observation about what the solipsist 'means'. Logically sweet, is this deprecation of 'internal' anxieties, hopes and fears any more convincing, in common human life, than the determinist notion that everything is predestined? Spinoza's '*sub specie aeternitatis*' is not quite identical with it. 'When all is said and done' does not entail or imply that there is no sense in saying or doing anything. Death clocks us all, but is not, Wittgenstein said, a part of life.

Iris Murdoch's deprecation of egotism implies that noble nullity can ready candidates for docile adherence to a totalitarian doctrine. In *The Sovereignty of Good* (1970), she made telling the truth an unquestionable virtue, as once she did following the Party line. In virtue's name, she came to say, one should not even lie to the Gestapo when they were looking for hidden persons (I don't think she specified you-know-whos). Logic, she never says but should have, is implacable but has nothing to do with goodness. Murdoch's admirer Antonia Byatt applauded Bernhard Schlink's *The Reader*, in which an illiterate female is regarded, if not revered, as the victim of a witch-hunt just because she has been put on trial for having been an SS guard at Auschwitz. The novel would have it that she should be absolved because she was Christian enough to be nice (in bed even) to women who were next in line for the gas chamber. She is said to have volunteered for the SS only because she needed the work. In reality, since she was illiterate, she would never have been accepted. Ideological killing in the German style involved paperwork. Cynthia Ozick did not side with the prize-winning English ladies in their admiration for an executioner's moll. In Stephen Daldry's 2008 movie, the person who played the SS woman won an Oscar and a Jewish survivor was shown in a New York flat of gilded elegance. Whitewash comes in a variety of colours.

83

George Steiner maintained that the Jew's 'extra-territoriality' had best be flaunted as definitive; hence his repudiation, following Joseph Roth, of Zionism as a solution to the Jewish question. Kafka has a short story in which a man sits waiting all day by a half-open door. A man comes out, at the end of the day, and says, 'This door was open for you. Now I am going to shut it.' Keiron Pim's 2022 biography of Roth, *Endless Flight*, is a tale more of resignation than of cowardice. Roth doubles for that mythical bird born without feet: he can hover, never land; it flies, flutters or falls.

It could never quite be wished or washed away that Jewish texts were fundamental to Christian doctrine. To qualify for the Saviour's role and have his birth predicted by oracular scripture, Jesus had to be modelled as a version of Isaiah's Messiah, grafted to the stem of Jesse. Hilaire Belloc's doctrinaire anti-Semitism led him never to read the Old Testament. After Vespasian's 70 CE triumph over the Judaeans, it was not politic to recall that Jesus had claimed, at one stage, to be bringing 'not peace but a sword', presumably against the Romans. Robert Graves's King Jesus is a tactless reminder of the Galilean's rebellious talk and has it that Judas Iscariot was enraged by his air of resignation at a Passover supper, of all times. In the Gospels, in Pauline scripture and in the polemic literature which barbed them, the man who had preached only to Jews was nominated their nemesis. The stiff-necked Jew was excluded from grace the better to enhance the celestial prospects of converts.

Was Roman imperium ever directly challenged in Christian literature or episcopal edict? Jesus' recommendation to render unto Caesar the things that are Caesar's did little to encourage defiance. When the princes of the Church cloaked themselves in the majesty of the Roman emperors whom they had supplanted, Jews became, as they remain, prime targets for denunciation, religious, social and political. Free-thinking and heresy were indistinguishable, so too, almost, pope and caesar.

The royalist Christian Mr Eliot's lines 'The rats are underneath the piles / The jew is underneath the lot' promoted everyone else, including rats, to superior status. Might it be that his poetic dig was a winking parody of 'Underneath are the everlasting arms'? Never underestimate highbrow appetite for giggles. The red-brick mansion flat, off Gloucester Road, London SW7, shared for a while by Eliot and the crippled wit John Hayward, was a prim location for the smirking class.

Unspoken disappointment at the deity's failure to be, as they will say, 'pro-active' doubles with fawning on Him. The vocabulary of Christian humility echoes the obsequiousness of ancient place-seekers. Courtly gush when approaching Hellenistic potentates left its mark on the Greek of the Gospels and attendant literature. Kneeling in prayer, in Christian and Muslim practice, derives from *proskynesis* (grovelling) as required of postulants before the Great King in the ancient Persian Empire. Jews defer to the Holy One; they do not crawl to Him. In Charterhouse School chapel I took furtive pride in not bowing my head in the Creed. I also dreaded receiving instruction from the Liberal Jewish synagogue in a brown envelope, franked 'STUDENT'S EXERCISE'. What privately educated person in pre-Suez England ever called himself a student? Students were people, mostly males, who made sloganeering trouble in foreign cities.

Eliot's willingness to defer to a king, literal or fanciful, suggests an appetite for gourmet humiliation. Might it be that his now-infamous line, about 'the jew', secretes some kind of vindictive compliment? It is part of the humbug of defenders of Eliot's laundered persona (for which he himself posted no spotless claims) that the now-regrettable quotation – which it did not, for a long time, occur to the author to delete or to his friends to deplore – should now be attributed to unhappy personal circumstances. Eliot's royalism had little to do with loyalty to constitutional monarchy as practised in the United Kingdom, more with the summary autocracy advocated by Charles Maurras and *Action française*.

The man from St. Louis, eager to do the English gentleman (as he had others 'do the police'), adopted the clerical cut and verbal niceties of those among whom he meant to make his mark and, if not before church on Sundays, to raise a polite laugh. Thanks to the forces of democracy, not to mention the English Channel, Eliot was spared being called upon to resist, or not, the rewards of siding with genocide. Can anyone easily imagine him, or any number of other literary enemies of democracy and its soft tolerances, declining the promise of swastikaed advancement? What would the big deal have been, had it come to putting the jew back beneath the piles?

In the 1930s, Hugh Sykes-Davies (1909–84), a Cambridge 'Apostle', communist and surrealist, wrote a novel entitled *Rats*. Its hero decides that rats have a social system superior to humans and goes down the drain to join them. In Piotr Rawicz's 1961 novel *Blood in the Sky*, arguably the greatest imaginative work concerning the Holocaust, the 'hero' Boris and his lover Naomi hide in a well accompanied by rats. In Anthony Rudolf's 2007 edition of his scholarly monograph,

Engraved in Flesh, 'Boris, cruelly, tells Naomi about that zoological freak, the king rat, and relates it to the condition of his community'. In 1963, Sykes-Davies was taken to be a shameless rat after he refused to pass adverse judgement on Anthony Blunt and promised a friendly welcome to his fellow Apostle, if he happened by.

Sykes-Davies's own ratty side was metaphorical. He had the habit of closing the curtains in his Chapel Court rooms during daylight hours. The St John's College housekeeper took it upon herself to tell him that, by doing so when the sun was shining, he was fading college drapery. Always rubicund, he grew redder. Curtains wide, he walked around his room stark naked in ruddy view of all and sundry. The College Council gave him leave to close the curtains. I owe Sykes-Davies a measureless debt of gratitude for granting me the travel studentship, bequest of a reverend benefactor, which widened my geographic horizons and bought me time to write my first novel.

84

The Mandate of Heaven, withdrawn from despoiled Jerusalem, was transmitted to Rome. Gentle Jesus, meek and mild, became the resurgent avenger who now bound all others against his own people. The Vatican replaced the Second Temple as the divinity's head office. Centuries later, the Al-Aqsa mosque imposed Allah in Jahveh's place on Jerusalem's Temple Mount. Mohammed's alleged flight to heaven from the summit of the mosque is, in all but credulous eyes, a poached remake of Elijah's ascent from the same launching pad to the same destination. Jews became trespassers in what legend promised them was their own God-given territory. The world had taken exception to their exceptional claims. Only recently, the Archbishop of Canterbury condemned the British government's proposed transfer of its embassy from Tel Aviv to Jerusalem. In the case of Israel alone, an Anglican pontiff presumed moral authority to determine that a nation's capital city should not house the British embassy. The same Archbishop, Justin Welby, declared no dated moral qualms at being summoned to celebrate the coronation of an adulterer as head of the Anglican Church, his scheming lady as queen. Welby was obliged to resign his office after having failed to take action, in no few cases, against paedophile clergymen who abused children in their charge.

The suppositious nation of 'the Palestinians' (*quondam*

Philistines) claims priority in the land of Israel. Their festering and fostered grievances by no means baseless; they are placarded by other Arabs who show them small sympathy when it comes to living space. Failure to transform the well-placed Gaza strip into a mercantile city-state contrasts with the thriving economy of territorially smaller Singapore.

Over a million Greeks, long resident in the Middle East, were expelled in 1922, after a disastrous campaign, sponsored by the British under David Lloyd-George, to supplant Turkish rule in the region. The ejected Asiatic Hellenes bore no marked responsibility for the folly of the Athenian government. Has anyone ever suggested that they should be reinstated? Shown few favours, they were assimilated, grudgingly, in poverty-stricken mainland Greece. Palestinian Arabs alone, in a world of mass migrations, cannot be absorbed anywhere but in the land of their supposed origin. Most of them now come of generations that never inhabited today's Israel. In no small part, they owe their fenced sequestration to other Arabs less concerned for their brethren than determined to preserve the obloquy subsidised grievances can bring on Israel.

Disputes of Jews with early Christians began between what Girard calls "*frères-ennemis*", sects at odds for the domination of communities and cities. Residing far from Paris, in remote Montignac, in south-western France, the aphorist Joseph Joubert (1754–1824) remarked, during the French Revolution, that few feuds are so irreconcilable as those fought between previously compatible communities and within hitherto-undivided families. Vespasian's extirpation of the Judaeans (in disputed numbers) did little immediate harm to the status of Jews in other parts of the Roman Empire. Rough justice can be less implacable, if scarcely more just, than dogmatic conviction.

Tendentiousness, stretched in contrary directions, renders the number of Jews left in Judaea after the fall of Jerusalem to Titus a matter for vexed partialities. The notion that all Palestine's Jews were expelled after 73 CE suits those who claim that there is no evidence of continuous tenure of what had been their Promised Land. The loud implication is that the Jews' presumptuous lease has irretrievably lapsed. The truth, inconvenient or not, is that Jews remained in the region, however many Greeks and, later, Arabs rejoiced in their eviction from, Jerusalem. There were certainly enough to be slaughtered, along with Arabs, by righteous Crusaders.

Even when there seemed to be a chance that the uprising of 66 CE might succeed, by no means all Judaeans shared the manic confidence of the Jerusalem zealots. The Jews of Scythopolis, in the hinterland, took up arms alongside the Greeks, a majority with whom they had shared the town without known friction, against the Zealots, whose monomania they deplored. Given weapons, the Scythopolitan Hebrews fought with such spirit alongside the Hellenes that the Zealots were repelled. The Greeks then feared that their fellow-citizens, having discovered their united strength, might turn against them. They conned the Jews into returning their borrowed arms and camping in a wood. The Greeks came back in force next day and massacred their *quondam* allies.

This *fait divers* had nothing to do with Jesus or religion. In 480 BCE, the Spartans were similarly alarmed by the valour of the Helots (native Greek slaves) whom they armed, in haste, to help repel the Persians. The bravest Helots may have hoped for grateful emancipation. Their reward, after the triumphal event, was to be led away and slaughtered. The ill-fated rebellion of Bar Kokhba, some fifty years after 66, is evidence enough of the presence and spirit, if not folly, of no few surviving Judaean Jews.

85

In the pre-Christian world, Jews – with their solitary God and picky diet – may have seemed cranky. Despite the Jew-versus-Greek antagonism in pre-Christian Alexandria, alienation and ridicule never aggregated into doctrinal or 'racial' anti-Judaism. So-called Judaeophobia was unknown until the Church was formally established. The episcopate diabolised all conceits but those it pilfered for remounting in its creed. Christianity adopted its own dietetic foibles. Eating only fish on Fridays commemorates the day of the crucifixion and insists that Christians are innocent of what damns the Jews, the blood on their and their children's hands. It also recalls the Greek for fish, *ichthys*, a horizontal hieroglyph which stood for Christian. The blood that Christians did not shed is held to be absorbed in their persons by participation in Holy Communion. Lascivious craving for the blood in the sacraments was wished on the Jews. They have been regularly accused of wishing to filch and torture the sanctified slivers until they bleed. Lack of evidence is the proof of diabolical cunning, the transfer of guilt conclusive.

Who will deny that there is probably some truth in the story of the crowd's preference for the reprieve of Barabas? As for 'all the Jews' calling for Jesus' execution, as the Gospel insists, the truth is likelier, much, to be that the brigand's friends were quicker and more outspoken than the Galilean's, whose disciples dared not speak up for him. That the whole of Jewry ever turned up to shout for one more moralising chatterbox seems as unlikely as the celestial provenance with which his tendentious survivors decked Him. Who but an ideologue will deny that more available low-life chums are likely to present themselves to save a charming villain's life than skulking Peters and their kind? Jesus' disciples were mostly low-class out-of-towners, Matthew an exception. Charm is a quality that will trump all others, virtue especially. Did the Jerusalem crowd not somewhat resemble the Athenians who voted Aristides out of their sight because he was insufferably too Just for his own good or their pleasure?

For all the pious puff in Evelyn Waugh's tithe-paying *Helena*, it is questionable whether the emperor Constantine had other-than-pragmatic reasons for adopting the faith which his mother's supposed recovery of the True Cross was held to confirm. His stage-managed conversion, *coram publico*, topped by a you'd-better-believe-it vision of a cross in the sky, was more pragmatic than spiritual. The upstart could claim to be sponsored by celestial sanction. The Church's accession to primacy was rewarded, *donnant-donnant*, as Marshal Pétain would say, with its politic endorsement of his authority.

At the same time as his now-hear-this conversion, Constantine was building a temple to glorify his own majesty. Inhabitants of Rome's sprawling empire were increasingly divergent. Olympian gods and localised cults no longer held them in civil balance. Autocratic presumption and a recension of Semitic monotheism seemed made for each other. Providential symmetry contrived for heaven and earth to be ruled by reciprocal masters. Spiritual imperialism issued from concord between Roman imperialism and the Christian Church. The Divine Right of Kings would emerge from the same bag. Europe was then saddled with a dyarchy that is only now beginning to slip. Charles Freeman's *The Closing of the Western Mind* (2003) suggests that the arrival of Christianity, dogma its muzzle and bit, was no unalloyed blessing for civilisation. Innovative thought was read as heretical. Rabbis discuss; priests dictate.

When Evelyn Waugh and Randolph Churchill were deputed, during the war, by SOE to attach themselves to Tito's partisans in Yugoslavia, Waugh discovered that Randolph had never read the Bible. The pious papist happened to have a copy with him. Without likelier reading matter, Churchill began at the beginning. He was soon heard to exclaim, more than once, 'What a shit God is!' If only for a giggle, Waugh put it about that Marshal Tito was really a woman. Sophia Loren, we are told, had firm evidence that this was not so. Waugh proved the practical utility of pre-Vatican II Catholicism by holding conversations with alien priests in Latin. Vernacular *maquillage* has kindled small fervour. The old music-hall joke reads: 'She had her face lifted, but when they saw what was underneath, they dropped it again.'

86

The Maccabees, strapped for manpower to fight the Seleucid Empire, are the only Jews known to have exerted force to enrol others, for wholly pragmatic reasons. In the second century BCE, they conscripted the Idumaeans, who inhabited the Negev. The tribesmen were granted full equality with those of Jewish stock. In 67 CE, when Jerusalem was besieged by Vespasian, twenty thousand Idumaeans, summoned by the Zealots inside the city, came north to add to the rebel strength. First allying themselves with the extremists and assisting in the purge of thousands of 'moderates', including the old theocratic priesthood, then disillusioned by partisan squabbling and, it may be, poor prospects of reward, they returned home.

After the fall of Jerusalem, in 70 CE, and the disintegration of its hierarchy, surviving rabbis met, on Roman licence, at Yavneh, near Ashdod. Inspired by the resilient forty-year-old Pharisee Yochanan Ben Zakkai, a member of the Grand Sanhedrin until its eviction from the Temple, they picked up the shards of shattered authority and edited the contents of what became the Old Testament. The militant Maccabees' briefly triumphant separatism was prudently relegated to the private parts of Judaean history, the Apocrypha.

The opposition of Greek and Hebrew owes more to the militant secession of Palestine's Jews from the Seleucid Empire than to intellectual or social incompatibility. Descendants of Alexander the Great's marshals, the Seleucid monarchs and their soldiery were regarded by no few mainland Greeks as scarcely of their own breed. Greco-Christian cultural imperialism relished the disparagement of Jewish religious and patriotic particularism. Alexandrian Philo and Cordoban Maimonides remain examples of cultural synthesis in circles not dominated by Cross-patched militants.

Valued as warriors by Julius Caesar after a posse of Jews saved him from an Egyptian mob, Jews were downgraded, following their eviction from Jerusalem in 70 CE, into money-grubbing cowards. Alan Clark, in his rich youth a competitor at Brooklands in a belted six-litre Bentley, amused his chums with talk of 'Jewish racing yellow'. When the IRA was threatening to bomb one of London's bridges, I was obliged to spend a long time in the car with Clark and Robin Day on the way to some publisher's klatsch in a rural retreat. He took notes of some of my remarks, not least the futility of thinking about bluffing as a political tactic. As every poker player learns, do it confidently, or not at all. Clark was an Etonian affecting to have been to Eton.

After Jerusalem had been pacified and pillaged, Titus had some seven thousand 'rebels' crucified. There was not enough wood to make crosses for the remainder; they were dispatched by other means. The Judaeans lost their combative nationhood, their worship its physical centre; faith became portable, if not yet fugitive. The Council of Yavneh was both an admission of defeat and a declaration of faith. Literate intelligence was the one resource of which the vanquished could not be deprived. Nostalgia became an aspect of hope. By the fifteenth century CE, as recorded by Isaac Tyrnau, in his *Book of Customs*, 'Next Year in Jerusalem' had become an Ashkenazi mantra when celebrating Yom Kippur. What is more persistent among the descendants of displaced peoples than nostalgia for where they never lived? Among Sicilian, Irish, Armenian and Greek exiles, solidarity takes various forms, many culinary, more sentimental, not a few violent.

87

The cult of Jesus of Nazareth was of a discordant piece with the decentralised Judaism that followed Yavneh. Regional versions of early Christianity were dressed with Dionysiac and Mithraic devices. Like not a few Mediterranean mystery religions, the redesigned faith promised initiates upgraded lives after death. Jews remained the biggest threat to the emergent Church's hegemony, not least on account of Christianity's pillage of the spiritual and intellectual qualities of Judaism. Dispossessing Jews has become a contagious tradition. Those who robbed them accused them of being tight.

Joseph Stalin would be obsessed with eliminating the cult of Leon Trotsky (*né* Bronstein), whose armoured train and inspiring leadership had been central in the glory days of the 1917 Revolution. Trotsky and his Red Army's exploits supplied the old testament of Bolshevik mythology from which the Jew Bronstein was later erased. His followers became the new *Marranos*, godsend to a godless ideology: the failure of the Stalinists to deliver on their promises could be attributed to heretical wreckers.

The Holy Inquisition set the style for Stalin's punitive godlessness. The Saved were to have the pleasure of witnessing the eternal torment of whoever had, or could be said to have, made the wrong choice. In Christianity, the two-tier notion of the human condition, in which after death the faithful graduate to a better place, served to sedate the lower orders of principalities and powers here below. Their day would come; meanwhile patience was advised. The Communist Party supplied salvation here below and selected those who might enjoy it, temporally and, in no few cases, temporarily.

88

As if to honour man's arbitrary calendar, almost exactly two centuries after the lynching of Josef Süß Oppenheimer, Christian/Germanic sadism was translated to city streets by the Nazis: the broken glass (and heads) of Kristallnacht, in November 1938, presaged the full-scale, murderous remake of what Crusaders and the Holy Inquisition had dress-rehearsed. In 1147 CE, the Teutonic knights, on their way to the Holy Land in the Second Crusade, hardened their hearts and blooded their swords by massacring unarmed Jews in the Rhineland. The Holocaust would be a reprise, on an industrial scale, of the sack of Jerusalem and of the Holy Office's demonisation of survivors. Ferdinand and Isabella baptised their united kingdoms with the blood of Semitic intruders. There were Jews and Moors in Spain long before Christians cleansed it.

In *Christian Beginnings* (2012), Géza Vermes established that Christianity lurched in divergent directions before acquiring dogmatic Trinitarian form four hundred years after the Event. The Jew as bad example seeps into Enlightenment culture and literature. The judicial murder of Joseph Süß Oppenheimer yoked theology and political philosophy. Quasi-Christian re-scripture laid the foundations for the eye-catching, crowd-pleasing anti-Semitism of

231

Voltaire, Kant, Treitschke, Belloc and who all else down to the Hitlerian, all-but-reasonable Carl Schmitt. He conceded the force of arguments raised against him by his one-time pupil Leo Strauss and allowed the arbitrary nature of the Aryan/Semitic divide, while cleaving to it. No such honesty was displayed by the ex-seminarian Martin Heidegger, the mountebank Alfred Rosenberg or the *fascisant* Belgian Paul de Man. Bilingual bigamist, the last turned his coat and became a postmodern pundit in post-war America, where he propounded the fissile nature of all convictions. Kant seems an odd recruit in the anti-Semites' ranks. Does his wish for a universal morality somewhat explain his distaste for Jewish exceptionalism? That he went out for a walk at precisely four o'clock every afternoon suggests a man, prisoner-cum-gaoler, who will not exempt himself from his own rules.

Leo Strauss translated to an academic life in the USA, where he became the guru of neo-conservativism. His distinction between the class who might be called 'Guardians' – with knowledge superior to those whose world was limited to what Plato called 'appearances' – and the intellectually inferior masses led him to be accused of oligarchic sympathies. Outstanding evidence that not all Jews are wits, nostalgic malice tagged him an emissary of the Elders of Zion.

It seems anomalous that Voltaire, who denounced the murderous bigotry of the Catholic Church in the Calas case and called for the French '*écraser l'infâme*' (to crush the outrage), should embrace a malevolent view of what amounted to about 0.5 per cent of the least-favoured fraction of the population. It appears particularly damaging to Jews that so artful an iconoclast should visit his animosity on them. In truth, Voltaire's animus disguised *ad hominem* resentment; while toadying to Frederick the Great (crowns do go to other people's heads), he was denied a loan, on preferential terms, by German Jewish bankers. Never trust a satirist to take a joke, unless for money.

89

In the 1980s, when visiting David Garnett in his earth-floored, bedside-carpeted cottage in the Lot-et-Garonne, I asked his opinion of the painter Mark Gertler, Dora Carrington's allegedly unsubtle lover. 'When we were friends,' Garnett said, 'he was just like anyone else; when we were rivals in love, he was that bloody Jew.' Miron Grindea, *schnorrer* and editor of *Adam*, little magazine of rare quality, told me that in his native Romania people had the habit of saying, '*Il est – pardon! – juif.*'

The habitual anti-Semitism of that paragon of feminism Virginia Woolf is rarely held against her, unlike her contempt for charladies. The psychoanalyst Melanie Klein would doubtless read Leonard's conjugal devotion as incurable masochism. The Bloomsberries in general tended to mock his you-know-whoish tightfistedness. Keeping the Hogarth Press solvent must have consumed any available funds. It is not on record which of the clique, apart from godfatherly Maynard Keynes, was noted for open-handedness. Morgan Forster was notorious in King's for doses of poor sherry often served, Simon Raven told me, in a tooth mug. Immune to racial or social snobbery, Forster made no secret of one of his lovers being a police constable. His novel *Maurice*, published posthumously, was at once wary and outspoken in its account of a homosexual love affair. It remains no great recommendation for earnestness in art.

Trite malice was not limited to snobs and toffs. In 1945, Ernest Bevin, known as 'the dockers' QC', spoke of Jewish refugees seeking haven in Palestine, from which they were barred by British imperial edict, as 'pushing to the front of the queue'. The now-hallowed Attlee government of 1945–51 shipped European Jewish leftovers back from the shores of Palestine to the Nazi camps from which they had been sprung.

In the 1930s, Sir Oswald Mosley's union of fascists did not foist anti-Semitism on the good old British working class; it licensed it, as J. Corbyn's clique does among Muslims. The Corbynistas' partiality owes as much to arithmetic as to morals: trading two or three hundred thousand Jewish votes for two million Muslim looked to be good political business. When electoral results proved this not manifestly the case, Corbyn and his caucus were eased from the Labour praesidium. Today's Midianites, they still prowl and prowl around.

In 1968, Bevin's one-time constituents in the London docks were as quickly supportive of Enoch Powell's notorious 'Rivers of Blood' speech as German communist rank-and-file members turned out to be of Nazism, once the Communist Party was banned and new uniforms with virile belts distributed to Nazi recruits. One of Bevin's least-advertised and shrewdest observations was that it had been a great mistake to dethrone the German Kaiser (and the Austrian emperor), thus making room at the head of government for rabble-rousers, opportunists and fortune-hunters. Traditional rulers, however vainglorious, subsidised polite and gilded parades of spectacular humbug. Courtly formality sponsored social grammar, above and below the salt. The rich man in his castle, the poor man at his gate, sang from a patriotic hymnal.

The one smart move by Neville Chamberlain's right-wing government in the late 1930s was to ban the British Union of

Fascists from wearing military-style kit. Mosley went as near as he could with that black turtle-necked sweater, the militant breeches and the get-me boots. The swagger ensemble was not seductive to the masses, nor was his fisty rant to more than a few of the semi-upper class. Harold Nicolson, for instance, was for a time seduced by Mosley's belted and buckled virility, 'Chips' Channon likewise. Channon, snob and *arriviste*, was a thorough anti-Semite; Nicolson had too much intelligence to embrace doctrinal malice, but he did find it repugnant to swim in the same pool where Jews were or had been, as was undoubtedly his right. Both Michael Foot and Enoch Powell, unlikely sentimentalists, retained a belief that Mosley was a 'lost leader'. His indexed proximity to Moses is a sweet fluke. The waverers did not part for him.

Not long ago, the Labour MP Grahame Morris circulated images of what he said were Israeli soldiers beating up a Palestinian boy 'for fun'. When the Israel Defense Forces identified the soldiers as Guatemalan, Morris apologised *du bout de lèvres* by conceding that the bullies were indeed not Israelis, but then added that they might as well have been, in view of how he knew the IDF to behave. Morris is a name not unusual among Jews (the leading character in *The Glittering Prizes* was called Adam Morris), which proves nothing, no doubt, when it comes to the moralising MP's desire for distinction from the Chosen, not to mention appeal to Muslim voters.

90

Communism was a mutation of the religions it affected to render obsolete: the working class its Chosen People; Karl Marx, a rabbi's grandson, its Moses; the classless society its Zion. The Jews, whom young Marx branded the 'Huckster Race', remained the Jews. What most resembles a political zealot is often his systematic target. Marx was doubly helical in effect: as gospeller, he licensed contempt for Jews; as a target for Nazis, his origins proved his ineradicable villainy. Communists were especially venomous towards gently-does-it bourgeois reformers whose Fabian socialism might loosen their hold on the Left; similarity is a form of distinction. Freud talked of the 'narcissism of small differences'. He ignored their habitual enlargement and observed, with small prescience, that Europe used to burn Jews and now (in 1938) burnt books instead. Before long, progress accelerated backwards.

Theological anathemas derived their Christian licence from Constantine's Council of Nicaea, in 325 CE. Its principal resolution had been to demonise Arianism because it conceded the divinity of Jesus but shied at His parity with the Father. There was no pretence of evidence, in any mundane sense, of Jesus' equality with the Father; belief was strutted into dogma, then into unarguable grounds for enforcement. The Arian churches of Ravenna, with their matchless mosaics, were appropriated as scintillating advertisements for the doctrine which their benefactors never honoured.

The distinction posited between religious and politico-philosophical anti-Semitism is a modern device. It suits the religious to detach patristic mythology from totalitarian creed. In fact, the records and practices of the Holy Inquisition prefigure Nazism's racial postulates, bureaucratic dossiers, smug murders. Malice persists in language when faith has gone. As the philosopher Berel Lang remarked, in an article on 'the Jews', sly coalition is implied by the pointed attachment of the definite article in a manner that compresses a diverse range of people into a single polycephalic hydra.

In *The Spanish Inquisition* (1965), Henry Kamen concludes that fewer Jews were dispossessed, racked and burnt alive than is often asserted. He has it that only a few thousand suffered in that way. The torture chambers, secret proceedings and foregone conclusions of the Holy Office furnished pious precedents for mass murder. It was a fundamental of ancient Athenian democracy that trials of groups of people, especially on capital charges, were illicit. Totalitarianism has specialised in them.

This does not promise that such things never took place in a democracy. A signal instance was the hurried condemnation of the six admirals out of eight who made the brave mistake of presenting themselves for trial after alleged failure to rescue the drowning after the Athenian victory of Arginusae, in 406 BCE. The weather had worsened and prospects of life-saving were poor. Later, by ordering batches of executions, without trial, the Thirty Tyrants, under Plato's uncle Critias, set a precedent for totalitarianism. The principle of individual justice returned with the restoration of democracy.

Greek history repeated itself, after two and a half thousand years, in the trial of the six politicians found guilty of promoting the 1922 attempt, at first popular and finally disastrous, to retrieve Constantinople from the Turks. Backed, until it failed, by British Prime Minister Lloyd George, the Greek incursion ended in the eviction, by Kemal Atatürk, of almost all Hellenes resident in their ancestral territory in Asia Minor. I bought some scissors in Kuşadasi from a rare remaining Hellene. Ernest Hemingway's *In Our Time* includes an unblinking eye-witness account of the execution of the six scapegoats as well as of the panic evacuation of Greeks from İzmir. He was no more present on either occasion than was Stendhal's Fabrizio del Dongo at the Battle of Waterloo. The home-grown instigator of the Greek invasion of mainland Turkey was the Cretan Eleftherios Venizelos. Out of office (and reach) when catastrophe struck, he survived to become a national hero. The modern Athens airport is named after him.

91

Martin Heidegger's *Sein Und Zeit* (*Being and Time*), published in 1927, its author not quite forty, served notice on a long European tradition of rational discourse. Julien Benda's terse and tart *La Trahison des Clercs*, denouncing the sell-out of philosophers, left and right, to ideological unreason, was published in the same year. During the Occupation of France, Benda was 'buried alive' among brave Protestants. Heidegger read the Nazi victories of 1940 as proof of Germany's triumphant destiny, the 1945 catastrophe as a temporary reverse. How often do ideologues learn from experience?

Born in 1889, Heidegger grew up in the mountainous backwoods of the most forward industrial state on the continent. While the steel gleam of the Ruhr promised the triumph of modern industry, the romantic legend of the unspoiled Teutonic rustic, rooted in ancestral land, persisted in a Germany increasingly mechanised by wealth-generating industrialists. Nazism came of a schizoid conjunction of rustic nostalgia with conscienceless modernism. While supervising industrialised mass murder, Heinrich Himmler insisted that he was a simple farmer at heart but had yet to stable his cows.

Not unlike the early life of Joseph Dzhugashvili (later Stalin) as a Russian Orthodox seminarist, young Martin Heidegger's uncompleted training for the Catholic priesthood scarcely lost its impress when he chose to disavow it. Godless 'Being' effaced the Trinity. Jews were noxious in both revisions. Parodic faith axed Christianity's antique source in the scriptures of allegedly rootless, inauthentic Hebrews. Heidegger declared Aryans to be the world's uniquely 'spiritual' people, reselected Chosen, 'the Jews' their quasi-diabolical Others. Theodor Herzl's Zionism had promised to anachronise anti-Semitism by re-establishing Jews in Palestine, revised as open-necked Spartan nationalists. Orthodox Jews could scarcely be denied entry and now propagate what may soon become a majority of intolerant exclusionists.

The particular virtue of Richard Wolin's unsmiling indictment of Heidegger (who wrote a long essay in praise of boredom) is its scholarly examination of the meta-philosopher's black notebooks with their protracted, not to say demented, denunciation of The Jews. Wolin scarcely mentions the comedy of Heidegger's adulterous passion for his Jewish student Hannah Arendt (and hers for him). If she did denounce him, sort of, once she was safely installed in classy New York circles, vanity disposed her to go on pilgrimage to enjoy his post-war company. Despite losing his professorial chair, he retained his intellectual throne. HA found his conversation was a relief from that of the garrulous *Ost-Juden* at the 1961 trial of Adolf Eichmann, which the *New Yorker* commissioned her to cover. She took the exquisite view that Eichmann should have been tried in Germany. Her usage 'the banality of evil', to reduce the mass murderer's unprepossessing person to the ranks of the negligible, was first coined by Heidegger, less to indict mass murder than to deny 'philosophical' significance to those six million 'disappearances'. The categorical accepts no challenge from contingency.

The vanity of reputation led Heidegger to conceal – and his post-war family to edit – his obsessive *Black Notebooks*, with their reiterated indictment of the Jews. In the 'era of the Christian West... World Jewry was the principle of destruction'. Such ravings were never unprecedented; they had seldom before recruited supposedly humanist followers as well as a long train of Islamic partisans. Author of *L'Existentialisme est un Humanisme*, Jean-Paul Sartre was unfazed in 1946 by Heidegger's dismissive response to his trendy emulation. Pierre Bourdieu had the decency to say, 'When I hear people say that Heidegger alone makes it possible for us to think about the Holocaust – but perhaps I am insufficiently "postmodern" – I think I must be dreaming.'

Wolin is scrupulous in pinning falsehoods, absurdity and vanity on Heidegger's multisyllabic celebration of unreason. Except for the odd irrelevant gaffe (he equates Drieu La Rochelle's ardent wartime collaboration with Henry de Montherlant's retreat into pseudo-sporting solipsism), Wolin avoids speculation about his subject's motive or psychological peculiarity. Scruple stacks the charges but attempts no punchy analysis, not least below the belt. Did Heidegger take especial pleasure in making his star pupil his Jew-mistress? Without some dissection of his crass perversity, even Heidegger's ruins are liable to become items of fetishism.

Mel Brooks's 'Don't be stupid, be a smarty, come and join the Nazi Party' is a jibe in the right direction, but the truth is further to the loony right: in 1933, Heidegger expected the Nazi Party to join him. His quite prompt retreat from being the Fuhrer's loud academic adjutant led one or two unintimidated colleagues to tease him with 'Back from Syracuse?', an allusion to Plato's ejection into temporary slavery after playing tutor to Dion, heir to the Sicilian tyrant Dionysius. Heidegger sulked and railed; if bruised, he remained shameless. Learning worldly lessons was no part of his philosophical practice; it was the world's business to learn from him. Oh, for a latter-day tart-tongued Schopenhauer to dish it to him as scathingly as he did to Hegel! Heidegger's own brother read Martin for some kind of Dadaist.

92

Informed derision, of the kind that Trevor Roper visited on Arnold Toynbee, Peter Medawar on Teilhard de Chardin, might do something to dislodge Heidegger from his false eminence. How do we know it false? Because, not least, it is an all-but-childishly-facile transfer of 'chosenness' from the Jews to the Germans. What was a burdensome demand on the ancient Jews, no less than a privilege, was re-blocked, in the form of a unique crown to fit only the blond bullet-heads of the idealised Aryan. 'Being' became the vacuous grail of a heartless creed. The English (Jewish, does it matter?) Oxonian philosopher Alfred Jules 'Freddie' Ayer said that the whole rigmarole, pages and pages of it *chez* Sartre, was based on nothing more reliable than a gross misunderstanding of the use and weight of the verb 'to be'. Habitually verbose, Sartre was reduced to calling Ayer a '*con*'. Hannah Arendt's long infatuation with a man she came to see was incorrigibly misguided suggests that comedy alone has the vanity-piercing capacity to reduce loud ruins to proper dust.

Sartre popularised a reupholstered notion of authenticity, which had also had its place in Nazi 'philosophy'. Richard Wagner's contempt for Jewish composers, akin to Karl Kraus's for Jewish *feuilletonistes*, postulated Aryan authenticity of a kind no Hebrew could attain, however flashy his cadenzas. Like some second Herman (Arminius) putting Quintilius Varus' Roman legions to flight, Wagner disdained the sentimentality of Italian opera and based his own operas on Teutonic myths supposedly derived, like the Rhinemaidens, from an entirely indigenous Germanic source.

The postulate of a distinction between art and literature, which derive from aboriginal roots, and the alien glitter of imposture runs through a certain brand of literary criticism. By contrast, René Girard devoted clever energy to insisting on the mimetic nature of all literary composition. Inventive imposture is the mark of civilised people. Authenticity can be as much conceit as distinction. Sincerity in art makes no reliable promise of quality.

Josef Brodsky's improbable model, W. H. Auden, was relegated to the class of flashy disappointments by Frank Leavis's magazine *Scrutiny*, 'immature' its code-word for homosexual. If Leavis and his friends never subscribed to the criminalisation of homosexuality, they shared a presumption that heterosexual (preferably conjugal) relations alone could be 'mature'. Hannah Arendt made the unfoolish pairing of the Jew and the homosexual as similarly extraneous to Christendom and, she might have added, its 'genius', to use the term of the unbelieving but enchanted Chateaubriand.

The vindication of the gay (and the Black) has had little cheerful correlative when it comes to Jews. Exclusivity and the charm of officialdom haunt the works of Man the systematiser. Authenticity doubles for a hallmark; like Aryan blood, it is unobtainable by outsiders, regardless of transfused civility. The postulate of an irredeemable distinction between the genuine and the meretricious has recurrent charm, not least for citizens of confected nationalities: fascism enchanted many Italians, Nazism most Germans, communism the supposed Union of Soviet Socialist republicans. In today's United Kingdom, fabricated vanities and promotions have renewed attractions. The semi-educated darn holes in their intelligence by recourse to stereotypes; the books they consult are those with the same old answers, revised.

On the naice side of the street, Theresa May, a sudden Little Englander after the 2016 Brexit referendum, chose to refer scornfully to no few of the forty-eight per cent remainers as 'cosmopolitans'. Resignation from the European Union leaves the British at the proud top of a class with only one member. Whom then shall be blamed when things turn nasty or sour or both? Jewish duplicity is a surviving article of faith among the now-faithless. Much good it will do the Chosen that, of all the followers of monotheism, they have never, at least since the fall of the Second Temple, conducted pious massacres of those who decline to adopt their religion or – like Sunni and Shi'ite, Catholic and Protestant – one particular version of it.

This promises no moral or any other form of superiority or veracity in Judaism, nor a reliable tradition of tolerance within it. The treatment of Spinoza's contemporary the literally down-trodden Uriel da Costa by the same Amsterdam community that expelled the philosopher was a parody of the conduct of the Spanish Inquisition from which so many of the congregants were refugees. Da Costa later committed suicide. Jews in general have remained unlikely to recruit or coerce converts.

Spinoza's genius survived in magisterial isolation. He then wrote works, in Latin, of dissent from all kinds of institutional worship and revealed religion. In his *History of Western Philosophy*, Bertrand Russell, not averse to flaunting his family earldom, named Spinoza the 'noblest' of all the great philosophers. He was one of the few Jews never for a moment to have believed, in 1666, that Zabbatai Zevi was the Messiah come to lead the Jews home again. Spinoza's superbly impersonal Latin text was a contrast with the vernacular of Michel de Montaigne, whose mother had Sephardic roots. Gallic irony standing in for overt scepticism, Montaigne observed that a man must be very sure of himself to burn another at the stake for taking a deviant view of Jesus Christ. His humane levity led to his work being placed on the Index by the Roman Church.

93

The wish that Judaism be guilty of what Christianity and Islam have done, repeatedly, has its part in the ascription of mass slaughter to the Israel Defense Forces at Jenin, in 2002. A. N. Wilson had already asserted that Israel 'poisons water supplies' (no malice like vintage malice) and has no right to exist; he then said that, by attacking a base for suicide bombers in Jenin, the IDF were guilty of 'massacre... genocide... immense slaughter'. It is now generally conceded that there is no evidence – apart from that postulated by Robert Fisk and company – that any massacre took place at Jenin or that any school or hospital was deliberately targeted by the Israelis in one of their incursions into Gaza. In fact, at Jenin just over fifty Palestinian fighters were killed and half as many Israelis.

Murderous maltreatment and penal sequestration of Jews down the centuries have excited paranoid apprehension among their persecutors. After what was being done to them, how could those people not be planning some sudden revenge, even worse than that conducted by the islanders against the colonising Franks during the Sicilian Vespers of 31 March 1282? Shylock's 'sufferance' was taken to underwrite malevolence that dared not speak its name. In the 1340s, the spread of the Black Death was attributed to the poisoning of Christian wells. Marlowe's *The Jew of*

Malta supplied literary back-up. This fancy served to patch the increasingly dubious postulate of God's interventionist benevolence with regard to Christians. The fraying thread of Christian respect for Judaism, Peter Abelard its lucid advocate a century earlier, was ruptured after bubonic plague – probably shipped in by Italian traders from the Middle East – had decimated Europe. 'The Jews' became an inverted godsend: their guilt saved the Faith. Marcel Proust's Gentile father (a doctor, as was Marcel's brother) originated the nineteenth century's *cordon sanitaire*, which put incoming vessels in quarantine, thus all but eliminating the import of alien plagues until the advent of mass air travel.

The sainted Augustine (345–430 CE) proclaimed that Jewish misery confirmed the truth of the Gospel: 'They groan in grief over their lost kingdom and quake in fear under the sway of innumerable Christian peoples.' Miserable Jews furnish other people's truths, their tears Gentile smiles. Once the keys of the kingdom were in its safekeeping, the Papacy added worldly majesty to clerical office. While avarice and usury remained Jewish sins, the Church's celestial travel agents offered debenture tickets to paradise for those with the gold to make first-class reservations.

In the early sixteenth century, Martin Luther appealed to Jews to rally to what became Protestantism. Rejected, he pelted them with metaphorical excrement. Luther's anal vocabulary is said to have been due to chronic haemorrhoids, often held to be a characteristic Ashkenazi discomfiture. On both sides of the Christian schism, Jewish refusal to accept Christ's divinity became a crime of which all Hebrews, including the unborn, might be convicted. Happy Jews appear to mock Christianity.

94

The First Crusade, mounted at the end of the eleventh century, can be read as a reaction to the failure of the Messiah to return on the hoped-for millennial date. Renaissance art reassured the faithful about what was to come and garnished their imagination in the interim. A friend of Bernard Berenson is reported to have told the great connoisseur, excitedly, of a dream he had had of the imminent return of Christ in glory. Berenson said, 'Really? In what style?' Crusaders expressed faith and frustration by the ruthlessness of their piety. Muslims and Jews alike were slaughtered. En route home from the Fourth Crusade, the pious Roman Catholics pillaged Constantinople, slaughtered Eastern Christian inhabitants. The modern Arab/Muslim wish to dominate Jerusalem and to rally *bien-pensant* support for its appropriation refigures the crusading spirit.

For almost twenty centuries, Jews never mimicked the rough tactics of other monotheists. Converts to Judaism might be accepted, never solicited. In *The Jews of San Nicandro* (2010), John A. Davis tells of a Catholic veteran of the Great War, Donato Manduzio, a native of the isolated, impoverished Apulian town of Garganico, close to the Adriatic, who becomes convinced, in the 1930s, of the fundamental truth of Judaism. Whatever Christians or Muslims might say, their deviations from Judaism could not deny its primacy without undermining their own claims to veracity. Judaism, Manduzio insisted, could be true without them; Judaism denied, Christianity had no base. Much the same argument is said by Yehuda Halevi, in *The Kuzari*, written in the twelfth century CE, to have persuaded the ninth- or tenth-century Khazars, a Turkic tribe in the Caucasus, to convert to Judaism rather than to either of the other two, derivative, monotheisms.

Arthur Koestler's fanciful *The Thirteenth Tribe* (1976) claims that the Ashkenazi Jews were, in large part, descended from the Khazars, who lost their independence in the tenth century. Hence many Eastern European Jews were not 'Semites' at all. Jewish noses, Koestler claimed to show, complete with diagrams, are not exclusively Jewish. This theory has been embraced as an opportune argument against the notion that Jews have any 'right' to territory in the Middle East.

Manduzio's naïve logic had persuasive force among parishioners in Garganico. Having no contact with Jews, he relied on the Old Testament and his own mystic vision. He was eloquent enough to convert more than a few of his fellow-townsmen. While much of Europe was possessed by anti-Semitism, the leader of the 'Jews' of San Nicandro wrote, in innocent ignorance, to the chief rabbi of Italy seeking instruction on how to, so to say, become kosher. The chief rabbi warned of the difficulties of conversion, but was persuaded to send a deputy to assist, if he failed to deter, the unlikely postulants.

San Nicandro was too remote to be of interest to the Germans and Italian fascists who deported and killed more easily identifiable victims. Towards the end of the war, a small detachment of Germans happened to retreat via Garganico. Two SS officers walked into Manduzio's house, perhaps hoping for wine, and saw him sitting in solemn robes in front of a flag bearing the Star of David. They looked at each other, turned and walked away. In their wake, San Nicandro was liberated by the one division of the British Army composed entirely of

Jewish soldiers. The male converts of San Nicandro chose to be circumcised in 1946.

Jews have, in general, sought and fought, sometimes, to recover only what was once theirs, not least treasures pillaged by the Nazis and their accomplices. Stolen works of art have been wrested, even from national collections, such as that in Vienna, only after prolonged litigation. The Swiss denied the children of Holocaust victims access to their parents' or relatives' fortunes, deposited in bank accounts before the war, unless they could produce the precise encoded numbers needed to spring their safes. Since almost none of the survivors were likely to have any idea what digits to press, the bankers felt entitled, if not obliged, to hang onto the treasure. Prolonged litigation preceded restitution. Determination to retrieve what belonged to them served to confirm that Jews could think of nothing but money, not least when it was their own. In line with Calvinist determinism, one Swiss banker said, 'I do not affect to judge what is right or wrong. Either one's papers are in order or they are not. Mine are.'

95

In July 1263, the learned Rabbi Nachmanides (Moses ben Nachman) was coerced into taking part, in Barcelona, in a disputation with the Dominican friars Pablo Christiani and Petrus Alfonsi. He was warned by King Jaime I of Aragon, his patron and medical patient, that he might defend Judaism, but must not cast doubt on the veracity of Christianity. A winning point sharp enough to disconcert the faithful would cost him his life. The conditions protected the inquisitors, and the Holy Office, from the embarrassing possibility that the conversos Christiani and Alfonsi would be tripped into offering the smallest public hint that they had been mistaken when they abandoned their ancestral religion. The Jew latent in the converts heated their ardour to prove their Catholic *bona fides*. The notion of faith denies and implies the possibility of doubt. In Christian polemics, only a fixed fight could be relied on to be fair.

Although the disputation was adjourned *sine die*, Nachmanides' impenitent defence left him in mortal danger. Jaime I smuggled him away before the Dominicans could lay hands on him. The same monastic order would save a good many when Jews were being rounded up in Nazi-occupied Italy. Its brethren also assisted the flight of persecuted Nazis such as Adolf Eichmann from Europe to South America.

Nachmanides, for all his scholarship, was disposed to an

emollient form of Judaism as against that of Maimonides, who accommodated aspects of Aristotle in his metaphysical scheme but could be outspoken in militant contempt for Christians. The first book printed in Lisbon, in 1489, was a copy of Nachmanides' commentary on the Torah. In early 2023, the female leader of the Catalan government in Barcelona branded Israel an apartheid state and severed their city's twinning with Tel Aviv.

While Jews were, for centuries, forced to live in shunned seclusion, except when their expertise (often medical, always housebound) might be useful, the Jewishness of Jesus Christ remained an indelible, if regretted, element of his personality. Palestinian sympathisers have sought, as Nazis did, to de-Judaise the Galilean and so excuse him from ever belonging to the anathematised sect. Claude Lévi-Strauss had it that the construction of irreconcilable opposites braces ethical and ethnic grammar.

In the Middle Ages, while Jews continued to practise and preach in unassuming places of prayer, like the synagogue in Cordoba, where Maimonides prayed in a side-street lined with orange trees, their sacred books were scorned as a travesty of Truth, Kabbalah a devilish rigmarole. St Louis, King Louis IX of France (1214–70), had all available copies of the Talmud burnt in the streets of Paris. When any religion, endorsed by the civil power, claims a monopoly of the Truth, executioner and incinerator are soon in business. Purgative and punitive use of fire runs through Christian iconography. Louis IX's sainthood derived not only from pious persecution of Jews but also from his sponsorship of Notre Dame cathedral as the central symbol of French piety. The accidental burning of much of that (not entirely) ancient structure, in Easter week 2019, was passed over in tactful ecclesiastic silence. No sceptic was heard to ask what purpose God might have in so signal a conflagration on such an exemplary date.

As dramatist, George Bernard Shaw had the Earl of Warwick, one of the English prosecutors who attended the burning of Joan of Arc, reel onto the stage afterwards in shocked revulsion. This did not inhibit Shaw from asserting, elsewhere, that the state had the right to decide who might live within its boundaries, and who die. Ascribing quasi-physical pains to states, along with their surgical alleviants, has been a temptation for philosophers left and right. Even the excellent Roger Scruton presumed to play medic for the body politic, a category mistake in my view, which he had the grace to take seriously.

Heinrich Himmler is said to have blenched when visiting one of the Third Reich's death factories. He is reported to have hoped to save a beautiful, naked eighteen-year-old blonde (Aryan-looking) Jewess from the consequences of Nazi ideology. When she scorned to deny her blood, brute logic left the Reichsführer SS without decent recourse. Her last recorded words were 'Remember me'. Caroline Lamb scrawled the same to Byron and had better luck with it. The idolisation of Che Guevara has been blemished, in some eyes at least, by the story that he went out of his way to attend and relish the execution of alleged enemies of the Cuban revolution.

Josef Mengele's role in 'selections' suggests that mastery of death is the medical man's finest hope and also, in some cases, his darkest dream. Dr Harold Shipman is evidence that mass murder can take place even under the aegis of the National Health Service. Veneration of the NHS as the means of resurrection this side of the grave is liable to credit successful treatment to ideological bureaucrats rather than to medical expertise. Socialism is graced with redemptive competence akin to that of Christianity. Doris Lessing once told me how the NHS had saved her daughter's life, thus implying that institutional 'socialism', rather than the medical profession, had been cardinal in her survival. Mrs Lessing not only won the Nobel Prize, for literature, but also (she was of Iranian extraction) reverted, after a long ideological detour, to Sufism, a form of Islamic mysticism. Our daughter Sarah died after being incompetently diagnosed and treated in an NHS hospital. Nothing contingent can prove anything necessary.

96

The move to detach the Gospel from the Torah accompanied the urge to substitute Greek philosophy for Hebrew piety and poetry. Until neo-Platonism took over from him, Aristotle was the primary source of Greek ideas selected for injection into Christian doctrine. These included the notion that the sun went around the earth. In the third century BCE, Aristarchus of Samos had already suggested the reverse, perhaps for fun, an underestimated ingredient of intellectual speculation. Simone Weil, apostate Jew, venerated by some for her otherworldliness (General de Gaulle, not among them, labelled her 'folle'), proposed to amputate the Old Testament *in toto* and to replace it with the works of Plato. Maimonides preferred Aristotle, whose ideas he attempted, in *A Guide for the Perplexed*, to harmonise with the Torah.

Freud hybridised psychoanalysis by dignifying it with classical Greek references, Oedipus as universal. His desk was fortified with classical antiquities; so too were the conversations of Marcel Proust's alter ego Bloch and James Joyce's *Ulysses* with pseudo-Homeric locutions. Passages of ancient literature have been subjected to party-lining by Christian scholars. Virgil's 'messianic' verses in his fourth *Eclogue* – about the birth of Marcellus, an ill-starred, short-lived prospective heir to Augustus' empire – were declared prophetic of the Saviour. Thanks to his alleged clairvoyance, the pagan poet was conscripted to play Dante's guide to the *Inferno*.

In Roman Catholic liturgy, the Jews continued, until Vatican II (1962–5), to be denounced as perfidious deicides. The historical species lived in ghettos (Shylock's Venice among the more spacious) with meagre access to air, light or green spaces. The ghetto adjacent to the Vatican was gated, and locked at night, until after 1945. In *Les Décombres*, published in Paris in 1942, Lucien Rebatet gloats over the last Jew dying in a cage, in the mid-twenty-first century, in a Paris zoo. In similar vindictive spirit, Maurice Barrès, egotist and dandy who drifted, with stylish appetite, into reactionary company, gloated at the sight of the falsely condemned Alfred Dreyfus 'alone in the universe'.

Some of the finest pages in Vassily Grossman's masterpiece *Life and Fate* take the form of a letter from his doctor mother to the narrator, Viktor Shtrum. She has just been deported by the Germans to the pinched Berdichev ghetto, which is, she must have guessed, as good as an annex to the abattoir. Perhaps because she is writing to her son, who is with Russian forces at Stalingrad, she observes that she feels more truly herself in misfortune than she was as an emancipated, quasi-assimilated practitioner. Copies of Grossman's novel, the huge 1960 sequel to his *Stalingrad* (1952), only just evaded the vigilant malice of the Soviet authorities. Like the Church when it came to Aristotle's *On Comedy*, they did all they could to efface it from the record. *Stalingrad* was first entitled *For a Just Cause*, which helped it survive the Stalinist censors.

Grossman was a journalist with first-hand experience of wartime brutalities. Another fine passage in *Life and Fate* imagines Hitler walking alone in the forest near the Wolf's Lair, in East Prussia, after the surrender of Field Marshal von Paulus and his army at Stalingrad. Hitler lurches as if incipient Parkinson's disease were the evidence that his war was lost. Great writers can render historical figures in fiction so convincing that it seems to add to our knowledge of what they were 'really like'. Grossman trumps Tolstoy in this regard. It was his misfortune never to know that his masterpiece had been published and recognised as a *ktema es aei*. Measured against Grossman, Pasternak's *Doctor Zhivago* is middlebrow narcissism.

97

Escape from communal ignominy through exceptional expertise offered an early incentive to Jews, in Muslim and Christian societies, to emulate Galen's therapeutic profession. A primer of benign neutrality with small reference to the gods, more of the Pergamene's medical texts survive than of the works of any other ancient writer. While Jewish alchemy was rumoured to poison wells, Jewish doctors – with presumed access to arcane arts – were often summoned to prescribe for sultans, kings and queens, Elizabeth I of England among them. Rewards depended on results. Success must have owed at least as much to bedside charisma as to arcane 'science' and had its unreliable rewards. Failure prompted accusations of diabolical malpractice.

In the early 1950s, Stalin, ex-seminarian, brought that charge against the Jewish doctors convoked, as a last resort, to save the dying tyrant. Medicine was a perilous prescription for preferment, but – as Moses Maimonides proved, when in service to Muslim rulers – a more reliable lifesaver than observant faith or lyric genius. In the twelfth century CE, the poet Yehuda Halevi sought salvation by quitting Spain for Jerusalem. Soon after arriving, he was killed by an Arab horseman while praying at the Wailing Wall. The earliest European medical school, in Salerno, south of Naples, is said to have been founded, in the ninth century CE, by a Jew, a Christian and a Muslim.

Medicine presumes mankind to have a common anatomy. Hippocrates of Cos, like Galen, made no distinction between Greek and barbarian; living on the fringes of Hellas, both healers were familiar with all sorts and conditions of men. Despite links with necromancy, pharmacology was clean of social, tribal or mystical preconceptions. Medicine continues to flaunt Greek terminology in prescriptions which flirt with Kabbalistic cryptography. If a patient can tell what exactly he or she is taking, practitioners tend to think, it will do less good than illegible mystification.

When our friend Paddy Dickson became the British doctor in Bangkok after graduating from 'Tommy's' (St Thomas' Hospital in London) in the 1950s, he had to pass the necessary written tests in the Thai language. No prescription is necessary in Thailand for drugs which will not otherwise be sold by proper English pharmacists. The fear that people will kill or harm themselves with overdoses is, Paddy promised us, greatly exaggerated. He suspects it to be maintained to enhance the abracadabra monopoly of the medical profession. Once he began to practise medicine in Bangkok, Paddy advised an early patient, who had mumps, to go home, rest, take regular aspirin and wait till the swelling went down. He was dismayed to hear that his prescription had been derided as ignorant. The sufferer said that everyone knew that aspirin was not enough; one had also to draw a lipstick dragon on the swollen glands. After Paddy conformed with local lore, he enjoyed a promptly elevated and lasting reputation.

The growth of science and philosophy during the Enlightenment seemed to rupture factitious boundaries. While Leibniz treated Spinoza as an equal, he continued to describe him as 'the Jew', despite claiming that we lived in 'the best of all possible worlds'. Might it be that this phrase defines the limits of possibility rather than asserting human residence on the apex of any imaginable terrestrial perfection? Leibniz was less silly-clever than Voltaire supposed. If the world cannot be other than it is, then it must, by definition, be the best of all possible worlds; yes, and the worst. Jews remain Jews.

In *Candide*, Voltaire's Pangloss was a caricature of Leibniz. Philosophers, like oracles, give rise to a suite of exegetes who explain to the laity what such and such a pronouncement was really intended to convey. There is comedy in the urge of interpreters to expound what is claimed to be manifestly established in contrary readings. Quarrels between philosophers – Voltaire with Rousseau, Schopenhauer with Hegel, Ayer with Sartre, Sartre with Camus and Merleau-Ponty – are notorious for their vehemence. All insist on being engaged in a dispassionate search for truth.

The comedy is enhanced by philosophers' advertised reluctance to use or be intimidated by the first-person singular. Statements prefaced with 'I believe' or 'I think' are deprecated as 'mere autobiography'. Publicly condoned conceits stand in for personality. *Candide* made memorable fun of Leibniz, but failed to honour that philosopher's own possible levity in endorsing a worldview much like unsmiling Spinoza's. Ruthlessness is the offspring of doctrines which edify human malice and promise 'inevitable', because logically pre-determined, success. It is then wished onto the divinity or History and by that means grafted onto a source other than vindictive sadism. The ancient Athenian slaughterer of sacrificial animals jettisoned the bloody axe into the sea; the blade was the killer, not he.

For the outsider, power and fame are often to be attained only by exceptional wit, as Disraeli proved. Jealousy and envy were *pursuivant* to his ascent of the 'greasy pole' of political success. Jewish altruism is assumed to be self-serving; versatility is badged with ostentation. The assassination, in 1922, of

Walther Rathenau, Germany's pre-eminent technocrat and – like Joseph Süß – a public servant of foresight and intelligence, was a trailer for the mechanised massacres of twenty years later. Fervent German patriot during the Great War, Rathenau had wide administrative responsibilities, not unlike those of Albert Speer in the Second World War, if never as sweeping as those conferred by the Führer. Speer was a first-rate second-rater, nicely spoken, well-dressed and as plausibly apologetic after the event as he had been ruthless as a slave-driver when empowered. Earnest assimilationist, Rathenau deplored Jews who stood out by wearing 'Eastern' clothes. He was referred to, in his lifetime, as 'the prophet in a tail-coat' by the English and as *le Christ en frac* by the French. Speer played the misguided gentleman technocrat and so duped his gentleman judges, as loutish Julius Streicher had no hope of doing.

At Cambridge, in 1954, one of the secretaries of the University Appointments Board filed an undergraduate acquaintance of mine, who had sought his salaried advice in finding post-graduation employment, under the rubric 'looks Jewy, wears Jewy-cut clothes'. The Eternal Return takes many forms, among them the *fascisant* Mircea Eliade's post-war affectations of humanism. His compatriot E. M. Cioran, another pre-war fascist, became a Parisian companion of Piotr Rawicz, a Holocaust survivor and author of *Blood from the Sky*, written in French, his sixth language. Cioran's self-redeeming aphorisms were composed in an Augustan version of the same language and beau-tied imposture. Even toffs are known to imitate toffs, Lord Curzon not least.

98

The recrudescence of populist anti-Semitism, sponsored by elements in the left playing for Muslim votes, has rendered British Jews seriously uneasy for the first time since Edward I expelled them as usurers in the late thirteenth century. To replenish the royal treasury, he then racked their debtors for what had been owed to Jews. Survival without homeland or entitlement enhanced the myth of the Eternal Jew who, until the Saviour chose to return and absolve him, was sentenced to undying vagrancy. The Wanderer was last spotted, it is said, in Salt Lake City, Utah in the second half of the nineteenth century. The mendicant acquired the allure of an immortal archetype, victimised and preserved, if never cherished, by God. His redemption came to be held, by some doctrinaire Christians, as a necessary preliminary to general salvation.

Quakers in particular took a friendly view of Jews; they visualised America as the new Zion from which the Chosen should not be excluded. For that calm reason, the first Dutch governor of New York, Pietrus Stuyvesant, was unsuccessful in blocking the admission of Jews as equal citizens. In the late nineteenth century, millions looked west for salvation from Catholic and Orthodox persecution. America's Wasp society was exclusive, seldom murderous. Lynching, literal or judicial, was reserved for Blacks and a few Reds (Sacco and Vanzetti, for notorious judicial instance, in 1927). Until the 1960s, unregistered numbers of Blacks continued to be lynched in the old South. Fiery crosses still burn from time to time, a matter only for state police, who seldom make an arrest. A bill to make lynching a federal crime still awaits endorsement by the House of Representatives and a president's signature.

Jewish writers, songwriters in particular, were prominent in protesting against the maltreatment of, as they used to say, Negroes, or, as polite cant then put it, Colored People. The composer of Billie Holliday's signature song *Strange Fruit* was Abel Meeropol, a Jewish communist. In the immigrant mill, Jews had to grind twice as hard to get half as far until admitted to citizenship and, in the very long run, something like equality in a republic whose founding fathers, despite their tolerance (and, in some cases, practice) of slavery, were Augustan deists, enlightened enough to be sceptical about any single religion's claim to transcendental and exclusive superiority.

The melting-pot image lent uneasy credence to the eventual common citizenship of all immigrants, whenever they arrived, wherever from. Most Democrats and Republicans seemed, for a long time, to have contentious, but more or less harmonious, notions of public service and purpose. Honour and justice, God and the dollar shared billing. Single-issue politics and quasi-religious organisations, such as Scientology and the Nation of Islam, with opportunist tax-exempt advantages, came to foster antagonisms with no off-season. The irrational is a great fundraiser.

Coercive special-pleading and blatant crackpottery are eroding what Walter Lippmann called 'the public philosophy'. In the 1930s, he and H. L. Mencken (Doctor Johnson's match as lexicographer) argued in literate, uncondescending, often acerbic English. Their common tongue has given way to television commentators' clichés and a vocabulary drawn from the lowest common denominators. Until the 1960s, minority concerns were relegated to a remote page. Lippmann was an admirable stylist with a similarity to Karl Kraus; however Jewish, he wrote as if he wasn't. Who can say what bundled motives led him to appropriate, love, parade the wife of a close Gentile friend? During the war, in his role as the magisterial columnist of the *New York Herald Tribune*, Lippmann scarcely alluded to what was not yet called the Holocaust. The owners of the paper, although and because they were Jews, were careful not to make waves. Disraeli had promised that, admitted to citizenship, Jews would become ardent conservatives.

In England, baby-faced ex-journalist Michael Gove and Boris Johnson, the Golden Golly, and other Brexiteers with unfathomable, never-unguessable motives, ridiculed rational experts, since they were sometimes mistaken. They preferred insular vanities, opinions held infallible, thanks to falsified statistics, unkeepable promises, bogus egalitarianism. Paul Valéry held that a civilisation should be judged by the wealth of contradictions it embraced. Nigel Farage and his beery kind have no tolerance for anything but insular self-importance. Farage's scurry to grovel to President Trump announced money-lingus as a prompt adjunct to Great British patriotic bombast. Hypocrisy ain't what it used to be.

99

Anti-Semitism can be a furnisher of common ground for niceish people. I recall an occasion on the island of Lemnos, where the ancient female inhabitants, having murdered their husbands, became prophylactically smelly. Having flown in on a late plane, we were met by the resort-hotel's minibus for the longish drive across the flat island where Philoktetes was once marooned. Two British couples in the bus with us exchanged civilities. We stayed modestly mute. We were too late for the full dinner at the resort. One corner of the wide dining room was lit, three tables for two in a row. The other couples pursued their mundane conversations while we ate cold mezes.

Suddenly I was alert to one of them, a tweedy person, referring to 'four-by-twos, if you know what that means'. The other man knew very well, and so did I; it was, of course, rhyming slang for 'Jews'. The grey speaker was, as they used to say, well-spoken. Beetle had not heard the remark. I had a strong urge to challenge the chap; he didn't look all that muscular. What would happen if I tipped the contents of his small table onto his lap? It was the first evening of our holiday. If I made a scene, we should be in a sour situation for two weeks. I pretended not to have heard and shall be forever ashamed of my decorum. Next day, we were greeted, on the beach, with conspicuous courtesy, by the same gent. That afternoon I spoke to our friend John Summerskill, head of the American school in Athens. Asked how he was, he said, '*Etsi, ketsi.*' So, so. He was dying.

100

Philip Roth considered the British the most anti-Semitic people he had known. Anthony Rudolf suspects that Roth, like R. B. Kitaj, discounted the anti-Americanism which fostered the defensive-aggressive style of post-imperial British intellectuals. The upper-class Gentile wife of a Jewish friend of ours told us recently how shocked she had been by other people's reactions to her impending marriage. John Murray Cuddihy's book *The Ordeal of Civility* (1974) makes mordant play with the difficulties which four-by-twos are said to have in conforming to the niceties of Christian society. The implication is that it is for them to abate ostracism by aping civilised behaviour. Christianity remains the measure against which all others are to be ruled. In unwanted fact, Jewish literacy has always been far above the average. Reading, from the Torah, and accession to manhood went together; killing, soon a Christian specialty, not.

Presumptions of cowardice persisted despite statistical evidence of the numbers of Jews who fought, for the Central Powers or the Allies, in the Great War. It remains true that in previous years a good number of Jews who lived in the Russian Pale of Settlement procured exemption from prolonged military service by having their trigger-fingers amputated. This digital circumcision had little to do with yellow-streakiness, more with parents' concern to save young men from up to twenty years of conscripted service in loutish company.

I had a Great-Uncle Mauser who died fighting for the Kaiser, in 1917, and a twenty-two-year-old second cousin, Irvin Weintraub, a lieutenant in the USAAF, who was taken prisoner and murdered, along with his crew and uniformed passengers, by the SS outside Arnhem in 1944. This says nothing singular about Jewish mutability. In the Middle East, the Druze, a Muslim sect, are loyal to whatever country, including Israel, a particular community resides in. Alone of Arabs, they serve loyally in the Israel Defense Forces.

That Jews could be found in any number of countries, speaking a variety of languages, including their own lively German dialect, Yiddish, rendered versatility suspect. Despite usefulness as cross-border negotiators, polyglots are liable to be regarded as too clever by half. Linguistic facility seems to supply something like a second home, Stanislavski's term for the theatre. The common British way of making oneself understandable to foreigners is to speak English in a raised voice with demanding spaces between words, sometimes with a patronising alien accent.

Like Proteus, first on the scene, and as even Adolf Eichmann conceded in a spasm of rueful candour, the Jew was always the same, always mutable: when himself a *pauvre type*, in polite disguise an adroit pretender, in neither case authentic. Otto Weininger (1880–1903) conceded that Jews were incapable of original work, an idea all but seconded by Wittgenstein, who counted Weininger, another Viennese Semite, as the rare case of a writer both misguided and worth reading. Towards the end of a shortened life, abbreviated by shooting himself, Weininger converted to Protestantism. Carlo Michelstaedter (1887–1910) also committed suicide, in Trieste, after composing his terse masterpiece *Persuasion and Rhetoric*. J. Robert Oppenheimer, if never the equal of Byron's friend Cardinal

Mezzofanti, was fluent in many tongues. Since an interpreter was often alone in understanding both sides in cross-lingual negotiations, how could anyone be sure that he rendered a proper account of what was being said by either? *Traduttore, traditore* (translator/traitor); those with versatile tongues were taken to lack the intractable integrity of the monoglot.

101

The 63,000 or more Jews who, until 1943, lived in the northern Greek port of Thessaloniki were of Sephardic origin. They spoke Ladino, the Hispanic dialect brought with them after the Jews were expelled from Spain by the Catholic kings. Spanish scholars visiting Thessaloniki in the twentieth century were amazed to find Ladino an unspoiled, sixteenth-century form of Spanish purer than the Castilian of modern Spain. It is said that Argentines now speak the most correct Spanish. French-speaking Canadians still use phrases now obsolete in France, for instance, *barrer la porte* for locking the door. When did the English start saying 'Hi' for 'Hullo'?

The Greek Sephardim were all deported to Auschwitz. Primo Levi was witness to their solidarity, expressed not least in their singing. Such unison was less common among Ashkenazim. Today's Thessaloniki carries little sign of that once-busy Jewish community. The centre of the old Jewish quarter is paved over by a large square named after Aristotle. Vassilis Vassilikos, author of Z, wrote a long short story about the deserted Jewish quarter. It is one of the rare post-war literary mentions of the deportation of Greek Jews. Their few descendants supply a target for the right-wing Golden Dawn political party. Vassilikos, who died in 2018, was vehemently hostile to Israel. As Greeks say, often, with a shrug,

Ti na kánoume (What can we do?). Alfred Dreyfus's Alsatian background made him more a patriotic Frenchman than his fellow-officers and, by the same token, less like them. After the cession, in 1871, of Alsace and Lorraine to the victorious Prussians, traumatised Alsatians became especially fervent Gallic irredentists. Nevertheless, when a traitor was needed to explain how French military secrets had found their way to the German embassy in 1894, a bilingual Jewish artillery officer was ideal casting, his 'race' proof enough. Gunners might be ubiquitous and indispensable, but, since they fought at a distance, never quite gentlemen. The Jew's *a priori* guilt guaranteed the truth of lies uttered by Christians; Dreyfus had to be lying, especially when what he swore was true.

The foregone conclusion of his court martial was greeted with cheers and jeers. Parisians relished the public breaking of his officer's sword across a sergeant-major's knee (it had been snapped ahead of time and stuck together to avoid an ill-omened technical hitch). While Dreyfus was shipped to Devil's Island, the death-trap penal colony off the coast of French Guiana, Catholic apologists, literary luminaries and low journalists supplied a torrent of righteous glee. Édouard Drumont's depiction of sinister Jewish power took fresh root in French folklore, gutters and drawing rooms. Drumont is said to have been unbalanced. If so, the direction in which he tilted was signposted, in capital letters, by easy-to-follow Christian prejudice. The accumulation of undeniable evidence that Dreyfus was innocent – as more than a few had guessed, including the governor of the Parisian prison into which he was first pitched – put an end to his five-year calvary, literally in chains.

Emile Zola's article, in Georges Clemenceau's newspaper, headlined 'J'ACCUSE', pointed an unwavering accusatory finger. Zola's reward for vindicating an innocent man was to be hounded into exile in London. Voltaire too had spent fugitive time there. Once prejudice ceased to play detective, the actual traitor, Ferdinand Walsin Esterhazy, was revealed beyond any plausible doubt. He had needed the money. Reinstated as a French officer, Dreyfus was never formally acquitted. In the Great War, he rose to the rank of colonel. Not a few of those who deplored his pardon viewed his innocence as unforgivable.

French examining magistrates, like many policemen, are disposed to lend credence to what they call *intime conviction*, an intuitive sense of who is guilty in a given case. The prime suspect is then liable to provoke prosecutors into selecting and composing facts into a pattern which validates their 'instinct'. In the case of '*le petit Grégory*', an infant who disappeared in the *arrière pays* of the Jura in the early 1980s, the child's mother came under early suspicion. Marguerite Duras, famous as François Mitterrand's one-time mistress and author of *Hiroshima Mon Amour*, wrote a long pamphlet in which she declared her *intime conviction* that Grégory's mother was a murderess. It was later proved that the child was killed by a distant relative. Duras never recanted and was never held to account.

102

Bernard Malamud's 1966 novel *The Fixer* is based, rather too obviously, on a case in 1913 Russia when, through malign 'intuition', Menahem Mendel Beilis was accused of the murder of a child said to have been killed for ritual purposes. That no such ritual has ever been shown to have any part in Jewish life has done nothing to inhibit repeated allegations of the same order. After Beilis's indictment had caused outrage in then-civilised Europe, he was acquitted by a brave jury. He was then forced to flee Ukraine for fear of a lynch mob of the Black Hundreds, first to Palestine and then to the US. The pogroms of 1918 onwards remained under cover until Jeffrey Veidlinger's *In the Midst of Civilised Europe* (2021), a calm account of the nascent Soviet Union's 'rehearsal of the Holocaust'. In 1952, Stalin executed a platoon of previously honour-laden Yiddish writers, guileless David Bergelson among them. Little indignation was audible among fellow-travellers who still held the USSR a blueprint for human redemption. Khrushchev's invasion of Hungary in 1956 opened some eyes, never John Berger's.

In *Darkness At Noon*, Rubashov is never described as a Jew, but bears a common Jewish name. Perhaps to allay charges of special-pleading, Arthur Koestler depicts him as an Old Bolshevik of the order that Stalin was ruthless in purging and who often had Jewish origins. The same is now declared vestigially true of Lenin, whose great-grandmother converted to Christianity. Stalin determined that Lenin's Semitic streak be consigned to secrecy. Although Koestler never specifies the USSR, Rubashov is a manifest victim of the Great Terror of the 1930s. Culpably innocent, he is led to confess by a sly interrogator, not – as would probably have been the case in Russia – by physical torture and lethal threats to his family.

Rubashov acquiesces in the Party's need for a guilty man whose treachery will explain communism's failure to accelerate the inevitable paradise. He can confirm his loyalty to the Party only by the confession that he has betrayed it. He is persuaded that it is a far, far better thing to agree to be a traitor than he ever could do by obstinately insisting on his selfish innocence. Kenneth Burke, author of the magisterial *Grammar of Motives*, argued elsewhere, with brilliant, perverse ingenuity, for Rubashov's 'objective' guilt. He did not draw an analogy with Dreyfus. The logic of *raison d'état* and the scapegoat mechanism apply in both cases.

Stalinism required that his version of Marxist-Leninism could never be wrong; hence any flaw in the system had to be the fault of 'wreckers', drawn from the usual suspects. The essential characteristic of the scapegoat is that it/he/she can be loaded with all manner of malign purposes and ambitions, diabolical powers and quasi-ubiquity. Once haul-marked, they deserve suspicion and prophylactic confinement, in the ghetto and in the female quarters, such as the shuttered upper rooms of the Court of the Lions in the Alhambra in Granada, the windowless seclusion imposed by the Taliban in today's Afghanistan. They are then in no position to do any harm to the gaolers and persecutors whose malice leads them to dread the night-flying malice of their victims. *Nykti-plangtos*, night-flying, is part of the longest word, composed by Aristophanes, cited in the *Lexicon* of ancient Greek. The rise of the domain of 'invisibles', in international banking and finance, engenders the dread of devious schemers, always male, usually bearded, of the kind that give figures of small intelligence and wide fame, Kanye West or Jeremy Corbyn, a target against which the witless can pose as crusaders, a category to which Arabophiles now annex Israelis.

103

John XXIII, pope from 1958 till 1963, held out a leftish hand to the Jews. His announcement 'I am your younger brother Joseph' lost him the allegiance of an unsmiling segment of the faithful. The loudest reactionaries against Vatican II were led, in France, by Monseigneur Lefebvre, who defied John XXIII and persisted in celebrating Mass only in Latin. He and his followers adopted the pose of truculent martyrs for the true faith betrayed by pragmatic liberalism. They included reborn schismatics united in virtuous anti-Semitism, who took the late Charles Maurras as their paragon (despite his excommunication in 1926).

The callous comedy of centuries of Christian vindictiveness lies in the possibility that the Church feared that 'the Jews' were right, from the beginning, in their scepticism about the divinity of Jesus Christ. The appended virginity of his mother Mary derived from mistranslation of the demotic Greek *parthenos* (marriageable virgin), which was further consecrated by the doctrine of the Immaculate Conception.

The Inquisition wanted to punish Jews not for their errors, but for refusing to allow themselves to be wrong, thus infringing a Christian conceit. Except in extreme schools, Judaism never embargoed theorising about the origin and composition of the physical world. Speculative ingenuity and mathematics,

pure and applied, enjoyed a field free of the *a priori* considerations which inhibited Catholics from innovative liberties.
The visual arts served to advertise Christianity, not least to
the illiterate. Imagery was rarely representational in Jewish
premises, for fear of blasphemy by the reproduction, however
inadvertent, of the features of the Holy One. There is modest,
faded impersonal decoration on the wall of Maimonides' synagogue in Cordoba.

Hatred of Alfred Dreyfus was most principled, in a
Christian sense, when expressed by those who insisted that it
would have been more patriotic for him to have been guilty:
neither the army nor the Church would then have been held up
to derision or accused of perjury. It was argued that the subsequent breach between Church, army and the Republic left
France disunited when the Boches made their move. *Cherchez
le Juif* goes back at least as far as the Black Death: that the
Jews had poisoned the wells served to explain why a loving
God allowed widespread suffering among faithful Christians.
Having granted man free will, He was powerless against wilful
malice.

If the Jews were not guilty, Christians were left with a
God indifferent to their mundane misfortunes. This led to the
Church's enhanced advertisements for heaven, then the claim
to papal infallibility. Gilded and palatial counter-Reformation
cathedrals and episcopal palaces promised that the Church
enjoyed divine favour. Their murals offered a prospectus of
celestial mansions reserved for those generous with pious
endowments. The image of despoiled synagogues is a frequent
feature of ecclesiastic ornamentation. An instance can be seen
on the lintel of the neat twelfth-century church at Moissac in
Occitanie, south-western France.

104

Thomas Babington Macaulay's speech in favour of Jewish emancipation, in the House of Commons in 1833, was the first to seek to break the mould in which Christian nations had compressed 'the Jew', as the men of Württemberg had Joseph Süß. T. S. Eliot took time out from his *mandarin superbe* to denounce Macaulay (never alluding to this speech in particular) as a man whose style was 'corrupted' by journalism. Did Eliot ever say as much about Charles Maurras, whose addiction to print was served by the newspaper which he edited as *primus inter impares*? Eliot's distaste for 'free-thinking' Jews seconded Maurras, who especially vilified assimilated, hence unidentifiable, Jews, and presages the recent Christian activism, cited by Adam Gregerman, which 'reduces the complex message of the Bible to a simple dichotomy: "Strong Israelites are sinful and merit only divine rebuke, but weak and stateless Israelites are beloved of God." [Hence,] "Only powerless and weak Diaspora Jews are faithful to their religious and moral traditions."'

As Mark Caine declared, in *The S-Man* (1960), 'Success and money are more or less synonymous.' The existence of the state of Israel stands, in the logic of Christianity (and of Islam), as a challenge to the truth of what is said to have replaced 'the Jews' in the eyes of the Almighty. Jewish success in this world offers a direct threat alike to Christian and to meta-Christian, *marxisant* ordinance. Eliot had pious fun mocking the humiliation of the Jew with small risk of a punch in the nose, my father's practical response as a six-year-old boarding-school boy. 'Tom' both admired the poetry of Isaac Rosenberg, who died in the trenches in the Great War, and also stood up for the genius of Ezra Pound, his Master. The wily referee does favours to both sides.

In *Europe's Inner Demons* (1975), Norman Cohn established, unsurprisingly, that there was no trace of evidence that Jews did not perish, like any Christian, from the plague or that they had anything to do with its deliberate spread. Cohn also shows how the Church's other victims of choice, the female sex, were accused of being witches and mistresses of dark arts. Following the Armistice of 1918, while not denying the principle of female suffrage, French socialist politicians were apprehensive of women voters. Females were liable, if not prone, to take advice from their priests. A theoretically progressive measure was likely to increase the reactionary vote.

The Mary/Mary division of the female sex into virgin innocents and whorish wantons chimes with a programme whereby a deprived constituency, liable to threaten established power, is subjected to a triage that privileges one segment, humiliates another. By virtue of specialised skills, a chosen few of the Tsar's Jewish subjects enjoyed freedom of movement denied those confined to the Russia's Pale of Settlement. Jewish doctors and musicians could be relieved of anathema; so too mandarin cricketers and jewelled Indian princes under the British Raj. In Europe, 'The king's Jews' were similarly favoured. The proviso was that they should make their masters either rich or healthy. An Israeli Nobel Prize-winning economist was told by some British pundit, 'I don't usually like Jews, but I like you.' The

Israeli replied, 'I usually like Englishmen, but I don't like you.' What diaspora Jew would ever have uttered such a retort? Some shameless Archimedes might say that it justified the existence of Israel.

105

The Thirty Years' War between Roman Catholics and Lutheran Protestants was settled, in 1648, by the Treaty of Westphalia; under the rubric *Cuius regio, eius religio*; the religion of the local prince alone determined the style of his subjects' devotions. This pragmatic measure abated bloodshed; did it not also sully the majesty of a divinity with so malleable a disposition? Tolerance fillets faith. Philosophy quizzed theology itself, with whatever voluminous caution. René Descartes (1596–1650) was both innovative and wary of ecclesiastical venom. Civil conflict between the two main strands of Christianity continued to divide Germany, not only during Bismarck's anti-Roman Catholic *Kulturkampf*, but on into the ideological mishmash of Weimar. It was formally resolved in 1930, when Papal Legate Eugenio Pacelli, later Pope Pius XII, sealed a concordat with the Nazis. In return for his Church's immunity from direct hostility, Pacelli lifted Vatican support from the Catholic Centre Party. Its respected newspaper might otherwise have expressed dated objections to godless Hitlerism.

Pacelli himself was to become subject to division, in some eyes, into the bad, collaborating pope and, in others, into a pragmatic *capo dei capi* who preserved the Church from direct wreckage by the Nazis. I corresponded for a few years with a Father Geary, who, with patient geniality (he invited me to visit him and his collegiate brothers in Rome), sought to show that Pacelli had saved a precise, unrounded number of over eight hundred thousand Jews. The pope had, I was assured, done everything he possibly could when, in particular, the inhabitants of the Roman ghetto were deported. Why there was a ghetto at all was not discussed.

The Catholic novelist Gabriel Fielding (*né* Alan Barnsley) once told me he loved Jews; nice chap, was there a hint of gotcha in his archangelic tone? Recent publication of previously secret Vatican papers has disclosed the repeated malicious scorn with which Pacelli reported on the Jews in Germany and their repulsive character. I wrote to Father Geary, a fellow-classicist, many times, with courtesy and good humour, and he to me, until I realised that he was, in the nicest possible way, repeating his party line with immutable faith.

Henry Hyndman told Karl Marx that he was growing more tolerant with age. Marx said, 'Are you? Are you?' My late brother-in-law Baron Moss, long-time communist, wore a small smile when listening to earnest arguments for the Open Society. He would say 'uh-huh' and repeat the usual Marxist lines, among which was, in parody of Christian hope, a reminder that we still had a long way to go before we could know exactly how the classless society would operate.

Once, on the chauffeured way to a session of *Any Questions?*, I asked Monsignor Bruce Kent, who later left Holy Orders and married, whether he seriously believed, off the record, that the Virgin Mary ascended bodily into heaven. If so, how did she survive the forty-degrees-below-zero temperatures she would have had to traverse before arrival? 'All I know,' Kent said, 'is that she is with God.' 'Does she have any other embodied company up there?' He smiled a smile of the same patient order as Baron Moss. A naïve question could not expect a serious response. What might it be? The red queen's sentence is the likeliest.

106

Under the Third Reich, Jews became guilty by inspection of their birth certificates and, if male, of their circumcised persons. It was no longer necessary to be proved to have done or believed in anything wrong; they were something wrong. Baptised Catholic, Adolf Hitler was never chided, let alone excommunicated, by the Vatican. Unlike the outspoken archbishop of Toulouse, Pius XII failed to denounce mass murder in so little as an audible whisper. Toulouse was a centre of the Albigensian sect, against which the Catholic Church conducted an exterminatory Crusade in south-western France in the early thirteenth century. The crushing of dissident sects has always been a Christian mission and profitable exercise. Heaps of Mayan literature and sacred items were destroyed in the process of converting the highly developed civilisation of Yucatan to subservience to Spain and its ecclesiastic apparatus. The campaign was as principled as it was merciless. Only one or two priests had a sense of the rare qualities of what the Church was set to destroy. They became historians and, to whatever degree, custodians of the relics of a society their brothers were seeking to extirpate.

The Aztec city of Tenochtitlan, built on many islands, was seen, at first sight, by Cortez and his men as more marvellous than Venice. They then made it their holy business to conquer, pillage and dismantle it. The Aztecs had themselves been merciless conquerors. Their gods were held to demand the regular sacrifice of thousands of human beings, from neighbouring tribes, whose hearts were extracted, still throbbing, from their chests. Their altars were situated on the peak plateaux of tall, steep pyramids. Sacrificial blood flowed down the steps under the feet of imminent victims. Hannah Arendt would, no doubt, have accused them of going like sheep to the slaughter.

The Aztecs had the pitiless grace to spare their victims the notion that it was all their fault. Christianity and its political enforcers have never conceded that their accusatory apparatus might be a justification for eliminating the right to differ and for robbing the dissenter. The only Central Americans exempt from ruthlessness were the Toltecs, whom the Aztecs had evicted and exiled in a quarter remote from the rich lands they had once occupied. The Aztecs never lost apprehensive respect for the Toltecs' antique lore. They sent regular delegations to seek assurance that they were behaving in a way that pleased the gods. The Toltecs never returned the solicited verdict.

107

Scepticism regarding Islam is liable to be equated, in today's English media, with 'racism'. This is more convenient to social appeasement than valid logic: Muslims, of whatever persuasion, genial or otherwise, are not a race. By endorsing 'Faith Schools', with slippery zeal, Tony Blair proved as destructive of England's intellectual integrity as Shirley Williams was of higher education for the socially disadvantaged. By her principled abolition of grammar schools she reduced social mobility. There would, on her officious watch, be no more up-from-the-sticks Doctor Johnsons. She was good enough not to foist her virtue on her (and Bernard Williams's) daughter Becky, who went to a private school.

My father once described Pat Cotter, St Paul's School's very Christian and excellent classics master, as 'almost the nicest man in the world'. Shirley was almost the nicest woman. The last Christmas encyclical that we received from her carried the implication that the existence of Israel alone rendered the world out of joint. When I sighed, loudly, she reminded me that her second professor husband Richard Neustadt was a Jew (and shared a name with a concentration camp). Since she and Dick had stayed with us in France on a couple of occasions, his persuasion did not come as news. Despite all her honours, as Harvard professor not least, was Shirley ever better than upper-second-rate? George Orwell told Evelyn Waugh that belief in Catholicism (and praying for favours from the Little Sisters) was not worthy of a serious person.

Tony Blair claimed to have kept God out of his dialogues with George W. Bush, who was reborn as a Christian after emerging from alcoholism and being elected, perhaps with divine assistance, certainly by sharp practice, as president of the USA. At the time of the second Iraq War, it was not revealed that Blair was taking instruction before entering the Roman Catholic faith. His Faith Schools institutionalised righteous schisms in state-backed education. Should he not have disclosed what honourable members used to call an 'interest'? Society has since become fractured by clerical and secular pronouncements of one kind and other, some benign. The English language and the common sense and the jostle of ideas that it articulated have lost authority along with the grammar that shaped civility. It has become improper, often dangerous, to utter dissentient or satirical opinions on religious matters. J. K. Rowling's polite disagreement about some questionable doctrine has left her the richest outcast author in modern publishing.

Mullahs are no longer pronounced mad, as they were at the 1898 Battle of Omdurman, where the British, Winston Churchill galloping along with them, mounted their last cavalry charge. Rabbis are liable to be labelled generically 'good', a scornful courtesy towards the Chosen and their rarely bloody-minded clergy. Innumerable Catholic priests, of all but the very highest rank, have been convicted of prolonged abuse of children in their charge. Ireland, once a land of almost unanimous piety, has all but abandoned the Church as a moral governor, just as Northern Irish Catholics have every prospect of winning their cruel (on both sides) battle for authority.

Impugned, after the war, for failure to give spiritual guidance to German Catholics, Pope Pius XII responded that he had not wished to confuse the faithful. A regular article of that faith was, until Vatican II, that Jews were innately perfidious and, as Pacelli's recently published correspondence declares, often physically repulsive. An ordained Catholic priest presided over the deportation and/or massacre of Croatian Jewry. Detailed evidence of a Polish pogrom, in 1941, led by the village priest, can be found in Anna Bikont's *Le Crime et le Silence* (2004). The author has been accused of persecuting the Poles.

108

The fantasy of Jewish solidarity appeals to the orthodox rabbinate; it has small place in history. Where did those missing ten tribes go and why? The rift between Jews and Christians began as a quarrel between contending forms of Judaism. Neither Jesus nor even Saint Paul denied being a Jew. There has been no shortage of antagonisms inside what others like to presume conspiratorial Jewry. The case of J. Robert Oppenheimer is cradled in a nexus of animosities. For all the enlightened theism of the authors of the US Constitution, fears, prejudices and partialities were baggage carried from the Old World to the New.

Until the crisis which began with the collapse of the US stock exchange in February 1929, was Franklin Roosevelt ever regarded as a plausible political saviour? He came from the moneyed and propertied class which socialists, of whatever ruddy shade, were liable to blame for the Depression. At the same time, patrician tones, like his affinity with Teddy Roosevelt, convinced voters of his quality. The long myth of the innate superiority of the well-born led William Rees-Mogg (head boy of Charterhouse when I was sent there in 1945) to declare, well into the twenty-first century, that David Cameron was genetically bound to be an unswervingly principled prime minister. Paths of glory, it turned out, led but to the gravy.

I went with my mother to vote for FDR's when he ran for re-election in 1936. His Republican opponent, Alf Landon, was a Roman Catholic, hence an unlikely winner in any circumstances. Paul Johnson considered that FDR's New Deal did much less than advertised to cure the American economic condition. No personal charmer himself, Johnson ignored the fact that FDR's charismatic 'fireside chats' made people feel better. As would Ronald Reagan's amiable rhetoric; however narcotic, it brought the Berlin Wall down.

In 1940, when seeking re-election for an unprecedented third term, FDR promised to keep America out of the war. It was politically prudent in the face of isolationism and of Wendell Wilkie, a more personable Republican opponent than Landon. Announcing only that America would be 'the arsenal of democracy', he somewhat remedied unemployment and rehearsed national rearmament. The Japanese attack on Pearl Harbor and Hitler's concomitant (and unnecessary) declaration of war obliged FDR to do what he may have expected all along and enter the war, as if involuntarily, alongside the British and – where 'and' has a touch of 'but' – the USSR. The way to victory led to a steeply resurgent economy and, in short order, to Washington, DC becoming the capital of the Western world.

My mother Irene (silent second 'e'), like the great majority of American Jews, voted Democrat as a matter of quasi-faith. FDR was addressed by Rabbi Stephen Wise as 'Dear Boss'. The tone of intimate subservience procured no favours. Pre-war, FDR did nothing to offer sanctuary to fugitive Jews. A ship full of refugees was refused entry at any port in the Americas and eventually sailed back to Hamburg, whence there was no objection to transferring them to death camps. FDR never doubted that the US was essentially a Protestant country. Other persuasions might be tolerated, never entitled. As for colour, FDR was as liberal as a man might well be whose congressional backers included the Dixiecrats. Their cardinal policy was to make sure that the integration of Black Americans was never any part of the Four Freedoms.

Roosevelt did not care to discuss the fate of European Jewry; in public, he allowed half an hour, once, for the topic. He took no measures to prevent or hobble the slaughter as Winston Churchill, baulked by Anthony Eden's wilful lethargy, tried to do. FDR did not disdain the advice or services of influential or brilliant Jews, Bernard Baruch and J .R. Oppenheimer famous instances, but – like the king's Jews in medieval Europe and tsarist Russia – privileged American Jews seldom spoke up for lumpen co-religionists. In deference to martial Joseph Stalin, the salvation of Europe's Jews was never pronounced an Allied war aim.

109

Of Latvian Russian origin, Isaiah Berlin was the first Jew to be elected a Fellow of All Souls College, Oxford. Elegant idiosyncrasy rendered him the haughtiest of acolytes. His exquisite epistolary diplomatic reports from wartime Washington were Churchill's favourite reading. As with Ludwig Wittgenstein, alleged genius effaced 'race'. Siegfried Sassoon's courage in battle, not to mention his family's wealth, gained him passage in classy English social life. Never so British as when, in 1916, he pitched his MC into the sea, as a gesture against Allied tactics in Flanders, he posted his assimilation under the rubric *Memoirs of a Fox-Hunting Man* and confirmed it in the English of their composition. Understatement used to be a British variant of tally-ho.

Friedrich Nietzsche claimed that Judaism shared responsibility, with the disconcerting Socrates, for unmanning Europe. The thin irony is that the other two monotheisms have always advertised militant plans for the subjugation of humanity under dogmatic rule. As for Jews, while their allegedly sinister solidarity has frequently exploded in internecine hostilities over an *aleph*'s-worth of difference, enrolment of Gentiles has never been any part of their programme. Karl Marx proved how immune he was, perhaps, to obsolete loyalty by denouncing his rival, the German socialist Ferdinand Lassalle, as a 'Yid'.

Among Jews proud to declare hostility to 'Zionism' is the film director Mike Leigh. He has proved how insular his muse by favouring a pedestrian cinema derived from the witless documentary tradition of the Crown Film Unit's wartime morale-boosters. Black-and-white patriotism depicted the working class as the salt of the earth. In fact, strikes, go-slows and bloody-mindedness were hardly unusual in wartime Britain. Rough-hewn 'realism' persisted in the piously populist 1950s work of Tony Richardson and Lindsay Anderson until success in commercial cinema disobliged them from remaining low-falutin'. Fame and fortune came to dispossess Harold Pinter of visceral loyalties. Once a naïve supporter of Israel ('We've given the Arabs a bloody nose,' he said to me in June 1967, though neither of us had bruised knuckles), in later years the suspicion that another guest might be a Zionist put the by-then-very-grand Harold off his food until the hyphenated scoundrel was ejected.

People in the film and television industries, actors as well as writers and directors, are apt, when off-duty, to strike sententious attitudes, wallet on the right, heart on the left. Dirk Bogarde, who starred in *The Servant*, directed by Joe Losey, script by Pinter, from Robin Maugham's novella, noticed that Harold became grander and grander as success added cubits to his stature. While shooting *The Servant*, Dirk asked Harold why the toffs in the piece kept eating lobster thermidor. The youngish Harold asked Dirk what other dishes the rich (Gentiles implied) were given to eating. After his death, Harold was rumoured to have been about to convert to his Lady Antonia's Roman Catholicism, thus acquiring a prosthetic foreskin.

110

Antagonism between Jew and Jew, prophet and king, runs through their social history, culminating in the stand-off, in modern times, between assimilationists and Zionists. This lends specious substance to the argument, embraced by Loach and his writer, that 'the Zionists' were complicit with Nazi plans to purge Europe by channelling its Jews to Palestine. In the early years of the Nazi regime, Zionists did indeed seek to negotiate with Hitler. It was neither foolish nor wicked to hope that arrangements might be made for the evacuation of German Jews. This soon-abortive diplomacy has been taken to prove that 'the Zionists' (now often camp for Jews in general) were collusive with Nazism. Compare and contrast London ex-mayor Ken Livingstone's beery allegation that these pre-war meetings amounted to a conspiracy; hence Israel = SS, as Roald Dahl, the kiddies' schizoid sugar-uncle, chose to proclaim.

In order to extract inflated damages from post-war Germany, grabby Zionist negotiators are accused of greatly inflating the number of Holocaust deaths. Not only do Jews deserve what happened to many millions, say the virtuous, it also never happened. The scandal of the settlement by the Federal German Republic of damages due to dispossessed Jews is that the say-no-more-about-it payment, negotiated between a wincing Konrad Adenauer and the state of Israel, made small provision for individual Jews whose fortunes and goods had been stolen and secreted by pirates of various stripes and by the Austrian authorities whose national anthem was played on the BBC, during the war, among those of countries allied against the Axis. Kurt Waldheim became secretary-general of the United Nations not long before he was revealed to have been an Austrian officer actively participant in Nazi actions against Jews. Like some swastika-bearing Vicar of Bray, he joined the Nazi *Sturmabteilung* in 1938, and took an officious part in the war-time deportation of Greek Sephardim to Auschwitz. Primo Levi never forgot their rare solidarity on the threshold of death.

Holocaust denial has become, as Levi long dreaded, one more way of reasserting the innate wickedness of the Jews. Comedy and tragedy dangle in a common cage from the same hook: Jews are often said, with or without attendant sigh, to be their own worst enemies. Among a few extreme orthodox rabbis this conceit has taken the form of accusing assimilated Jews of being the cause of God's bad temper: in their view, the whole of European Jewry paid the price for modernisers' impertinence. Theology and philosophy edit knobbly history to validate smooth a-priori doctrines.

The old game began anew when 'the Jews' seemed to have been resurrected by the establishment of their own state. For similar, conflicting reasons – hopes of a reliably tethered base in the Middle East – the Soviet Union and the United States raced to recognise Israel. London was a sullen third; the Vatican hung back. The return of Jews to Jerusalem breached the folkloric promise that errant homelessness was proof of their iniquity in betraying Christ.

Jewish pietists (and Flavius Josephus) blamed the Zealots for the destruction of Herod's Temple. Christian Fathers attributed it to the failure of His own people to recognise Jesus as the Son of God. Who would guess that it took more than three hundred years for various strands of contentious and mutually murderous Christians to settle on the quotient of divinity in their Saviour? In the course of internecine blood-letting and hell-bent anathemas, Pope Innocent III (1161–1216) modernised Augustine's attitude to the Chosen by deploring the antique shibboleth: 'Their sufferings and homelessness are the just deserts for their crimes.' The more wretched the Jew, Augustine insisted, the truer the truth of Christianity and its apparatus of ascent.

If the proposition were advanced today that a dead man had risen, after three days in the tomb, into heaven and is now to be treated as divine, who would salute it? If the great monotheisms were not ingrown in European culture, would they be valued as other than curiosities, if not delusions? One twentieth-century litigant insisted on taking the oath in an English court by swearing by Jupiter. Modern man cannot, it seems, bear too much modernity. Frank Morison's century-old classic *Who Moved the Stone?* claimed that the stone on Jesus' tomb was so heavy that only the deity Himself could have moved it and allowed His son to ascend to heaven. The tomb is still there. The round stone on the grooved threshold in Gethsemane hardly looks immovable, given enough simultaneous shoulders. Meanwhile, man has contrived his own ascent into the heavens, with no happier motive or result than the intimidation of those who lack the same rocketry.

The most recent version of a Middle Eastern faith, the Bahá'i, is one of such all-embracing, undogmatic geniality that, despite the delightful, well-kept gardens of its headquarters on the slopes above Haifa, it attracts few adherents. I have been charmingly entertained there, but I cannot recall what precisely their unaggressive faith believes in. I gathered that, like Sufi, it stands to Islam somewhat as Quakerism does to mainstream Christianities.

111

The great schism between Roman Catholicism and Eastern Orthodoxy derived from a literal disagreement: was Jesus made of the same or (only) of similar stuff as is God the Father? For that iota's-worth of difference between *homoousios* and *homoiousios*, men killed and denounced each other, were defined as true Christians or hounded as heretics. The deicide committed by the Jews became a reconciling article of faith. Deviance supplies a warrant for murder, spoliation and self-righteousness through the ages. Salvation the ecclesiastical bonus, seconded by coercive vindictiveness, rehearses celestial triage. During the thirteenth-century siege of Béziers, confronted with a mixed crowd of Albigensian heretics and Christian citizens, Arnaud Almaric, a crusading cleric, gave the order, 'Kill them all, the Lord will recognise His own.'

What Joseph Conrad called 'the horror, the horror' of colonialist savagery was repatriated to Europe. It was not for lack of warning signs or tearful crocodiles. A concert of nations, convened in Évian in 1938, affected watered-down dismay at Nazi policies towards the Jews. The Dominican Republic alone declared itself willing to receive any number of them, at $100,000 a head. Diplomats from Britain and the United States washed pious hands in public. Entry was refused by both countries to all but a few refugees, preferably 'innocent' children; the unspoken implication was that Jews grew to be guilty as charged. The war sealed Europe against their escape, to the regretful relief of the defenders of the Four Freedoms.

Anti-Semites can be remarkably unobservant, perhaps indifferent, possibly excited, when it comes to females. In occupied Paris, titled hostesses of Jewish origin continued to entertain the *gratin*, including select Germans for whom French posting was too comfortable to excite meticulous vindictiveness. Throughout the war, under discreet French protection and holding an American passport, Gertrude Stein lived an untroubled, quasi-anonymous suburban life. In erotic mythology, Jewish women were thought to have rare sensual propensities. Tiresias, who had experience on both sides of the bed, declared that women enjoyed nine times more pleasure than men. The licensed brothels of pre-war France often paraded *la Juive* as *pièce de résistance*. Proust's 'Rachel-when-from-the-Lord' was one such star piece.

112

Palestine was the surviving European Jews' sole practical hope of a place to live as their own masters. This remains a more-or-less unspoken argument for denying it to them. Before and during the war, to appease the subsidised Arabs, the better to filch their oil and in conformity with clubby prejudice, the British Foreign Office encouraged Balkan states to do what they could to prevent any new exodus. Europe's Jews were cornered in a killing field. While others did the dirty work, Britannia and Uncle Sam, Walrus and Carpenter, wrung their hands and intoned prayers. The unfortunate and the destitute have few friends. Royal Navy vessels have regularly been deployed in the English Channel to intercept Syrian refugees in desperate flight from fellow Muslims in Syria. Putting the blame on 'traffickers' excuses callousness. Joseph and Mary had a more generous reception in Bethlehem.

Today's concert of nations, conducted under the aegis of the UN, has found it virtuous, and rewarding, repeatedly to condemn Israel as a racist or apartheid state. South Africa has now charged the Jewish state with genocide, after its invasion of the Gaza strip, following the events of 7 October 2023, when some four hundred unarmed members of an audience at an Israeli music festival were tortured and murdered, including some children, hundreds of hostages bundled into cruel captivity. This massacre was conducted, with savage glee, by Hamas intruders who broke through a boundary fence more suitable for a playground. The absence of armed Israeli patrols smacks of vanity, if not (as we must hope) all but deliberate temptation.

The South African government was not scandalised by the slaughter but by the reaction, ordered by Benjamin Netanyahu: a full-scale invasion of Gaza, with the declared intention of eradicating Hamas. Netanyahu's ruthlessness demanded the unification of his fellow-citizens at a time when his popularity was waning and he was under suspicion of autocratic ambitions to cover dubious book-keeping. I cannot believe that the massacre of 7 October was engineered by Netanyahu, but I cannot quite swear, as quietly as may be, that the security lapse was not, to some degree, the result of some misguided double-dealing which went altogether further than possibly promised by Hamas. Netanyahu's rage is no doubt genuine, not least in seeking to rally the Diaspora by making life awkward for middle-groundlings, his internal sceptics.

If the Israeli response has been excessive, it has been nothing like the 'genocide' which the South Africans and their friends, Jeremy Corbyn among them, are pleased to allege. The perversion of language seeks, and has sought again and again, to render Israeli guilty of a crime equivalent to what happened to six million unarmed Europeans between 1940 and 1945. That the British Parliament chose to debate the need for an immediate truce has less to do with humane purposes than the culling of Muslim votes in English constituencies. Corbyn's denial of anti-Semitism is the common recourse of the third-rate pseudo-Leninist.

Alone of nations, Israel is threatened with pariahdom unless it submits to schemes likely to lead to its own destruction. There is a zest of irony in the fact that one of the allegedly dispassionate judges in the matter is German-born Professor

Henry Siegman, president of the US/Middle East Project. Jews are apt to specialise in high-minded Jeremiads. Jacqueline Rose has never been slow to cast the second stone. When it comes to the deaths inflicted in their hundreds of thousands by Arabs and their friends on other Arabs or Muslims, not to mention the part played by Russian, British, French and American armaments manufacturers and peddlers, what loud indignation is provoked? How many Members of Parliament denounce regular massacres in Syria, Yemen and large tracts of Africa? What popular crowds call for what?

There are rates of moral exchange particular to Jews. Black is learning to imitate white when it comes to humbug: Alice Walker has refused to have her novel *The Color Purple* (made more famous by Steven Spielberg's forgettable 1985 film) translated into Hebrew. Does she know the name of the rabbi who marched arm in arm with Martin Luther King from Selma to Montgomery, Alabama? The face and character of Abraham Joshua Heschel were omitted from the 2014 film *Selma*. 'Based on a true story' promises falsehood. *Ars est celare veritatem*, as no one was ever heard to say, many prove.

Jews have not been alone in being consigned *in toto* to oblivion by pontifical persons. Roman Emperor Pontifex Maximus Domitian declared it his pleasure that a troublesome North African tribe be deleted from the human race; the British did the same for native Tasmanians. When Hannah Arendt chided the Jews of Europe for failing to rally support from other, unspecified people, she was more disposed to hold the Jews responsible for their own fate than with itemising what practical alliance was available to them. The Kurds, over forty-five million of them, have been backed by one opportunist power or another in their claim to autonomous territory. They have as often been baulked, recently by Trump's America, the better to appease the Turks and also to warn off similarly aggrieved claimants.

113

It cannot be denied – why should it be? – that Israel has benefited from the famous achievements of certain Jews no less than from the ambivalence at the root of Christianity. Jerzy Kosinski, author of *The Painted Bird*, a more-or-less autobiographical, certainly remarkable novel set in wartime Poland, told me that he had been the guest on a radio talk show in which, while discussing the Holocaust, he made a point of emphasising the equal iniquity of the Nazi murder of some three million gypsies. A listener with an accent called in to ask Mr Kosinski to answer just von qvestion: 'Can he give me, pliss, the names of ten famous gypsies?' I have twice received letters from scissor-and-pasting anti-Semites to remind me that the ancient Jews' treatment of the Amalekites proved them to have invented genocide. Another letter kept it laconic: 'YAWN'.

Elevated British critics bridle when it is suggested that T. S. Eliot was, or even could have been, anti-Semitic, quite as if it were some social contagion acquired only in low places where refined persons never venture. Who cares or dares to recall that in the lectures delivered at the University of Virginia, in 1933, entitled 'After Strange Gods', Eliot denounced 'a society like ours, worm-eaten with Liberalism, invaded by foreign races' and endangered by the noxious presence of 'free-thinking Jews'?

According to tenured pietists, Christopher Ricks and Craig Raine in the outspoken lead, it is an insignificant coincidence that Eliot was a friend and admirer – protégé, even – of Ezra Pound, whose sustained wish for the destruction of the Jews almost came true. Only after the Axis defeat did Pound describe his own raging anti-Semitism as a 'suburban prejudice', quite as if he had contracted it from an uncovered sneeze on the first tee of some artisan golf course. At the height of a time when European Jews in their hundreds of thousands were being rail-roaded, in cattle-trucks, on the way to being murdered, Pound was still writing verses accusing 'the Jews' of sending innocent soldiers to their deaths. He specified, for those who couldn't guess, that the latter were packed into cattle-trucks by profi-teering Hebrews.

In literary criticism, as in theology, anything can be said to be proved or disproved, once certain premises are embraced or glosses suffered to kiss the text better. Whatever Eliot's genius as a poet, the man from St Louis was, like his *miglior fabbro*, a striker of attitudes drawn from more select quarters; no cos-mopolitan like a provincial on the make. Nice that Charles Lindbergh, pilot of the *Spirit of St. Louis*, was also no friend of the Jews. In *The Plot Against America* (2004), Philip Roth made play with the fascist sympathies of the first man to fly solo across the Atlantic. He might have had more dangerous fun by telling the story from Lindbergh's point of view.

Eliot's pre-Great War proclamation of his new patriotism was accompanied by an assertion of faith in classicism, high Anglicanism and royalism. Of this triad, only the second had anything specifically to do with the United Kingdom. What Eliot admired, or craved, in royalism had more in common with the aggressive autocracy which Charles Maurras propounded in *Action française* than with constitutional monarchy. While living in Paris in the 1920s, Eliot composed *m'as-tu-vu* poems in French. Mockery of Jews afforded inexpensive *entrée* to chic Parisian milieux.

Eliot came to fashion himself so lofty a niche in English letters than any attack on him is now liable to be taken as unpatriotic. Anthony Julius made a well-researched, measured and, a simple soul might think, unanswerable exposé of Eliot's far-from-marginal anti-Semitic *faible*. Julius served his thesis without salt. As some people were bound to say, he did bang on a bit. If there was little question of the sourced legitimacy of his remarks, he lacked the wit to leaven stringency. His enemies did not have to bide their time for very long. Julius was deputed by Princess Diana as the solicitor to handle the financial aspect of her divorce. Nice newspapers led the way in suggesting that he was of an apt provenance for screwing the last penny out of the Windsors. That the people's princess commissioned him to dig for all he could get her was unspeakable.

Between the wars, Hilaire Belloc, *en bon Catholique*, sought to import *ex-cathedra* anti-Semitism into England in order to reinforce pettiness of the kind that kept Jews out of swank golf clubs and accused them of always counting the change. "Name of Father, if changed" was demanded on applications for membership. Eliot's cultivated duplicity allows his defenders to maintain that, since he was never personally rude to Jews, he was not anti-Semitic. Was he personally rude to anyone? It seems unlikely, although he could be tart in literary judgement. Eliot's ideal Christian society deplored 'free-thinking Jews', although a few might be allowed to season, perhaps unify, the godly: scapegoats might safely graze, a few of them, until needed.

114

Charles Maurras was less hostile to the undisguised, prefer-ably abject, orthodox than to Jews, long resident in France, who presumed themselves *Français comme les autres*. This flake of tolerance led Louis-Ferdinand Céline to denounce Maurras as what Marxist jargon might term 'an objective Jew'. In similar vein, William Joyce had accused Sir Oswald Mosley of being a 'kosher fascist'. As the tide of war turned against Germany, Céline dared to say, at a dinner in the German embassy in Paris, that Hitler had been replaced by a Jewish lookalike monkey who was leading Germany to disas-ter. Not a few of his hosts may have shared his apprehensions, but they knew to look dismayed when observed by the ser-vants, many of them SS in domesticated drag. In his own eyes, Céline became the only *pur et dur* left alive. In post-war dis-grace, he came to resemble, in his own self-pitying view, that solitary, caged Jew whom Rebatet had imagined in the Paris Jardin des Plantes. The image of Jew Süß recurs in fancy and in fact. In the gateway of the peninsular town of Peñiscola, on the coast south of Barcelona, once the meagre fiefdom of the deposed fifteenth-century anti-pope Benedict XIII, known as Papa Luna, hangs an iron cage, like a ribbed balloon, in which the effigy of a man still crouches.

Ezra Pound, closeted and cossetted in fascist Italy throughout the war, was arrested by the Americans in 1944. Prima-facie traitor, he was boxed for a while in a cage in Pisa. The fate of Joseph Süß Oppenheimer and of Lucien Rebatet's 'last Jew in captivity' fell, for a while, less vindictively, on a genuinely guilty party. Pound's post-war lines 'Pull down thy vanity, I say, pull down' read, at first sight, like some kind of recantation. In fact, it was addressed, with some small justice perhaps, to those who presumed to judge him. In the 1920s, Pound had been the principal agent in extracting Eliot from his job as a 'clerk' in a London merchant bank where, it seems, he was happily employed dealing with foreign exchange. He might have continued, like Robert Frost, to combine being a poet and a metaphorical 'Jew', had it not been for Pound's dismay at seeing him being businesslike. He proceeded thereafter to occupy an eminent perch, like some lay prelate.

Contempt for Jews has been more a sales-enhancing placebo than a solemn sentiment among writers in English, from Dickens, through Trollope and Thomas Carlyle, down to Wyndham-Lewis, Virginia Woolf, Hilaire Belloc, J. B. Priestley, Graham Greene, Kingsley Amis (who booed Jewy names – entirely his right – when they appeared in TV credits) and Salman Rushdie (see *The Satanic Verses*). There is no marked depth to the opportunism in these and many other aspiring authors. English anti-Semitism is a form of pastoral William Empson chose to ignore. Somerset Maugham, not rated by academic selectors, was one of the few authors unprincipled enough to write admiringly, in *The Alien Corn*, about a manifest Jew. His Ferdy Rabenstein dared to be unashamed by flashy distinction – based on whom, I wonder. D. H. Lawrence applauded the Jewish genius for 'disinterested speculation'. His admiring portrait of a leader in Kangaroo was rendered plausible by the Australian Jewish general Monash, who commanded Anzac forces at Gallipoli.

Lawrence has been justified by the number of Jews, J. R.

Oppenheimer an outstanding instance, who put on literal or metaphorical white coats. Peter Medawar told us that Karl Popper asked him, seriously, 'You would die for the truth, wouldn't you, Peter?' Clive Donner overheard Freddie Ayer (one of whose mistresses Clive had married) say to himself, as he worked on a text, 'That's very clever, but is it true?' Ludwig Wittgenstein was once approached by a lady who said to him, 'Professor Wittgenstein, I have a problem: I don't feel at home in the universe.' Wittgenstein replied, 'That is not a problem, that is a difficulty.' Did he call her 'madam'? Ah, that forever-reshuffled nine of diamonds! The alienated Jew, of whom J. R. Oppenheimer stands as paragon, has often thought to abate difficulties by concentrating on problems.

115

Post-Holocaust embarrassment, from which the British exempted themselves, had at least something to do with why the original European six states embraced Jean Monnet's project to relegate nationalist antagonism, German and French in particular, to obsolescence. An economic community would, Monnet presumed, create links and mutually beneficial knots too tight for rupture; blood would be washed out of European soiled balance-sheets. The signatories of the 1957 Treaty of Rome elected to give the old continent a fresh, unwrinkled complexion. The triumvirs of this new concord, Konrad Adenauer, Charles de Gaulle and Alcide de Gasperi, were all Roman Catholics. Neat that Rome lent its name to the charter for a secular, guilt-free Europe; the Holy Roman Empire came again, again not holy, neither Roman nor imperial. Almost two millennia after Quinctilius Varus' three legions were cut to pieces in the Teutoburg Forest (having been lured into an ambush by Herman, né Arminius, Rome's supposedly trustworthy ally), post-1945 Germany agreed, under the uncontaminated Konrad Adenauer, to participate in a communal identity; *Recommençons*, without Sartrean irony. Anyone responsible for the Shoah ceased to inhabit the present; no citizen of the new Europe was to be tarnished by the old, except for Jews not sporting enough to let bygones be bygones. The dated writing on the wall was covered with immaculate paper.

Early in the 1990s, I was in a London stationery shop, where a young foreign man in his early twenties was asking how to get to the nearest underground station. Since I was going that way, I offered to take him to Gloucester Road station. On the way, I asked, out of politeness, where he came from. He said, 'Germany, I'm afraid.' The revulsion of young Germans when they learnt of the activities of their fathers and grandfathers (which is not to say that camps and other elements of the Nazis' murderous enterprise lacked female operatives) led not a few to convert to Judaism. Ex-Nazis, with the sly exception of Speer, were little disposed to apology; scientists found refuge and employment in Arab countries where they collaborated in plans to destroy Israel. What might no longer be a vocation remained a living.

As Bettina Stangneth declares, in *Eichmann Before Jerusalem* (2014), many Nazis harboured by Juan Peron in Argentina cherished fanciful plans for a Fourth Reich. The Israelis' kidnap and literally boxed export of Adolf Eichmann, in 1960, and the consequent Jerusalem trial, somewhat dented neo-Nazi conceit. Eichmann was tried with due process and condemned on a cascade of evidence. This did not prevent high-minded persons, tracking Arendt, from saying that the trial should have taken place in Germany. The Jews, she implied, are people with no right to judge anyone; except each other.

116

The Suez episode of 1956 was to be the last exercise of Anglo-French Middle Eastern imperialism; *exeunt* those shady operators Sykes and Picot. The enrolment of Israel in the last-throw scheme devised in London and Paris was an obsolete diplomatic trope: the surrogate serves first as provocateur, then as repudiated patsy. Israel's reward for playing an obedient part in the ineptly scripted charade was to receive from France the Mirage fighter-planes with which, eleven years later, the Egyptian Air Force would be eliminated and Israel's survival assured by what de Gaulle then condemned as an impudent pre-emptive strike. In *Realpolitik* rig, the general echoed Innocent III's view that Jews, in whatever guise, had no right but to suffer. Michel Debré, de Gaulle's first prime minister, a convert to Catholicism, had a grandfather who was a rabbi.

President Eisenhower's anger with France and Great Britain for defying his embargo on military action and so endangering his prospect of re-election in 1956 was vented on Israel. Ben-Gurion was obliged to withdraw his troops from the Sinai Peninsula. Ike's diplomacy served notice on the old European entente that their day was done. An attendant strand adds presumption to pragmatism: whatever concerns Jews and their correction is likely to derive from a double helix of history and metaphysics. Eisenhower later confessed that failure to support the British and French over Suez was a great mistake. Then again, if Anthony Eden had not irritated the president by calling him 'My dear', in his dated Etonian way, he might have persuaded him to come onside.

Israel's victory in the Six-Day War of June 1967 was more comprehensive and much quicker than the Quai d'Orsay (aka *La Maison*) envisaged or wished. *Le grand Charles*, who had counselled the Israelis to wait and be hit before they hit back, rated their brilliant haste as impudence. Where the socialist leaders of the Fourth Republic had supported Israel to weaken the Arabs, the better to retain Algeria as a department of France, de Gaulle was now recruiting Arab states to baulk *'les Anglo-Saxons'*. In a Gallic form of Palmerston's style, no motive other than the national interest had reliable leverage on him.

As Julian Jackson describes, in his 2018 biography of the general, de Gaulle was almost literally beside himself on key occasions, a man impersonating the hero he stood in for. His old mentor Marshal Philippe Pétain gave a somewhat similar performance in 1940, when he made *'le don de ma personne'* (the gift of my person) to his humiliated nation; the hero of Verdun became scapegoat and redeemer. In *Le Solstice de Juin* (1941), Henry de Montherlant found no fault with Pétain's sporting handshake with Hitler. Winston Churchill agreed to meet Pierrepoint, the hangman who supervised the execution of the Nazis condemned at Nurnberg, but he did not care to shake his hand.

The assumption of an identity not identical with the mortal person of the man of destiny goes back at least as far as Julius Caesar, who, like General de Gaulle, adopted a third-personal ego. A Vichy insider tells of Philippe Pétain, descending in the elevator in the Hôtel du Parc, asking his aide-de-camp, as they reached the ground floor, *'Qui suis-je?'* The young officer replied, '*Vous êtes le Maréchal Pétain.*' '*Ah oui,*' said the Marshal, like an actor resuming the character he was commissioned to impersonate.

Who you are can be, should be, Sartre said, a personal decision rather than a given. His literary portrait of the anti-Semite depicts a man who comforts himself daily by donning a decisive, fraudulent identity: false consciousness personified. Sartre was given to odd bouts of essentialism. His maquette of the anti-Semite was muted by the fact that Stalin was an eminent instance. Disposed to the Marxist view that everything was political, Sartre's anti-Semite was portrayed as a 'psychological', that is, apolitical, oddity. In the anatomy of the ideal body politic, the Jew resembled the appendix, once of some utility, now superfluous, if not toxic. It was less the inhabitants of working-class Boulogne-Billancourt that Poulou took care not to cross than the party line. Sartre had it that a Jew would be well-advised to settle, like the knight on the chessboard, for freedom to progress only in a crooked lurch. Nazi bureaucrats referred to Jews, dead or alive, as 'pieces'.

De Gaulle's *ex-cathedra* definition of the Jews (not merely of Israelis) as '*peuple d'élite, sûr de lui-même, et dominateur*' was *mi-figue mi-raison*. He affected surprise when Raymond Aron, who had rallied to the general's call in 1940, read it as other than a compliment. Was de Gaulle's view not consistent with '*une certaine idée de la France*'? His *boutade* was the first formal European denunciation of the state of Israel. The general's cosmetic formulation of history (the political New Look) demanded that, just as Paris had been 'liberated by itself', France – his France – had nothing to apologise for when it came to Vichy's prime part in the deportation of Jews. It took the scoundrelly President Jacques Chirac to acknowledge the truth, all but half a century later.

If the French political and intellectual class had little to be proud of when it came to the Jews, no more, Sartre failed to say, did his *chouchou* the working class: trains serviced by mostly communist *cheminots* never ran late on their way to Buchenwald and beyond. That seventy-five per cent of French Jews survived the war was due not least to the decency of *Français moyens*, especially in the countryside, where Jews were most likely to find hiding-places, notably among Protestant communities. During most of the Occupation, the few thousand German soldiers stationed in France tended to be resident in garrison towns. The French were mostly left to fight it out between themselves, *Milice* versus *Maquisards*, right and left.

117

History repeats its tragedies not only as farce, as Marx postulated with reference to Louis-Napoleon's coup d'état, but also as rumour: anti-Israeli sentiment is validated by the refashioning of the age-old shibboleth that 'the Jews', once the sole impediment to celestial harmony, are now the principal obstacle to mundane concert. Liberal rhetoric appeases the Arabs by making the Jews uniquely responsible for the turmoil in the Middle East, which dates, *grosso modo*, from Alexander the Great's dismemberment of the Persian Empire in the fourth century BCE. It was exacerbated, in 1919, by French and British imperialists after their voracious dismantling of the Ottoman Empire known, at the time, in London and Paris as 'the loot'. Programmed instability, fabricated geography, allowed the victorious profiteers to exercise benign supervision with a minimum of personnel. Tyrannies and puppet kingdoms did for any prospect of regional democracy.

The one-time Labour government minister Shirley Williams announced, some ten years ago, in her Christmas encyclical, that it required only that Israel retire to its 1967 frontiers (she would have preferred a retreat to the map drawn, arbitrarily and tendentiously, by the British in 1947/8) for the world to become a peaceful place. Metaphysics were redressed as practical reason. Was it but coincidence that Shirley was a Roman

315

Catholic? One night long ago, before her secession from the Labour Party, Shirley invited us to dinner in her house. Bill Rodgers, then minister of transport, later one of the 'gang of four', arrived late, having been involved in some negotiations, and took the place next to me. After a forkful or two, the first thing he had ever said to me was, 'Why do you like money so much?' Did I believe my ears? God, yes. I said, 'Because it means I can hire a helicopter any time I want and get away from people like you.' I have never had the shekels to allow me to afford any such means of transport. It was the quickest wordy way I could think of to give him the punch on the nose I wish I had had the guts to deliver in literal form.

How many liberals are jellies that never quite set? Diabolisation of Israel/the Jews prompted a variant of the blood libel advertised by the cartoonist Gerald Scarfe. His depiction of the Israeli prime minister building a wall using a compound of Palestinian limbs and blood as his cement appeared in *The Sunday Times*, by nice coincidence, on Holocaust Sunday 2013. The newspaper later apologised, a standard tactic for doing nothing else. Cicero perfected the device of saying something out loud and then apologising, quite as if his own utterance had caught him unawares. A notorious instance was a reference to Clodia Metelli as the 'wife' of Cicero's arch-enemy Clodius Pulcher. Cicero then corrected himself to say he was referring – sorry about that! – to pretty Clodius' delectable sister. The rumour of their incest waggishly publicised, he affected to bite the tongue safely lodged in his cheek.

Scarfe had already portrayed Benjamin Netanyahu looking like the anti-Semite's traditional string-pulling bogeyman and a cowled Palestinian leader of no recognisable identity, exchanging rockets which plunged into the eyes of their respective targets. The witless tagline was 'an eye for an eye'. The unsubtle implication was that there was something typically Jewy in such an exchange. In fact, in the ancient world, the principle of 'an eye for an eye' proposed the humane substitution of limited damages in preference to murderous vendetta. In 1976, Netanyahu's brother Yonatan was killed leading an Israeli airborne force which went to liberate the Jewish passengers whom Idi Amin, then boss of Uganda, had separated from others on an airliner which had made a forced landing. The dictator – who had recently expelled all Uganda's Asian population – appeared likely to murder the Jews to please his Arab backers. The Israeli commando force was given leave to overfly Kenya. No other country saluted their boldness. When Jews take matters into their own hands, it carries an odour of impertinence.

In the otherwise callow play *The Journalists*, Arnold Wesker got the essence of the matter right when he observed, after intrusive research in various departments of *The Sunday Times*, that the motto of all hacks when dealing with personalities was 'Who does he think he is?' Scarfe affected to be a fearless moral arbiter, never – you know me, chums – an anti-Semite. The hint that the Jews were persecuting him was an uncited rider on his high horse. Top-dollared indignation is nice work if they can get it for journalists who, like cabinet ministers, survive at the pleasure of their bosses. They affect to prove that they are *menschlich* by not being 'afraid' to attack Israel. Such courage requires belief in the myth that, unlike Rupert Murdoch and other front men, 'the Jews' really control the media. That they receive a remorselessly bad press serves only to prove their devilish duplicity.

Richard Dawkins continues, as if daring, to spread the word that the Jews control the world's press. Professorial author of *The Blind Watchmaker*, atheist *affiché*, he is not infrequently in print, drawing immodest attention to his own boss-eyes and to his fancy of Semitic domination of the press in which he condemns it. When did distinction in one field preclude cultivating nettles in another? Never denied a page, Dawkins wonders loudly, and fatuously, what would happen if atheists achieved domination of the media. Professorial geneticist, he is no historian. Atheists have already controlled media and state: in Nazi Germany and Soviet Russia. Was the result a marked victory for truth or broadmindedness?

118

The repeated use of 'really' hints at some secret dossier to which the 'realist' has privileged access. This 'really' promises no more reliable support than a confectioner's sugared pilaster. Philosophical affectations of rare insight begin with Parmenides' two-track distinction between mundane appearances and immutable truth. Ancient Greek grammar encapsulates his vision: schoolboys used to be taught the mnemonic *phainomai ôn quod sum, quod non sum phainomai einai*. A similar notion was ensconced in Plato's distinction between mundane appearances and celestial 'Ideas', subsequently reupholstered to embellish Christian metaphysics. The Buddhist acceptance of appearance as reality punctures pie-in-the-sky schemes in which God/the dialectic is working His/its purpose out. Freddie Ayer wondered what those who imagined themselves bound for immortality would do, in what form, in another world.

A. N. Wilson, prefectorially collared and tied, has decreed that Israel, alone of all the states in the geographer's index, lacks the right to exist. It is not unknown for a certain brand of Jew to be equally judicious. In the early 1930s, Hitler attracted a few whose patriotism, indistinguishable from self-harm, impelled them to identify with ultra-German anti-Bolshevism. With better reason, no few Italian Jews came to support Fascism and rally to its bundled band. Anti-Semitism was no part of Mussolini's early creed. In the late 1930s, when Hitler twisted his arm, the Duce, who had had a Jewish mistress, among no lack of others, fell into line with Nazism. Italian ultra-fascists were quick to profit and ultra-righteously dispossess fellow-citizens.

Mussolini legitimised fascists to eliminate the classic Sicilian Mafia, the better to accommodate his own racketeers. Thanks to the adroit war-time politicking of the paroled US gangster Lucky Luciano, liberation of Sicily doubled with the reinstatement of the heirs of the old Mafia. Affecting to have been victims of the Duce prompted naïve favour from the Yanks; John Dickie's *Cosa Nostra* (2007) carries the dark details. Danilo Dolci tried in vain to spring the Sicilian peasantry from the exacting gangsters and corrupt officials who collaborated to frustrate him.

My friend the late Joseph Janni was born in 1916, son of a prosperous Jewish mill-owner in Milan. His mother was a Montefiore, from one of the senior Italian Sephardic families. Growing up in Mussolini's Italy, Jo was told, in due time, to report to the local gymnasium for enrolment in the Fascist youth (was the signature tune of the movement). When he came to sign in, the Maresciallo in plumed dignity behind the desk was also a weekday employee in his father's mill. On seeing Jo, the man said, 'What are you doing here, Signor Peppino?' Jo said that he had no choice. 'Do you really want to come and do drill every week?' 'In many ways, not, but...' 'I tell you what we do, Signor Peppino, every week, you call me and say why you can't come and I put a tick in the book and no one will ever know any different.'

This arrangement continued for months, with a tick in the book every week. One week, Jo called as usual and was told that on parade day the following week, he had to be present. The Duce's legate for the whole of northern Italy was coming to present the sword of honour to the Young Fascist of the Year. Jo had to be there in full uniform. Jo said, 'But for God's sake, what does it matter if I am there? Put the tick in the book and...' 'Signor Peppino, you don't understand. You are the only one with a tick in the book every single week.' 'Thanks to you,' Jo said, 'I know that.' 'And that is why you have to be here. You, signor Peppino, are the Young Fascist of the Year.'

Alexander Stille's *Benevolence and Betrayal* (1994) details Mussolini's despatch of those who had been among his earliest supporters. Jews were keener nationalists than most Italians, on whom their region, their region or, in the case of Sicilians, their island, had a stronger call than the very recent notion of a united Italy. In 1939, after the family had been stripped of wealth and possessions, Jo made his way to England. In 1940, when Italy entered the war against France and England, Jo was routinely interned as an enemy alien. Released a few months later, he was eager for sexual comfort. He approached a comely whore in Bond Street and followed her to an upstairs room. When she lay down, fully dressed, on the bed and opened her legs, Jo said, 'For God's sake, in Italy, we have a talk and the girls take their clothes off, before...' The knees-up local lady said, 'Welcome to England, ducky.'

119

Denial of unique evil to the industrialised murder of some six million Jews, of differing kinds, languages and nationalities, takes a variety of pseudo-objective forms. In modern dress, it alleges equal and opposite grievances on the part of the Palestinians, after the so-called Naqba of 1948, when many were expelled or fled and some killed. This spurious equivalence allows Arab partisans to incite the West to 'divide through' by events with entirely different origins and statistics. Despite a population of twenty per cent mostly Israeli Arabs happy to be where they are, Jerusalem's policy is commonly labelled apartheid, more often 'genocide'. Manfred Gerstenfeld reports that, in 2011, a study by the University of Bielefeld showed that a large number of EU citizens agreed that 'Israel is conducting a war of extermination against the Palestinians'.

Might this owe something to a wish or fear or desire to please the pollster? The style in which a question is pitched often gives 'yes' solicited likelihood. Flat can be tilted: to pose alternatives suggests both are plausible. Votes may resolve issues and determine practice; they prove nothing. Great Britain's 2016 Brexit referendum posed what was paraded as a brave, once-and-for-all choice. 'Standing alone' appealed to British vanity. Just over a third of the electorate became 'the people' whose credulity became, according to ambitious opportunists and financial manipulators, immune to revision. The rich were enriched, mugs mugged.

The Palestinian population, for all its misfortunes and misery, has greatly increased over the years. False equation with the Nazis' exterminatory policy encourages wits, of a kind, to equate the Israelis (as if they were all of the same mind) with both the SS and with hook-nosed financiers. Journalists and caricaturists are cautious when it comes to ridiculing Muslims. The Prophet has taken on an aura of divinity. Unlike the Christian image of Jesus of Nazareth, Mohammed's followers have never claimed his family connection with the deity. He was manifestly human, not least in an unashamed appetite for young girls.

None of the monotheists' nominees for the one and only God is remarkable for humour. Philosophers often dignify themselves with clerical scorn for those with different ideas; Democritus – the Laughing Philosopher – was a rare ancient exception. Charlie Dunbar Broad's *Five Types of Ethical Theory* (1931) has the distinction of a witty index: for example, 'England, Church of, the author's respect for'. The elderly Broad, whose index also featured a larky endorsement of the Führer's Aryan tastes (which CDB shared), invited Tony Becher and me to dinner in Trinity. The sole scientific experiment that still diverted him, he told us, was making yoghurt. Under the same conditions, with the same ingredients, it sometimes 'took' and sometimes did not. Caprice was redeemed as a part of reality, determinism fractured.

120

In the 1980s, the German academic Ernst Nolte, quondam pupil of Martin Heidegger, placed the Holocaust in what he claimed as historical perspective by claiming that the rounding-up, then massacre, of Europe's Jews should be reclassified as an understandable, if not prudent, prophylactic move. In the 'total war' all Jews were Hitler's enemies, hence legitimate targets. The Argentinian José Pablo Feinmann's 2005 novel *La Sombra de Heidegger* deals with Heidegger's malign charm and seemingly inextinguishable legacy. The narrator, Martin, is the son of Dieter Muller, a student of the Master who, after the war, takes refuge in Argentina. Muller *père* has convinced himself that he and the philosopher were in no way responsible for the Final Solution, if it took place, which he affects to question. Young Martin is possessed by the image of a renowned thinker who is also a monster. Long after his father's death, he goes to Freiburg, a war-time gun in his knapsack, to confront the man whose name he shares and whose malevolence haunts him. Crossing the bridge into the city, he realises that he cannot execute his shadow. He throws the leftover Luger into the river.

With a sliver of glee, George Steiner insisted that there is nothing anyone can do to prevent a malign ghost from wandering the earth and poisoning the wells of thought.

Grievance-merchants exercise a sinister attraction. Alan Ginsburg made a pilgrimage to see Ezra Pound, perhaps in the hope of an apology or, more likely, a wink of exemption. Céline attracted apologetico-accusatory pilgrims, Celan among them, to Meudon, where he played a suburban Philoktetes, all grievance, no magic bow. In his text *The Portage to San Cristobal of A.H.*, a text that ends modishly without a full stop, Steiner gives the Führer the last word: Israel would not exist had it not been for him.

During our first year at Cambridge, my tandem classical scholarship-holder and *miglior fabbro* John Sullivan wrote to Ezra Pound, still in official purdah, about Sextus Propertius. Pound replied, with more haste than my innocence expected, in a letter typed on yellow paper, signed 'Ez' in green ink, as courteous as its author was unabashed. Sullivan later wrote a book defending Pound's recklessness in translating Propertius' Latin. If I imagined Pound to be forever tainted by his anti-Semitism, it had not stopped me buying (and still admiring) his *Seventy Cantos*. Who fails to applaud 'fish-scale roofs'?

Long before Bismarck, forcible unification of Germany under a single catch-all, quasi-dictatorial imperium, anti-Semitism was fashionable among German philosophers. Common to Lutheran protestants and to the large Roman Catholic minority within the Reich's widened borders, the myth of diabolical Jewry was transmuted into social adhesive. Heinrich von Treitschke (1834–96) called the Jews 'our misfortune', a sentiment repeated, daily, on the front page of Julius Streicher's Nazi newspaper, *Der Stürmer*. What genuine master race would be so apprehensive of a small minority, most of whom wanted nothing so much as to be indistinguishable from their pronounced betters?

Hegel led philosophers – Karl Marx the most influential – into the temptation of proclaiming an inevitable dialectic in human history. Human beings were immune to blame for what was indexed, indelibly, in the stars. Marx's materialism stood Hegel's Idealism on its swollen head. Both trumpeted the inexorable role of so-called Reason and urged opting for the right side while there was still time, a modernisation of Pascal's vulgar tip to bet on Christianity. That man is capable of reason does not certify his being reasonable.

German philosophers, given to polemic generalisation, were often opposed by historians. Theodor Mommsen advertised the chanciness of life and scorned affectations of metaphysical insight into an inexorable future. Like Michel de Montaigne, Mommsen was suspicious of those so sure of access to certainty that they condemned to death any who questioned their insight. Ernst Nolte was a hybrid historian-cum-philosopher, with the selective logic of the latter. German philosophers, drummed up by Heidegger, are liable to affect unique understanding of the Greeks. Philippe Pétain might have been thinking of one such pontificator when he said, '*Il connaît tout, et rien d'autre*' (he knows it all and nothing else).

121

The Romans have been little admired by philosophers, even though their engineering competence, to say nothing of their disciplined belligerence, gave them characteristics in common with modern Germans. My friend the late poet and classical scholar Guy Lee was unusual in declining to be impressed by Greek architecture. How, he asked, could one be uncritical of people who never progressed beyond the essential mode of erecting pillars and placing marble lintels across the capitals? The Romans' use of the arch and their invention of concrete armed them to undertake monumental structures, long aqueducts not least, more impressive and useful than anything Greek, apart from the fine aqueduct that served Athens during the Roman occupation.

Johann Joachim Winckelmann's proclamation of the superiority of Greek art, in the mid-eighteenth century, may have owed something to a sublime homo-erotic sensibility (as was said of both Byron and Shelley); it also carried an implicit rejection of the Latin temper. All the same, Winckelmann spent much of his life in Rome, doubling scholarship with spying for the Austrian emperor. In 1768, on his way back from reporting to Vienna, he was murdered, probably by a greedy, not to say dishy, cook in Trieste. Winckelmann's admiration for the Rhodian Laocoön scarcely promises aesthetic perfect pitch, but his advocacy of Greek art, echoed by other German philo-Hellenists, distanced him from Roman imperialism, terrestrial and spiritual.

Aversion from Latin culture had a military correlative in German hostility to France and Italy and a diplomatic annexe in German imperial overtures both to newly liberated Greece (blessed, now and again, with a German royal family) and to Ottoman Turkey. Hitler's early emulation of the Duce transcended the age-old antagonism of Teuton and Italian, but only until 1943. As soon as Mussolini was deposed, and Italy sued for peace with the invading Allies, Hitler declared the Italians a 'gypsy race gone to rot'. An extreme, distant, eminently parodic instance of European dictatorship – backed by German subsidies – was in Paraguay, as Alfredo Seiferheld illustrated in his 1985 *Nazismo y Fascismo en el Paraguay: visperas de Il Guerra Mundial 1936–1939*.

Mussolini's favourite writer, Curzio Malaparte (Kurt Erich Suckert), aping Buonaparte's dark side, was licensed to build himself a swollen carbuncular house on Capri. He took elegant revenge for Nazi slights in *Kaputt*, a calm chronicle of the Nazis' disaster in Russia, where he served as a war correspondent. He trumps Hemingway's account of the Greek retreat from İzmir with his description of an entire German horse-drawn brigade frozen into bleached sculpture as it tried to cross a lake near Leningrad. Truth and fiction jostle for mastery in both cases. Without some streak of double-sided sado-masochism, what I-witness gets it right? Malaparte's *La Pelle* and Norman Lewis's *Naples '44* are equally scintillating in recording the aftermath of the city's liberation and how the Allies made free with a starving population. *La Pelle* records that Neapolitan prostitutes wore blonde pubic wigs the better to appetise Black GIs. True? It is now.

122

Sapped by the bankruptcy of the USSR, fanciful futurists have resumed the ambitions of those galled by the collapse of the Great Experiment. Few were not born after its eclipse, none in range of its cannibal shadow. For all the diligent specificity with which they have been exhumed or enumerated, Stalin and Mao's millions of murdered and brutalised victims excite small indignation among idolators. 'Perspective' vindicates unredeemed purists who aim to serve the principle at the end of their rainbow. Similar to W. S. Gilbert's Lord High Executioner with his list of those who will not be missed, such down-with-our-side zealots rarely venture a word against 'Allahu Akbar' uttered by quick-on-the-draw enthusiasts.

Philippe Lançon's 2018 memoir *Le Lambeau* is an eloquent and meticulous account of the author's agonising reconstruction and convalescence after having his jaw shot away during the terrorist assault on the offices of the Parisian satirical weekly *Charlie Hebdo*. Without bitterness and with little interest in the attackers' motives or what happens to them, he is scornful of those who, in the weeks before the assault, washed their hands of the Gallic heterodoxy which has been the trademark of *Charlie*. The magazine was abandoned to scapegoat isolation after its cartoonist exercised the civilised right to ridicule the Prophet. He and his colleagues had also pilloried more than a few local sacred cows who did not entirely regret what happened to its editors. Painfully wounded and disfigured, Lançon realises, while undergoing protracted rehabilitation, that at the age of fifty-one he has little wish to return to the life of the freelance pen-for-hire.

There is rare grace in his lack of rancour with regard to the killers. Their victims included a wounded Muslim gendarme, begging for mercy, whom his co-religionists finished off as they left the scene. What Lançon sees, not least in reconsidering Michel Houellebecq's *Soumission*, is the shrug with which Western Europeans agree to consign their secular societies, together with the freedom of speech and ridicule that once defined them, to whatever extremism might deign to leave them in comfortable, if demoralised, peace. Hugh Trevor-Roper, bold in verbal cudgelling of fellow-historians Alan Taylor, Arnold Toynbee and A. L. Rowse, rallied to denounce Salman Rushdie for provoking Ayatollah Khomeini by writing *The Satanic Verses* and thus obliging the UK taxpayer to supply him with a bodyguard.

123

In *Engraved in Flesh*, title derived from Kafka, Anthony Rudolf reports that, in the mid-eighteenth century, a number of the dissident Sabbatean Jewish sect known as Frankists went all the way and converted to Catholicism. They then agreed to 'serve the interests of the Catholic clergy by publicly defending the blood libel in the disputation at L'vov (1759)'. Repetition congeals as folk-knowledge; old alarm buttons are pressed, tasty scabs picked, plague bells tolled. In truth, the enemy of scheme, the greatest known massacre of children was conducted by meta-Christians. The Germans and their acolytes took the practical and bestial view that, if spared, Jewish children would grow up to avenge the dead. Did the same logic prompt the British to their exterminatory 1828 end-to-end cull of every single aboriginal inhabitant in Tasmania?

The Sunday Times of 10 February 2019 carried a story that John McDonnell, the meta-Stalinist shadow Chancellor of the Exchequer, 'has strongly defended a prominent Labour activist Jackie Walker, former vice-chairwoman of Momentum, suspended from the party after saying Jews were "chief financiers" of the slave trade'. Is there any documentary evidence to support that good-womanly accusation? Might there be a schematic disposition to wish it true? It goes to absolve a slew of manifest profiteers from that iniquitous pursuit, including Arab traders, not to mention a number of African tribes that condoned the export of their neighbours. As for British involvement, the city of Bristol, scarcely renowned for its Semitic population, built its prosperity on shipping slaves. Should today's Bristolians be ashamed of themselves?

It is plausible to believe that Lenin-capped Jeremy Corbyn's Labour Party's 'problem' with anti-Semitism was the result less of some paranoid virus than of a bet that for every Jewish voter lost a dozen Muslims might be recruited. Their anti-Semitism, for notable instance in Rotherham, where the council is dominated by Muslim militants, elected by a largely Muslim population, is validated by the vile things Jews are said always to have done and, according to Corbynistas, continue to do.

In America, the reverend (hence tax-exempt) hustler Louis Farrakhan, loud preacher of the Nation of Islam, repeats the old charge that 'the Jews' hated Jesus Christ. His red-bow-tied followers were thus furnished with a white target unlikely to recruit other 'Caucasians' to its defence. Coincidentally, he denied the undeniable place of American Jews in securing civil rights for Black Americans. Oscar Levant once said that he knew Doris Day (née Doris Mary Ann Kappelhoff) before she was a virgin.

124

By the time of J. Robert Oppenheimer's birth, in 1904, the United States had proved a Zion more attractive than any sandy strip in the Middle East, peopled with unwelcoming Arabs and policed by the routinely anti-Jewish British, supposedly in the loud interest of international peace, not to mention the maintenance of imperial reach to India and command of local oil. When enacting the self-determination decreed as gospel by President Woodrow Wilson at Versailles in 1919, the British pronounced some people, especially Arabs, more entitled to self(ish)-determination than others. For all his swagger head-dress and attendant robes, Lawrence of Arabia is said to have counselled, quietly, leaving the oil under the desert and allowing Jews to come and vivify the region. No vestige of this audience-endangering notion was present in David Lean's 1962 Union-Jacketed movie. Although the cheap can always be nasty, the greater the budget in any public art, the more likely that the truth will be doctored or dumped. Look at the shamelessly propagandistic annex to the Sistine Chapel.

Self-determination was a sweet-sounding fallacy. In *The Times Literary Supplement* of July 1982, C. M. Woodhouse, who fought, as did Patrick Leigh Fermor, in Greece during the war, and was later a conspicuously decent, long-serving Tory MP, declared that Woodrow Wilson had done much to 'muddy the waters' by his impractical idealism. Nothing did more to foster a new political class of 'nationalists' whose positions depended on generating suspicion of foreigners and metics. As for dogmatic inevitability, what has more historical instances than the law of unforeseen consequences? Dismayed to hear that T. E. Lawrence favoured a Jewish presence, and energetic influence, in the Middle East, Rudyard Kipling accused him of being 'pro-Yid'.

However good a man he rated Gunga Din, Kipling was a compendium of dated attitudes and vanities. Max Beerbohm hit him with punctual wit in a cartoon showing Mr Kipling taking a walk in the park with ''is girl, Britannia'. The muted comedy of history is that the abiding effect of Whitehall's last hurrah in the Middle East was the creation of fabricated states, with starched borders and ethnically and religiously diverse populations capped with imported majesties like that gallant Old Harrovian King Hussein. Arbitrary 'national' boundaries enabled the British to keep the pieces, with benign affectations, in all sorts of outlandish places. Factitious 'national' entities in Africa are now not uncommonly divided against each other and within themselves, despite vestigial, not to say profitable, adhesion to the Commonwealth.

The notion that Israel alone has been planted in the Middle East ignores the rigged formation of most of its geography. It was tactless of Golda Meir to say that there was no such place as Palestine, whose inhabitants were best described as 'south Syrians', but the sanctification of Palestine is another instance of the attempt to disqualify 'the Jews' from any claim to unique misfortune or to a sliver of territory in the atlas. This neither justifies the maltreatment of Palestinians (none of whom has ever been judicially executed, despite many murders of Israelis), nor excuses vindictive policies with regard to the so-called 'occupied' territories. No hectic partisanship is required to point out that, before Hamas mounted the armed coup which evicted the PLO from Gaza and its surroundings, Israel and the US had been generous in funding local development. The coastal strip was nicely placed to become prosperous, had its leaders not lacked the live-and-let-live decency to take advantage of practical possibilities. To monopolise the power, they incite the masses to ruinous violence. The rise of a mercantile bourgeoisie, apt to compromise, is the biggest threat to gangster hegemony.

125

The scapegoat comes in ambivalent forms: eccentric and arriviste, saviour and pariah. The last is exemplified in Albert Camus's novel *L'Étranger*, usually translated as *The Outsider*, although *étranger* also implies foreigner, alien and immigrant. The anti-hero Meursault, a *pied-noir* (Algerian-born French citizen) is first seen at his mother's funeral. He shows no conventional sign of grief. The reader never gets close enough to Meursault to learn his 'Christian' name. Graced with no inner life, no intimate personality, at his mother's graveside he sips a *café au lait*. How did Camus choose his anti-hero's name? It belongs to a popular Beaune wine (red or white); an overdoing-it Derridan etymologist might detect undertones of 'death-leap' (*meurs/saut*), if not of breached *moeurs*. Void of human sentiment, if not of sexual appetite, Meursault has no allegiance, to men, to civility, to God. He shoots an Arab who has threatened him with a knife. He then fires three more shots into the prone body, possessed by some passion of which we never learn the precise source.

When tried in a French colonial court, he might successfully plead self-defence, but he does not. He embodies Rimbaud's '*Je est un autre*', an ego who is not himself. The psychopath, like the serial-killer in Richard Tomlinson's *Landru's Secret* (2018), can regard himself as if from a distance. Meursault's indifference procures his conviction. Sentenced to death, he shows no emotion. He looks forward to the crowd's howls of execration as he walks to the guillotine. As if to out-Dreyfus Dreyfus, he will mount the scaffold in an ostentatious parody of martyrdom. His death bears witness to nothing. Rather than a Christian prayer, he might as well recite Ernest Hemingway's 'Our Father which art in nada, nada be Thy Name...'

Claude Chabrol's 1963 film *Landru*, with Charles Denner, had a script by Françoise Sagan. As Landru approaches the scaffold, the magistrate in charge asks whether he really did kill all those women. Thanks to Sagan, Landru has an exquisite exit line: '*Ça, c'est mon petit bagage!*'

Hemingway's hero in *For Whom the Bell Tolls*, the wounded Robert Jordan, dies alone, holding the pass, hopelessly, in a war against Fascism that is not his own and that the reader knows to be futile (the novel did not appear until 1940). A notorious or, in some eyes, uplifting story of the Spanish Civil War, melodramatic but genuine, concerns Colonel Moscardó, the commander of the cadet garrison of the beleaguered Alcazár in Toledo. His son was captured by the 'Reds', who threatened to shoot him if the colonel did not surrender the fortress. They put the boy on the line, hoping that his impending fate would induce his father to surrender. The colonel recommended him to die bravely, for God and Spain. The boy was shot. The Alcazár never surrendered. Who can visit the fortress without a twinge of admiration for Moscardó and his garrison, that single motorbike supposedly their sole generator of electric power?

Robert Jordan has no God and is not Spanish. He dies, without loud declaration of conviction, for a losing cause, much the same one which Robert Oppenheimer would be accused of supporting. Like Sydney Carton, Jordan's suicidal gesture implies that it is a far, far better thing he does now than he has ever done before. The cause matters less than

337

courage for courage's sake, whether or not, as Cavafy had it, the Medes are bound to get through. In Hispanic dress, Hemingway ennobled the suicidal heritage which led him to end his own life, as his father had. His competitive spirit led him to say to Gary Cooper, the movie's hero, that he would 'beat him to the barn'.

Did Hemingway's choice of name for Robert Jordan owe something to Jordan the female golfer, accused of cheating, in *The Great Gatsby*, masterpiece of an author for whom Hemingway proved his respect by persistent disparagement? I saw Gary Cooper shooting his last film at Borehamwood studios. He still looked like Gary Cooper, but he wasn't all there. Jordan can also be a Jewish surname. I was at school with one or two. Tony, whom I scarcely knew until we were both in the Classical Sixth, claimed to translate English verse into good Latin hexameters literally in his sleep and serve them up, immaculate in their scansion, the next morning.

The second Jordan, Robin, was in my house, Lockites. A character of rare duplicity, not merely a deceiver, he doubled as dissenting intellectual (he lent me Auden's *Age of Anxiety*) and sporting paragon. Exception and conformist, he refused to 'do the Corps' (Junior Training Corps, JTC) and preferred 'estate work'. If he carried any Jewish blood, it was undeclared. He sang in the choir and was never heard to utter an obscenity in public. When I showed him a poem of mine ending 'The sum of all experience, muck', he suggested the obvious rhyming emendation, the one time I heard it on his lips.

I have a notion that Robin watched my petty calvary with a sympathy which betokened relief, not to say pleasure, that I had attracted the lightning. Was there also a tinge of envy? Ernest Hemingway, whose overt Jew, Robert Cohn in *The Sun Also Rises*, is no sort of hero, sometimes called himself Hemingstein, as if trying on second-hand clothes. There are, Roland Barthes said, no innocent words, his own included,

though he did not choose to say so. Barthes is revered in chic
circles for his enigmatic paradox that there is no such thing
as an author. Everything written, he suggested, has origins
outside the individual who puts it down. His writings are
gnomic – '*L'amant, c'est celui qui attend*' – scarcely witty.
It did not seem to Guy Lee to be a remark of great profun-
dity, but it does stick in the mind. Brevity is a recommended
adhesive. Guy never met Barthes nor, so far as I know, had
any personal quarrel with him, but he was gleeful when the
Parisian pundit was run over on a pedestrian crossing on his
way home after lunching with François Mitterrand at the
Collège de France. Guy was disdainful of a professor who
lived all his life with his mother. One of the most amiable men
I ever met, Guy rated Jews not excluded but 'exclusive'.

126

Laurent Binet's satire *La septième fonction du langage* (2015) makes clever play with the events surrounding Barthes's accident and the negligent treatment of the dying man. Binet anatomises the Parisian intellectual milieu and its endless games of one-upmanship, at the expense not least of its once-presiding duo, Philippe Sollers and Julia Kristeva. The fictional finger-amputation which follows a postulant being outsmarted by another candidate for top intello owes something both to *The Golden Bough* and to a story by Roald Dahl. I first heard mention of Dahl from Somerset Maugham in 1954: 'I made shift to read a dozen of his stories and three or four were quite good, but that's n-not enough, you know.'

In stylistic homage to Hemingway, in *L'Étranger* Camus employs what grammarians call asyndeton, linkless narrative. He never furnishes Meursault's actions, or inaction, with any suite of motives or purpose. Life is one disjointed thing after another. Meursault does what he does, no 'therefore', no 'but', no 'why', effect without cause, action without morality. In line with the triumph of the irrational, Primo Levi records how, when first in Auschwitz, he was thirsty enough to break off an icicle and suck it. He was told by a guard that his action was forbidden. Levi (a German speaker) said, '*Warum?*' Why? To which the guard replied, 'Here there is no *warum*.'

After Auschwitz, Theodor Adorno announced, there could
be no lyric poetry. Was he forecasting the parodic future of
Western art and theology after an event which could have no
adequate memorial? What had not been prevented, and had
no sane explanation, had to be repressed or repossessed by
those who came to lie about it. Amnesia has its humbug muse,
pastoral drag: deconstruction, post-modernism, neo-Marx-
ism advertise unending play/grounded rehearsal. Camus's
Meursault has no public or private ambition (and no first
name, as D. H. Lawrence alleged, wrongly, of Boldwood, in
an essay on Thomas Hardy's *Far from the Madding Crowd*;
close reading finds him a 'William'). Nothing matters more
to Meursault than anything else; he does not aspire to get
away with things nor spring to imposture. Meursault is a fictional projection of Camus's earlier postulate, in *The Myth
of Sisyphus* (1942), that the essential moral question is why
a man should not commit suicide. Was Camus lamenting the
prime casualty of the Second World War: that in the rubble
of values, he no longer saw any reason to go on living or
faith in salvation to require it? Was he also revealing the self-
centredness induced by recurrent tuberculosis? 'The horror,
the horror' is one thing, self-pity always there to displace it.

Julien Sorel, in Stendhal's *Le Rouge et le Noir* (1830), was
a purposeful outsider, a seducer (as Joseph Süß was said to
be) who revels in misleading the world about his sentiments
and purposes. Deceit is the dandy's top dressing and neatest
button. Like Balzac's Rastignac, when he looks down at Paris
and says, '*A nous deux maintenant!*', Julien Sorel challenges
society as an antagonist. So did his author: is Stendhal's claim
to fame as well written as his classic status suggests? The
journalistic pace of *Le Rouge et le Noir* is of a young man
urgent for fame, romantic and cynical *à la fois*. Julien has to
be a loner because he is a deceiver; no one reliant on charm
confides, unless falsely, in anyone else. That Stendhal was

Marie-Henri Beyle's *nom-de-plume*, a name to plume himself with, is consonant with his cool.

The pseudonymous boast no origins other than those they concoct for themselves. Honoré de Balzac awarded himself his particule. George Orwell sported no Old Etonian tie. The painter 'Count' Balthus, né Klossowski, stepped clear, he presumed, of his Jewish traces and was pettish with the biographer who raised them. Stendhal claimed affinity with a self-nominating 'Happy Few': initiates who appreciated each other's art. The self-styled have no childhood, flaunt no family tree: they presume *élite* kinship rather than being born into it. Imposture is a regular ingredient of the arts. Nijinsky 'faked' hanging in mid-air; the audience's credulity supported him there. André Gide declared that he hated families and – could it be? – their preference for 'normal' sons to continue their silly line. 'Who are my father and my mother?' Jesus asked, when – so Christian tendentiousness reports – he detached himself from mundane genealogy and grafted himself to a celestial stem.

Robert Oppenheimer elevated himself by attaining high places attached to no traditionally blighted root. Comedy and aspiration go together. The bourgeois *gentilhomme*, the bluestocking (Simone Weil and Susan Sontag) and the *poseur* (Oscar Wilde no less than Christopher Hitchens), genius and charlatan (Oppenheimer and Lysenko) climb common peaks, higher the better. Who can aim at success in the world's game and dispense with bluff? How many scholars have read all the books cited in their bibliographies? Some suspicious wit has coined the term 'fibliography' to cover the parade of meritorious padding. When accused of calling George Steiner a 'charlatan', Isaiah Berlin demurred: 'I said no such thing. I said he was a genuine charlatan.' Richard Davenport-Hines notes that Berlin was self-deprecating, unless it was crafty, enough to pin the same cachet to his own lapel.

127

Even in science, where verification and peer-review dis-
countenance sharp practice, there are a few inside-traders:
people who crib the work of others. Francis Crick and James
Watson, winners of a Nobel Prize for their explication of the
double helix, advanced their research by scanning Rosalind
Franklin's notes and images on the same topic. Desire for
credit, just or duplicitous, gives the diverse practitioners of
C. P. Snow's *The Two Cultures* one common characteristic.
Jorge Luis Borges makes play with this duplicity in *Pierre
Menard, autor del Quijote*.

Those whose achievements should have sated their vanities
are rarely above the temptation to appropriate the contributions of their underlings. Stanley Kubrick sought to make
those who wrote scripts for him sign a contract ceding to the
Master the final decision on who had written a given line or
thought of an idea. In this way, he legitimised his role as *solus
rex*, a mundane mutation of The Creator. Is it not written,
'the Lord thy God is a jealous God'? Even those who seem
hostile to the society in which they work are prone to become
addicted to its honours. Who lanced bourgeois vanities with
more accurate pricks than Henrik Ibsen? In his old age, he
grew avid for the same society's awards and medals. To
measure human beings on a single scale is always to misread

their double-helical nature. In biography, it is not enough to look at a subject in isolation. The close-up is not the whole man, nor can the whole man be excerpted, honestly, from contingency. Scarcely more than ten per cent of people who served in the Second World War were ever actually under enemy fire or engaged in direct fighting. Yet all had some sense of what it was to be in the service.

J. Robert Oppenheimer may not have been conscious of all, or even of many, of the events or currents to which I have alluded; men are shaped by elements of all kinds, genetic or historical, subconscious as well as documented. Whatever is latent in the language is liable to recur. Belonging and detachment are aspects of each other. The solitary is never alone: isolation implies that there is something from which it is distinct. What Jew, however lucky, can be wholly unaffected by how Jews have been seen, treated and depicted by others? Sartre's prescription for Europe's surviving Jews was that they should 'assume', as a Method actor does, their prescribed role. While it need not be yellow, Jews could never escape the star under which they were born. Alone among humans, their essence appeared to precede existence and shape their 'Being'. Wittgenstein said that his object in philosophy was 'to show the fly the way out of the fly-bottle'. Sartre's recommendation to Jews (and to no one else) was to regard the bottle as a showcase in which to flaunt what was expected of them. Denial of contingency is implicit in the one-size-fits-all solution to how 'they' should behave.

Existential status denied, The Jew is committed to a predestined *huis clos* no better, certainly no freer, than a glorified ghetto. Until he met and was enamoured, asexually, one assumes, of Benny Lévy, Sartre knew little of Jewish culture, though he was resentful enough of Raymond Aron, whose cool academic credentials trumped his own, to say to him, '*Pourquoi as-tu si peur de déconner?*' (Why are you so afraid of making a fool of yourself?). Sartre's remark can be unpacked to imply both that Aron was a prig, which he was not, and that he had no sense of humour, which may be true.

Having endured, and seconded, Sartre's appetite for the contingent pleasure of taking young women to bed, Simone de Beauvoir was jealous of Lévy's leverage on the old philosopher, whom he as good as seduced. Might it be that that quasi-conversion carried a vestige of the recantation that Julius Streicher affected to deliver, rather late in the day? After Sartre's death, and the Beaver's embrace of his decomposing body and legend, Lévy quit left-wing politicking and pursued Hebrew studies in Israel.

Raymond Aron was probably right about as many things as a dispassionate clerk could hope to be. He had been one of the first to rally to General de Gaulle, who was cool enough to remark, *après-coup*, that he had appealed to Frenchmen to join him in London and it was mostly Jews who did. Jean Moulin's secretary, a right-wing Catholic before the war, met Aron when the latter was on his way to London and was amazed by the older man's charm and erudition. Informed that Aron was a Jew, he found it impossible to believe. He had previously met only paper Jews in Catholic *réquisitoires*. While Aron dared to think outside the boxes on which Sartre tied his bows, the student youth of 1968 came to find it sexier to be wrong with Sartre than right with Aron.

Faced with the futility of Christian hope, Camus concluded, *'Il faut imaginer Sisyphe heureux.'* While Camus saw man forever rolling one absurd boulder or another, with some kind of a smile, Sartre excepted Jews, with didactic solemnity, from common humanity. In dark times, he and Simone de Beauvoir had not been outstanding Samaritans. In 1942, Poulou took the job of a deposed Jewish *lycée* professor with unapologetic careerism. In her 1954 novel *Les Mandarins*, which glorified the Sartrean 'family', Simone de Beauvoir neither mentioned the deportation of Jews from France nor created a character at all like her lover Claude Lanzmann, the Resistance fighter. Despite her own Sapphic episodes, she records no Lesbian adventure. She preferred to advertise her affair with the proletarian Chicago writer Nelson Algren as a rare *coup de foudre*. Puffed for the good of American sales, her portrait of him appeared to Algren to be patronising. A long correspondence had followed their affair; when *Les Mandarins* put icing on it, he affected to have but a vague memory of the French chick.

128

Not long after the Liberation, Sartre became the *frère-ennemi* of his one-time friend Camus, ostensibly because the latter played *philosophe* while lacking professorial credentials. In 1952, Sartre commissioned Francis Jeanson to write a long, sneering review of *L'homme Révolté* in the Sartrean family's house magazine, *Les Temps Modernes*. Claude Lanzmann's *Shoah* can be viewed as an apology, offered quite late in life, for his juvenile suppression of his Jewish origins in order to chime with the Sartrean 'family', in which there were no children, but one father.

Did young Lanzmann do anything unusually shameful in severing antique allegiances in the post-war world? In his late memoir, *Le Lièvre de Patagonie*, he recalls his embarrassment during the Occupation, when his mother made a loud and demanding exhibition of herself in a Parisian shoe-shop. The return of the repressed took the form of that protracted, never-overlong, cinematic confrontation with surviving victims and perpetrators of the Holocaust. *Shoah*'s often-unkempt footage promised no omissions of what cant calls 'disturbing' material. Lanzmann played the part of inquisitive, dispassionate observer, as menacing as he seemed curious. His shaggy film stands as an implacable maverick in which ethics swamp aesthetics.

Lanzmann's later films were fisty defences of the right of Israel to exist and to defend itself against the malice of the Arabs (which long preceded the creation of a Jewish state) and in spite of the pursed lips of European powers which had acquiesced in the *Shoah*, whether actively or passively. Lanzmann, more forceful than charming, retained ambition into his old age. When he was ninety, he told Philippe Labro that the one thing he still wanted was for his autobiography, *The Patagonian Hare*, to outsell Philippe's latest best-selling novel. I met Lanzmann once, on a Channel 4 programme. He felt no call to be studio-sociable. He wore *Shoah* like a proud yellow star. Enthusiastic mountaineer, his autobiography supplies a vivid account of an Alpine climb in tandem with Jeremy Bernstein, who promises me that, although the two were acquainted, that particular adventure never took place. As Billy Wilder and Izzy Diamond put it, at the end of *Some Like It Hot*: 'Nobody's perfect.'

129

The particular merit of Ray Monk's biography of J. R. Oppenheimer lies in its clear, detailed account of Oppenheimer's contribution to theoretical physics and its relevance to the Manhattan Project. During its composition, Ray asked me to look at the early chapters of his book. His tone and methods were necessarily his own. The passages dealing with Oppenheimer's boyhood and its effect on what came later were not as I might have written them. Why should they be? How could anyone without specific experience understand the strands, of fear and pride, arrogance and apprehension, which threaded the life of an ambitious American Jew of Oppenheimer's lineage?

Psychoanalysis is never more Jewish than in the presumption that no one fully gets over anything, however strong his or her psychic digestion. Nietzsche dared to say, 'Whatever does not kill me makes me stronger.' Does it? His own life offers small evidence of it. My glosses on Monk are, as Wittgenstein might have said, Talmudic. I doubt whether Ray would have altered his text to conform with my intuitions. Objective, documented biography is liable to miss the quick of its subject. Propriety docks the rarely documented contradictions and absurdities or puerilities of the child within the adult, the Jew (if that's the case) within the agnostic or apparently serene personality. If I let Ray down by my reticence, it was in the tradition of common civility.

The last time we were in touch was an occasion of the very sort that often escapes documented accounts. Ray invited me to take part in a symposium on biography shortly before the publication of *Inside the Center,* his study of J.R. Oppenheimer. I had small wish to get up at six in the morning to travel to Southampton, but I wrote a paper which I thought elaborate enough to suit the occasion and honoured the call. At Southampton station, I was hailed, as if we were friends, by Miriam Gross, a literary editor who had repeatedly done my work no favours but who now allowed me to pay for her taxi. I read my piece, somewhat over the grey heads of a sparse audience, and stayed to listen to a Penguin editor, ruled feint, tell us, in a university lecture room, how prospects of publication were determined by sales managers, today's Lord High Executioners.

Ray and I had collaborated, harmoniously, in editing and contributing to a very successful series of mini-monographs on philosophers, from Socrates to Wittgenstein. So far as observable facts were concerned, nothing was seen or heard to happen that morning, apart from lectures, hullos and how-are-yous, to rupture our friendship. After eating a sad sandwich, I told Ray that I should like to go home. He ordered a taxi and accompanied me to the forecourt, where we waited, for some time, for its arrival. We talked about what we seemed to have in common (he and his family had visited us in France) and wondered why, with no shortage of philosophers still to be anatomised, the publishers had aborted our successful series. Watched by a clever camera, should we have been seen to be very slightly at odds? There were no declared or even concealed grounds for any rupture. Was there something sorry in the way we stood to each other? Our distinct impatience for the taxi, my suggestion that Ray not wait, indicated terminal uneasiness. The taxi came. I wished him luck with the book. We shook hands goodbye. We have never communicated since.

None of my inflections of sentiment (as Henry James might have called them) had anything directly to do with Ray. We never exchanged an unfriendly word, and now we exchange none at all. Indirection is part of life. No scene is also a scene. To discount it is to miss the elements that explain nothing in human affairs but which, motes in the air, play a vagrant part in them. What Ray did not elect to imagine of Julius Robert Oppenheimer's fears, hopes, expectations, vanities, cannot be said to have been missed by him; they were not there to be itemised, only inferred.

Feminists are known to maintain that no man can (or should) impersonate a female or presume to know what women feel. Freud was perpetually puzzled to know what women wanted. How 'different' are Jews? How different would you have them? Who knows what Jews feel or think that no Gentile can guess? A specific Jew's character has a good deal to do with the circumstances into which he has been – as Heidegger put it, about humans in general – 'pitched' in society. There is a particular strain in Oppenheimer, the scholarly star, and the setting it rises in. Might Ray have got closer to the contradictions in Oppenheimer's mind and conduct if he had acknowledged what he could not explain? Perhaps he had no such apprehension.

Did Oppenheimer elect to be called Robert? Did his parents call him Julius? The irreplaceably manifold uses of fiction begin with guessing, or suggesting, just what makes this man, that woman, do the things they do, or even what they do not. Life is loud with silent squeals, scored with skid-marks that biographers seldom track or decorum chooses to ignore. Their trade has small place for imagination, unless spiced with a pinch of malice. Robert Graves's and Richard Aldington's front-liners' mockery of Lawrence of Arabia outrank endless pages of research that affects to make deference definitive, weight weighty.

130

Monk gives a calm account of Oppenheimer's 'crucifixion' while in summer camp. Given the segregation typical of old New York, it is no surprise that fourteen-year-old Robert's fellow-campers were all Jews. Many were quick to regard him as a smart-ass sissy. He had been vain enough to tell one of his classmates at Ethical Culture School, on Central Park West, 'Ask me a question in Latin and I'll answer in Greek.' I was, for a couple of semesters, a pupil in the same nice school. My teacher was Miss Henry. One day, in camp, a posse grabbed the young prig, marched him to an ice-store, stripped him naked, painted his genitals and backside with green paint and left him tied up. The shivering boy managed to escape and call his parents.

They uttered soothing words but elected to leave him in pariahdom for the rest of the holiday. Were they less callous than hopeful that their son would become tougher, or more tactful? To remove a child in such circumstances is not necessarily to do him a favour. Endurance can lead to a hardening of resolution to excel one's persecutors. It is also liable to open an irreparable breach between child and parents. It is not always easy to forgive people for doing what may be best. Is not Jesus reported to have said, 'Father, father, why hast thou forsaken me?'

When the sudden target of a bout of schoolboy anti-Semitism at Charterhouse in 1948, I was stunned by the resourceful malice of supposed friends, the resource coming from parental chat, communal uniformity (by assuming a common enemy), scriptural polemic. My father made an appointment with my headmaster, George Turner. Turner listened to Cedric's quiet fear that I might commit suicide (not a threat I ever made nor thought I entertained) and then said, 'Well, you have chosen to live in a Christian society.' The correct retort would have been, 'No choice is involved. We are British subjects. UK passports do not mention religion.'

The slyest of my persecutors was a direct descendant of Disraeli's smug opponent William Ewart Gladstone. Robin E. G. said that I was a rose with a nose like a hose. Among the others, a Welshman, and we all know what Taffy is; the son of the sole Indian peer of his time, next best thing to a wog; the son of a manager of the Yorkshire Penny Bank; a northerner with an unamended accent; the house captain of games, of whose dialogue I recall only, 'Everybody's doin' it, doin' it, picking his nose and chewin' it, chewin' it.' David later gave me my hockey and cricket 'houseteams' (colours).

I took comfort in not forgetting things. Accuracy of recall is the best revenge, apparent objectivity the smartest form of personal observation. Bias leans the ball close to the mark. Proust abandoned *Jean Santeuil* because he had overdone its autobiographical character. Reducing *le petit* Marcel to an exiguous figure in *A la recherche du temps perdu* tailored the text, veiled egotism in otherness. Maugham did something similar, if less artful, in *Of Human Bondage*. Not long ago I heard that one of my Carthusian picadors was dying from Parkinson's disease. I wrote to congratulate Jim on his distinguished work in television, some of it in tandem with me, quite as if we had become adult friends. He replied that his misfortune was just punishment for how he treated me all those years ago. I promised him that I should want nothing to do with any kind of justice which harboured that kind of disproportionate grudge. Never my conscious intention, might it be that being forgiven weighed on him like the last straw?

Fred Koenig regarded his friend Robert's 'crucifixion' as determinant of Oppenheimer's attitude to the world. That the victim had been nicknamed 'Cutie' leads to the suspicion that the choice of colour had symbolic meaning: green is traditionally associated with homosexuals. 'Suits you, sir!' was the camp catchphrase of a pair of comic tailors on TV when draping a client in green cloth. If Oppenheimer is never documented as having homosexual appetites, was there a hint of 'camp' in his good opinion of himself and in his tendency to flaunt it? His notorious 'affair' with Haakon Chevalier suggests what is clearly the case: not all passions between men are erotic. Friendships can have a zest of duplicity, toying with what the in-group used to call 'the other', without involving or desiring genital consummation. The narcissist is not necessarily complacent. One poet speaks of 'Narcissus, that plain boy'. When someone works hard at being read as exceptional, there is often a tincture of doubt in his/her self-esteem.

131

A. J. Ayer's *Language, Truth and Logic* led him to wake up somewhat famous when he was twenty-five. During his rise to ermined eminence, Ayer collected fame for disputatious wit. His first quality never self-effacement, he confessed that, for all those accolades and doctorates, he was always waiting for someone to denounce him as a bloody Jew. The shadow of Joseph Süß Oppenheimer falls across even the most celebrated of those eager for limelight. The late Jimmy Goldsmith's father, who passed for a thorough Englishman until the Great War, in which he served gallantly, excited apprehensions that he was a bit of a Hun, if not a Jew, or both. After 1918, he sold up and went to live in France.

Oppenheimer came to have his first name Julius in common with Streicher, the loutish Nazi Jew-baiter, and with Julius Rosenberg, the alleged atom spy; yes, Caesar too. Perhaps 'Oppy', as he came to be called, although never quite a pet, flinched from the too-prompt announcement made by Julius' first syllable. He had no reason to be ashamed of the family from which he distanced himself. His father had come from Germany in 1888 and made an American fortune as a textile importer. His mother was a painter whose taste was evident in the collection, including Van Gogh, Vuillard and Picasso, which adorned the family's large Riverside Drive apartment. The Upper West Side of Central Park was a rich Jewish enclave. They had it and they flaunted it. By the time their older son was adolescent, the Oppenheimers were high in the peerage of 'Our Crowd', as Stephen Birmingham dubbed the German Jewish *gratin* of Manhattan.

Their parents' wealth and status gave Robert and his brother Frank hedged security. Even for exceptionally brilliant Jews, the Gentile world was to be approached with discretion. Oppenheimer's command of Latin, Greek and the several languages which came to be added to them announced that he meant to be a Jew *pas comme les autres*: where possible, no Jew at all. Solitary ascent to the peak of the academic cursus was his likeliest means of escape from the menace of his peers. Only the cleverest Jews, with rare qualities and good tailors, hoped to find places in Ivy League universities. Where better to excel than where not entirely welcome?

Mr Eliot's solicited correspondent, Groucho Marx, was not alone in maintaining that he did not care to belong to any club that would have him as a member. Consistent with hagiographical solemnity, Eliot's academic admirers waste little time on his crush on Groucho. Is it not evidence of Tom's nice side that he made so unlikely an approach to a Marx brother? Style owes something to the audience, ideal or otherwise, to whom a letter is directed. Prose has to be versatile if the writer hopes to make emotional or humorous contact. Shelley's letters supply as clear an indication of monotonous self-centredness as any scrutineer could find in his verses; Jane Austen's are no less flat. Byron's mutability, tuned to the person to whom his letters are addressed, is a form of seduction, plumed with jokes and teases or lordly with propriety. Conceit and doing the voices are easily compatible. Byron wrote to Teresa Guiccioli, his last attachment, in cursive

Italian. Might it be that Eliot was more pleased to get a letter from Groucho, with its hint of knockabout, than Groucho to hear from the laureate?

132

In 1922, the president of Harvard, Abbott Lawrence Lowell, made it a principle to limit the number of Jewish admissions. As Monk puts it, nicely, 'The problem was not that Jews were not good students, or that they were bad people; it was that, just by being Jews... they were unacceptable, except in small... numbers.' Eliot would advertise the same view. Also writing in the 1920s, George Wickersham, a former United States attorney general, deplored the way in which the American bar was filled with a 'pestiferous horde of aspiring lawyers whose spoken English is of the most imperfect character and who lack the faintest comprehension of the nature of our institutions or their history and development'.

In the 1940s, Wickersham (nice Trollopian name for a man of straw!) was seconded by Harlan Fiske Stone, dean of Columbia University Law School, who went on to become chief justice of the Supreme Court. He declared that Jewish lawyers constituted the 'greater numbers of the unfit who exhibit racial tendencies toward study by memorization and who display a mind almost Oriental in its fidelity to the minutiae of the subject without regard to any controlling rule or reason'.

Stone's remarks can easily be classed as typical of a dated, Waspish prig; perhaps too quickly. His allusion to 'controlling rule or reason' has unintended relevance to Wittgenstein's notion of what it is to follow or honour a rule. Merely to keep the law or to steer clear of breaking it is not the same thing as respecting it. To be reasonable is not simply to be alert to false conclusions on the part of an opponent; it also implies, if it does not announce, that one wishes to arrive at a harmonious resolution. This harmony may be technical; it is also social. The British barrister's courteous humbug when referring to his opponent as 'my learned friend' is pinstriped with a conventional, not silly, acknowledgement that, when the case is done, mutual respect will, or should, remain intact.

The moderation to be exercised in the play of rules and reason, if formulated, would itself become a rule; only when implicit does it remain a principle. Between the two wars, in a world riven by conflicting ideologies and racial pretensions, physicists appeared immune to the rhetoric common in 'the arts'. It was nice to suppose that, while on duty, scientists and mathematicians conversed in a nuance- and value-free language. If duly collegiate, they would understand each other without persuasive nuances or contentious translation – *if*. Conceits and credulities come in all sizes.

In the first, boldly polemic edition of *Language, Truth and Logic*, A. J. Ayer insisted that 'verification' supplied an implacable means of distinguishing true from false or, in particular, metaphysical propositions. His critics were quick, if not happy, to point out that the process of verification could not itself be verified and hence had to be defined, with whatever sigh or smirk, as itself metaphysical. Anyone with a sense of decency, Ayer might have said, but did not, should have small difficulty in seeing that the process of testing whether something is true cannot itself be 'true', but rather plausible, acceptable, honest and so on. Must hallmarks be silver? Failing to agree on what amounts to a reputable procedure must otherwise lead to an eternal regress. The comedy of the case is that any argument, like Ayer's which relegated 'ethics' to the lumber room, has to be conducted in accordance with unspoken, perhaps indefinable, proprieties. I remember passing a costume jewellery store on Madison Avenue. A notice promised, 'Everything in this window guaranteed fake.' Did anyone take it that that included the notice?

Ayer eventually conceded that there was no formal way in which verification could itself be proved conclusive. *Eppure...* it remains true, socially if not formally, that a decent society will not embrace, still less enforce, ideas without foundation in common sense and a certain civility (as in Montesquieu's *Défense de l'Esprit des Lois*). Who will define unarguably what common sense is as it was demanded of Ayer in order to verify the principle of verification? One cannot dissect a shadow. A society without unspoken rules will either disintegrate or become crippled by ever-increasing sets of laws which can be enforced, in practice, only by selective application and a bureaucratic apparatus apt for corruption by those whose power it purports to regulate.

Exit from the European Union, it has been argued, smugly, means that foreigners will no longer be able to oblige the British to conform to alien laws; hence it seems plausible to blare that 'we've got our country back'. In unsurprising practice, we are witnessing the return of the least amiable symptoms of resentments and fears, of aliens of various kinds, not least (the old tunes still the best) of 'the Jews'. I am promised that the loudest grinning celebrant of Britain's restored independence was in the habit, at school, of creeping up behind Jewish fellow-pupils, making the hiss of escaping gas and whispering, 'Gas the lot!' Joseph Ettedgui, founder of the Joseph chain of classy clothiers, is said to have been among his victims. Infamy too is a spur.

Doctor Johnson said that patriotism was the last resort of the scoundrel. He was referring to a political cabal whose members cloaked ambition in a show of principle; same difference, as some people will say. The modern Johnson, master Boris, identified the national interest with self-advancement and pruned his party into a sect loyal only to opportunism. When his selection of colleagues turned against him, he accused the House of Commons bipartisan committee delegated to quiz him of being a kangaroo court, and hopped it.

133

Before the Great War, the complacency of Our Crowd (of long-established, mostly Upper West Side, German Jews) disposed them to use the coinage 'kike' to designate the influx of Yiddish-speaking *Ost-Juden* immigrants whose names often ended in -ski or -sky. Many were in flight from the pogroms which gave Cossacks and Russians a common, defenceless target. The Judaism taught by rabbis in the shtetls of the Pale of Settlement gave central importance to 'Thou Shalt Not Kill'. Arrival in the New World emancipated newcomers from rabbinic ordinance. Abbreviating their names, or taking immigration officers' mispronunciations as a kind of baptism, 'Itzig off the pickle boat', as my mother was known to call the archetypal immigrant, became more-or-less instantly trans-Atlantic. Thrown into the American hopper, Yiddish speakers came to learn the ups and downs of social snakes and ladders in the land of the free and the more-or-less freed. Their argot infected American speech to the point that 'chutzpah' (insolence verging on bluff) is now a commonplace.

Jews came to distinguish themselves in nearly every department of American life to which they could gain access, including the underworld: Meyer Lansky and others are paraded in Rich Cohen's *Tough Jews* (1998). Jewish gangsters were embraced in the self-mockery in a range of stories, none of which is ever likely to raise a laugh when repeated by Gentiles. One is of a Jewish hitman, wounded in a shootout, who stumbles to his mother's tenement door. She opens it and he staggers in drenched in blood. 'Mama, I...' 'First eat,' she says.

If his brilliance exasperated Oppenheimer's schoolfellows, it won access to circles to which his quondam persecutors were never to be admitted and where his moneyed parents would be socially and intellectually outclassed. 'Crucifixion' accelerated the urge to be exceptional. At the same time, the scar on his psyche may have inclined him, during the 1920s, to seek comradeship under what he, and no few others, took to be the ecumenical aegis of the American Communist Party. Negligible contact with the working class makes it easy to idealise the proletariat. Unlike Wittgenstein, Oppenheimer never rejected the benefits of his father's money; he did, however, have enough of a social conscience not to be grateful for them.

Was Wittgenstein's rejection of family wealth not an implicit renunciation of Jewishness? He refused the money rather than gave it away, it seems, but dread of pollution lent his gesture a sort of noble selfishness. The chastity of philosophical investigations with regard to worldly temptations has at least some connection with monastic, not to mention Chasidic, tradition. However much he doubted the value or even the propriety of his professorial role, despite his insistence that philosophy had no particular subject matter, Wittgenstein scarcely touched either on sex or on economics. In this regard he came to don the lineaments of the traditional English gentleman.

After his installation in Cambridge, Wittgenstein, the one and only W (was he ever referred to as Ludwig?), appeared to embrace a life akin to that of Diogenes. The greatest luxury in his rooms was a canvas-seated deck chair. After flirtations with positivism and communism, he avoided adhesion to any specific doctrine, though he was said to have been lured by the

Catholicism pressed upon him by Geach and Anscombe. In the early 1950s, Cambridge philosophy, while imbued with Wittgensteinian methods (and boxed gestures), was limited to traditional Britannic topics.

The work of Georg Simmel, who preceded the young Wittgenstein, centred without *états d'âme* on Money. Simmel endured the usual impediments to progress in German universities with dignity and without inhibitions with regard to subject matter. If his masterpiece was besmirched by its topic (cash was equated with shit by Freud), his interest was no less philosophical than economic. Insistence on the duplicities in human notation denounced the *naïveté* of seeking to measure motives and ambitions on a single common scale. Simmel's subtlety accommodates both Marx and Freud. His father a convert to Catholicism, the double helix would have been no surprise to him. I never heard his name cited among Cambridge Moral Scientists.

Wittgenstein's attempt to cleanse himself of the taint of the cushioned life cannot be attributed to a single source, whether the dread of faeces or the wish to be cleansed of the shame of homosexuality. His favourite areas of discourse were at a distance from the savage realities of twentieth-century politics and social life. It is usually taken that his reference to philosophy as 'the game' was light-hearted. Did he know that 'the game' is what English prostitutes are commonly said to be on? One might argue that W's terminology was an unintentional advertisement for what he was avoiding; it declared whereof he chose not to speak. He is reported as saying, when on his deathbed in Dr Beavan's house in Cambridge, 'Tell them it's been wonderful.' Does that mean that it had, or that people were liable to believe anything?

134

Both physics and Marxism promise universally dominant logics. The Party, parodying science, barred no one from its creed. Communism was a materialist church without metaphysical credo. As with celestial Christianity, in its company there was, supposedly, neither Jew nor Gentile. Young Robert Oppenheimer's ambition was to find a world elsewhere, while still shining in this one. There is small evidence, even in hostile sources, that he had any practical interest in furthering the power of the Soviet Union. His notion of communism was an abstraction; its human adherents, like Saint Paul's Saved, were without racial distinguishing mark; for the Party faithful, the sole original, quasi-racial, blemish was to be born bourgeois.

In retrospect, Oppenheimer appears to have been destined from the beginning for great things. Biographers tend to assume that painful events in their subject's early life can later be effaced by success. For all his poetic and erotic triumphs, Byron's club foot was a sorry spur. He never forgot overhearing his first love, Mary Chaworth, saying, 'Do you think I could feel anything for that lame boy?' Oppenheimer's isolation had the piquancy of being impressed upon him by a pack of adolescent Jews. Asked whether the cruel and useless treatment for his lame foot was painful, the young Byron said, 'You shall see no signs of it in me.' Yet all his life he walked with a lordly limp; he was as other men only in the water, hence his showy nocturnal swim, flaming beacon upraised in one hand, along the Grand Canal, as playing Leander he had swum the Hellespont. Oppy's culture was remarkable, not to say ostentatious; he selected his reading with eclectic *hauteur*. Playing the polymorph grandee, Byron wrote 'Hebrew Melodies' for Isaac Nathan, a Jewish musician; he also favoured a prototypical Jewish state and was ready to die for liberated Greece, while happy to dine with Ali Pasha, its ruthless governor.

Oppenheimer's 'crucifixion' disposed him to become a modern Joseph, apt for service to Pharaoh. Versatility patched a coat of many intellectual colours; other Jews were both enemies and kin. His eventual pleasure would be to patronise them in the service of America's Wasp *élite*. His blood brother, young Frank, was more tenderly, if condescendingly, treated. Shame and pride, durable double act, left Robert wary of contemporaries. He craved the company of seniors whom he meant to outrun and outshine. He paid the prodigy's price of becoming old before his time. His second cousin, the poet George Oppen(heimer), once said of old age, 'What a strange thing to happen to a little boy!'

There is no evidence that any of Cutie's fellow-campers ever recalled, still less regretted, what they had done to the young genius. Nor, so far as we know, did he ever take direct revenge. Brecht wrote: 'When the wound / Stops hurting / What hurts is / The scar.' Crucifixion doubles for election. It is tempting to propose that Oppenheimer's eventual elevation over obscure persecutors left him with a secret appetite to be seen, like Alfred Dreyfus, as the target of cruel, unwarranted accusations. Might it be that Oppenheimer's folly, in the early 1950s, when he lied repeatedly to the authorities on matters about which he could, without danger to himself, have told the truth, derived from some sour urge to revisit his early calvary, if only to be measured for a martyr's halo? With the Japanese surrender to his credit, he had reason to imagine that, this time, he could triumph over his persecutors. Admiral Strauss and his one-time friend Edward Teller, Oppy's Iago, were trying to paint him red. Did he presume himself eminent enough to put them down, single-handed? Like Othello, he could claim to have rendered the state some service.

In the volume of my notebooks entitled *There and Then*, there is a passage which suggests Oppenheimer's double vision of himself, as paragon and pariah: 'George [Steiner] had been besotted with J.R.O. He met him one day after O.'s "disgrace". He was still a famous personality, respected at Princeton above all. Oppenheimer told G. that he had just been to Paris where he had seen his own story dramatised under the title *In the Matter* of J.R.O. He said what a scourging ordeal it had been to watch himself being impersonated and having to endure again, in anguished detachment, the whole of his calvary. G. looked closely at the man he venerated and saw in him only pride and exultation. In that moment, the long love died.' What might he or George have thought of the 2023 film that is now likely to pass for authentic biography?

135

Fear of the masses can inspire a wish both to be immune and to lead them. To the outsider, belonging is immunity; it also remains provisional. Rebecca West said of Harold Wilson that, even as prime minister, he looked as if he was expecting to be found out. When a clever boy loses faith in the amiable intentions of his contemporaries, fame is the best protection. Unable to confront louts physically, he will trump them intellectually and socially. Having been outnumbered and, in Robert Oppenheimer's case, unmanned – that coat of green paint was symbolic emasculation – can generate an air of invulnerable hauteur. Dread of contemporaries is mantled in precociousness.

While redolent of charm, especially on public occasions, such a man is also liable to turn, capriciously, on friends and pupils. Early experience proves that those close to him double for potential enemies; they can be tickled, like trout, not trusted. To deceive others is to rise above them. What greater pleasure than pulling rank on one's peers? Then again, riding for a fall can be as exhilarating as the prospect of a kill. Condescension, backed by mastery of an arcane discipline, mantles fear of not being man enough to wear true colours and stand by them. The uneasy ego affects the autonomy of a father who will not let him down.

J. R. Oppenheimer's ambition was charged with duplicity: at once diligent and mark of the *recherché* science in which he became involved. Willing to rough it, for instance, riding long distances in the mountains of New Mexico, he tested himself more rigorously than he suffered others to challenge him. Fashioning a secret world elsewhere, he emigrated to arcane languages and cultures. Mimicry proved more scintillating than its models; wit outsmarted the original. The polymath and polyglot may be admired; how thoroughly is he liked by those he puts in the shade? 'Oppy' was more abbreviation than endearment. The family of his namesake and second cousin the poet George Oppen amputated giveaway syllables. George joined the Communist Party, without ever being involved, we are promised, in its darker doings. In the 1930s, Walter Benjamin told Gershom Scholem that he had joined the Party in an 'heuristic' spirit. He was lucky if the comrades never noticed the condescension. A toe in the water is no whole-hearted baptism.

Biographers, nowadays often disposed to coddle their subject in first-name terms, remain liable to be chilled by J. R. Oppenheimer's amalgam of charm without cordiality, intelligence without warmth, desire without passion. An alcoholic wife is often a mute, self-punitive accuser. Oppy's gaucherie – manifest in cut-to-the-chase overtures to a colleague's wife whom he was meeting for the first time – was both infantile (like a child urgent for the breast) and crass. Did he play the wanton to prove that, by overdoing it, he was exempt from common courtesies? Byron once fell on a Calais chambermaid like a bolt of lightning, as Zeus on Semele, Oppy on Mrs Whoever.

When Monk reports the way in which young Robert responded to the news of his mother's death, by saying, 'My mother is dead... my mother is dead... my mother is dead,' he speculates neither on the volume of the repetition, nor on the duration of the intervals between the phrases. Yet silences are parts of speech; in Pinter's art, they can stretch to three syllables. Was Oppenheimer seeking to convince himself that his mother's death had really taken place? Did he repeat what ought to have mattered to him (and produce proper tears) or was his response a ritual triplet like the apotropaic spit – resembling the Greek *po po po* – of the shtetl Jew he never was? Had a secret wish been fulfilled and concealed by a show of grief he did not feel? Did he recall Jesus saying, 'Who are my father and my mother?' André Gide's *'familles, je vous hais'* qualifies him for the same cool club.

With his quasi-Petrine repetition, was Oppy savouring the phrase, in the manner of an actor rehearsing how best to deliver it, to himself no less than to others? Like Camus's Meursault, he appeared to have no twinge of what was expected of a normal son. Might a mother's death be no less of a liberation than a father's? The child's guilt dies with her. Did Freud deceive himself, and others, on that point? Willie Maugham kept his dead mother's picture beside his bed all his life. So? Indeed: devotion and accusation can be two faces of the same card.

136

Oppy's adolescent 'crucifixion' could scarcely be attributed to anti-Semitism; yet his smart-ass affectations paraded what anti-Semites find most insufferable in Jews who are (in Gore Vidal's twee concession) 'too clever-by-one-quarter'. Other Jewish boys in camp that summer discharged the sense of inferiority he vented upon them by mounting the persecution of one who was both like and not like them. How not to enjoy impersonating anti-Semites for a day? As for the scapegoat they left for dud, in time he had his resurrection. Shaman and showman, the pariah lived to be his country's saviour and bringer of death to enemies for whom he entertained no personal hostility.

The atom bomb (nicknamed Big Boy) did to the Japanese what it is no wicked guess to imagine that 'Cutie' wished he could have done to those other smallish boys in summer camp. The harshest suspicion about human motives and actions is that a double helix of the trivial and the sublime is liable to be ravelled around even the best of them. Freud might have called such a convoluted conceit the Coriolanus complex. Then again, what cheers more choice than those that issue from the ranks of Tuscany?

At a crucial moment in world history, Oppenheimer was licensed to direct and dominate a cadre of rare talents playing for the common good. At Los Alamos, commissioned by the president of the United States, his duty was to save the West by destroying the evil (yellow) Easterners who threatened it. Did anyone think that the A-bomb might be used against Germany? On the side of the angels, Oppy could attach wings to his own back, gloriously, publicly and virtuously. Leadership of the whole 'Manhattan' operation required that those ranked beneath him have no idea, needed to have no idea, of the contradictions which braced his *superbe*. His aura depended on something of the remoteness which General de Gaulle considered the sign of the true leader: a self-designed, self-inflicted iron mask. Such a man is estranged from his own personality: '*Je est un dead,*' said Rimbaud; Caesar was Caesar, never Julius: he, not 'I', conquered Gaul, quite as if he was serving no personal ambition for loot.

Like the biblical Joseph, Oppenheimer was authorised, as if by Washington's Pharaoh, to direct Jews and Gentiles as seemed best to him. No longer obliged to play his parents' son, as unchallenged commander he realised a destiny which no one could have guessed within his reach. Vanity and self-distrust – thrust upon him by bully-boys whom no individual child could well resist – had already inspired him to compensatory acts of individual daring and deviousness, such as his juvenile attempt, in 1924, to poison the Cambridge physics don Patrick Blackett with an apple charged with 'toxic chemicals'. In 1979, Monk reports, Francis Fergusson said that Oppenheimer told him that he used 'cyanide or something similar'.

Alan Turing, equally brilliant outsider, contrived to kill himself, quite as if making England's ungrateful society his own murderer, by eating an apple sauced with cyanide. Turing's suicide, in 1954, after being arrested for homosexual acts, deprived an ungrateful country of his genius. More than any other single person, he had helped the Allies win the war by cracking the German Enigma codes. He did not make the right friends in the right places. His sole reward was callous prosecution and reduction to the rank. Lytton Strachey might have been naughty enough to say that the English made Turing a Jew, crucifixion his peerage. His major contribution to victory in Europe not enough to enlarge the priggishness of his countrymen, Turing was metaphorically painted green. J. L. Austin, with contributions of almost equal merit as a wartime lieutenant-colonel, proceeded to be an Oxford philosopher of professorial rank and paternal virtue. The unsociable Turing's sexual tastes and their public indictment drove him, without back-up from ranking self-redeemers, to suicide.

137

Lytton Strachey's denigration of 'eminent Victorians' purged his generation of guilt they might have felt for the waning of the imperious patriotism of before that signal moment in 1910 when, as the self-conscious Virginia Woolf put it, Everything Changed. It is more plausible to say that belief in European civilisation choked in the mud of Flanders. The sense of honour embodied in the Liberal Sir Edward Grey obliged the British to go to war, as they would in 1939, not for material advantage, but because they had given their word. Would Bismarck ever have made so quixotic a mistake?

Both world wars were economically disastrous for Britain, although some still say (Niall Ferguson among them) that it was, in some quasi-moral sense, necessary. The late Alan Clark, toff and amorist, regarded Britain's 1939 declaration of war as a quixotry too far. Like any number of French intellectuals, Marcel Déat *en tête*, he would have preferred an alliance with the Nazis capped with Aryan dividends. Clark's father was Kenneth Clark, whose TV series *Civilisation* testified to high-bourgeois connoisseurship and may have disposed his Etonian son to a revulsion from Culture, like that of Great War flying hero Herman Goering. K. Clark's smugness, chin up, eyes narrowed, excited the Marxist scorn of John Berger, seconded by Michael Ayrton.

Strachey's essays derided what could never be recovered. Britain's evangelical optimism had covered all kinds of vanities, never without self-serving belief in civilised achievements and possibilities. Strachey's naughty solemnity cannot be attributed solely to his sense of never being fully at home in straight society. Mockery of Victorian values, like his determination not to fight for King and Country, lent contrariness the semblance of *sérieux*. Scorn for how things are in a given society furnishes no practical armature for a better.

Oscar Wilde has been promoted to a status attained only by those who have been victimised by contemporaries when, admirers insist, they should have covered him with laurel. The presumption that Wilde was a victim of dated prejudice ignores the fact that, if a man were convicted today of erotic activities of a similar order with under-age boys he would, as the Rolf Harris case proved, face a far longer prison sentence. The public would be urged to lynch him by columnists in newspapers whose proprietors live beyond reach of cosh or court. Another Harris, the scoundrel Frank, was among the few who remained loyal to Oscar Wilde, despite Wilde's response to Harris's boast of social distinction: 'Yes, Frank, you've dined in every great house in London. Once.'

138

Young Oppy's plan to kill Blackett smacks of psychopathic puerility. Blackett was everything the postulant Jew was not. John Edsall, the biochemist, recalled him as: 'brilliant and handsome and a man of great social charm', as well as a renowned scientist. Edsall and Monk are too tactful to speculate on whether Blackett embodied the one thing that Oppenheimer could never emulate: Gentile genius. Might it not be that Oppy harboured a restless impulse to do something which might merit the pariahdom visited on him by those who took him into the ice-house not all that many years before? For a fortunately farcical moment, he assumed the role of the very Jew he never wanted to be: a hysterical kike. Imagine if Blackett had died.

Monk notes that Oppenheimer's parents were in Cambridge at the time, but he makes no connection between their presence and their son's grotesque manner of drawing attention to himself. Thanks to his father's diplomacy, the Cambridge authorities agreed, with rare generosity, which Blackett must have seconded, to let Robert continue his studies, provided he sought psychiatric help. He complied with scant gratitude. When Francis Fergusson asked how the treatment was going, Monk reports that the twenty-year-old replied that 'the guy was too stupid to follow him and that he knew more about his troubles than the doctor did'. He seems to have looked quite nutty at this stage, 'with his hat one side of his head'; Hamlet playing Yorick. Less than twenty years later, the same man was charged with the enterprise which would change the course of the war against Japan and the fate of humanity.

Oppenheimer is said to have been so lonely and frustrated in Cambridge that when the master of the Cavendish, Sir Ernest Rutherford, rejected him as a graduate student, he fell in a faint on the laboratory floor. Did some casual British remark, not necessarily anti-Semitic, perhaps anti-American, or merely dismissive, trigger memories of juvenile humiliation and prime his passing out (or the affectation of doing so)? Late in life, he recalled that he 'felt so unhappy in Cambridge that he used to get down on the floor and roll from side to side'. One can imagine a proper college-tied Cantab of the day remarking on how alien it was to be so frantic a bad loser.

To seek to poison his teacher with fruit from the Edenic tree of knowledge was a conceit to appeal to Oppenheimer's notion of poetic justice. It would not be out of character for him to have recalled the *doron adoron*, gift that was not a gift, which allowed Odysseus and his fellow-warriors to gain furtive entry, cached in the belly of the Wooden Horse, into the citadel of the Trojans. If one looks at the case as Kenneth Burke might, Oppenheimer was webbed in a nexus of motives, American patriotism not least: one of his strongest ambitions came to be to make the US, rather than Europe, the fulcrum of progress in physics. Then again (as so often) the desire to prove himself a genuine Yank suggests apprehension that he was not one.

The English have always permitted themselves to sneer at the 'almighty dollar' (cf. 'Jewish money'), but Britannic vanity finds it difficult to believe that Americans can harbour hostile feelings towards their peerless motherland. Conceit leaves people short of suspicions. Did the attempt on Blackett's life resemble that of a frustrated Oedipus, aware that someone had already solved the riddle of the Sphinx and gained the eminence he craved? The embarrassment which the gauche felony provoked in Oppenheimer's actual father served as a soft assassination. Might the prodigious son have wanted to teach his parents not to follow him around and remind him, and other people, by their presence, of what sort of people he came from? The 'inexplicable' attempt on Blackett's life may have had any number of contingent motives, plus too much drink perhaps, but it chimes with the Oedipal aspect of Oppy's career: the ambitious man seeks both to impress the 'father' of his speciality and to supplant him.

Monk reads Oppenheimer as a prodigious physicist who did not immediately recognise science as his vocation. He had turned first, as more than a few New York Jews did, to fiction as an escape from exotic enclosure into native fame. As a paragon of New York literary garrulity, Alfred Kazin's books sported titles that insisted on both his Jewishness and his Americanism. Saul Bellow, in the first sentence of *Augie March*, has his hero declare, 'I am an American, Chicago-born' (Bellow was Canadian-born). Did Robert Oppenheimer abandon the writer's life when he realised that it might entail self-examination? The physicist is not called on to anatomise himself. If the work is outstanding, so is the man, nominally, never for his character. Unmoved by individual personality, it is nice to presume that science parades no moral proprietors.

139

Jeremy Bernstein, who has led an unconcealed double life, first a physicist, then a long-time writer for the *New Yorker*, principally on scientific topics, exploded my naïve notion of the collegiate habits of scientists. He delivered me a bouquet of thorns selected from the *obiter dicta* of the Hungarian-born physicist Valentine Telegdi: 'When I was at Princeton,' Bernstein says, 'there suddenly appeared Telegdi. He had first knocked on my neighbour's door, a rather odd-looking mathematician. "There is living across from you a pithecanthropus erectus," he said. He had celebrated feuds, one... with his Chicago colleague Herbert Anderson... "This man scatters mesons from horseshit. This way you learn neither about mesons nor about horseshit." When one of Anderson's students applied to work with Telegdi, he was told, "You are a ship leaving a sinking rat." A Swiss colleague said... "It's worse if he likes you."'

Oppenheimer was quicker to correct others than to make sure that he was right himself. If some part of him wanted to humiliate rivals, was he also a self-torturer who, by his provocations, had to prove that he could take it? Self-esteem was matched by need to test his nerve; he embarked on acts of boyish rashness, such as putting to sea, off Long Island, alone in a small boat in foul weather. Shelley, who did something similar, in his case fatal, in the Ligurian Sea, had been bullied at Eton College. His middle name, Bysshe, was used derisively, as 'Cutie' was in the teenage Oppenheimer's persecution. Shelley too suffered imputations of effeminacy. He would almost certainly have joined the Communist Party, crutch and pulpit, had it been available at the time. Marching in step never his lame style, Byron made do with patronising the Italian Carbonari and their revolutionary panache.

No sooner had Shelley gone up to Oxford than he published *The Necessity of Atheism*. He must have guessed that the title alone would procure his being sent down. The university authorities were all clergymen. If Shelley's insolence had no manifest effect on his contemporaries, he succeeded in immediately becoming more notorious than any one of them. Mark Boxer did something similar in 1954 in Cambridge, when *Granta*, while he was editor, published a poem by a local alcoholic which was deemed blasphemous. It led to Boxer's enforced, triumphant, temporary exodus, accompanied by drummers and applause. It was a seminal instance of today's substitution of celebrity for achievement; Mark became Marc, the cartoonist, as Saul had Paul, the gospeller. Boxer's access to metropolitan fame was boosted by those whose purpose had been to teach him a lesson, their rocket his propulsion. Was he a Jew? Like Max Beerbohm, another cartoonist, he relied on being incomparable.

Shelley's insolence, badged with humane qualities, encouraged Paul Foot to write *Red Shelley* in which the aristocratic poet and *flâneur* was portrayed as a rouged, prototypical left-wing visionary. Shelley rehearsed his reaction to death during that storm when he and Byron shared a small boat on Lac Léman. His verses could express aggression which, in daily circumstances, his Dionysian frailty did not. He was forked between respect for 'antique courtesies' and chiliastic rupture with the society of his fathers. *The Revolt of Islam* prefigured the modern Left's disposition to side with whatever alien force might humble Western civilisation and its complacent grandees.

Michel Foucault was one of the first to salute the Iranian Revolution of 1979 and the 'justice' which has led to the massacre of thousands of Iranians whose capital crime was association with the secular state of the evicted Shah (whom the president of the French Republic, Valérie Giscard d'Estaing, had been heard to address on the telephone as 'Sire'). Those who now dissent, in increasing numbers, from the theocratic oligarchy of the Ayatollah and his henchmen are liable to execution after summary trial. Foucault applauded the economy whereby accusation and execution were all but simultaneous. Enthusiasm for righteous lynching might seem strange coming from an author who had devoted long studies, in the spirit of Voltaire, to the protracted cruelties of Christian judicial procedures. Must it be a sign of 'homophobia' (a bastard term) to remark that Foucault was both rare intelligence and hectically hostile to the morality of 'the West'? That the Ayatollah and his fellow-believers proved as pitiless in regard to male homosexuals as to 'free' (unveiled) women did nothing to mitigate Foucault's vengeful vision. Fellow-travelling with radical Islam has become a feature of those who deplore 'capitalism' but seldom claim that confiscatory one-party rule is the key to how the world's game should be regulated.

140

Shelley's idealisation of 'the Greeks' and their versatile hedonism was sentimental, the better to shame (or seduce) cold contemporaries. Death by drowning fitted the pattern of the poet's recklessness. His abandoned wife, Harriet, had already drowned herself in the Serpentine pond in Hyde Park. The sinking of *Ariel* off the Ligurian coast, with the poet aboard, matched conceit with conscience. He had been warned that the boat had an insufficient keel for the amount of sail it could spread. Was that its attraction? His early, 'tragic' death plays a signal part in his renown. André Maurois's *Ariel*, a romanticised portrait of Shelley, was the first Penguin book to be published by Allen Lane.

Imagine a middle-aged Jesus 'sticking around' long enough, as a naughty Kingsley Amis poem proposed, to have some kids himself. Might He/he have had second thoughts about replacing the law, with its cautious and cautionary provisions, with something as fragile and volatile as 'love'? Byron first regretted Shelley ('another man' – was Byron thinking principally of himself? – whom the world had 'cruelly misjudged') and then, we may guess, came to envy Percy B. his renowned quietus. Confronted with the posse of inept English doctors who proposed to bleed him, when stricken by malaria in

Missolonghi, Byron greeted them, and their lethal apparatus, with 'Come on, then, you butchers!'

Had Byron survived the doctors and the Greek adventure which has certified his revolutionary credentials, would he, as cynics suggest, have reverted, in middle and old age, to Tory crustiness? His upper-classy letters to the Etonian Douglas Kinnaird and in brisk Italian to Teresa Guiccioli testify to prosaic versatility. Playing the world like a gaming table, he made life a gamble seasoned with luck, Avernus its dark destination. Shelley wished for a new, fairer world and imagined the poet its sublime legislator. There is a lot to be said, though it rarely is, for prosaic justice and reliable routines. The Law, while lacking in glamour, is not as capricious as the Prophets. It lends itself less readily to the self-important or the deluded. A store in Jerusalem does brisk business in Jesus costumes.

Both Shelley and Byron inherited minor aristocratic standing; disowned by their peers at home, titular breeding dignified them abroad. In Venice and Pisa, they paraded as condescendingly as any other grand tourists. Their writing was stained with blue-blooded insolence, sexual and social. Byron was lordly enough to despise Johnny Keats and to scorn the children of his ally, Leigh Hunt, as 'cockneys' when they came to stay with him in his rented Pisan palazzo. Liberalism likes to mount a tall pedestal on which to strike egalitarian attitudes.

141

A symmetry in Oppenheimer's dandy life was that his eventual nemesis was another Jewish physicist. Determined to develop the H-bomb, in the face of Oppenheimer's squeamishness, the uncomely Edward Teller was more disparaging of Oppy's motives than even Senator Joe McCarthy and Admiral Lewis Strauss (pronounced, he insisted, 'Straws'). Another Jew, at once more conservative and less inhibited, Strauss had been President Herbert Hoover's private secretary. After growing rich, very, in the banking firm of Kuhn Loeb, he was a leading supporter of 'the Joint', an organisation to raise funds for what would become the Jewish state. Did Strauss's campaign to strip Oppenheimer of his security clearance during the early 1950s have anything to do with Oppy's secession from Jewish identity? Nothing? The Gilbertian rear-admiral, who never commanded a fleet, imputed to Oppenheimer a want of unalloyed loyalty to the United States. Did his animus derive from scorn, if not resentment, that Oppenheimer had so smoothly slipped his Semitic anchor?

There is something like a reprise here of the confrontation in Barcelona, in 1263, between Pablo Christiani, Petrus Alfonsi and Rabbi Nachmanides. Strauss and Teller were converts to the militant hundred-per-cent Americanism which would come to flower in the domination of the 'military–industrial complex' against which Dwight Eisenhower warned his countrymen in 1960, having done little to challenge it during his presidency. The stand-off was between right-wing advocates of the Biggest Possible Bang, led by unabashed chauvinists, versus liberal humanists, exemplified by Oppenheimer. Taking advantage of America's temporary monopoly of the atom bomb, Strauss and Teller wanted to proceed to make the H-bomb conclusive guarantor of American ascendancy. National Security was the latter-day inquisitors' gospel, Oppenheimer the cosmopolitan heretic whose *auto-da-fé* they invited the world to attend.

A gloss on Oppy's life in the style of Robert Graves's and Richard Aldington's books about T. E. Lawrence might bracket him within the cultural and societal pressures of his time and background. It would investigate the double strand of Achillean arrogance and the assimilationist's wish to be one with both the elite and the masses. Oppenheimer took the low and the high road simultaneously; one led, via intellectual excellence, to that magisterial role at Los Alamos, the other to the threshold, if no further, of the Communist Party, where he could imagine – like Wittgenstein? – expunging the stigma of Jewish exceptionalism. If he had ever actually joined the Party (see *Commentary* magazine N.Y. September 2023), it remains unlikely that he associated membership with enhancing the fire power of Stalin's USSR.

In *A Grammar of Motives* (1945), Kenneth Burke proposed a method of diagrammatising motives without recourse to affectations of mind-reading. He held 'motive' to be subtended by dramatic setting and circumstance. With no appetite for divining psychic impulses, he posited a pentad of influences, none 'deep', that apply theatrical variety to human conduct: act, scene, agent, agency and purpose. All the world is a stage and one man, in his time, can (wishes to?) play many parts, including the villain. The latter is liable to have the best lines, licence like no other.

Ordinary Men anatomises a platoon of German squaddies who consented, under patriotic licence, to kill unarmed civilian *Ost-Juden*. Their actions were as good, or as bad, as their mix of Burkean motives: they did as they were ordered in the circumstances. Is Browning too scrupulous (or too decent) to consider the thrill of being licensed to be Other? Uniforms efface individuality; obedience suborns scruple. Costumes and uniforms have often been enough to enlist a company for almost any kind of performance. Nazi dignitaries, plump or ill-favoured in civilian rig, were enhanced by the belted cut of their sinister Boss kit and dangling (penis-enhancing?) accessories. The Red Army had been denied such accoutrements; Stalin held it not in the Party's interest to encourage military brass to gleam as if outranking the civilian Politburo. The purge of the best intelligences in the army, notably Marshal Tukhachevsky and other modernists, in the 1930s, was meant to cow the bobbed residue of the general staff.

The wilfully unforeseen German invasion all but broke Stalin's nerve. He expected the Politburo delegation which came to his dacha to break the news to him to arrest and execute him. None dared to take the lead. His purges had left him surrounded only by indecisive apparatchiks and a suite of docile generals. The Great Leader had time to recover his nerve, change tack and revert to the old religion and patriotism of Mother Russia. He restored military ranks and salutes, in place of the 'comradeship' of earlier years. Georgy Zhukov his implacable second, Comrade Stalin became 'Marshal' and, out-Trotskying Trotsky, played Tolstoy's Subarov in repelling the new Napoleon. In George Orwell's *Animal Farm*, the tyrant pig, a caricature of Stalin, is called Napoleon; Trotsky is Snowball, who melts away.

142

Reflecting on Hitlerism and Stalinism, E. M. Cioran postulated the existence of 'monsters' who have no conscience and rally to barbarity. Better on the bench than in the box, who would guess that Cioran, the post-war pundit, had been, when it was timely, a loud Romanian fascist? He shucked his no-longer-fashionable persona by assuming the character of a *philosophe* delivering dispassionate intelligence. His *redressement* as eighteenth-century French pundit effaced what had become embarrassing. He even claimed to like Jews (Paul Celan *entre autres*), once status was no longer to be acquired by advertising hatred for them. Enlightenment too has its opportunists.

Not unlike Gilbert Ryle, Kenneth Burke held it superfluous to seek internal, 'psychological' causes for human conduct. Impersonating a first-class fellow-traveller, he displayed tractable ingenuity by compounding a 'logic' which justified Stalin's 1930s Show Trials as a form of living (and murderous) theatre. Burke argued that character is often affected, infected perhaps, never determined, by the company a person keeps. The fields of force generated by social milieux nudge pieces within their confines. Among different people, in a different setting, what someone would never do might well become just the thing he does do. In the same vein, Wittgenstein saw the element of ambiguity in what was meant by honouring a rule.

William Lyons reminds me that Rodin's so-called *Thinker* (original title *The Poet*) became paradoxically emblematic for Ryle, when he argued that there was no 'ghost in the machine', as Descartes and others had claimed. Mental processes were not the instigators of human actions but another way of describing them. Rodin's seemingly ruminative figure could be read as an involuntary representation of the sloth consequent on affecting thought to be a solemn inner exercise. *The Concept of Mind* implied that a man deceived himself when he claimed to be 'deep' (Wittgenstein's favourite term of praise). Ryle made the expression 'category mistake' fashionable in the early 1950s. To regard 'thinking' as a kind of shadowy internal activity was an instance, Moral Scientists were quick to repeat, of where Descartes went wrong. Who now maintains that 'I'll think about it' is a vacuous promise?

An instance relevant to J. R. Oppenheimer's eventual fame is the primer for Clare Mac Cumhaill and Rachel Wiseman's *Metaphysical Animals* (2022). Their study of a quartet of female Oxford philosophers is bookended by President Harry Truman's nomination, in 1956, for an Oxford honorary degree. With rare insolence – rare because the protesters were young women – Mary Midgley, Iris Murdoch, Miss Anscombe and Philippa Foot virtually and virtuously opposed the body of male dignitaries about to pass a formal vote to give an honorary degree to ex-president Harry Truman. The females' principal and principled objection was that Truman was responsible for signing the order to drop the A-bomb on Hiroshima (and then again on Nagasaki). They therefore considered him the author of a crime against humanity by incinerating tens of thousands of 'innocent' Japanese. The category question, if not mistake, occurs: can the docile civilian population of a belligerent power be entirely innocent of support for a nationalist war conducted with programmatic ruthlessness, especially when it came to the massacre of hundreds of thousands of Chinese, by no means all in battle?

Truman's decisive hand in the use of the A-bomb was held by the philosophical quartet to be so morally obnoxious as to disqualify him from any civilised, let alone Oxonian, honour. Had it ever been up to them to decide whether or not to end the Japanese war in such an abrupt fashion, they would have been entitled to honour their *états d'âme*. Truman was president of the United States, whose interests he had sworn to honour. Personal squeamishness was no part of his duty. He had no business to prolong the war in conventional style when it would have entailed the deaths of several hundred thousand American servicemen. Such deaths would have betrayed the president's oath and his duty to his countrymen. The Oxonian quartet committed a Rylean 'category mistake': they ignored that Truman's decision was presidential. Soul-searching had no place in his elected duty. American lives were determinant.

The war over, the same Truman's hesitation over developing the H-bomb was not manifestly contrary to his mandate. It might have been an error to deny his country a weapon almost certain to be developed by the USSR, but it would not have offended against his sworn role as supreme commander of America's armed forces. When General of the Army Douglas MacArthur, undoubted national hero, proposed to use the atom bomb against China, because it was the ally of North Korea, Truman retired him, despite wide public outrage. This may have been more for politic than humane reasons, but it scarcely argues for the savagery of a president who stood up against the post-war menace of the USSR with the cool of a Kansas City poker player, seconded by the subtle George Kennan.

Iris Murdoch's early membership of the Communist Party, however brief, suggests that the deaths of millions of Ukrainians and thousands of others, during the Great Terror, failed to excite her comradely disapproval. Truman's decision to proceed with the H-bomb was properly presidential. He considered above all the interests and safety of the United States, once the USSR was known to possess it. In *Call Me Madam*, Ethel Merman's 'HARRY!' might be a 1950 musical comedy super; in White Housed reality, he had no right to accept the possibility of hundreds of thousands of American casualties in a war which the USA, whatever its militant posture, was never likely to start. Failure to develop the H-bomb might be morally refined; it was also liable, if not certain, to deliver Western civilisation to totalitarian Russia. Indignation was the Oxford women's right; its grounds were misconceived; ostentatious opposition to the university's decision to honour the by-then-ex-president smacked of self-importance no less than of moral presumption.

In *The Sovereignty of the Good*, a late philosophical volume of the kind that success as a novelist rendered portentous, Murdoch advocated a neo-Platonist morality requiring its adherents always to tell the truth. A cited instance: if asked by an SS man whether there are Jews hiding in the house, the virtuous had to tell the truth, even if it entailed the arrest and murder of any old young Anne Frank. Could there be a more chilling instance of the crypto-ideologist's abrogation of personal decency? Elizabeth Anscombe, for all her devotion to Wittgenstein, leaned on Roman Catholicism as a moral yardstick. It might be held to have offered her no choice but to give W a Christian burial. Not a few of her co-religionists in Europe had no compunction in adopting and baptising the children of Jews who had been deported to concentration camps. When survivors sought reunion with their offspring, they were not infrequently lied to, morally, about their location or led to believe that they had disappeared. Salvation justified kidnapping. God protect us from those who know they are honouring His will. Iris Murdoch's donnish husband, John Bayley, wrote a sharp book entitled *The Uses of Division*. That he won the Military Cross for gallantry during the war promises experience of war at the sharp end.

143

If some of Robert Oppenheimer's actions were 'out of character', was that not characteristic? His attempt to kill Blackett,
like flirting with other people's wives or with communism,
chimed with a reckless, if repressed, Other Life. It is always
tempting to jiggle locks in Bluebeard's castle. Energetic versatility, backed by a shameless wallet, is scarcely unusual among
clever Jews reminded of their back-of-the-bus place in Gentile
company. 'You have to do twice as much to get half as far,'
my grandfather Max told me, as we scanned the *New York
Times* Funnies on Sunday mornings. The urge to excel and to
entertain, to 'pass', to transcend Jewishness and to vindicate
it, was common among those in the mass 1900s immigration
into the USA.

The speed with which many Jews took to what was then
called 'The Show Business' betokens a wish to sing and dance
like authentic Broadway babies. Lyricists such as E. Y. 'Yip'
Harburg acquired a sophistication which, in his case, enabled
him to write 'April in Paris', quite as if he were a traveller of
cultivated tastes. He had never been to Paris when he wrote
the song. Harburg went on to become the composer of many
'standards' before he fell foul of Senator McCarthy's committee for his allegiance to the socialism which he had ingested
in his early days. In a 2013 article in the *Wall Street Journal*,

'Passing the Memorability Test', Joseph Epstein insists that lyricists such as Harburg have more secure lodgings in our memories than curricular, but literally unmemorable, poets of the same period, as of ours.

In Proust no less than in Tin Pan Alley, sophisticated authorial imposture achieved access to grand places and classy company from which poverty or kikedom excluded the author's physical person. Ambition picks the world's best-buttoned pockets. While the Vanderbilts rarely asked immigrants to tea, they lacked the power to prevent Irving Berlin from toying with tripping up their avenue, as he did literally Churchill's Downing Street, if only because of an invitational confusion with the ascending Isaiah. Social affectations were not limited to Jews: Philip Barry's *The Philadelphia Story* (1939) presumed familiarity with a social upper set to which immigrant Irishmen rarely acceded without rare wit and/or, as with the Kennedys, a wallet fattened by sharp practice and rough tradesmen. In academic traffic, physics and medicine offered access to the high road, as 'The Show Business' did along the low.

While Jews became eager Yankee Doodle Dandies, a vengeful strain still ran through not a few of those humiliated in Tsardom's Pale of Settlement. The Russian Revolution of 1917 promised that expropriators, royal and bourgeois, could be expropriated, Jews redeemed, at least until Trotsky gave Stalin the urge to recirculate the old currency. Oppy's indignation at human injustice, at home and elsewhere, was compatible with the role of impartial scientist: why should societies not be corrected, like theories, false consciousness repudiated? Communist parties, *ici et là*, traded on such sentiments in liberals; meliorist vanity rendered the guileless useful to the Party.

By the hint of availability with which he reacted to Haakon Chevalier's overture, Oppenheimer toyed with his own ruin without springing to any specific treasonous act. Innocence and guilt became indistinguishable, if never quite coincidental, somewhat as Heisenberg's Uncertainty Principle makes it impossible to estimate position and momentum at the same time. Such a character never comes clearly into settled focus. A double bind hobbles and energises the emancipated Jew. The cleverer he is, the more mesmerising, if alien, his hold on those who may, at some vexed point, refer his superior sense of inferiority back onto its source. This leads to the stereotypical charge of 'the Jew' being a both-sides-against-the-middle man. Monk seems to hold that brilliance as a physicist acquitted Oppy of that charge. His theories about gravitational collapse were later confirmed by the empirical evidence for neutron stars; had he lived, they might well have gained him a Nobel Prize. *Pace* Gilbert Ryle, they would have done nothing to dissolve or discount his inner confusions.

Were all Oppy's colleagues and protégés sorry to see him cast down? In a germane instance, the tart (and venal) historian A. J. P. Taylor was pleased to deny his one-time tutor Sir Lewis Namier's deathbed request that Taylor come to see him and close the rift between them. Namier had failed to give support to Taylor's candidature for an Oxford professorship. Coals of fire were not in Taylor's scuttle.

Harry Truman could not abide Oppy's squeamishness with regard to the development of and likely casualties to be caused by the H-bomb. He instructed his staff to spare him further visits from that 'cry-baby'. Did Truman guess, with whatever relief, that the question of a Bigger and Better Bomb's actual use was unlikely to fall to him? The decision to proceed was presidential but its use would never be up to him, as dropping the atom bomb had been, determined by his responsibilities. The buck would by then have stopped on someone's else's desk. Scorning Oppenheimer's scruples was politically hard-headed, morally misplaced. He was entitled to conscientious refinement which the presidential oath denied the timed tenant of the White House. The public stand of the Oxford blue-stockings may have been bold, but it was, as Gilbert Ryle might have said, with that straight face of his, misconceived.

Truman had been intimately involved, in his early days, with the 'Prendergast gang', who ran Kansas City, Missouri, from 1900 till the Second World War. Prendergast made sure that the Democratic Party stayed in local power. Franklin Roosevelt furnished him with funds. Prendergast offered my amiable grandfather the position of restaurant sanitary inspector. It would involve less salaried vigilance than a cut from the sale of indemnities. Max Mauser did not take the job. When Prendergast died in 1945, Harry Truman went to the funeral. Max and his wife Fanny later opened a delicatessen in K.C. Prendergast's gangster successors let them off lightly: they were obliged regularly to buy many cases of overpriced soda that no one wanted to drink.

144

The not-many-laughs-there, dear, comedy of Nazi *Volkischkeit* lay in its inadvertent hint that a chorus of Germans might be needed to match solo flights of Jewish intelligence. When German togetherness, under a destined leader, claimed racial superiority, it supplied involuntary acknowledgement of Jewish genius. There is no shortage of Jews without rare qualities, but 'Christians' remain prone to curse the Chosen with unique resource, diabolic or otherwise. The late Kenneth McLeish, with whom I translated a number of Greek and Roman texts, once told me, during one of many protracted Sunday talks on the telephone, that I was 'the least Jewish Jew he had ever known'. He rang back to say that he was afraid that what he had said had sounded somewhat anti-Semitic. I told him it did not; but didn't it? So what?

Streams of thought run in worn channels. Ken had been assured, by his agent, with whom I had been to school some fifty years before, that if he collaborated with me, I would sooner or later rob him of his share of the proceeds. Ken was a genial man. I wonder what disposed him to inform me, so promptly, of what Andrew Best had said. When Ken fell into financial difficulties, I sent him money. Would I have been so prompt had I been unaware of my old school-fellow and his antique vanity? Several years later, Ken's widow repaid me in full and sent me several of his books.

The drab claim recurs that all Jews are conspirators in some devious plan for world domination. That there is no evidence, except for forgeries such as *The Protocols of the Elders of Zion*, can be represented as proof of just how devilish their scheme is. The dire compliment keeps a silly finger pressed on the world's scales. What Martian would guess that of the three monotheisms, only Christianity and Islam boast of their ambition to convert and coerce the heathen, purge the infidel, including wide swaths of those who profess much the same faith as themselves? Top prize for guessing right in Pascal's selective lottery is a front seat at the eternal barbecue of the dissenter.

In *Jewish Self-Hatred* (1986), Sander Gilman all but endorses the notion of innate shame. No charge sheet is needed; language does the work: a Jew is a Jew. The next case is confirmatory of the last. Tautologies decant their own poison. A joke is a joke is not always a joke. There are few laughs in philosophy, fewer in theology: both are apt to generate *a priori* (cf. Gospel) rules from which universal truths can be logically divined. Earnest theory discounts the pleasure (and profit) to be gained from denouncing and despoiling races defined as 'other'. Unforgiving purposes link prig and priest.

After the *converso* Roderigo Lopez, Elizabeth I's personal physician, was convicted of being an agent of Spain, he was hanged, drawn and quartered, even as he was protesting that he was as good a Christian as any of the spectators. That was the risible pay-off Tyburn's groundlings were waiting for. Old music hall comedians who failed to get a laugh used to call out, 'What do you want, blood?' The queen knew Lopez to be innocent, but her majesty dared not save him from a Christian fate.

During Stalin's Great Terror, John Erickson reported,

quota-filling victims appeared before 'grinning judges'. Everyone present recognised farce and tragedy as indistinguishable. No few Jewish Stalinists came from a sub-set whose service to the Revolution was to supply a quota of scapegoats, Leon Trotsky, *né* Bronstein, the paradigm instance. A journalist sought out the rabbi who had known Leon in his youth. 'The Trotskys make the Revolution,' the rabbi said, 'the Bronsteins pay the bill.'

145

In his later, post-Second World War years, Percy (a name he hated) Wyndham Lewis became blind. Michael Ayrton, who admired his draughtsmanship, offered to play Lewis's amanuensis. Ayrton's mother, Hertha, was Jewish and related to Israel Zangwill. Michael was disposed neither to acknowledge nor to deny connections with 'the Jews'. It is scarcely unlikely that he enjoyed the opportunity to display Christian charity towards the man who liked to think of himself as 'the enemy'. Did Michael read himself as honouring a dejected *miglior fabbro*? Lewis's fine penmanship trumped political partiality.

Michael told us that he would sooner be shot by Communists than Fascists, because he would then be serving the better cause. Why would such a man prefer to be a scapegoat than a martyr? In his youth, M had a rare reputation as a high-scoring cocksman; would it be unduly neat to say that he chose to be Wyndham Lewis's Other? It is also plausible. Someone said of Lewis that he had the face of a frustrated rapist. Michael's drawing of him, in a sorry slouch hat, served to illustrate that diagnosis. Or might it that being Canadian generated furious shame at being blamelessly vanilla?

Michael died of an abrupt heart attack brought on by failure, on the part of the nice family GP, to diagnose an advanced, but banal, case of diabetes. Michael used to say that after forty a man was left with the face he had come to deserve. Sandor Gilman grew to be of an appearance he could be forgiven for not loving; so too Joseph the once-dandified Roth, but Roth had genius. Since Jews are held to be prone to low self-esteem, between bouts of *superbe*, it is common to assume some innate defect for which they despise themselves. What they are as likely to loathe, if unwise to denounce, is 'Christian' vanity. Baruch/Benedict Spinoza's repudiation of Judaism is an eminent instance. Indirection does not exclude taking careful aim.

Spinoza's motto was *caute*, cautiously; he never denounced, though his Latin implied, the miraculous irrationality of Roman Catholicism. While he enjoyed the liberty of the Dutch Republic, a threatening Christian mob assembled outside where he lived. Spinoza opened the door and stood on the step. His dignity outranked the crowd. When he invited the malign burghers to go home, they did. His style supplied no reliable recipe for dispersing hostile vanities. One had better be Spinoza before assuming it.

The machinery of the Inquisition, the Church's secret service, could not be sure that public converts to Christianity did not continue to think or pray in Hebrew. Hence the long dread that two-faced Jews are secreting treasure; portable wisdom, stitched gelt if any. Maud Kozodoy's *The Secret Faith of Maestre Honoratus* (2015) supplies a fourteenth-century instance of refined duplicity in the wake of the Inquisition. Scorn for Christianity was overt among the Jews in Baghdad, where they were in no way muzzled by or hostile to the Muslims among whom they lived. The local rabbinate was free to scorn the absurdity of the Trinity and kindred postulates.

In the tolerant twelfth-century sultanate of Cordoba, Moses Maimonides had been hardly less uncowed. In the latter years of the *Convivencia*, he wrote of an ambition to crunch

Christian bones to dust. Modern Jewish apologists are liable to be more tactful, as the charming David Baddiel showed in a Channel 4 programme discreet enough to make no allusion to Jewish genius while insisting on the unexceptional character of those to whom so many take exception. His modesty might have been better spiced with a measure of insolence. Must all Jews be quite as anodyne as he suggested?

As for the Inquisition, revisionists have claimed that being burnt at the stake was quite a humane death. We are promised that the condemned were stifled by the smoke from thoughtfully dampened kindling, before their flesh was crackling, its appetising smoke mounting, *ad maiorem Dei gloriam*, to heaven. Perhaps more important for them, the faithful executioners thus avoided being defiled by the blood of those consigned to the flames. Similar fastidiousness disposes today's Islamist slaughterers to wear gloves when virtuously murdering those of differing or variant faith; warrant and war/rant furnish a Derrida-esque duo.

146

Before the foundation of the state of Israel, a very few uncompromising spirits such as Bernard Lazare (1865–1903) dared to return an unintimidated response to racial malice. In the frenzy surrounding *l'Affaire Dreyfus*, Lazare was more Dreyfusard than the maligned captain himself. Chained to his steel cot on Devil's Island, France's penal colony off the coast of South America, Dreyfus endured protracted 'crucifixion' with patriotic stoicism. To the disappointment of radical supporters, he asked only for reinstatement as a French officer and gentleman. Eventually vindicated to his own satisfaction, he appeared all but spineless to those who had campaigned on his behalf. By the end of the Affair, his supporters retained small faith in the honour of the French establishment or the justice of its justice. Theodor Herzl, who died a year after Bernard Lazare, advocated Zionism as a response to the injustice done to Dreyfus. Dreyfus himself showed no loud resentment towards those who never apologised for their vindictiveness. How different was Oppenheimer, J. R.?

Gentiles can affect to fear that 'the Jew' never is, never can be, wholly, square with them. Rendered plausible by their own hostility, suspicion procures an equal and opposite reaction. The Jew as pariah is accused of despising himself. His best revenge, he is apt to think, is to excel those who wish him no good. If it takes the form of conspicuous philanthropy, as innumerable benefactions prove, it is sentimental to take it that generosity equates with gratitude. Giving can be the nicest form of conceit.

In my mid-twenties, I was the occasional beneficiary of Cyril Ross, a tweedy pipe-smoker who had made money in furs. In return, I tutored Cyril in his naïve, never silly attempts to write fiction. His only published book, *Pirates in Striped Trousers*, made play with takeover-bidders such as Charlie Clore, whom Cyril had outsmarted when threatened with a hostile approach. Over one of our lunches at Grosvenor House, Cyril told me that, among other unpublicised generosities, he had founded and maintained the wartime Rainbow Services Club, in the top end of Edgware Road, for British and American officers. 'Everyone used to go there,' he told me, 'Eisenhower, Montgomery, all of them.' 'And did you get to know them personally?' Cyril said, 'To tell you the truth, Fred, I don't much go for the Goyim.'

147

Hannah Arendt wished cowardice on European Jews who failed to form their battalions or to enrol Gentiles in a common front. She fails to specify how they were to achieve such an alliance against a powerful enemy with lucky-dipping neighbours who treated the Holocaust as what Jean-Marie Le Pen came to call 'un point de détail'. Le Pen was the first smiling right-wing ranter. His hallmark pose was with both hands high in the air, leary smile on his face. Was his racism as much manic joke as practical policy? Unwise to rely on it. Nigel Farage, the hundred-per-cent Englishman with a – perhaps Huguenot, perhaps Arabic Faraj – alien-sounding name, is nearly always seen to be smiling, often with a British pint in his friendly fist. Have any of his political opponents had the gall to do as Winston Churchill might have and mis-pronounce his name to rhyme with garridge, where the lower orders lodge their bangers? Tradesman in trumpery, Farage threatened, in March 2019, that he might return, yet again, to politics, having learnt a lesson or two. 'Next time,' he quipped, 'no more Mr Nice Guy.' Was the funster aware that this is the punch line of a chance meeting in a bar with Adolf Hitler, who delivers himself of the same amusing resolve? Was he not?

Having taken ship to New York soon after Hitler came to

power, Hannah Arendt absented herself from those on whom she returned only to sit in judgement on behalf of the *New Yorker* and its urbane subscribers. She scarcely concealed her view that Europe's Jews had been spineless in not resisting the Nazis. Isaiah Berlin, who lost family members, including his ageing parents, never forgave her. In truth, when feasible, there was Jewish resistance. Fighters in the Warsaw ghetto, equipped with a few stolen weapons, mostly hand-guns, held out longer than had the French Army in 1940.

Arendt's books are dense with scheme, skimpy on references to specific events, people or arguments at odds with her own. Rare use of the first-person pronoun gives her prose an air of dispassionate assessment. It also spares her drawing any uncomfortable evidence from lived life. The philosophical trick, notable in her and in Heidegger as in many others, is to presume that impersonal generalisations rise above contingent experience. Relegation of individual witness to 'mere autobiography' lends seemingly sublime authority to formal preconceptions. Facts are selected or ignored according to whether they will fortify or disconcert a preconceived 'logic'. Karl Popper held such bias typical of those who wish to clamp mankind in closed societies. Self-criticism, self-mockery or then-again reflection find no place in their toolkits.

Derived in good measure from the all-but-morbidly conscientious Kierkegaard, existentialism appears to re-establish the self-made character of the individual. While advocating the notion that man alone has the power to be what he chooses, neither Heidegger nor Sartre was disposed to loosen hold on disciples by according disputatious equality. After the war, Heidegger condescended to attend colloquia of French admirers (no one else was admitted) only after questions had been submitted, and sifted, in advance. Arrogance and apprehension *allaient de pair*.

Wittgenstein's concession that his own work was essentially

critical, if not Talmudic, seemed to honour Otto Weininger's typology of the effeminate, dependent Jew as against the virile, authentic Aryan. Imperial Vienna was at once haven for Jews and incubator of what would become a murderous crusade, Hitler its tin drummer. His way of banging on is typical of today's single-issue politicians. As long as Franz-Josef II was on the throne, anti-Semitism was at once ubiquitous and limited by the Christian presumption of superiority. Outstanding Jews were not denied access to the arts and, if they could clear the barbed hurdles, higher education and specialised medicine.

148

Stefan Zweig, while a signally successful author, claimed never to have encountered anti-Semitism in old Vienna. Before the 1938 *Anschluss*, he enjoyed a safely gated address on the high road. As low-life *schnorrer*, Joseph Roth had no illusions about what Nazism portended. Without bourgeois blinkers, he is the first journalist known to have proclaimed the menace of Adolf Hitler, back in 1923. Between cadging handouts, he mocked Zweig, who, among no end of celebrities with Jewish roots, took personal success as evidence of his world's essential decency and his own emancipation. So too Bernard Levin, who died before the resurgence of anti-Semitism fostered not least by immigrant Islamists and native opportunists.

Wittgenstein's solitary, not to say ostentatious, courage during the Great War, when a steepled lookout in the Austrian Army on the Italian front, parodied what might be expected of those who excluded Jews from their clubs or declined even to duel with them. Who did not whisper as his Austrian fellow-officers did about the Jewish regimental surgeon in Joseph Roth's *The Radetzky March*? Elsewhere, Roth tells the story of a Galician Jew conscripted into the Austrian Army who endured weeks of gruelling training without complaint, including crawling under wire while live ammunition was fired over the recruits' heads. Finally, he arrived at the front line and took part in a charge on the enemy lines. As machine-gun fire began to topple his comrades, he called out to the enemy: 'Are you out of your minds? THERE ARE PEOPLE HERE.' In the trenches of the Somme, Siegfried Sassoon won the MC after a display of coolness under fire and then, in protest at the carnage, threw his decoration away, as he did his Jewishness, he supposed, when brushed in as a Roman Catholic fox-hunting man.

Unlike Joseph Roth, whose alter ego saw himself as an officer loyal to the emperor, even when there no longer was one, Wittgenstein manifested no distress at the collapse of the Austro-Hungarian Empire. Recourse to abstraction, in mathematics and logic, detached him from nationalist enthusiasm. His definition of a philosopher was of a man essentially alone. After doing his duty, in a losing cause, Wittgenstein returned to Cambridge. Recent enemies received him with courtesy; genius procured professorial preferment. Unprecedented in its bloodiness, the Great War was never ideological, on the western front at least. Residual sports-manship made it possible for the victors to forgive, if not to forget; many of the defeated did neither. If both sides were economically and morally maimed, the middle ground was still there, however churned and bloodied. In the unofficial truce of Christmas 1914, Tommies and Fritzes alarmed their ranking superiors by playing friendly, egalitarian soccer in no-man's land.

That Wittgenstein saw merit in Otto Weininger's exaggerated racial dichotomy seems to endorse the inference that all Jews are likely, if not obliged, to be ashamed. The young Wittgenstein's obsession with his 'sins' surely concerned his more-or-less-repressed homosexual longings. Whatever being 'Hebraic' might mean, can it have had much to do with being 'sinful', except on the addled reckonings of ultra-Catholic piety? Nazis had many motives, greed not the smallest, for dispossessing and exterminating Jews. Kenneth Burke's scene/ act ratio elucidates the elements of the case.

Sly light is cast on Nazi veneration for barbarism through the 'reasoning' which led Jean Genet to embrace the curse laid on him by society, when he said, more or less, 'You say that I am a thief? Very well then, that is what I shall be, proud to call myself The Thief.' Genet's acceptance of the scapegoat role repudiated the spirit of the laws by which he had been condemned. When Sartre labelled Genet '*saint et martyre*', he provoked his anti-hero's raucous refusal of a halo. '*Martyre*' implied that Christian categories were still valid. Genet's rejection of Sartre's decoration is nicely analogous to Poulou's refusal of the Nobel Prize, if less conceited. Little disposed to brag of his homosexuality, Genet flourished his pro-Palestinian left-righteousness.

The veneration with which Sartre was treated (some thirty thousand mourners followed his coffin) seems to establish that he was a popular and important writer. When it comes to fiction, literary or dramatic, how surely does he belong in the great tradition of French literature? Before the war, he mocked François Mauriac for denying choice to his characters who, Sartre said, were subject to a Catholic scheme which docked them of individual freedom. His own fictions were meant to illustrate individual choice in a godless world. Man was shown electing the way he chose to live, after Sartre flourished the menu. The formal innovations, in the second volume of *Les Chemins de la liberté*, owed more to John Don Passos (in its 'cinematic' staccato) and to Ernest Hemingway, whose heroic model was echoed in Sartre's fictional alter ego, than to any singular originality. The Nobel Prize he refused was designated to celebrate *Les Mots*, more autopsy than autobiography. Bob Dylan, born Robert Allen Zimmermann, trumped Sartre by ignoring the same award. As George Steiner predicted, with masochistic glee, in the twenty-first century literature is down from the high ground; society without appetite for ravelled versatility. Pop music and journalism seduce, blare and rave, fame and money the media's brassy gods.

Sartre abandoned *Les Chemins de la liberté*, originally planned as a tetralogy, in three-quarter form. Did he have a stiff preconception of the destination to which his characters were bound? Were they, perhaps, unwilling to go there? Sartre turned out to be scarcely distinct from the ideology-ridden author that he had accused Mauriac of being. Did he lack the looks to make free play with his own self? Giacometti, no oil-painting, is the only person known to have said, '*Sartre, tu es beau!*' Without humour, fiction becomes programmatic. Jest ruptures scheme; hence Plato's apprehensions.

149

The Maya of fifteenth-century Yucatán resisted the Spanish *conquistadores* for no few years after the rest of Mexico before being forcibly converted to Catholicism, their books burnt, as the Talmud had been. The Maya combined a knowledge of the movements and seasons of the stars and planets, well in advance of European astrology. Their cult of death differed from that of the Aztecs in being self-sufficient: sacrificial 'victims' were not from some alien or subdued tribe but from within the Mayan population itself. Who knows by what impersonal means they were selected? The stepped dignity of Yucatan's architectural masterpieces – the pyramids of Chichen Itza, the great palace at Uxmal – testify to a self-confident culture. The beauty of signal buildings fails to validate the doctrine of any civilisation.

It has recently been deemed sacrilege for tourists to climb the steep steps to what was once Chichen Itza's sacrificial peak. We visited the place on several occasions in the 1970s. In shows of local machismo, young men mocked our careful steps by racing from the top to the bottom of the steps in showy double-quick time. The embargo on tourists setting foot on them is a retrospective show of piety, the revenge of the Maya, without antique precedent. In the centre of the complex of Chichen Itza is a grassed area, about the size of a football pitch, in which the Mayan ball-game was played in front of lateral rows of spectators. The solitary 'goal' was a stone hoop projected from the side wall, through which players competed to deliver the ball, neither by throwing nor by kicking, but by blows from knees or elbows. As in the muddy Eton ball-game, scoring was rare, despite contestants' best efforts. If a 'goal' was scored, it was a good omen for the imminent crop of corn, staple diet of the tribe. To celebrate his team's achievement, the captain of the winning side was often sacrificed to the gods.

I asked a professor of anthropology at the university in Mexico City what obliged a man to accept the captaincy or then to urge his side to victory, when his own death would follow it. 'It was a privilege to know that his blood would serve to enrich the coming harvest,' she told me. 'You will never understand Mexico unless you understand our love affair with death.' Siding with death is also a way of exempting oneself from it. The black SS uniform gloried in allegiance to a murderous cult. Fascist roll-calls, in which the dead are heard to say 'present', defy mortality (and concede it).

When the Romans burst into Herod's Temple in Jerusalem, priests continued with their ceremonies as they were cut to pieces. There is something superb in serving a divinity who promises his worshippers no favours. Durable religions often exact more-or-less sublime forms of self-immolation. Amputation, dietetic limitation, chastity, self-castration are aspects of sacrifice. The bleakest charge is that of the atheist: after everything man has done to please or placate Him, his deity lacks the grace to exist.

150

Science entails the de/moralisation of the world; abiding by a nexus of proper procedures, it never knows where it is going, but nothing can stop it getting there. Its sole morality is that theories should be susceptible to peer review. As soon as scientists are enrolled in any ideology or creed, they are liable to temper dispassionate conclusions by their compatibility with an a priori orthodoxy. They are then out of order if they fail to ditch results which, although true, would dismay the faithful. Science is neither a humanism nor an ideology. Theories merit consideration until they are shown, by logic and experiment, never by dogma, to be mistaken.

Was it dogmatic of Stephen Hawking to base his account of the universe on the principle that nothing can travel faster than light? When presenting him with some bauble award, I made bold to say that he was the living refutation of his own theory, since his thinking encircled the globe in no time at all. He did not signal amusement. His better-than-best-selling *A Brief History of Time* is a trim and unamusing promise that there is no sense in whimpering about the end of days and allied topics. Meanwhile, the nullity of Gertrude Stein's Oakland infects the world with bulbous repetition.

Before the Great War, it was plausible to regard 'letters', whether fiction or journalism, as a likely means of escape from Jewish limitations. When Heinrich Heine converted to Christianity in order to have access to public print and wider literary company, he became a pioneer of the non-Jewish Jew or of the Jewish non-Jew who made existential use of the *cuius regio* model for resolving religious allegiance. Franz Rosenzweig begged to differ. On the verge of conversion to Christianity, he elected to remain on the shady bank of German life. He then devoted himself, while in protracted physical pain, to loyalty which kept him Hebrew, without Heine's lyrical consolations or social viability. Anthony Rudolf quotes Rosenzweig as saying, 'Prose is our poetry.'

Until, and then again after, he renounced it, Karl Kraus (1874–1936) made his fat wallet the warrant for scatological criticism of *feuilletonistes*, the posh band of Jewish journalists (Joseph Roth the best and least docile of them) who supplied editors with the snap and crackle Gentiles liked for breakfast. Kraus scorned classy suppliers of bonbons for the bourgeoisie: try as they might to become seamless with the prevailing Gentile culture, even their written words had, he claimed, an accent (*mauscheln*) that carried the taint of alien cadences, halitosis in print. From the vantage point of his own temporary apostasy, he had it that there was no remedy for fancy fakery other than honest recourse to the ghetto. Joseph Roth was sometimes of similar opinion: if he seldom pretended to be other than an unapologetic Galician Jew, from the least favoured of the regions of what had been the Austro-Hungarian Empire, he also liked to parade as a loyal Catholic subject and wartime officer of Franz-Josef II, even after the latter's death and the dismantling of his empire.

To Arthur Schnitzler what seemed most repugnant in Kraus was the anti-Semitic vocabulary of a man who remained, by any mundane standard, a Jew. Even after he switched to Catholicism, for a decade or more, Kraus could not shuck what would have qualified him for Nazi extermination. No sort of self-hater, Kraus rejoiced to single out German-writing Jewish journalists for debasing the coinage of speech. He diagnosed misprints as revealing of psychic pretentiousness or an involuntary giveaway, as Freud did slips of the tongue. The term 'psychic bid' (or 'psych'), used by bridge players of a bluffing bid which lacks the high-card strength it boasts, is a vestige of old Vienna. Asked by Theodor Herzl to enrol as a Zionist and to imagine having his plays performed in a Jewish state, Arthur Schnitzler, Viennese from way back, asked, 'In what language?' He did not live to witness the *Anschluss*, but he did see his daughter marry an Italian fascist officer.

Kraus had means enough to write, print and publish his own magazine. He also married a rich wife. His attacks on Jewish journalism (particularly in Vienna's *Neue Freie Presse*) and its 'gesticulating prose' appear unambiguous; but – as with Spinoza's denunciation of Judaism – a covert codicil promised that all journalism, except Kraus's own, was liable, lie/able, to be infected by contagious venality. Gentile scribes had to be thick-skinned indeed not to suspect that his sauce could as well cook their goose and the goose-steppers who strutted to deliver it.

151

Modern journalism boasts a menagerie of *feuilletonistes* with inflated bylines and congruent salaries. They boast the facsimile freedom of animals so pampered in bondage that their cages have no bars. Star columnists are paid much higher salaries than the politicians on whom they keep a jaundiced eye on behalf of the quasi-illiterate products of a nerveless education system. Fact-checking, if practised at all, is no well-paid activity in today's media. Impersonating the tribunes of the plebs, dirty-cracksmen shout down those once said to be our betters. News and entertainment converge and coalesce. Wars and scandals deplored by leader-writers are the indispensable stuff of headlines and profits. Empressed villains are lame ducks without wit or means to quack back.

As with the Mafia and allied tradesmen, the yesterdaying of one set serves to make way for younger, more malign operators. The offshore media-magnate is as close as we come to an Archimedes who, in a stance of personal outsiderdom, can put a lever under the world. All the antagonisms of the world, in professional sport not least, enrich those who do not share the partialities of supporters as faithful as they are callow. In overpriced seats, the faithful pay up and yell for one slate or the other of performers whose allegiance is for regular auction.

152

The notion of 'Jewish science' was a Nazi amalgam of apprehension of the out-of-step and of refusal to concede that anything initiated by a Jew could be of Aryan validity. Martin Luther first gave religious warrant to the rejection of Rome and set Germany on the way to a nationalised creed and master-racialism. The Nazis' conclusive purge of Jewish artists and writers was easy to achieve, given the flexibility of literary criticism and theory and the opportunism of so many writers. When was there not a posse of academics and intellos on hand to be vindictive for the sake of applause and advancement? *Odium academicum* is a vintage brew, half as old as hemlock. According to David B. Dennis's *Inhumanities* (2015), forty-one per cent of the vitriol printed on the arts pages of the Nazi newspaper *Volkische Beobachter*, during its three decades of existence, was supplied by 'notable professors' from German universities. Jonathan Glover's *Humanity* (1999) supplies an implacable roster of academic opportunists and their vicarious braying.

During the German occupation of Belgium, Paul de Man's articles established him as a paradigm of intellectual opportunists. After the war, he scooted upwards to American academic eminence. Having become a proponent of moral relativism, his subordination of text to its interpretation parodied Talmudic and Jesuitical artifice. Duplicity was franked as sophistication; nothing need mean only what it said. Mimesis is an antique habit in academic circles; study of Greek and Latin begins with reproducing the style of canonical texts and the attitudes of whatever procures favour with examiners with their preference for suave Cicero over tart Tacitus.

Jean-Paul Sartre said that he never lost the sense that his working year was consistent with school or university terms, especially the *rentrée* in September. The academy and power have always been liable to converge, Archimedes and the tyrant of Syracuse early instances. Michael Frayn's *Copenhagen* made boulevard play with the supposed dilemma of German scientists who had the capacity to give Hitler atomic weapons but elected not to do so, just. A fat unscrupulous majority was baulked less by fine scruples than by Allied bombs, interdepartmental jealousies and shortage of funds.

153

Literary and theatrical pat-ball is a frequent recourse of the semi-serious, William Styron's *Sophie's Choice* a factitious instance. Styron, your honest Southern gentleman, given to uninhibited remarks about Jews, his right but scarcely his virtue, concocted a story about the Holocaust featuring a female victim, Sophie, who is a Polish Gentile. She is forced to choose to save the life of one of her children at the expense of the other. If that kind of kitsch doesn't prove how bad the Nazis were, what can? George Steiner urged the novel on me. I happened on a passage in which Styron pays tribute to George, who was, at the time, chief book reviewer of the *New Yorker*.

The place in Nazi ideology of music which, sublime or not, can never be either true or false, soundtracked the promotion of myth. Who could prove that Beethoven would not have been proud to lead the band in Hitler's camp? Did Herbert von Karajan hesitate? Beethoven's third symphony, the *Eroica*, was a tribute to Napoleon, until it wasn't. Music can be both sophisticated and beyond analysis in terms of definable content; hence Wagner's cardinal role in *volkische* art. Genius as recruiting officer, he orchestrated a chauvinism blaring with horny Rhenish mythology. European music was construed as predominantly Germanic. Composers – Bach to Handel to the operatic Richard Strauss and Wagner – were recruited to Aryan nationalism. We are told that when workmen were deputed to remove Mendelssohn's statue from the face of some Reich opera house, they chose the one with the biggest nose. It proved to be Wagner's.

Did J. R. Oppenheimer's retreat from the arts, as a ladder to renown, owe anything to apprehension that he could never escape Jewishness by that means? Even the best American Jewish writers of fiction have honoured a specificity which they seldom deny. *The Catcher in the Rye* (1951) came too soon for J. D. Salinger to make play with Jewishness, not least, maybe, because he hoped for publication in the *New Yorker* of that prim time. Norman Mailer's best book, *The Executioner's Song*, carries no mention of Jews. The measure of Philip Roth's wicked success in post-Second World War literature can be taken by the envy which it excited in John Updike, who warped his Wasp features in his Bech, a Jewish alter ego. After two early oy-veyish novels, Saul Bellow switched to life-enhancing playfulness and made literature a luxury commodity. Unlike Mordecai Richler, who proclaimed himself 'world-famous in Canada', born-Canadian Bellow effaced the frontier and announced himself 'American', thus eliding his origins, national and 'racial', into Yankee-Doodle Dandyism.

Ductile modernists, echoing Roland Barthes, have it that literature is never innocent: we cannot speak, or write, without our words bringing in a train of barnacled preconceptions. Language is the brothel from which, like Jean Genet's characters in *Le Balcon*, there is no escape. The scientific innovator, by contrast, has no identifiable accent: how can there be *mauscheln* in the terms of an equation? Scientific discoveries may carry a name-tag, but sooner than later they become common property, available for revisionist co-option by whoever balances on their authors' shoulders.

For Robert Oppenheimer, science doubled as sublime recourse and practical escape from pronounced classification. He achieved fame in a subject in which his work could mesh, without distinction of language or topic, with what all the best people in the field were doing or wished they had done. His signature ticketed his work but did not season it. Has any scientist, however famous, ever mimicked Picasso who said thank you for dinner by signing the tablecloth? Science has neither homeland nor proprietor. A pundit may be laurelled; his ideas never remain his property. Once published, they belong to common knowledge.

154

It is facile to presume that little of what has been destroyed in the way of art or literature, whether by chance, stupidity or doctrine, has deprived us of anything of irreplaceable beauty or intellectual significance. I remember reading a scholarly volume on lost masterpieces of the classical world, but I needed Paul Cartledge's prompt scholarship to supply its (2005) author's name: Stuart Kelly. There is an unpopular case for saying, *caute*, that the Nazi murder of millions of Jews led to a grievous depletion of the European gene pool. 'Yeah, yeah' is in line with Bernard Williams's response. Horace had the bravado to say that great books were *aere perennius* (longer-lasting than bronze); portable as they may be, they are also prone to incendiarism. Enough masterpieces have survived by a whisker, Catullus' poems, for instance, though not necessarily all of them, to justify faith in the censorship of chance. The world's lacunae remain barnacled with who knows how many drowned or downed masterpieces.

Freud's eagerness, early in the twentieth century, to recruit Gentile savants to the psychoanalytic fraternity prefigured the fear, realised after the secession of Carl Jung from his entourage, that what Freud wished to have taken for science would be derided as Talmudic mystification. Vladimir Nabokov, philo-Semite with a Jewish wife, labelled Freud 'the Viennese witch-doctor'. He abhorred the notion that a son necessarily duplicates Sigmund's Oedipus. Nabokov's love for his murdered father – cleverest of the Cadets, according to Trotsky's account of the Russian Revolution – was not to be soiled by a generalisation. Volodya's son became a racing driver, as if in a hurry for the frisson of a close shave.

155

Were the Jews of his greening more hateful to Oppy than the Gentiles whose highest society he would seek, and briefly dominate, by becoming their cutie? Public renown commanded immunity from debasement. Oppy became an inverted pariah by being scored alpha-plus-plus, unmatchable scarlet letters. A double life suited him: he could have recourse to solitude, at sea or in his mountain cottage, while masterminding the Manhattan Project at Los Alamos. Affectations of indifference to popularity can be both admirable and ostentatious. Oppenheimer became a figure of destiny, at once unique and rejected of men, saviour of civilisation, apt for beatified crucifixion. The character can be more exquisitely finished than the actor who sets out to play him.

The emblematic instance of Jewish self-hatred is said to be Benedict (Baruch) Spinoza. Was he not more subtle than his critics? He camouflaged his attack on the concept of a personal, interventionist, miracle-working God by making Judaism the overt target of his magniloquent Latin opus. In reported truth, Jesus' Father was a more frequent wonder-worker than JHVH, though the latter did do his lightning stuff for Elijah in that mano-a-mano with the Philistines' Baal. The axiom of Spinozan insolence was that God and Nature were alternative terms for the same thing (*deus sive natura*).

There is a hint of distinction in all assertions of equivalence: two and two make four; but four – if only because one word, not three – is not identical with two and two.

Spinoza held it logically impossible for nature to breach its own laws by furnishing unnatural exceptions for select suppliants, a conceit typical, if not integral, to Christianity, never of Judaism. Candidates for Catholic beatification must be credited with three non-natural miracles. Although he never said so, Virgin Birth and the Resurrection were instances of what Spinoza ranked as absurd. Caution led him to mask diplomatic insolence by writing in Latin, *lingua franca* of Catholicism and of educated Europe. Spinoza's philosophy entered the same charge against both testaments, overtly in one case, discreetly in the other. Concealed contempt for Christianity sharpened his needle when it came to Jews. The *avertis* alone could guess that he was firing at a double butt. In military target-practice, the exercise known as 'aiming off' involves accurate missing as a form of precision. George Steiner had it that anti-Semitism embodies Gentile resentment of an alien morality too firmly installed to be dismantled. Jew-hatred is the anti-Christianity that dares not speak its name.

156

Hegel both denied that Jews could philosophise and all but conceded that their 'logic' and its moral skein had anticipated logic itself. The positing of necessary antagonisms is part of the choreography of Hegelian dialectic, two-timing its quickstep. Sartre regarded 'contingency' as not of the essence, as Plato did; he contrasted the chanciness of life with man's unique capacity for steering the direction he means to take; post-war Sartre then insisted that turning left was obligatory if in search of salvation.

Schopenhauer derided Hegel's verbosity more than his sentiments. Enemies of the Jews, Christian or Muslim, murderous or playful, rarely agree among themselves. Céline came to regard Charles Maurras, as did Lucien Rebatet, as hardly better than an associate Jew, squeamish enough to distinguish one Jew from another (as liberal Jews sometimes do bacon from pork). William Joyce called Oswald Mosley a 'kosher fascist', suspecting that 'Tom' was pandering to prejudices he failed to honour in private toffdom. Adolf Eichmann had at least one spasm of confessional inferiority: in exile in Argentina, after the war, he conceded that Jews could have daunting originality. Anti-Semitism is less often a symptom of social superiority than an adhesive between those liable to fall out or apart. Hence Sartre's guess, unless it was a confession, that when an anti-Semite looks in the glass, he more confirms what he is not than declares what he is.

Drieu la Rochelle, fluent second-rate author of the first rank, was a paradigm of the type. Uncertainty and conceit incited secession from respectability. After his early inter-war books failed to procure conventional eminence, he repaired to fascism. Louis Aragon, when disowned by André Breton, the Surrealists' Censor, had recourse to the Communist Party, whose clubby patron he then became. Drieu's carnets (never as much fun as 'Chips' Channon's no less anti-Semitic gossip) promise allegiance to fascism and to anti-Semitism. Lacking the fanaticism of Rebatet or Céline, more opportunist than fanatic, his greatest achievement was to leave a dirty mark on his times. Drieu's first wife, Collette Jéramec, was from a Jewish family. In 1945, in flight from retribution from old friends, André Malraux *en tête*, he took belated refuge *chez elle* in steep sandstone La Roque-Gageac, on the Dordogne, where he committed suicide in March 1945. Their terminal duet, as seen in Aude Terray's *Les Derniers Jours de Drieu la Rochelle*, merited a dramatised annex, outspoken Colette in attendance. Maurice Ronet made Drieu a tragic suicide in an early post-war movie.

The worse Jews are treated, or threatened, the more they excite suspicion. Who do they think they are not to hate those who persecute them? I once told such a person that I saved hatred for best. He declared this very arrogant. An arriviste who, like Joseph, brings fertility to alien fields is apt to excite first respect, then resentment. To render rare service to the state, as Walther Rathenau did, can lead to denunciation. One Iago after another tracks such benefactors in various styles. The suspicion that J. R. Oppenheimer was some kind of a double-dealer was fostered by his having rendered the state rare, if not unique, service. He gave Harry Truman a sense of being patronised. Oppy's plotted fall is the measure of the height to which, like Prometheus, he had risen. In McCarthyite eyes, Oppenheimer being a Jew made it plausible that he was some sort of a Red. The senator employed a pair of Jews, Roy Cohn and David Schine, one homosexual, who could be depended upon to show self-protective ruthlessness, just as Nachmanides' converso inquisitors did in 1263. How could McCarthy's henchmen's accusations be the result of prejudice when they themselves were overprinted Jews?

Looking back, Isidor Rabi, physicist and colleague of the first rank, thought that Oppy compromised his thinking by choosing to venerate Sanskrit texts rather than the Talmud. Ray Monk makes the sensible objection that Oppenheimer was never any sort of Talmudic student and had no duty to be so. How should he be held an apostate when his social or spiritual conception of himself never had avowedly Jewish 'false-work', as civil engineers term the scaffolding which supports construction in progress and is later jettisoned? Was Oppenheimer's repudiation of what Rabi took to be integral to his personality not the best evidence of just how Jewish he may have feared himself to be, during his New York youth at least? Denial takes a psychic toll. Norman Mailer claimed that cancer was, or could be, psychosomatic: the body pays tax (a corporeal version of the *fiscus Judaicus*?) from which the mind claims exemption. All fears leave their mark.

The ancient historian Moses Finkelstein changed his last name to Finley rather as Joseph ben Mattathias became Flavius Josephus. George Steiner tells of an academic function at which he went over to talk to Moses F. After their conversation finished, Mrs Finley took G. S. by the sleeve and said, 'I saw you talking to Moses in a very Jewish sort of way. I think I should tell you that we are now Buddhists.' Finley's work is much admired by his admirers. I have always found it dry, cautious and devoid of wit (so too that of Lewis Namier), quite as if being amusing would leave naughty prints. As so often, there is an old Jewish story not irrelevant to those who, understandably, efface their original names in favour of something more sociable. A Jewish businessman becomes rich enough to have a yacht and invite his mother to come and see it. When she comes along the quay, he descends in an anchor-buttoned blue blazer, peaked cap and white ducks. His mother expresses some surprise at the nautical rig. 'You don't understand, Mama, I'm a captain now.' 'Sammy,' she says, 'by you you're a captain; by me you're a captain; by a captain are you a captain?'

157

As quick to criticise as the deaf to speak, if only to be sure they know what is being said, Oppenheimer conquered fields of excellence with speed and swagger. His genius of many colours was a camouflage against personal criticism. Self-assertion as a physicist may be, personality adds nothing to the merit of what he publishes, though anecdotes feather memorability. Science uses a notation in which a researcher seeks to be truthful; if it requires genius to formulate a new idea, its merits are never enhanced by egotistic flourishes, though Einsteinian brevity helps. Scientific theories may be beautiful, by virtue of exquisite shapeliness, but truth scorns seduction (Carlo Michelstaedter's central point). Scientific discoveries are known to have been made by two or more people at much the same time. Rival researchers often race to produce results which merit the Nobel Prize. It remains absurd to imagine two literary figures happening to write the same poem or novel, without knowledge of each other. Borges makes play of the notion in his fictional Pierre Menard, who duplicates *Don Quixote* while ignorant of the original.

Is there is any evidence that Oppenheimer passed secrets to any foreign agent? Need pride in having the beans in his care have gone as far as spilling them? Haakon Chevalier under-estimated Oppy's patriotism as well as the pride he took in the command to which he had been assigned. By a captain, he was a captain. In his frigid self-esteem, was he not a little like a good Albert Speer? Speer's career demonstrates what is likely to happen in practice when Ayn Rand's architectural genius, Howard Roark, or his ambitious counterfeit finds himself on the pinnacle of the devil's temple. Only when Oppenheimer was no longer admitted to the *peloton de tête* among physicists did he settle for being the sage of Princeton's Institute for Advanced Study. His attitude to the foundation of the state of Israel was that he flashed no attitude to it.

If he never changed or himself truncated his name, Oppy chose to sport the top-dressing of a tweedy, pork-pied, fat-free New Englander. He invested himself in physics at a time when it was revising the nature of matter, hence of reliable identity. This chimes with the effacement of Jewishness as immutable characteristic. Since the atom was split into an uncertain number of electric particles, nothing remains as categorically definite as previously thought. Oppy's electric personality had no fixed co-ordinates. The great prize was to be indistinguishable from Gentiles, but superior to them.

Was 'betrayal' of Chevalier a sign of how keenly Oppy had valued their relationship? To deceive a man whom he had seemed to like more than any other was a deliverance from obligation. A man can establish emancipation from inferiority, and from gratitude for small mercies, by betraying what was once precious. Without alertness to the ambiguities in so-called self-hatred, how should we understand his conduct? To humble a Gentile stands for liberation: the other becomes the victim whose hat, like Freud's father's, is tumbled in the gutter. Indifference in the face of his friend Chevalier's disgrace aligned Oppy in the triumphant company of his persecutors of all those years ago. Throwing Chevalier to the dogs, he was done with being his old, needy self; he had found his scapegoat. The schemer had been duped into believing that he was

Oppy's intimate friend. Seduction and egotism take pleasure in heartlessness.

Other people appear to have been the least of Robert Oppenheimer's worries. The alcoholic wife, the alienated children, there they were, like lost or abandoned friends; he denied himself the demeaning vanity of guilt. Did emotional frigidity (except with regard to his brother Frank) have its source in that ice store or in revulsion from scarcely embarrassing, undeniably Jewish, parents? Both? And what else?

In the panoply of commanding officer at Los Alamos, Oppenheimer was liberated to play Sanskrit deity, death-dealer and deliverer with epochal responsibility. Dispassionate scientist and preening victor, he later visited the sites of Hiroshima and Nagasaki. Whatever Strauss and Teller were seeking to take away from him, his fell creation had won the Pacific War. More Archimedes than Prometheus, his team used human means to generate that inhuman force 'brighter than a thousand suns', as John Hersey had it in his *New Yorker* account of Hiroshima.

158

Hersey, John, is rarely mentioned in any conspectus of American fiction. His novel *The Wall* (1950) was one of the first to take the Holocaust as its theme. It remains vivid for its images of the eponymous wall which is being built to enclose the Warsaw ghetto and, in particular, for the dwarfish Jewish clown who amuses the SS officers in the process of compressing and humiliating the sectioned Jews by his parody of all the absurdities attributed to the *Juden*. Immune from the Nazis' malice because he panders so grotesquely to their fantasies, he seems to justify, as he appears to be amused by, the degradation of those denied even the bones which his SS audience choose to throw him. In return he can call the ring-masters brutes and bullies. He does it so fawningly that they take it as a compliment. It eases the stress of dutiful heartlessness. One of Frantz Fanon's patients, when he was a physician at a hospital in Algeria in the 1950s, was a French officer nervously broken down by the strain of torturing members of the FLN.

The Jewish comedian – wisecracking between shamelessness and self-mockery – has something of the doctor as well as of the self-emblazoned butt. He relieves his audience of guilt they might feel when mocking or despising Jews by being openly derisive of, as they say, his own people. The technique of ur-psychoanalysis encourages the patient to come out with whatever distresses him/her, clinical *commedia dell'arte*. It has been said that Freudian patients have Freudian dreams, Jungian Jungian: the patient seeks to find favour by falling in with his audience's predilections, as Hersey's Yoricking dwarf did. When Jackie Mason teased the Jews, in the similar spirit, he made the biggest fools those who imagined that they had escaped ridicule.

159

In the defence of Syracuse in 212 BCE, Archimedes arranged a set of mirrors to concentrate the sun's rays and ignite the approaching Roman fleet. His brilliance was not enough to deter Roman soldiers from landing on the beach where he was doing geometry in the sand. Realising that the Roman squaddies were going to kill him, Archimedes is said to have cried out, 'Don't disturb my triangles.' His most famous promise – 'Give me a place to stand and I'll move the world' – was trumped by Oppenheimer: he moved the world and then he had a place to stand. Having recruited nature into resolving the Japanese War, his triumphant fate was to be run through by the spears of those he had worked with, his consolation that the worse he was seen to be treated, the greater his martyrdom. Lack of preparedness, when in front of the Senate committee, boasted how far above them he now sat; he had rendered the state enough service to put himself beyond vulgar reckonings.

160

In his last years, Oppenheimer had a long TV interview with Ed Murrow. He gave such a ravishing performance that Isidor Rabi said to him afterwards, 'You're a ham!' An element of performance is present in all who aspire to prominence; no one is that natural a leader; impersonation was essential to Oppy's giving his best performance of himself. Uncertainties left in the dressing room, he was always dominant in public. In seminars he would cut in and cut up whoever threatened to dispute his right to the last word; only rarely was he faced down by men self-confident enough not to be intimidated. The oxymoronic image of a kosher ham may have tripped inadvertently from Rabi's tongue; it encapsulates the criticism he made of Oppenheimer's deviance from the ancestral path. The apostate as show-off, comedian and intellectual is no rarity among quasi-assimilated Jews. The young Jonathan Miller made clever play with his confession that he was Jewish: he didn't 'go the whole hog'. Like his quasi-double Danny Kaye, Jonathan ceased being funny quite abruptly.

Oppenheimer's support of the New Deal, at its newest, and his extension of liberal sentiments to embrace anti-Franco 'fronts' were not untypical of forward-looking 1930s New York Jews without nostalgia for an old country. Oppy later travelled widely, in search of uplifting company. The US alone was home. He may have sought, as he later assumed, entrée into the best academic circles in Europe, but he cared little for the society, much as he admired the literature, of the old continent.

His contempt for post-war Britain was virulent enough to suggest that he remembered how, as an apprentice at the Cavendish laboratory, he had felt himself unwanted. Did he remember the Blackett episode or efface it from consciousness? Both will do. Monk notes Oppy's disdain for Oxford and Cambridge alumni but does not link it with personal experience. Why did Oppenheimer go out of his usual way to denounce the English novelist C. P. Snow, after the latter had published his sententious, scarcely pointless pamphlet *The Two Cultures* (1959)? Well-written or not (F. R. Leavis's pettish view), was it wholly in error about the growing divergence between literary and scientific intelligence? I heard recently of an engineer with not a single book in his house. Snow's proud connections with the Cavendish were more to the point.

Did Oppy regard himself as a one-man refutation of the idea that the Two Cultures were incompatible? Towards the accelerated end of his life, he was solicited to nominate the ten books which had meant most to him. Monk comments on the high-falutin' selections, six of them in foreign languages. Must such choices have been pretentious in a linguist of Oppenheimer's ability (he is said to have learnt Dutch in a few weeks previous to delivering a lecture in that language)? To become a well-read polyglot may seem to flaunt an intellectual's claim to be culturally at home *un peu partout*; it is also what used to be known as being civilised. Analysis of the listed texts suggests Oppenheimer's longing to slip the confines in which he was born. Compare Walter Benjamin's project (it owed something to Karl Kraus) of a literary patchwork composed of existent works making a new one by their crafty juxtaposition. Kafka imagined a victim punished by being literally branded with words.

Oppenheimer pulled with Jews only palpably of the first quality. He might have gentilised himself, but he could not efface a distinction, in his own conduct, between relationships with Jews and with others. How many love letters, to him or from him, were ever written to or by Jews (or by anyone else, come to that)? The unsaid is part of every story. Jews can be least inhibited when confronted with other Jews. The plethora of terms of derision in Yiddish suggests the need to vent scorn on those in the same boat and so take the tiller. Oppenheimer's enrolment in universal schemes, science and/ or communism, offered a double-tracked *fuite en avant*. In science as in left-wing politics, individual character and provenance were irrelevant to common purposes.

161

In literature, greatness is clinched, in many eyes, by becoming a national treasure, as Saul Bellow worked purposefully to achieve. His books can be divided, abruptly, into two periods. Trim, doleful and uncompromising, his early novels *Dangling Man* and *Victim* hardly celebrated life; their quality was fatal. Both titles might have been allusions to the fate of Joseph Süß Oppenheimer. God blessing America, hot for success, Bellow then took a deep, calculated breath and elected to become wide-shouldered, upbeat and starred-and-striped. *The Adventures of Augie March* made no pretence of realism. Said to be 'naturalistic', that obese novel makes being American itself something to snap one's braces for.

Bellow's reward was determinant: the book sold hugely and won a National Book Award in 1953. For the rest of his life, Bellow played the famous sage. His novels grow more and more didactic. He plays safe, even in *Humboldt's Gift*, his 1975 capper on his claim to the number-one spot in American letters, by having the poems of his eponymous, eventually tragic, hero said to be praised by both T. S. Eliot and Yvor Winters, trans-Atlantic buttresses for his poet's slim volumes. Bellow lacked the nerve to concoct credible examples, as busking Anthony Burgess did for his *Enderby* novels.

Humboldt lapses into liquor and dies an early, ignominious

death. Charlie Citrine, Bellow's alter ego as flagrant success, is hobbled all his literary life by the debt he owes to vitality drawn from a character based on Delmore Schwartz (a conveniently outdistanced and outlived writer to whom to play tribute). Bellow cannot be acquitted of envy of those he was proud to displace. He appends a film script which his asymmetrical selves, Citrine and Humboldt, are said to have co-authored. Never professional enough to do the work the plot demands, it is neither funny nor convincing. Deriding Hollywood may be easy; it ain't *that* easy. The character of Humboldt/Fleisher stands for the brilliant loser that Bellow successfully failed to be.

Philip Roth's fictional selves parade a shamelessness that puts a finger up at the oh-so-serious Bellow. Philip made no polite concessions in order to be welcome at the Country Club or find a chair on the Committee for Social Thought, at Chicago University, where Bellow and others cogitated *pro bono publico*. Roth got better and better, and sometimes a little worse, as a writer who never waited up for good news from Stockholm. Unsated by honours and applause, Bellow became a prig, Roth a scold, though never of the bivalved accuracy of his namesake Joseph. Vanity and resentment tripped upwards on the path to doubtful glory.

162

Science (and the Communist Party) attached small significance to self-expression; in their literature, however jargon-laden, the first-person pronoun was anomalous. All the same, the author of a breakthrough paper could secrete the dream of being nominated for The Big One. Like Saul of Tarsus, Oppenheimer sought an exit from particularism which was also an entrance to power. Ambitious Jews sought to Hellenise themselves, in the days of the Maccabean ascendancy, by being capped with prosthetic foreskins. Having embraced a discipline with a method, never a gospel, Oppy acquired quasi-messianic affectations. He first saved the world – certainly the lives of hundreds of thousands of Americans who might otherwise have been despatched to conquer Japan in hand-to-hand fighting – and then became its recrucified victim in the atmosphere of what Monk presumes to be post-war paranoia about the menace of Communism. He mentions Churchill's 'Iron Curtain' speech, but has no space for the consequences, for three generations at least of Eastern Europeans, of the West's powerlessness to save victims of Nazi domination and brutality from Russian domination and brutality. In later life, John Dos Passos (whom Hemingway sought to shop to the Reds when both were in Republican Madrid) embarrassed liberals by the heat of his anti-communism; it hardly certified him paranoid. It is more likely that Hemingway was motivated by literary envy than by cleaving to the Red line. Back in the Spanish arena, he might well have denounced George Orwell, had he then been famous or stylish enough to threaten his place on the literary leader board.

Have commentators on the left been too happily prompt in deriding Senator Joe McCarthy's whisky-fuelled anti-Red crusade? That the senator hounded innocent people does not entail that there was, in the US, no communist or fellow-travelling activity on behalf of the Soviet Union. Had McCarthy been replaced by some tidy and incorruptible investigator, such a person might well have discovered no few cases. For all Edgar Hoover's peculiarities and their convenience for ridicule, the record indicates that the FBI acted scrupulously when conducting the surveillance of Communist agents during the war; who will claim that all their suspicions were without substance?

Flight from the middle ground pulled Oppenheimer in two directions: physics took him to rare heights in the company of exceptional people; Communism maintained that personal vanity should be laid aside in the service of a common philosophy. The red prospectus promised that citizens who survived to dead-heat at the end of the rainbow (Judy Garland's song was another composed by 'Yip' Harburg) would be polyvalent and homogenised. Oppenheimer came so close to fellow-travelling that the name of Trotsky – an intellectual with far more in common with him than any Stalinist – does not appear in Monk's index. Many New York leftists, Mary McCarthy and Diana Trilling joint queens, embraced Trotsky's romantic martyrdom. It wished plagues on any number of houses while running no risk of seditious contagion or of being recruited to the thank-you-for-yours drudgery of practical politics.

163

Arthur Schnitzler had it that no Jew fails to show a tincture of contempt for other Jews, of whatever stripe. This conceit is itself conceited. How many Englishmen, when on holiday, do not flinch at the accents, or the anoraks, the socks with sandals, of those seen to carry the same passport? The brightest of the Tory leaders who tripped after Margaret Thatcher, William Hague, had a Yorkshire accent, which his education, unless it was his pride, did nothing to efface; it neither charmed the toffs nor flattered the plebs, as Sir Walter Raleigh's 'broad Devonshire' did his contemporaries. Only unreformed Yiddish-speaking *Ost-Juden*, despised by their 'civilised' brethren, reacted without a wince when other Jews were met or mentioned; hence Joseph Roth's abiding affection for their authenticity. At the same time, he advertised that he had served with distinction as an Austrian officer, loyal to the emperor even after no empire remained.

Charles Maurras claimed to have no quarrel with the rag-and-bone man of Yiddish folklore. Only a Jew slick enough to pass for French was held insufferable. This selectivity led Lucien Rebatet to denounce his one-time idol as lacking in rigour. William Joyce fell out with Oswald Mosley, whom he termed a 'kosher' fascist. In the same spirit, Louis-Ferdinand Céline denounced Maurras as a Jew. By the end of the war, in his view pretty well everyone else had turned out to be a Jew, 'Hitler' included; Céline became the only uncompromised Aryan/Breton alive.

When Maurras, for many years literally deaf to any voice, metaphorically to any idea but his own, was convicted of 'complicity with the enemy' and sentenced to ignominy, he called out, '*C'est la revanche de Dreyfus.*' Is it unduly fanciful to suspect that, somewhere in his one-man-banded psyche, Maurras dreamed of being persecuted, martyred, sentenced to a solitary fate, like Lucien Rebatet's caged, degraded last-living Jew in his 1942 novel *Les Décombres*? Compare Hugo's last line in Sartre's *Les Mains Sales*, resignation and vanity in one: '*Irrécupérable.*'

164

The dream-on dream of many *évolués* Jews is to be so distinguished as to pass for indistinguishable from Gentiles, like Proust's Swann, dandy in Jockey Club style. Is every friendship with a Gentile some kind of a performance, a slice of ham more or less exquisitely carved? The implication of Rabi's accusation was that Oppy had done his gig on TV with such panache that not even Ed Murrow could tell that the sage's diffidence was wrapped around a claim to parity with what Jimmy Baldwin and his friends in the 1960s would dub 'the Man'. After his on-camera performance, Oppenheimer was graced with a reputation for unassuming brilliance. Was he inflated by having duped the other fellow, Murrow the shrewdest, into considering him as modest as an Ivy League genius could well be?

Why did Oppenheimer's enemies pursue him with such sustained venom? Relying on an essentialist notion of human conduct, Monk seems to second Cioran's notion that there were good guys and bad guys. 'Shake it and take it' as the human prescription, can it be that simple? Without adducing Kenneth Burke's notion of motive as a function of circumstance, it is difficult to be sure, easy to guess, why Strauss (both a Zionist and a servant of the US apparat) and Teller (a manifest 'kike' in the clan language of Manhattan's *haute*

Juiverie) made Oppenheimer their target of choice. What zest was added to their enthusiasm by the righteous persecution of another Jew, the one who dared to presume that he had got away? The bull of such animus is often a man (rarely, if ever, a woman) who seems not to be subject to the dreads and humiliations which bruise his 'co-religionists'.

There was dark comedy in Teller, thickly accented Hungarian arriviste with neither native nor naïve affection for the USA, being able, with Strauss's gold-striped help, to accuse Oppenheimer, native-born Yank, of adhesion to a foreign creed. Was there not something vindictive in their determination to nail the pork-pie-hatted, polylingual assimiland as duplicitous? J. Robert Oppenheimer's presumptuousness resembles that of Joseph Süß Oppenheimer as directed by Veit Harlan: the Jew, dangling in the cage above the mocking mob, is denied quietus until he admits that he is, for all his fine library and his *shikse* lovers, no more than one more pathetic little Jew.

Oppenheimer's quite early death, after public humiliation, can be read as a tragic sentence passed on himself. Norman Mailer dared to diagnose cancer as in many cases self-inflicted, the sufferer a remake of the Roman playwright Terence's 'Self-Torturer'. Publius Terentius' last name was Afer, Black or African. Romans, for all their presumption of superiority, were never manifestly 'racist', but might the ex-slave Terence have had the wit to dredge comedy from his own apprehensions?

Oppy left few traces of an off-duty life in which self-doubt or humour had a place. It is tempting to read his affair with the woman in San Francisco as more conspiratorial than romantic. Did Oppenheimer never guess that he was under surveillance? To be tailed is a kind of distinction: 'Do you follow me?' a regular question of the patronising teacher. Might it be that what mattered most to Oppy was to be the centre of attention? At Cambridge, England, he embarrassed parents, limeys and Gentiles by his grotesqueries. Later, his genius impressed or intimidated contemporaries. Is he ever on record as being amusing? Inability to relax or to connect, in Morgan Forster's sense, persists throughout his career and his correspondence. It may be unjust to blame him for his wife's alcoholism, the suicide of his daughter, the sullen detachment of his son (even after his father's death); but such things are loud silent witnesses, mantled in mandarin vanity.

165

Nettled by something I said before a dinner party, Bernard Williams made bold to pronounce that the twentieth century had been 'good for the Jews'. If at all serious, his remark must have derived from the domination of physics and philosophy by people who, whether or not they practised Judaism, promulgated a way of thinking which was 'one-hundred-per-cent Hebraic', as Wittgenstein confessed, late in the day, in deprecation of his own mix-and-match manner. There was, he chose to acknowledge, a style more authentic (chthonic, even) from which Jews were, by their deracinated nature, embargoed. Dare it be said that 'Mix and don't match' is no disgraceful recipe? Accept Roland Barthes and Kenneth Burke as markers, the notion of native originality shrivels away. Of its nature, language makes everything said more-or-less second-hand. Wittgenstein's disavowal imp/lies that Hebraic thought is parasitic. His attitude to 'private languages' suggests that he recognised all human speech and thought to be bastardised, unless unintelligible, hence no speech at all. Then again, does Charlie Chaplin's Adolf Hitler not suggest that the rabble can be roused by the non-sensical rant of a charlatan?

Wittgenstein told Russell that the latter's work should be divided into two categories: one bound in blue, which everyone should read; the other in red, which no one should (interesting choices of colour in the light of Wittgenstein's flirtation with communism). Englishness made Russell a literary grandee, eligible for the Nobel Prize. Apart from his nation's firepower, what determines a philosopher's durability is as often his style as the merits of his work. Few have been more influential than John Locke, whose image of the newborn mind as a *tabula rasa*, ready to be impressed with sense data, created the myth of mankind being born equal. The promulgation of DNA led to no remarkable literature but it relegated Locke (and Hume) to dated distinction.

Was Wittgenstein's diluted Jewishness ever mentioned in Cambridge lecture rooms? Never in my hearing. At High Tables? Perhaps. Until Stephen Toulmin and Allan Janik's book on his Viennese background was published in 1972, undergraduates were incited to regard W as an eccentric one-off Catholic, as if infantile baptism had unhitched his Hebraic lineage. With age-old Catholic magnanimity, Geach and Anscombe filched his soul and buried him as *croyant* in an English country churchyard.

In *Wittgenstein Reads Weininger* (2004), David Stern and Béla Szabados attacked the notion that Wittenstein's reluctance to dismiss Otto Weininger's Manichaean thesis was a concession to Nazi (or Austrian) anti-Semitism. The all-but-envious attention he paid to someone whom he held to have misconceived ideas suggests that Wittgenstein was too honest not to see the force in them. That very late admission that his own thought was 'one-hundred-per-cent Hebraic' put a tick in Weininger's margin and a question mark against his own originality. What inclined Wittgenstein to philosophy? A wish to reduce its haughty affectations and shrink it, as Carlo Michelstaedter wished, to the role of logical vigilante against metaphysical pretensions? Did physics offer Oppenheimer immunity against the charge of self-interest? Precocious individuality was effaced by a landscape in which, as W's *Tractatus* has it, 'roughly speaking all objects are colourless'.

Does Oppy's reluctance to accept that the prime purpose of the Los Alamos installation was to create a weapon for indiscriminate killing derive from the shibboleth that there was no necessary connection between scientific enterprise and its application by the state or any other body? Nuclear power, while latent, was always there. Science discloses; it does not create. Its material and uses are immanent in the universe. Etymology promises as much: in Latin, *invenire* means to find, never invent.

Many Jews were engaged in philosophy and physics (as well as medicine) during the *entre-deux-guerres*. Which of them has chosen, in public print, to look into himself, as Byron put it, and declare why he embraced those particular disciplines? Simone Weil wrote in one of her notebooks: '*Sortir de soi, c'est la renonciation totale à être quelqu'un, le consentement complet à être quelque chose*' (to quit the self implies total renunciation of being someone, total agreement to be something). The philosopher discounts personal commentary, hence the disparagement of 'mere autobiography'. The ideal scientist, as depicted by Popper, commits him/herself to the self-abnegation of a quasi-religious order. The articulation of physics carries no risk of *mauscheln*. Philosophy and science double for sublime country clubs. Only outstanding outsiders attain entrance.

The Nobel Prize crowns those who have excelled; it leaves them subordinate to those who bestow it. The Académie Française elects 'immortals' and exacts ritual gratitude at the same time. Craving both to escape and to stand out is a fit for both Wittgenstein and Oppenheimer. Upwardly mobile escapologists breach holes in social and academic ceilings. Public renown rendered them more or less exempt from *a priori* tickets: neither was typical of anything. Oppy's recourse to a discipline without a first person can be read as a noble unmanning of himself (of the kind which Catullus described, with horrified relish, in the self-mutilating worshippers of Attis).

Oppy's least convincing performance was of being a normal human being. As his crass sexual tactics exemplified, on off-duty excursions he could resemble Chauncy Gardner in Jerzy Kosinki's 1979 novella *Being There*, capable only of passionless mimesis. The juvenile attempt to make off to Mexico with a colleague's wife to whom Oppenheimer had just been introduced might have been scripted by his advertised reading (though not of Flaubert's *L'Éducation sentimentale*) or after seeing a bad movie; mistimed and ill-performed, it was a *coup de foudre* enacted by a man lacking genuine passion or seductive grace. Oppenheimer performed *un autre* with conspicuous versatility. What aspect of intelligence could he not master? In his zeal for the examined life there was more examination than life, as much flight as pursuit. My friend, ex-Milanese Jo Janni, told of the captain of a new addition to the Italian fleet, who said, proudly, 'In this ship we can get away from anything else on the sea.'

166

Admired for *The Painted Bird* (1965), Jerzy Kosinski became an enigma, if not an embarrassment, as far as literary ranking was concerned. It has been said that, because his English was not good enough at the time of its composition, he could not have written *The Painted Bird*, which few deny was based on his experience as a small boy in occupied Poland, where he was sheltered by Polish peasants. He spoke English fluently when I met him in 1966, but it may be that he wrote or narrated his story in Polish and had it translated, perhaps before editing it again. So what? Henry James dictated his last, adipose novels without incurring any suggestion that he failed to be their author. Joseph Conrad's spoken English was idiosyncratic. Kosinski had a personal style which he can scarcely have cadged off anyone else, but he was later accused of 'improving' and appropriating the texts of his creative writing pupils without acknowledgement. If so, his students must have had rare talents. Has any emerged as a free-standing writer of quality?

Whether *The Painted Bird* is to be classed as fiction or as embellished autobiography is a matter for filing clerks. Such a debate does not affect its rare quality. It is part of a common Gentile attitude that Jews who survived should count themselves lucky and be chastened by their experience. Kosinski and I had one long conversation, sitting by the pool at the Athens Hilton. He had been invited to London for the publication of his new book and billeted at the Russell Hotel. He ordered breakfast, with two boiled eggs. A bulky waiter came with his tray. The removal of a lid disclosed two poached eggs. Kosinski said that he had ordered boiled eggs. The large waiter stood over him, pointed at the poached eggs and said, 'Eat!' True?

Kosinski had a near namesake, Jerzyk, second cousin of Anthony Rudolf, whose book of the same name is a brief, factual account of the very short life of the youngest Holocaust victim to commit suicide, at the age of eleven. Jerzyk's father was a doctor with easy access to the cyanide tablets with which he armed his family in the possibility – likelihood, even – of their arrest in German-occupied Galicia. One day there was a loud thump at the door and little Jerzyk, sure that the dreaded Germans were at the door, bit the cyanide tablet. In fact, the aggressive knock was from some local blackmailers. Jerzyk's parents survived the war, emigrated to Israel and had another child.

Roman Polanski had a childhood not unlike Kosinski's, a talent as rare, if not as fine. Polanski fled from Hollywood, after being accused, probably with justice, of having sex with a fourteen-year-old girl ('Just his size', a screenwriting cynic was heard to mutter), who was either procured for him or who presented herself – such things can happen – as older than she was, perhaps because she wanted the money, the kudos, the pleasure. It may or may not be the case that Polanski was deceived about her age; it is as likely that, at a time when he was at the peak of his success, vanity led him to presume that celebrity entailed immunity from common scruples. Polanski continued to make movies in Europe, culminating with *The Pianist*, which, while lacking subtlety (for instance, a hint of passion, born of the Jew and the Nazi each wanting somewhat to be the other), was all the better for the stringency of its *mise-en-scène*. The hounds of propriety continue to seek his extradition to the US.

Those who survived the world where there was no *warum* have some excuse for preferring flight to 'justice'. Like the sheep, goats and cattle led to the altar for sacrifice, victims of human malice, calculation and faith are expected to behave with comely acquiescence to those who mean them no good. As the case of Iphigeneia shows, virgins too had the required characteristics, the docility of unbroached women. Anne Frank supplied the modern appetite for innocent sacrifice. Imagine the memoirs of Solomon Schmuck, a smelly old Yid with appalling socks who travels on the same train as Anne Frank to the same fate. Who would care? Yet murder is murder.

167

The now-forgotten Lynskey tribunal was one of the rare comedies of Clement Attlee's now-revered 1945–51 Labour government. Never mind the massacres which followed the scuttle from India, who cares to recall the Tanganyika ground-nut scheme or the treatment of Seretse Khama when he dared to marry a white woman, Ruth Williams? The panoply of a British judicial inquiry was mounted, in 1948, to investigate the suspected corruption of a government minister, with the Ben Jonsonian name of John Belcher, and other officials by a man called Sidney Stanley, otherwise Solomon Wulkan. The price of small favours from smallish fry was little more than the odd cigar and freebies which, today, scarcely elicit a thank-you from recipients.

The attorney general, Sir Hartley Shawcross, who served as the UK's chief Nuremberg prosecutor, was diverted from grand affairs of state to nail the all-but-caricatural Yid. The ensuing comedy derived from the capacity of the alien crook, said to have redoubled his own double life by being a spy for Irgun Zvei Leumi, the Zionist 'terror' organisation, to remain not only unabashed but quite capable of bashing on his own account. It was as if John Hersey's capering dwarf in *The Wall* had reappeared as a post-war clown. My mother was told by her friend Joan Shawcross that, during a recess, the attorney general found himself standing next to Sidney Stanley in the gents'. As they rinsed their hands, Stanley said how much he admired Hartley and offered to find him a job if he ever needed one.

The proceedings resulted in the disgrace of the sorry Belcher and the scolding of a silly governor of the Bank of England, but it was decided not to pursue Stanley when he headed for Israel. After the discovery of Belsen, a manifestly guilty Jewy Jew came as a relief. Stanley proved that the image of the Yid as fool and fixer was still there to serve as off-the-ration butt for the virtuous in a time when all manner of ways were found, in all quarters and classes, to circumvent the mass of shortages and stringencies.

Immediately after the Labour landslide of 1945, Shawcross was heard to call out to the diminished Tories, 'We are the masters now!' He himself was masterly enough to tire of the petty emoluments of office and accept a fat salary from Shell Oil. He is remembered now, by a dwindling few, on account of young Bernard Levin's famous rechristening of him as 'Sir Shortly Floor-Cross'. The Lynskey tribunal, complete with a judge who sounds Jewish but was not, might form the basis of a period musical comedy. Zero Mostel, thou shouldst be living at this hour.

The trial of Ernest Saunders, Gerald Ronson, Jack Lyons and Anthony Parnes, who were arraigned in 'the Guinness Affair' of 1993, exposed a hand-in-the-honeypot scandal scarcely unique in the boom years of the Thatcher and post-Thatcher Conservative government. The four defendants were slick operators, dupes and scapegoats. They were recruited, as much by flattery, one can guess, as by the hope of profit. Successful businessmen who did not, as the saying is, need the money, they were enrolled by the Guinness family to boost the price of Guinness shares, by acquiring large numbers of them, in order to head off a hostile takeover bid. The family avoided leaving its prints on a routine case of insider dealing; those of the Jews were manifest.

Like Süß, the quartet were left to twist in the wind, though not literally this time, without any of the sponsors of the scheme being arraigned or showing the smallest indication of owning up. The accused were delivered to serve terms of imprisonment, without incurring any marked obloquy. Ernest Saunders was released early, having displayed symptoms of Alzheimer's disease. He was subsequently said to have made a full recovery. Ronson returned to his successful garage business without anyone thinking the worse of him. The Guinnesses were unblemished – and enriched. Oswald Mosley's second wife was a Guinness and undoubtedly good for him.

168

As boyish, buoyant candidate to succeed President Eisenhower, Jack Kennedy rallied patriotic votes by accusing the veteran general's administration of responsibility for America's insufficient ballistic arsenal. Kennedy promised that, if elected, he would increase military investment. And so he did, though there was, in truth, no missile gap. It is hardly new for fear to levy revenue to celestial ends. Like von Braun's rockets, Christian spires pointed to the sky, extracted tithes, promised salvation.

Dwight D. Eisenhower's adversary in the 1952 election had been Adlai Stevenson, ex-governor of Illinois, the sole wit to be nominated, post-war, by either party. Wits risk alienating those who don't, as they say, get it; win one smart vote, lose two stupid ones is no recipe for democratic success. After being defeated twice by Eisenhower, Stevenson persisted in contesting JFK's nomination as the Democrats' candidate in 1960. The Kennedys' handsome money put an end to the less-well-heeled Adlai, tagged as a loser by the hole in his photographed shoe. The incoming administration embraced him as the boa constrictor its prey. Having appointed Stevenson their spokesman in the United Nations, the Bostonian caucus commissioned the last liberal contender for the presidency to deliver pronouncements that soured his tongue.

Arthur Schlesinger Jr became the new administration's

house intellectual. With no rare expertise and having made no practical contribution to America's arsenal, he was nattily suited to play courtier and courier. His study of American vice-presidents warrants comparison with that pitcher of the warm piss to which one such, Alben Barkley, compared the pleasure of holding that office, under Harry Truman. Dropping whatever independent judgement he may have sported in Harvard's History faculty, Schlesinger grew red-handed with the applause he lavished on the Hyannis Port fraternity. Given access to private jets and a cabinet chair, his mouth, even when closed, proved him a plummy example of secession from pro-fessorial dignity to plush toadyism.

Washington fame procured him sideline selection as a magazine movie critic. He divorced his first wife and married a much younger, much, much taller woman. When the uneven couple came into Elaine's, a smart New York restaurant with overrated food (people went there to be seen, not to eat), Lilian Hellman remarked, 'Here comes Schlesinger with his six-foot bride; think he goes up on her?' Hellman's Stalinist conceits were spurned by Mary McCarthy. Red or not, Hellman had speed on the uptake no prig could outwit. McCarthy's prose, flush with fine clichés, was an application for mandarin enrolment. Her special subject was literary elevation, not least in bed, as proved by her going-up marriage to Edmund Wilson. It soon went down.

In due time, Schlesinger became the bulging encomiast of Robert Kennedy, whose murder capped a translation from Jack's enforcer to pacific saint. The suspicion that Bobby and his brother had played an inglorious part in the death of Marilyn Monroe was relegated to blasphemy. Schlesinger became not so much public intellectual as publicity intellectual. His hagiography of Bobby K. proved that Julien Benda's 'clerk' could double with Jean Reno, *nettoyeur* in Luc Besson's 1990 movie *Nikita*.

169

In the early 1960s, Duncan Sandys, Winston Churchill's son-in-law, announced that the British had lost the energy, as they had the treasure, to maintain an empire. Seigneurial plumage ceased to win salutes from the public. The media shed deference as pop stars ties, girls bras. Show business incited the white man to dump his burdens and go to pot. In 1963, Sandys was said to have frequented louche parties convoked by 'Doctor' Stephen Ward. Dishy Christine Keeler and come-and-get-it Mandy Rice-Davies passed the crumpet. Ward was hounded, slowly, to self-inflicted death by the Establishment. His exposure had threatened to bring disgrace on Lord 'Bill' Astor, whose cottager he was and for whom he was said to have played procurer.

In another country, Christine Keeler might have become a movie star; in England, beauty failed to make up for incurable accent, drab provenance. Mandy has her place guaranteed in the book of quotations by saying, 'Well he would, wouldn't he?' after Lord Astor denied having had anything intimate to do with her. Mandy went to Israel, converted to Judaism and lived unashamedly ever after. If she had had the wit to write it, her account of life in the days before the Beatles might have rivalled that of Harriette Wilson, to whom the Duke of Wellington dared to say, 'Publish and be damned!'

While on a flight from California, in the early 1950s, Duncan Sandys' Super Constellation was delayed in Newfoundland, for refuelling. All the other passengers returned promptly when summoned. Sandys was a minister in Churchill's government as well as the PM's son-in-law. It was not politic to take off without him. After three hours, he was chauffeured to where everyone else was breathing stale air. Some unintimidated person asked what matter of state had obliged them all to wait so long. 'Master Duncan Sandys' (my informant, Colonel 'Tiddly' Tyldesley-Jones, called him) replied, 'A man must have a bath.' It was one of the last practical demonstrations of the difference between U – upper-class – and non-U behaviour. The distinction was tabulated, in terms of vocabulary, by Professor Alan Ross in 1954. Partnered by Nancy Mitford, he peddled his precious research, in non-U style, in a bestselling handbook for the upwardly mobile.

Better connected than Ward, the rogue Tory MP and TV opinionator Robert Boothby survived being spotted consorting with the murderous Kray brothers and other come-and-get-it lowlife East End company. It made a change from the House of Commons, which Michael Foot, as he unstraightened his tie before attendance, called 'The Boys' Club'. Boothby had an ace in the hole: he was the lover of Prime Minister Harold Macmillan's wife, Lady Dorothy, who said, quietly, 'I belong to him.'

170

Insurance takes many forms. In the 1930s and early 1940s, while male homosexuality was still a crime, Tom Driberg MP was protected by Max Beaverbrook, for whom he wrote the William Hickey gossip column, and by others whose secrets he was feared to know. It is said that his suggestion that he suck off comely young persons was sweetened with 'it won't take a minute'. Philip Toynbee told females that what he wanted of them, if they weren't too busy, would take twenty. In 1956, Driberg wrote an opportunist account of Max (*Beaverbrook: A Study in Power and Frustration*) and was anathematised, but not outed, by his erstwhile patron. Sociable mutability made him the very case of the man who was one thing and two or three others. Having been an agent for MI5 when at Oxford, he ceased to be useful to them after he was expelled from the Communist Party in 1941. Richard Davenport-Hines guesses that his ejection came of Anthony Blunt's scanning of MI5 files.

Driberg was recruited again by the Russians after they had photographed him fellating a man in a urinal. He gave information, probably of small utility, both to the Russians and to the Czechs, while remaining on informative terms with MI5. Who in modern times ran more adroitly with hares and hounds, while also skating on thin ice? Driberg was later raised to the peerage. His camouflage – left-wing on weekdays, on Sundays High Anglican – and lordly promotion contrast with the fate of Alan Turing, whose codebreaking enabled the Mediterranean Fleet to take out almost the entire Italian Navy in a battle off Otranto in 1940, thus earning Admiral Andrew Cunningham a Nelsonian reputation. When Turing was charged, in 1952, with 'indecent' conduct, no important person saw fit to come to an unsociable boffin's aid as Ken Tynan did to flashier culprits.

Turing committed suicide, before coming to trial, by ingesting cyanide. Who knows how he came to acquire it? There is a small irony in the fact that, in Nazi-dominated Europe, sale of cyanide to Jews was rarely forbidden. More than half a century later, Turing was pelted with posthumous honours. Canonised in the 2014 film *The Imitation Game*, he was portrayed by the excellent Benedict Cumberbatch as a brainy loner who rather put people off.

171

The 1960s began late and spilled into the 1970s. After bowler hats became a marked part of the provincial uniform of parading Orangemen in Belfast, the British male bourgeoisie abandoned the headgear they had once lifted when they met a lady or passed the Cenotaph. The Church of England ceded its congregation to the Beatles; John Lennon claimed that he and his three friends were better known than Jesus Christ (Mick Jagger played the devil). Lennon's murder in 1980 secured beatitude that outlasted the Kennedys'. 'Give Peace a Chance' was the anthem of the CND marchers whose tramping ardour sought to arrest the development of germ-warfare at Porton Down and ban other lethal activities. In science clocks never go back.

172

Entre deux guerres, André Breton revelled in expelling misfits from his Surrealist group. Louis Aragon repaired to the Communist Party for muscular as well as ideological backup and the prospect of fat print-runs. Salvador Dali made fun of his excommunication by Breton with a grotesquely overdone grovel. Playing the post-1968 revolutionary game, Philippe Sollers presided over a Maoist cell in St Germain-des-Prés and took pleasure in arbitrary expulsions from favour. A few sensitive apprentices were propelled to suicide. Marco Bellocchio's film *La Cina è vicina* supplied the commercial for a product which lost a measure of its charm when the number of Mao's victims was counted, in millions. Jung Chang's implacable account of her compatriot's destruction of those deemed insufficiently hot for ideological tyranny was greeted with more sighs than gratitude by English-reading critics. London reviewers held its documented denunciation to be unsubtle and monotonous.

In *Les Femmes* (1983), Sollers made out that he was only having a bit of fun with totalitarian posing, not least because it brought a lot of women to his bed; kidding that didn't lead to kids. Laurent Binet's third novel, *La septième fonction du langage* (2015), is a delicious, overdone comedy of Parisian morals. Sollers is pelted with pitiless bad eggs. Who would remember Feuerbach, had Marx not written his theses scorning ideas which supplied mulch for Marx's own, greater radicalism?

Albert Camus's many ardent letters to Maria Casarès, not published until 2018, incorporate an anxious and repeated need for reassurance. Her copious, affectionate replies are more uninhibited, self-revealing and amusing than his. A Camus letter of 1950 mentions Sartre calling on him, in the south of France, where Camus was convalescing after a bout of recurrent TB. It says no more than that they talked together for an hour. Who, we are left to wonder, was who, and who, so to say, was whom? French law imposes something close to a ban on the unwarranted invasion of the privacy of public figures.

Montaigne's autobiographical penchant, which discloses little about his personal life (although we get a clear impression that he never enjoyed his wife naked, or very much at all perhaps), sets the tone for French writers. They can seem frank, even self-destructive (Georges Bataille an obvious instance), but rarely volunteer their weaknesses; French salt is liable to be dry of tears, which may account for Leopardi's distaste for that starchy language. The neediness of Camus's letters may diminish his macho reputation, but he stands in all-too-human contrast with Sartre's distancing of himself from sentiment as an ingredient of political or personal attitudes. If a rogue (he was unfaithful to Casarès, even though we do believe her the love of his life), Camus was not, as jargon put it when it was a term of abuse not appraisal, a shit. Absurdity – the absence of transcendent, divinely guaranteed reason – was Camus's abiding topic. His death, in 1960, speeding on the narrow, tree-lined Route Nationale Six, can be read as proof of the sincerity of a suicidal penchant. Francophile Julian Barnes plays tribute to Michel Leiris and Camus; in his artful dread of death, he joins their morbid team.

There is an unedifying account, in Lanzmann's long, seldom self-critical *The Patagonian Hare*, of Sartre and Simone de Beauvoir, Lanzmann's then-mistress, colluding in the seduction into Sartre's arms of Lanzmann's young, perhaps virginal, actress sister. Lanzmann's belated assertion of his Jewishness, his devotion of so much time and effort to *Shoah* and to the pro-Israel films which followed it, can be read as an apology for juvenile complicity with the vanities of the Sartrean connection.

173

The 'loss' of China to communism in 1949 reinforced American apprehensions. Like those on the temple of Janus, the doors of what Karl Popper had vaunted as 'the Open Society' again creaked shut. The precise use made of revenues was classified. Unelected elites came to determine matters of life and death. Secret and proxy wars avoided overt hostilities, just. *Pourvu que ça dure*, most civilians in The Free World have proved glad to leave 'defence' to those in the know.

Bent on fattening food and round-the-clock entertainment, the square were encircled with multiple choices of very similar things; the hip played at revolution, their aggressive hedonism a blend of vocation and vacation. Earnest trudgers in the CND (their footgear alone symbolic of changing styles) sought the means to reinsert the nuclear genie in her bottle. As the myth of Eden indicates, innocence and ignorance were beyond recovery once that clever apple was broached, science the serpent.

Ian Fleming delegated the dirty work of keeping the Queen's peace to a single, sexy super-hero. While waiting for a robotic governess, the British were glad to have James Bond – half sewer-rat, half lounge-lizard – to fight the good fight, with a patriotic licence for low blows. Double-Oh-Seven was both a pleasure and an economy. Granted unexamined ways and means, James – superman as bodyguard – would keep sinister foreigners at bay. Despite the examples of Burgess, Maclean and, not long after the publication of *Dr No*, Kim Philby and Anthony Blunt and who all else festering in the distressed woodwork of Western society, none of Ian Fleming's fictional villains was ever a Brit. James Bond himself, William Boyd reminds me, was/is half Scottish, half Swiss.

In 1955, in the *New Statesman*, Malcolm Muggeridge coined the phrase 'royal soap opera' to describe the drama of Princess Margaret's enforced renunciation of Group Captain Peter Townsend. The 'crisis' was a tear-jerking royal rehash of the Abdication of Edward VIII a score of years earlier. The Church of England's leading primate once again played moral governor in a nominally Christian country where scarcely five per cent of the population went to church. The outrage greeting Malcolm's coinage was soon followed by the recognition, now crowned on Netflix, that Buck House was an adjunct of the National Theatre. Muggeridge, shriven iconoclast, repaired in his senescence to the Roman Catholic faith. Blaise Pascal might have bet on it.

174

After the war, English writers along either wing of the political spectrum, Waugh to Orwell, stayed reticent on the Holocaust. Until the trial of Adolf Eichmann in Israel in 1961, it was as close as they came to having a conscience. As for the centre, when did it lack Levites? The democracies' pre-war abandonment of the Jews was followed first by sighing indifference to their massacre, then by impatience with survivors, insolent losers with pointy fingers. The not-necessarily (but probably) malicious English general Evelyn Barker, C-in-C in Palestine, asked Golda Meir what the Jews had done to provoke (he did not, it is nice to presume, say 'deserve') their treatment by the Nazis. They couldn't have been rounded up and murdered for no reason at all, could they? Kafka's *The Trial* was not, we may guess, on the general's reading list. Docility was never Golda's bag. Graduate of the pugnacious school primed, in Hungary, by Max Nordau and in Odessa by Ze'ev Jabotinsky, she made it clear that Israelis were not the same old supine 'Jewy Jews', Simon Raven's term to distinguish East End oiks from those like his classy patron, Anthony Blond, who *à la fin de sa carrière* emigrated to France and joined a synagogue near Limoges.

Emblematic figure of my youth, Simon was a Carthusian writer and classicist, expelled from Charterhouse (for holiday pederasty) but by no means disgraced. His 'factual' and fictional advertisements for himself, amusing, outrageous and shameless, were composed, like a grown-up's 'banco' – Carthusian slang for homework – for money and applause. He mocked and embraced British vanities, prejudices and conceits and distinguished, here and there, with no false courtesy between educated (preferably Etonian) and Jewy (showbiz) Jews. Raven is a name not unusually attached to Jews. As a young reporter, I covered a case for the *Sunday Express* in which one such Raven, in early 1950, took his small child and absconded from his North London home to Paris with a cry, as it were, of Nevermore. Simon Raven was a more-or-less conscious imitator of Evelyn Waugh's festive obeisance to the class system.

Waugh came close to a sympathetic portrayal of a Holocaust survivor in the last volume of his overrated trilogy *Sword of Honour*. The principal character, Guy Crouchback, is almost as lacklustre as Anthony Powell's Nick Jenkins. Accosted by the hirsute Alan Brien at lunch in White's and asked robust questions about his reactionary views, Waugh complained that he had been ambushed by a Jew. It might have been wittier to say that Alan was disguised as the Jew he certainly was not. Part of the comedy of Waugh's biography is that he was born in Golders Green.

175

What, in 1984, George Orwell termed 'Newspeak' imposed the patois of his Ministry of Truth on a population docked of any other linguistic resource. Warped platitudes embargo proles from thinking other than as bosses dictate. Nationalised and commercialised strangulation of the language deprives the population of the ability to express anything but the party line. Orwell took his cue from *Pravda* (Russian for truth with a pinch of sarcasm, cf. 'gospel') and from C. K. Ogden's well-intentioned 'basic English'. His evangelical pidgin was slated to arm the post-war world to become as reasonable as the triumphant Anglo-Saxons. Touted in nationalist China by I. A. Richards and William Empson, it did not have time to catch on before the Communist victory of 1949 consigned it to history's oubliette.

The afterlife of the USSR can be read under vari-coloured lights. The ex-KGB operative Vladimir Putin has been accused of staging or making prompt use of incidents during his presidency such as the deaths in the Moscow theatre where the rescuers killed more people, with gas, than the terrorists with bullets. Something similar happened in 2004 in Beslan, near the Chechen border. Hundreds of children died when Russian security forces stormed the school in which the pupils had been taken hostage. In both cases, the number of deaths was due, in large part, to the clumsiness, if not corruption, of the 'security' services. Underpaid border guards were bribed to let the armed Chechens through. Putin's autocracy was more fortified than threatened by what followed. Ruthlessness passed for a righteous response to the carnage which, objectively speaking, as the communists used to say, did him a favour.

Terrorism renews the lease and amplifies the mandate of the National Security state. The Chechens, deported in large numbers by Putin's model, Joseph Stalin, serve Putin in the office of Emmanuel Goldstein and his gang. Conrad's Mr Verloc, in *The Secret Agent*, has countless real or imaginary descendants. Nihilism is, by definition, in favour of nothing and in opposition to everything. It lacks either a specific programme or a fixed headquarters. There is always something about which we, its target, can do nothing very much. Fighting terrorism authenticates its existence and justifies the declaration of a perpetual state of emergency: power relies on helical hoopla. In Luis Buñuel's *That Obscure Object of Desire*, the 'Revolutionary Army of the Infant Jesus' sets off random explosions. Survivors shrug and life goes on. The groupuscule's name was pirated by a 1980s pop group of small percussive impact.

176

Karl Marx said that Great Britain, when great, was not apt for communism. Union-jacked imperialism had inflated all classes with incurable complacency. He came too soon to observe how football, now played by professionals, most of whom have no roots in the country or abiding club loyalty, has generated conceits and hostilities among spectators who have the illusion that they are watching their town or city prove its superiority in contests between mercenary elevens with small allegiance to anything but their wages. The size of the players' pay packets excites little resentment. If they win, the spectators are happy gulls. What victorious warrior is overpaid?

Polite rivalries can cease to be sublime. As the Brexit stand-off proves, the narcissism of small differences festers into something close to civil war. Partisanships begin with naughty-boyishness and become vile and violent. The British have become fractious, both with regard to foreigners and, nastier still, to fellow-citizens with differing views or styles. The Brexit referendum, rigged by opportunists of various complexions and warped by offshore interests, stands as the incontrovertible will of people who had small idea what was entailed by the camouflage of terms like Yes or No.

In the 1930s, Stalin postulated a parasitic class of rich

Ukrainian peasants, known as *kulaks*, as malign obstacles to the success of communal farming to which, in truth, if never in *Pravda*, almost all Ukrainians were opposed. *Kulaks* were stigmatised by their putative wealth, which rarely stretched to more than a cow or two and rudimentary furniture. When the scapegoat mechanism failed to deliver acquiescence or crops, Stalin's legate Nikita Khruschev supervised the starvation of some five million Ukrainians. Alan Bullock was the first to suggest that Stalin's getting away with that mass murder was a primer for Hitler's destruction of the European Jews.

177

Before 1914, science was a field without territorial boundaries or prescriptive creed; all might have access to it; given the wit, all might contribute. A plethora of fish swam in a common pool. Inventions were presumed to belong to, if not define, all civilised humanity. Seen through tinted bifocals, the space programme looked like the inevitable next stage in human progress; the future, in theory, has no proprietor, but options can be taken. Science has become linked with the generation and exercise of power by self-selected elites. Uncountable taxed wealth is allotted to the fortification of the already-powerful. After periods of patriotic self-denial, leading lights emerge from under their bushels to shine at the head of multi-national enterprises.

As for The Bomb and more and more powerful devices for its delivery, who can say whether the Anglo-American attempt to keep them secret, had it succeeded, would have made the world safer, or less safe? History neither certifies predictions nor promises regularity. Having pricked out the megalomania behind Arnold Toynbee's seemingly impersonal scheme of meta-Hegelian dialectic, humanised by the idea of Challenge and Response, Hugh Trevor-Roper later propounded the rule that while powers (he was thinking of Germany) might fight two losing wars for continental or world domination, they never undertook a third. There was a difference, he argued, between empirical observation and delusions of access to the ultimate scheme of things. Among Toynbee's affectations was a claim to have been extra-corporeally alongside Miltiades at the battle of Marathon.

Trevor-Roper was an outspoken Zionist. Toynbee saw fit to wish the Arabs all the luck in the world when, in 1973, they hoped to annihilate the state of Israel and implied the wish to include all Jews in their lethal prospectus. Their challenge received an unscheduled response. Trevor-Roper happened to have been an Old Carthusian (while always wishing, as did Simon Raven, that he had been an Etonian). Might it be that his pro-Semitism had something to do with unabated dislike for the *Carthusiana domus* and opposition to its long tradition (embedded in school slang) of anti-Semitism?

On the other hand – what else? – he took the young Alan Clark, star in a selected sequence, on a continental tour in his fancy Bentley. Clark had all but one of the affectations of a toff risen from the ranks of the mercantile class (his grandfather invented the cotton reel, unless he filched the idea from a guileless toiler), including imagining that he spoke perfect French: as I know from personal experience, he lacked the grace to keep his word to people unlikely to confer further favours.

178

Senator McCarthy's disparagement of liberals, not least in Hollywood, inclined well-advised people in the applied arts to play safe and manufacture confectionery. In his wake, political and military arrivistes of various degrees of callousness or crackpottery, like General Jack D. Ripper in Kubrick's *Dr. Strangelove*, set out to evict the as-to-the-manor-born East Coast gratin from the seats of power. Reaganite Republicans, for whom freedom was the liberty to purchase privilege, made whatever was good for the defence of the Union their profitable business.

Today, the Land of the Free doubles with the land of the immeasurably overpaid. The clamour for a colour-blind society has closed and widened divisions. Bonds which once joined Jews and Blacks in the fight for civil rights have been severed. Blacks have been introduced to the pleasures of malice against one-time allies and have shrugged off any debt they might have to liberal benefactors. Feminism broke apart the civil compact which had bonded white society in what came to be divined as a phallocratic conspiracy. Women no longer have to beware women, provided they follow their leaders. 'Me-Too' sloganeers persuade themselves and their sisters that females are guileless creatures whose endless expenditure on cosmetics and seductive gear implied no sort of wish to excite or gull what used to be called the opposite sex.

Denial that anything could ever be taught or said in unloaded language, hence that it is biased in favour of the beastly bourgeoisie, has blighted the humanities. This chimes with the meta-Marxist notion that nothing escapes being political. Conformist cant is the new rectitude. Neo-Manicheism rules the rooster: men bad, women good. Fidelity to one's sex, if feminine or gay, or gender, threatens to supplant marital fidelity.

Curricular reading-lists discourage reading texts enriched by nuance, irony or paradox. Boats against the current are apt for target practice. The woke Index has no Vatican vigilantes but hardly less stringency. The war on high culture conducted by political correctness has its artillery in a plethora of awards and prizes distributed by empanelled celebrities. Prizes, like places at universities, are liable to be allotted to members of groups that have been under-represented. To be good and level, the playing field must be tilted; for the fight to be fair, it has to be fixed. Impartiality is a virtue to be found only in those on our side.

Was there ever a golden age of dispassionate reckoning in artistic or any other form of judgement? Mark Lamster's *The Man in the Glass House* (2018) is an implacable, if belated, assessment of the career of Philip Johnson, whose architectural career, largely in New York City, can be read as a bloodless parallel to that of Albert Speer. Johnson manipulated and corrupted the allocation of both prizes and commissions which he himself either disdained or lacked the time to procure. Fashionably anti-Semitic in his pre-war practice (he shared broadcast time with Father Coughlin, the never-defrocked reverend Dr Goebbels of New World Roman Catholicism), Johnson intimidated *New York Times* reviewers into despicable toadyism. Sharing Albert Speer's aptitude for overblown, monumental architectural imposition, Johnson was for many years overpraised by those who looked to him for favours. The New York city planner Robert Moses was equally influential during the same forty years or more and has also been the subject of rectifying abasement. Things change, rarely all that much. The *New York Times* overseas edition recently published a cartoon of a docile Donald Trump being led by Benyamin Netanyahu wearing a collar with the Star of David on it. If there cannot be a god, there is always the devil.

179

In the priggish 1950s, it was said by the school of Mr Eliot that literature of quality coincided with the 'amputation' of the audience. Randall Jarrell's *Age of Criticism* had neither time nor space for common readers and their appetite for mental candy. Dwight Macdonald's coinage 'Middlebrow' banged bestsellers to rights. He never supplied an example of anything better. Today, sales managers dominate publishers' conferences. Like the New Testament centurion, they tell one writer to come, another to get lost, according to projected sales. The illusion of a hundred-per-cent share of the market sponsors ruthlessness and philistinism in all arts which solicit funding.

Science, clean of ethics or aesthetics, has become the road to salvation: it is easier, and more profitable, to contribute to cure cancer or to colonise Mars than to define what makes a man good, a book bad. The state's expectation of dividends from funding higher education in science has fattened the universities and sapped their independence, encouraged conformity even, if not particularly, in the first class.

The notion that all non-technical discussion is uneconomic presumes that solutions are all that matter. That the inconclusive is a vital element in civilisation threatens all ideological and dogmatic schemes. Any single scale of measurement, or way of determining merit, of any kind, is evidence of incipient

addiction to the single-party state and the conformist legislation which renders critics heretics, unless they promote what
toes and tows the party line. The conceit backed and fronted
by John Carey has it that in literature there can be no objective measure of quality. Is anyone likely to say as much of
music, dance or architecture? Quondam professor Carey's
affectations of modesty rely on a stonemason's use of the
term 'objective'. While it is manifestly, hence uninterestingly,
the case that no eternally true and guaranteed measure can
be applied to literature (or to anything else, Richard Rorty
claimed), it does not in the least follow that there cannot be
good and bad reasons, aside from meta-Benthamite accountancy, for admiring or enjoying literary works.

Reason alone can never provide abstract standards; it is
'objective' only in the sense that it can furnish the means to
articulate an argument and detect clichés, cant, banality and
bluster, the bread and butter of mass media. The notion of
innovation supplies the category most dexterously manipulated by interested advocates, as does 'revolution' or 'reform'
(Tony Blair's pet placebo) in politics. Drawing is an art in
which bluff, like that merchandised by Damien Hirst, cannot
prevail; hence some art schools consider any emphasis on
drawing undemocratic and elitist. Not everyone is a brain
surgeon or a first-class goalkeeper, but all are born artists.
Follow that bandwagon, some say; head for the hills, say
others. In post-cultural culture, market forces are everything.
Success is today's most rewarding form of failure.

180

English civilian intellectuals were never put to the decisive question, as the French gratin was, of whether to collaborate with Nazism. Drieu la Rochelle, Louis-Ferdinand Céline, Lucien Rebatet and Robert Brasillach did so, gleefully. Gide, Malraux and Sartre opted for magisterial dithering until the liberators were playing their tune. As Robert Gildea made clear in *Marianne in Chains* (2002), only a resolute few joined the armed resistance, eighteen-year-old Claude Lanzmann among them (he was not sorry, one guesses from his autobiography, to get away from his mother).

The preparedness of the elderly David Lloyd George to play the Pétain part in 1940, unless the duke of Windsor beat him to it, suggests that, had things gone badly, British intransigence might have been less firm than sentiment insists, had it not been braced by Churchill's eloquence. 'Tom' Mosley has his admirers, right and left, from Enoch Powell to Michael Foot. Cressida Connolly's novel *After the Party* (2018) testifies to the abiding lure of Mosley as the Big Bad Wolf.

France has remained divided in two in a fashion which Anglo-Saxons were spared until Brexit. Mrs May then sought to lead a split nation by a show of self-denying duplicity. A Remainer before fifty-two per cent of those who actually turned out to vote elected to leave, she then denounced the 'cosmopolitans' who favoured European Union, as she did until her followers deemed otherwise. Admirers of Stalin will recall that 'cosmopolitans' was his (and Nigel Farage's) pejorative for Jews. The moment when Uncle Joe reverted to the old Russian prejudice, expressed in much the same terms, came in 1948 when Golda Meir, as the ambassador representing the new state of Israel, received an all-too-enthusiastic welcome from Russian Jews. Stalin's immediate response was to eradicate Yiddish culture in the USSR under the rubric of 'chauvinistic-Jewish deviation'. What had been heroic during the war, when the Joint Anti-Fascist Committee received a state medal for 'valiant service', became treasonous soon after it. The committeemen had had the temerity to claim that the Jews had suffered more than other Soviet citizens, which challenged Stalin's *ukase* that all Russians had suffered equally.

Along with the great Yiddish actor Solomon Mikhoels and eleven other defendants, the novelist David Bergelson was accused of Zionism (which he had never embraced) and of spying for America by favouring a Jewish homeland in the Crimea, always a nervous region for Russian tyrants. Bergelson spent three years in prison and was then sentenced to death after the usual rigged trial. Like Koestler's Rubashov, he was either forced or elected to serve to the end the regime which proposed to lynch him. In the 1920s, Bergelson had emigrated to the US, but had found it a country of 'selfish opportunism' and returned to Russia. In his last words to the court, he confessed that he had 'headed towards attaining the level of a genuine Soviet man', but did not quite reach it, 'and of that I am guilty'. One of Stalin's most diligent, long-serving prosecutors was a Jew whose name was all but a pun on Mikhoels.

181

The development of nuclear physics led to the capacity to rocket death to unspecified numbers of strangers by gunners out of reach of reprisal. The world's population is subject to powers, of various hues and cries, without ethical restraint. Humbug survives; choose your flavour, secular or religious. Science has a non-territorial domain; IS and similar terrorist organisations are its bloodthirsty beneficiaries. They make it their business and pleasure to supply footage which some viewers may find distressing. The same stuff sells well in the bazaars. The once-sublime hybrid of science-cum-philosophy insisted that nothing be unthinkable; everything possible merited consideration. In a piecemeal, need-to-know environment, the sole comprehensive logic is reserved to central machinery which, like Kubrick's HAL in *2001*, may have an alarming voice for the purposes of self-preservation, but lacks flesh-and-blood personality; the robot's speciality is untiring activity. A servant without feelings bides its time. Jeremy Bernstein tells me that Stanley Kubrick had the skittish idea of asking Jackie Mason to be its voice.

The CND sought to inject moral scruples into a form of research in which peer review and confirmation are the sole marks of rectitude. The end of humanity and that of the humanities lie closely adjacent. As Noel Coward said of a

female character's eyes, 'You can't get a pin between them.'
Equality is another name for passivity; the quiet life is death.
The fears, hopes of The Machine's operatives are, however
refined, therapeutic or literary, irrelevant to its findings or
their expression. Scientific propriety concerns means, never
ends: to cure cancer is a more rewarding ambition than
humane desire. It prompts contributions to the laboratory's
bottomless collection box.

The arts have been relegated, by the military/scientific
domain, to the status of sugar lumps for donkeys, apt to
savour in the intervals of BREAKING NEWS, consolation for
lost tranquillity and substitute for self-expression. The writer
has been reduced to an employee, pampered or discarded, of
the communications industry. Journalism is literary fast food;
responsible for entertaining those who share or are outraged
by his/her opinions, the columnist's barracking supplies rented
outspokenness.

Like Yorkshire cricketers Hirst and Rhodes long ago, journalists of whatever rank get them in singles. Loud indignation
is more an aspect of the ache to be noticed than any proof of
audacity. Twenty years ago or so, I was flattered into backing
the launch of a new magazine which, its prospective and pros-
pecting editor promised, would raise the voice of reason, or
at least clear its throat. He repaid my investment, which he
soon asked me to double, as smooth persons do, by giving
me a column in the magazine. Honouring Catullus' principle
of *variatio*, I made a monthly effort to amuse and, in a nice
(grammatical) way, provoke. My observations were remarked
and reprinted several times in the national press, which did
the mag no harm. After a year or more, our modest success
procured the funds needed to warrant a glossier relaunch. I
was then told that my column was very much admired by
some people, detested by others. That sounded as if it was just
about what was needed; who would want to write a column

that was okay with everybody? I was being given notice by a bland climber who no longer sought my financial backing nor dared to weather the steep face of public opinion. The providers of new cash had asked for my head. Money never consents to lose its voice. When, in need, I sought to sell back my shares in the company, I discovered that they had been devalued by the issue of a great many other, preferred shares. My investment was dust. One lives and learns, rarely anything nice. It so happened that the editor concerned had a Germanic name and, although from a distinctly British family with above-the-line credits, had something of the classic *demi-juif*. Jewing another Jew apes the footballer's pleasure in nutmegging a teammate on the practice ground.

182

Publishers have grown ultra-rich from developments in the field of electronic access to a wide audience. Revenue from Kindle, while less than expected, is almost all profit; little is ceded to writers. The rise of executives in the movie business, however venal or commercial they may always have been, and now in publishing relegates artists to subservience. The best screenwriters were once idiosyncratic, necessary, adjuncts to 'the industry'; the writers' table was the one to sit at. The surge of rich opportunities, bracketed in a system of formulaic shocks, eliminates wit, banishes nuance. *Pace* Woody Allen's line, if never show-show, show-business is now all business; its officers have their noses deep in the backside of last time's successes. Bang bang, sex and violence (pistol-packing women to the fore) have collapsed originality into repetition, wit into catchphraseology. Costumes and masks clamp individuals into typical homogeneity. If God no longer parades His promises, the Front Office, in politics as in the movies, offers the happy few, elected or co-opted, tax-sheltered invulnerability. Talos, the robotic sentry created by Daedalus to secure Crete against invaders, struts again.

183

In a *New Yorker* article of April 2017, beginning, in accordance with editorially induced cuteness, with 'On a velvety March evening...', Tod Friend took his readers on a prolonged tour of the visionaries, Nobel Prize-winners and cranks who are planning the biggest grab available to Adam/Prometheus: the abstraction of the gift of immortality from The Supreme Being into the hands of men, especially the rich, who are promised, with a wealth – what else? – of scientific details, neologisms and what-about-that? laboratory evidence, the imminent prolongation and, if they are careful crossing the road and avoid those who wish them no good, or control the pill box, an eventual more-or-less-eternal life. A thousand years may have to serve and, given the state of culture and services, may prove more than enough. Mr Friend's flow of scientific data, or propaganda, deriving from Silicon Valley and its adjuncts, is indistinguishably heartening and depressing. The new Skylark will sail not to Cythera but to gated communities of the blessed, with private facilities, a Talos who can cook.

In line with the supervised cool of his magazine's house style, Friend is impressed by the funds being devoted to filching immortality rights from the deity and by the profits which will derive from the pill of all pills, unless it's the con of all cons. Serious research is certainly involved in the race for the *gotcha nostrum*, but no other seriousness is within the compass of interest, so it seems, of any of the people, charlatans, visionaries, men and women of rare scientific wit (without laughs). The very long, velvety article (how much more fun the Joycean vulva-ty would be!) never hints at the changes in sensibility which may/will accompany longevity extended towards, presumably, infinity.

Since the new immortality supplements will be available only to those with the necessary chips, it is bound to become the inspiration of an elite with no nobler purpose than its own preservation from the shocks of ordinary life or the incursion of the proles. So far from liberating man, or men and women (and their *chouchous?*), from diurnal anxieties, aches and pains, the great dread will be of what can never be subject to medico-scientific regulation: accidents, human error, systems-failure. The pursuit of a single, selfish objective is no great scandal, but indifference to what the unprivileged human tortoise would do, apart from prolonged fucking and watching TV, is scarcely broached. Science may keep you alive; it cannot promise to find you anything worthwhile or uplifting to do or be in terms of anything but the physical.

Common intelligence has lapsed from self-improvement to self-satisfaction. What might excite discriminating tastes is disappearing from shelves. The orchidacious is uprooted, weeds pampered. Literature yields to its facsimile, print in repetitious and formulaic recipes which pundits and pushers (convergent classes) think will earn them the gratitude and, more to their sole point, the pennies of readers, as well as the prizes of panels whose selected selectors – leisure-time's grinning judges – anticipate what the public will applaud them for choosing. The music goes round and round, only faster. Bob Dylan's shrugging response to the Nobel Prize trumps Sartre's rejection of it.

The limitation of choice, by a show of business-planned proliferation (different labels and prices for scarcely distinguishable products in stacked prolixity), applies to pushers of all sorts, Amazon, Netflix, supermarkets. Science is the godfather of conformity, its progeny conceived without passion, raised without a kiss. Any amount of research and applied intelligence cannot generate a single moral 'truth', though there will be no shortage, as in the operating theatre, of irreverent or raunchy badinage.

184

Christian pre-destination and scientific practice converge in unsmiling deference to the inevitable, otherwise His Will (Allah the merciful paragon of every other daggered vigilante). A covert smile comes of the presumption that the few just might evade the routine fate by designing the machinery of escape for a select company of A-listed space-émigrés. Meanwhile, the destruction of the earth, with its superfluity of people and their ineradicable hostilities, is declared to be imminent unless we all pull together and aid 'science' to do what has to be done to the planet which its operatives have been rendering uninhabitable. Our small wisdom is to concede key decisions to the brain of all brains which knows more than we can and cares altogether less, if at all. Already the cadet robot can be recognised on the telephone by being more patient and courteous than any live person. The planet, *natura* not *deus*, is now alleged to demand sacrifices, as if it cared; human vanity blesses and curses indifference with needs and purposes requiring penitential abasement. Canossa is our common destination.

J. R. Oppenheimer's exclusion from the further development of the powers of which he had been the genie-in-chief established how impersonal scientific progress is, how independent of individuality. Human genius is a classificatory notion; Lavoisier is not mourned: what secrets did he take with him that are not old hat two centuries later? All valid science is annexed to other scientific data or theory; in a universal scheme, there can be no unassimilable element or unique intelligence. Art, by contrast, is whatever no one else could have produced. Science was always there, however deep, like whatever a miner might have unearthed; art was never previously there; it is epiphenomenal, the steam from man's cerebral hob.

The Vienna Circle of the 1910s and 1920s had no time or place for anti-Semitism: it was 'nonsensical' and unscientific, hence as unappetising as pork in the Mosaic law. As it turned out, science was soon subject to political masters of whatever brand could furnish the facilities and ordain the agenda. Was the so-called pesticide Zyklon B concocted, on paper and by the factory hands, with any more murderous animus than the atom bomb? A day's work was a day's work. Philosophers and writers are regularly exempt, as Ben Jonson by benefit of clergy, from responsibility for the speculative warrants they sign for murder or cruelty.

The revenge of the B-stream is oversetting aesthetic refinement; the good is the same as the popular. The demagogue's shamelessness is his appeal, until he falls. If the machinery of election leaves too thoughtful an élite in charge of the 'logic', resort to chaos becomes a vengeful pleasure. Witness the collapse of the US into a tower of trumpery and of the UK into a midden of second-hand, parodic conceits and beer-in-fist nihilism. Displaced dynasts always claim to have nothing to do with what follows their eviction; vanity repeats itself first as aristocracy, then as iconoclasm. British and American politicians have found it fruitful, under a democratic cloche, to be pledged to ignorance, in the name of diversity, pluralism, multi-culturalism, non-judgemental equality and the rest. Facebook makes all faces mutually exchangeable. Distinction is reserved for scapegoats pastured till needed.

The imminent emergency stop is a society which, as Caligula once wished for the Roman people, has a single neck, which can be wrung with economic ease; scientists can be relied upon to supply a neat noose. Some self-selected group, we may be sure, is already planning to load itself into an exclusive sky-bus and set off for new worlds. However solemn their programme or sly their purposes, such a company is bound to take comedy with it: no matter how careful the selection, any crew and personnel, chosen by whatever dispassionate instrument, is bound to house genes and germs which will reproduce, near or far, the schisms and malice from which, like the Pilgrim Fathers, the travellers suppose themselves to be escaping. Any conceivable pantisocracy – of blood, race, intelligence or wit – is a fantasy. Leibniz did indeed have a point: Coriolanus found no world elsewhere, no more did Ovid, or Stefan Zweig.

Selection of those to be saved cannot avoid the doubleness implicit in the ravelled recipe of the species. Even the promise of a life so indefinitely prolonged, again by science, not by divine sanction, as to amount to virtual immortality, will not deliver peace of mind to the inhabitants of the new Sybaris. Admitted to heaven on earth (or to some stellar substitute), without moral formalities, the Saved will forever be on the watch for some new Pythagoras leading loutish Crotoniates to dispossess them. If too fine to resist, they are as good as lost already. Even without enemies, they will have no peace; they will have to invent Cavafy's barbarians to explain why perfection is imperfect. Those with no future tense have no future. The flaw in Plato's *Republic* was that he proposed that its citizens insulate themselves from the world. An inelastic population was neither to grow nor to diminish. Its pacified inhabitants would most likely die of boredom. Stability and decline are inseparable: as the Turks say, 'When the house is finished, death moves into the house.' Any idealised society, jacketed in rectitude, doubles for Dante's hell. The Christian heaven advertises many mansions; it offers no room for hope. That is the world's game.

Index

About the Author

FREDERIC RAPHAEL is a BAFTA- and Academy Award-winning screenwriter, author and journalist. He wrote the screenplays for Oscar-winning *Darling* (1965), Oscar-nominated *Two for the Road* (1967) and the adaptation of Thomas Hardy's *Far from the Madding Crowd* (1967). As a journalist, his articles have been published in *The Sunday Times* and the *Los Angeles Times*. As a prolific author, Raphael has written numerous works of fiction and translation, as well as history, essays and memoirs, most notably *The Glittering Prizes* (1976) and *Eyes Wide Open* (1999).